Journey

INTO THE LIGHT

THE THREE PRINCIPLES OF MAN'S AWAKENING

Also by Isha Schwaller de Lubicz:

HER BAK: THE LIVING FACE OF ANCIENT EGYPT
HER BAK: EGYPTIAN INITIATE
THE OPENING OF THE WAY

Journey

INTO THE LIGHT

THE THREE PRINCIPLES OF MAN'S AWAKENING

Isha Schwaller de Lubicz

Translated by Susan D. Resnick

INNER TRADITIONS INTERNATIONAL
New York

Inner Traditions International, Ltd.
377 Park Ave. South
New York, New York 10016

First U.S. edition 1984
First published in French as *La Lumière du Chemin*
Copyright © 1960 by Isha Schwaller de Lubicz

Library of Congress Cataloging in Publication Data

Schwaller de Lubicz, Isha,
  Journey into the light.

  Translation of: La lumière du chemin.
  I. Title.
PQ3979.S37L813   1984   843'.914   82-11894
ISBN 0-89281-038-6

The Publisher would like to extend his appreciation to Deborah Lawlor, Kendra
Crossen, John Mahoney and Sean Konecky for their assistance in the translation
and editing of this text.

Production consultants W.S. Konecky Associates
Printed in the United States of America

Note on the Cover Illustration

The "Path of Light" by Elmiro Celli is in the collection of R. A. and Isha Schwaller de Lubicz and hangs in the library at Bozawola. Elmiro Celli was their friend and collaborator during the epoch of the *Veilleurs* (1917–20), that socio-spiritual movement founded by Schwaller in an attempt to respond to the global crisis made evident by the end of the First World War. Schwaller, who had himself studied painting under Matisse, spent much time talking with Celli, who must have been greatly influenced by Schwaller's ideas. In 1919, the magazine *L'Affranchi* (the organ of the *Veilleurs*) sponsored an exhibition of Celli's paintings. In the anonymous introduction, Celli is heralded as the painter for today, for the new age; and in a lyrical essay, entitled "A Mystical Landscapist," which concludes the catalogue, O. V. de Lubicz Milosz writes:

> Celli is less concerned with grasping the image of the relative reality of things which come into his view, than with the higher, spiritual truth, with which objects of the physical world clothe themselves in the mirror of his religious contemplation . . . Landscapist of feeling, religious artist, for Celli earthly visions are, above all, manifestations of a spiritual reality; this is why his art expresses not only ardent love, but also profound and wise respect for nature. For him there is no place on this earth which is not a moving and mysterious garden of the Eternal Spouse, of the paradise of the conjugal arcanum. Delicate, pure adorer of all things, he halts both step and breath before the mystical landscape, and so contemplates at length, but always a little on the sly, the scene which reflects his spiritual state. For this corner of a forest or a garden is not just a thing whose inanimate image Celli the painter will fix for us on a canvas; it is a living, conscious being, a marvellous creature, endowed with feeling and thought, whose portrait Celli the mystic has already resolved to paint. Celli seems to me to be the portraitist of trees, flowers, clouds, waves. Thus he contemplates at length but secretly the places which have troubled him, a corner of Normandy or Brittany, a shady pathway, a vault of leaves and flowers, a misty stream . . . Yet Celli does not let himself be tempted by the joyous invitation of the wonderful path. It is enough for him to know that it is there, that one day he will be permitted to enter it without fear. Celli is rich in love, but richer still in renunciation . . . He understands as no other that this limited, veiled horizon, and this loving pathway through the foliage, and this door of brightness at the path's end, are not his poem's true subjects; that even the place which begins where they end, however far-off and nostalgic it is, is no more real. No, for places have no reality: the only truly real, truly situated place in this world is the immortal Isle of Patmos which we reach

with our eyes closed and inverted in unconscious prayer and detachment, not only from things, but still more from the sensible beauty which clothes them. Celli as no other knows the vanity, the childishness of the motto that paralyzed all artistic effort at the close of the XIXth century: Art for Art. Against this, he opposes, perhaps obscurely and unconsciously, the religious worker's motto: Art for Knowledge of the Truth. Nevertheless, the beautiful image which distracted him on his meditative walk is profoundly graven in his memory. He bears with love the earthly reflection of a place situated in the world of pure love, of liberated soul. For days,—for weeks, perhaps—he will let it pass through the fire of meditation and prayer; he will purify it until it mingles with the original substance, with the eternal and immutable archetype of which it is but the poor physical reflection fallen into the world of instants. Now, the sacrifice of renunciation is consumated, the moment of nature is spiritualized, religious feeling has grounded sensual emotion, and the mystic, satisfied with his humble victory, must lay himself down before the artist full of will and vigor. Triumphant, innocent, detached—armed with all the power of his chaste love—Celli now prepares to confide to the canvas the portrait of his friend and confidant, the Tree, of his gentle sister, the Christmas Rose, of his inconstant love, the Wave, of his wandering brother, the Cloud. This is the third moment of the creative act, that of the return of the earth, to the adorable, unsatisfied, brutal earth, the sublime moment of the work in Appeasement, in the acceptance of relative reality . . .

Contents

CONTENTS

Preface

Readers, if you are content with the satisfactions of this world, do not open this book, for it could prompt in you the desire to go beyond them.

Do not read this if you enjoy the fetters of your current impossibilities, if you are afraid of finding the keys to your suprahuman destiny, for this is the goal at the end of this path.

If you seek this goal, we shall travel the path together.

The horizon will take on different shades for you according to how you see the goal: either through your complexity or in your rediscovered simplicity.

The path must be "opened" and its direction, stages, and various obstacles described, in order to *explain* to the pilgrim the effective means of realization, to enlighten the traveler by awakening his consciousness to the initiatory value of each factor of existence.

It is no longer a question of marking time without moving. Nor is it a matter of "seeking," waiting, and hoping.

Weigh no more some haphazard progress; rather listen to your own sacred Voice.

Traveler! By drawing into yourself Your Presence, you are already advancing into immortality on earth.

Journey

INTO THE LIGHT

THE THREE PRINCIPLES OF MAN'S AWAKENING

1

The Conflict

The sky over Paris blackened. A sudden cloudburst unleashed a down-
pour that sent passers-by running for cover. Hailstones spattered over
the cathedral rooftop. A man, who had stopped to contemplate the
towers of Notre Dame in the strange light of this stormy sky, made his
way toward the front of the church to find shelter. Leaning against the
portal, he waited for the moment to continue on his way. A streak of
lightning ripped through the atmosphere and crashed at his feet with a
deafening noise.

Dumbfounded, the man groped for the entrance to the cathedral to rest
his half-blinded eyes in the darkness. The shock was brutal. Hardly had
he entered when he wavered and would have collapsed, had not a helping
hand intervened to break his fall and guide him over to the basin of holy
water. The cold water on his forehead brought him around. His guide
seated him next to a pillar. Little by little he regained consciousness and
stammered his thanks.

"It's nothing," he mumbled dizzily; "I wanted to take shelter from the
storm."

He barely heard the response:

"Notre Dame is a good refuge. It is not the first time that a man in
danger has been welcomed inside."

With half-closed eyes, he sought out the person speaking to him. In the
trembling shadows cast by the burning candles he perceived a vague
silhouette: a priest? a woman? or a traveler? The voice seemed distant.
His own ears were buzzing. He felt upset and ashamed.

"Do not trouble yourself anymore on my account. I'm quite all right now."

"How can you know?"

"Who are you?"

"Ah! It's of no importance! Perhaps a Good Samaritan."

The notion evoked a biblical image in his troubled mind. Afraid of wallowing in the dream, he dismissed the stranger:

"I'm weary," he murmured. "I want to be alone."

"Very well, be alone—if you can manage to do so in this cathedral so crowded with presences! I shall leave you. Its air of twilight is conducive to calming the nerves; you can rest a moment without being disturbed."

Closing his eyes, the man allowed the peace of his surroundings to enter him. It was a strange and unaccustomed peace that the harassed days of a life obsessed with work did not allow him.

A soothing drowsiness calmed the quaking that continued to agitate him. The time that passed before he was able to discern the uplifting feeling became insignificant. Nothing remained but the stone forms, which on so many other occasions he had scrutinized in vain: grimacing gargoyles, impressive statues of inhuman proportions, sibylline symbols, angels and devils that defied reason, with their terrifying mixture of the grandiose and grotesque. The man was tempted to accuse the inspired creator of this imbroglio of being an impostor. No doubt he had been too far removed from its medieval language. And despite everything, he was still obsessed—as if to defy his own scientific mentality—with what he would contemptuously call "primary symbolism."

A jarring crash of thunder awakened him, and what he saw made him doubt his senses: a curious character dressed in medieval garb was walking toward him. A crop of silver hair escaped from the small red cap he wore and contrasted sharply with his youthful face and the vital intensity of his expression.

The poor man, still recuperating, was subject to a new anxiety: Was this a dream or an optical illusion brought on by tired eyes? The lightning did cause some aftereffects, but could it have disturbed his mental faculties? He tried to regain his grounding in the "reality" of his everyday life; he forced himself to remember the important work that he was falling behind in because of this experience. Disturbing impressions tangled up his brain; the idea of "lost time" got sharper and tormented him: How much time? An hour, a century, or an instant?

Jolting laughter echoed like a bell, and a jeering voice answered the question . . . *which he had not articulated*:

"What time? What time? What is Time?"

The man refused to accept the possibility that he was hallucinating. Bringing all his senses into action, he forced himself to get in touch with the bare stone, the form of the stained-glass windows, the pillars, material *reality*! Again he received an answer to his silent thoughts as a retort to his doubting.

"Real! Real! What do you know of what is real, my child? Is the uncertainty of your thoughts more real than the Presence which expresses itself in a form conceived by very wise beings who understood its function?"

The man of reason's self-respect prevented him from answering; it would never be said that a moment of weakness could destroy the balance that he so fiercely fought to achieve. Regardless of age, a dedicated scientist is not allowed to sink into delusion! With clenched fists he stared the vision in the face and obstinately kept his mouth shut to keep from giving in to his curiosity.

His resistance seemed to encourage the old man. An amused smile came to his lips.

"Then stop doubting, young man of science, and believe in the reality of what I inspire in you; otherwise you might miss the chance to break through the barrier of your narrow mind. Five times seven years means you're a bit young to believe in your infallibility; and although man's maturity in your era comes early, you are not liberated enough from your atavistic bonds to recognize yourself. The self-delusion of which you are so frightened is less a threat than your foolish complacence.

"Dare to contemplate me with naiveté. I am certainly as real as your lame hypotheses. Who knows which of the two could teach the other about the things that are troubling you?"

"How could you solve my problems? Your appearance, the way you dress, seem to be from another era."

"That's quite right; *as I appear to you* I'm as old as these old stones, since it is through them that you have summoned me."

"What? Stone is inert, and these masterpieces of statuary are frozen images."

"They are not frozen, since I have responded to your summons."

"I could not have summoned you: I don't even know your name!"

"My name? The decent common folk have maintained the vernacular sense of it—the humble masses are the last guardians of tradition. Do you not know Maître Jacques?"

"Maître Jacques? Master Jack? The man of all trades."

"The soul of all trades."

"I don't think I've seen your image among the statues in this cathedral temple."

"Haven't you been listening? Are you deaf, or lacking in intelligence? The *Master Builder* of this cathedral, he who conceived it, knew the value of the Word; he remained speechless in order to allow each statue to express itself symbolically. And the totality of these statues is the truthful teaching of Nature's greatest secrets. In order to decipher them, one must learn to listen."

"Listen to what?"

"The voice of Maître Jacques, without which each image will be speechless for you as well."

"The way you speak is so different from my way that I have great difficulty understanding you. I'm afraid I'm deluding myself."

As he spoke these words, the silhouette of Maître Jacques seemed slowly to efface itself. The man suddenly realized that he feared the disappearance of his strange visitor.

"Don't leave me just yet," he murmured. "Tell me more about yourself."

"It is not I who is leaving. It is your doubt that is making me disappear before your eyes."

"Does this mean you're a figment of my imagination?"

"Are the keystones of these arches that assure the stability of the edifice figments of the imagination of those who contemplate them? However, if the man who built them had not first experienced from within the interplay of forces capable of offsetting the laws of gravity, he would never have been able to conceive such an ingenious form, whose secret is the *consciousness of these forces.* Each and every work produced through knowledge of Nature's fundamental laws is witness to human consciousness that has awakened from its sleep. You are dozing upon a treasure, my poor friend. And I, Jacques, am through my symbol the witness of the Knowledge of the sages who gave me this name."

"Are you a mere image, then?"

"Could I be teaching you this now if I were not real? Many is the time that I have heard skeptics like yourself express surprise that this source of Wisdom, if it does still exist in this world, could have dried up for long periods of time without leaving any surviving witnesses."

"You're reading my mind, no doubt!"

"Your blindness is to blame, because there are still surviving witnesses. Just think about the experience that you've just been through: when you were shaken by the shock, your brain ceased to cast a shadow over you, and my presence became palpable to you until the instant your distrusting mind took over again and almost obliterated me."

"I am experiencing your presence in two ways: one is with the almost childlike joy of a beautiful dream coming to life, an experience a child would be ashamed to admit to 'grownups'; the other is the fear I feel that by negating my faculties of reason, I shall lose the only means of support that makes me a man."

"You must never negate that faculty; your reason must be based on the ability to discern what is real from what is relative. Your education, however, has distorted the meaning of what is real, which for you represents the authenticity of what your senses perceive and what science recognizes as such. Science is in a constant state of flux: each new discovery undermines the stability of its assertions. The senses are fallible because the sharpness of their perceptions varies from one individual to the next.

"In your observations of the cathedral, have you never wondered why there are seven windows in the apse, two of which do not allow light to penetrate? Your five senses are your physical senses; the two other senses are also part of your humanity, but in most people they are still waiting to be opened."

"What function do they serve?"

"Your sixth sense is the one you started to open today," answered Maître Jacques. "The seventh sense is of an even subtler intuition. Opening that up is the result of mastering the functions and impulses of the human animal and of cerebral intelligence."

"Does that mean intelligence is an obstacle?"

"It can and should be a marvelous servant, as long as it is under the control of intuitive intelligence, for which the two subtle senses are the agents of perception. This constant control of the 'intelligent servant' by the intuitive consciousness produces *discernment*."

"Were the builders of the cathedrals educated in these things?"

"The true sages of all eras have founded their teaching on the knowledge of man, that is, the knowledge of the universe."

"You've lost me, Maître Jacques! If the Earth is a speck of dust enslaved by one sun among so many other wandering suns, how can man be anything but the slave to this speck of dust, even though he is the most highly evolved of its species? His only superiority consists in the power to reflect on the injustice of his fate. From the first cries of the newborn child to the final betrayal by death, man has been unable to bring to light other 'universal secrets' besides those of the forces of destruction.

"Isn't that where we end up? It's the great triumph of science and civilized peoples, the glorious finality of our humanity and so called revelations! Maybe there's nothing more to seek beyond that. Could that be the secret of your famous sages?"

"Do not blaspheme, my child; ignorance is forgivable, but presumptuousness deserves a lesson. You've already received it, however, through the liberation of your intuitive sense, which your reason has so jealously hidden. Alas! you're a child of your time. . . ."

"As you are a child of yours."

"You are still mistaken. You have not 'listened' to me: *I belong to all of Time.* This is the first time I am revealing myself to you, but I know who you are, Jean Thomas. Your very name explains your problem and your dual disposition. Until this day the being who inhabits your body has sought in vain to manifest itself: Jean [John], the intelligible Light, the disciple of the Heart. Your surname, Thomas, however, is the signature of your heavy heredity: the tendency of this century to secularize, to dissect and to profane the synthetic vision of the heart through analytic observation. Thomas is discursive reason, tyrannical skepticism that believes only in what is relative."

"If what you say is true, I am living between my two tendencies." Jean sighed. "This could explain my dissatisfaction, my revolt, and at the same time my admiration for the extraordinary power of scientific reasoning. Where have we gone wrong?"

"Led astray by their presumptuousness, men want to *invent* at all costs. Instead of adoring and adhering to the laws of Harmony, they would rather create monsters than become students of *that which* is *in truth*."

"What *is* in truth?"

"The Spirit, which animates all things, the only absolute Reality, which interacts with nature and forms the world of appearances and all these relative realities that are always changing. Everything that exists is an integral part of *Genesis*, which is a continual transformation."

"If that's the case, then we have no stability to hope for: man is incapable of creating anything that is indestructible!"

"He cannot create *Life*, but he can be of service to life in life's ultimate earthly form: the human being alone has the power to realize within himself the seed of an immortal being, which thenceforth makes him part of a suprahuman realm."

"What gives you the right to affirm such an extraordinary fact?"

"The right of him who knows the Spirit of Truth."

"And where do you fit in with regard to all this?"

"I am the servant of the Spirit of Truth. It is through him that I was able to revive your energies and reawaken your suffocating consciousness."

"But would it be possible to lead me into this state of subtle perception?"

"Definitely, if you have the courage to call me from within despite the resistance from your scientific mind. Doubting Thomas!"

"If the possibility that you have opened up is not another disappointing illusion, I might find that courage. However, I still need to have another proof, such as the certitude of meeting with you again. It's not every day that I'm struck by lightning!"

Maître Jacques started to laugh. Jean Thomas whispered: "Who was laughing? Maître Jacques or me?"

And Maître Jacques, who had started to drift away, suddenly spoke from very near. "Continue to think in this spirit, my son, and you will know how to find me again. I can meet you anywhere you please, but it's still too soon: you wouldn't recognize me. Come back tomorrow and we'll continue in this more favorable atmosphere. And if you dare to let Thomas into the house, I'll be waiting for Jean, so that I can teach him to listen to the silent voices.

"It's time to return to the tumult of the city. May your true desire allow you to create your solitude in the midst of it."

2

Maître Jacques: "I Am You"

Like a sleeper who awakens from a fantastic dream, Jean Thomas walked back into the surging life of the city amid the passing crowds. The violence of the crisscrossing lights from streetlamps and buses irritated him unbearably this evening. The luminosity that the living half-lights of Notre Dame had steeped him in made him sensitive to this artifice, which struck him as a grotesque anachronism.

This anachronism evoked in him the notion of simultaneity, stirring up an echo of Maître Jacques's words: "Time? What is Time?"

He made his way among the pedestrians, who were all obsessed with their own personal tasks, each one following his route like an ant among other ants.

In front of him a blind man poked his cane into potential obstacles along his path. Jean Thomas slowed down to observe him, surprised to liken the blind man's situation to his own. Was it certain that the blind man walked in darkness? Deprived of physical sight, couldn't he have been forced to awaken an inner vision that sharpened his other senses from the need to join their separate perceptions in a constant synthesis? Who could know if this synthesis was even more precise than the visual appraisal of appearances?

Where does the serenity we often notice in blind people come from? Can man live happily and serenely without light? Must one believe that an inner light can reveal itself once man no longer lives in the shadow of sensorial vision?

The experience that Jean Thomas had just been through made it impossible for him to deny systematically that which would have caused him to smile just a day earlier. For the first time, the "positive" scientist, certain of his equilibrium, was reluctant to classify the phenomenon he had been subjected to. This hesitation, however, did not disturb him. On the contrary, it gave him a motive for perpetuating the euphoria created by the strange vision.

Presenting his experience to the head of the laboratory was out of the question, since he had been hired on the basis of his biology thesis. The mere thought of doing so bothered him. What reasonable man could take this incredible adventure seriously? He could already predict the chief biologist's response: "Hallucination!" Why, after all, was he, the protagonist in this story, well known for his skepticism, already basing his defense on an undefendable argument: where was the evidence?

He suddenly felt tired, and was happy to find himself close by the building where he lived on the top floor. He had chosen this apartment because of its wonderful view, which revealed the silhouette of Notre Dame in the background.

Upon entering his apartment, he went directly to the window to look out at the site which had provided him with the vision that continued to attract him with irresistible charm. The fact that he continued to experience some of the emotion troubled him a bit, however. He sighed and shut the window with deliberation.

He was hungry and sat down to eat the cold meal that Anna, his late mother's faithful servant, had prepared for him. He did not try to stay awake. Too many contradictory impressions assailed him for him to be able to work productively. He applied mental discipline to try to fall asleep, hoping that sleep would allow him to clarify this confusing situation.

It was Anna who woke him from his half-sleep when she brought his breakfast.

"Here's your coffee, Monsieur Jean. You have a good day!"

"Do you really believe that it will be a good day, Sister Anna? What's your forecast for the day? Will it be beautiful or sad outside?"

"That's not fair, Monsieur Jean: 'beautiful or sad'! The weather is never sad, it's the way people see it that's sad. In the grayest sky a man in love will see blue! But that, of course, depends on what one's in love with.

"What do your eyes think this morning? They're a bit tired, but it looks as if the sun wants to break through a cloud."

"You don't know how right you are, dear woman. And yet you've no idea what happened to me yesterday!"

"I'm not asking you to account for your escapades, you scoundrel. After all, if a man doesn't frequent night haunts, he just isn't normal! But that's not what I see in your eyes this morning. . . ."

"What do you see, you old witch?"

"I see rain and sunshine. Where I come from, we'd say that it's the devil beating his wife, the angel. Rain and shine together. That's about all I can make of it."

"Anna, you're a philosopher and a mind reader to boot, because that's exactly how I'm feeling. Without giving it too much thought, tell me which one I should listen to."

After opening the curtains, Anna turned around to scrutinize her master. As she stood before the window, her profile resembled one of the figures on a stained-glass window. The scarf covering her head and shoulders, her tiny shawl, and her peasant skirt completed the illusion. Her folded hands indicated that she was thinking. She became serious.

"Mercy me, my child. If you're not just joking, I think you've got to be very careful. All my experience has taught me that the devil often disguises himself in angel's garb, but if you look carefully enough, you'll be able to see the tip of his tail! Never have seen the angel myself, but when they're fighting, you can tell that she's there."

"Old wise woman, how do you think you can tell them apart?"

"Come on, now. It's easy! The advice of the angel brings peace to the heart, like a refreshing northwind."

"Don't you think that Satan also brings with him small satisfactions?"

"Dear boy, you musn't confuse pleasure with joy. There's pleasure in ambition, pleasure in being right about something, and the pleasure of what I think . . . you're pulling my leg! You know very well how to tell the two apart. Why, you were no bigger than my bootstrap when I saw you ask for a spanking because you preferred the pleasure of getting an upset stomach to the joy of sharing your cookies with a beggar.

"Now, now, Monsieur Jean, don't you tease me! You can't fool the Good Lord, and it's not in the sky that I learned to look for him. If he sees us, he must very well know that one can't go spouting on about something one doesn't understand. I don't know much about anything, but I look at everything that lives and I say to myself: animals are more intelligent than plants, man is more intelligent than animals, and among men some are animals and some are scientists like yourself. But scientists don't know it all either, because they're always searching for things. They can go ahead and invent an atomic bomb that could destroy everything on this earth, but could they invent something to keep everything alive? Are they capable of inventing something that would make them intelligent, more so than animals and plants? And if they can't, is there someone even more intelligent than man, someone who is able to do all these things?

"Could man have invented angels, or are there beings who know more than the scientists know? I'm just a poor old woman, but I'm ashamed to see all these folks who are so satisfied with themselves that they can't even imagine there being intelligences more powerful than that of men!

"You can make fun of me, if you like, but I'd let them tear my eyes out rather than deny what I know for certain in my heart!"

"What you've just said is the strongest argument of all, Anna. It poses the true problem: what is it in man that gives him such certitude? Your certitude, Anna, which built the cathedrals . . . if it is true that laws unknown by science have been inscribed therein."

Somewhat embarrassed, Anna began to get his suit ready.

"Time to get up now, Monsieur Jean, or I'm going to catch it from you for making you late for work!"

Jean Thomas was not at all accustomed to hearing this kind of language from Anna, one of whose undeniable qualities was discretion. It had always been an unspoken pact between them that each one looked out for the well-being of the other without treading on more private matters: the deferential devotion of a quasi-maternal servant; the affectionate gratitude of "little Monsieur Jean," for whom she simplified domestic matters in his life of bachelorhood. He let himself be pampered, knowing very well that this big-hearted woman with healthy common sense, who knew how to join the simplicity of another age with an understanding tolerance of her own times, lived only for him. Everything was so simple with her that he would never have suspected she had been through difficult times.

Thomas was also a bit taken aback by her ardent declaration. It was proof of reflections of which he would never have thought her capable. Of course, he was aware that she liked the atmosphere of church festivals— the incense, the enchantment of the organ music, the colorful luminosity of the stained-glass windows; but he had never seen her fuss over the obligatory rituals in the "practice" of the faith.

Was her belief based on religious instruction, or simply on personal meditation?

As he followed his usual route to the laboratory at the Faculté de Médecine, the doctor was pensive. The question he had just asked himself made him slow his steps. He had no desire to dive into his work without first clarifying his own doubts. It was obviously these very doubts that sparked his interest in his housekeeper's answers.

In fact, he had to make a decision. Would he or wouldn't he go to the appointment at the cathedral? He noticed that he didn't dare add: the appointment with "Maître Jacques." He could already imagine the ridicule of his colleagues if he ever told them something so foolish.

The previous night had not brought him the answer he had been hoping for . . . unless . . . ? Impossible! Anna, for all her good sense, had no knowledge of his experience. Her conversation was gratuitous and offered no solutions whatsoever.

He arrived at the laboratory. He walked on for a few more steps just to assume an attitude that corresponded with his sense of "respectability." The very word unleashed in him such inner laughter that he blamed himself for getting carried away by a hysterical autosuggestion. Enough was enough! He would throw himself into his research, besotting himself if necessary, but it would never be said that Dr. Thomas sacrificed his firmly established reputation for having a balanced mind!

The day passed without incident—or, more precisely, it passed with the silence of a story without words. Could it be said that it was a productive workday? Possibly, if that is understood to mean that a series of contradictory observations led to the following conclusions:

"Each phenomenon is an arguable scientific fact that must lend itself to rational explanation.

"This phenomenon must be certified by the strict objectivity of a judging witness.

"The subject who is affected by this phenomenon is not competent to authenticate it, since his interpretation depends on his mental faculties, which could have been altered as a result of the aforementioned phenomenon.

"Nonetheless, it is certain that man is able to judge with certitude only if he makes use of these mental faculties.

"Man is essentially a material phenomenon, a component that ceases to exist at the very moment that death destroys the phenomenon known as *life*.

"Consciousness is the result of mental assertions.

"These assertions depend on the brain mechanism."

When the hour came at which he usually left the laboratory, Thomas invented a variety of pretexts to stay on, and forced himself to work out the program for the following day so that he wouldn't waste a moment in finding new proofs of well-demonstrated evidence.

Pleased with himself, he finally left the laboratory and headed with determination toward the bookshop to buy some materials he needed for his research. As he stood there leafing through the books, he realized that his thoughts were wandering far from the subject matter before him. After vain efforts to concentrate his interest, he left the shop to stroll along the banks of the Seine, deliberately going in the opposite direction of Notre Dame.

It was not long before he realized that he was running away from

himself so as not to give in to the temptation that was tormenting him.
He felt humiliated by this subterfuge. He tried to analyze his physical and
mental state to pinpoint the force that was opposing his reason, but he
was forced to admit that this had nothing to do with either the usual
animal instincts or the sudden explosion of a repressed passion. Being
steadfast enough to recognize the futility of "pro and con" disputes, he cut
them off and considered his situation with cold detachment.

The scientific rigor of his reasoning that he had experienced that very
day demonstrated to him the existence of an "unknown" in the elements
of his problem. His immediate priority was to find this unknown by
trying the same experience. Only this time it would be voluntary and
done with detachment. Would that not be a legitimate means of judging it
impartially?

He turned back and walked toward the cathedral with deliberation.

As he walked, his awakened curiosity brought a thousand questions to
mind: Would he be alone at the rendezvous? How would he be able to
find a visitor who didn't exist? Would it suffice to summon him, to call
him by his name, Maître Jacques? The name brought back the stranger's
last words: "If you have the courage to leave Thomas at home . . ." But
"Thomas" represented the rational intelligence he needed in order to
judge. To judge what? The dispute between Thomas and the imagination?

It was then that a voice with Maître Jacques's intonation answered
from within: "Not the imagination, but the intuition. But how can
Thomas be both *judge and party* in the dispute between himself (reason)
and Jean (intuition)? Who will be the intermediary? If you can solve this
aspect of the problem, you'll have your answer."

Jean Thomas was even more disturbed by this unexpected dialogue
than he was by the visual presence he had instinctively come to desire.
What was the use of resisting? He surrendered to the haste that carried
him toward the cathedral, and took up his vigil for the strange encounter
with a feeling of relief.

Eyes closed, he forced himself to take a clear stand. He would not
refuse to listen to his reason. Was not his reason the only defense he had
against illusion? After all, the problem was not himself, but Maître
Jacques.

"No, Jean Thomas, the problem is yourself."

Jean Thomas tried to control his emotions. Maître Jacques was before
him. So be it! Illusion or reality, he had to take advantage of this presence
to find the reason for its occurrence. He went to the heart of the
matter:

"Regardless of who you are, answer me, Maître Jacques. You claim that
I am my own problem. However, before I met you this problem didn't

exist. You are the source of my worry, and it's up to you to explain your presence."

"That would serve no purpose. Only when you know yourself will you be able to understand me."

"I fear I've fallen victim to a case of autosuggestion. What impelled me to return here tonight?"

"Your dissatisfaction, your secret suffering for having contented yourself with continual uncertainty."

"That's a possibility, but the acceptance of this uncertainty is a source of honor for those of us whose ambition lies in extending the scope of human knowledge without assuming we'll find definitive answers. One can always hope to go beyond actual conclusions with new discoveries. That, however, is at the heart of our dedication, and even more than that, it's the source of our courage because every scientist works for his successors, and remains unfulfilled in terms of himself."

"To remain unfulfilled would not be tragic, because the man who is satisfied with his earthly state will never rise above his own inferior humanity. But what you are speaking of deals with *knowing* and not with true *knowledge*. Knowing depends upon your mental faculties and upon your sensorial and technical possibilities of perception. It constantly relies on the phenomena, not on their *vital* causality, which your science does not allow you to discover.

"Nonetheless, your courage is praiseworthy, and your sacrifice would have merit if there were not another solution besides your succession of hypotheses. But what if one can prove the possibility of a direct knowledge that reveals the reason for the existence of phenomena and gives us the keys to the laws of their genesis (*of which I am an active agent*). Admit that it would be useless to refuse this, just as it would be useless to construct a building without first having established a permanent foundation."

"I'll agree to that, if one can prove the existence of this knowledge," replied the scientist.

"The builders of this cathedral and of numerous other temples of initiation have left their testimony. But will you have the humility to admit that your incapacity to decipher them is due to an error in method and not to the reality of its existence?"

"Where is the error in the method?" murmured Thomas.

"In the pride you take in mental prowess, which you place at the summit of your possibilities through ignorance of a higher faculty. If you understand me, Jean Thomas, it is this intuitive faculty that understands. The jolt that awakened it merely dissolves the mental mist that until that moment had obscured it."

Momentarily shaken, Thomas tried to hold fast to his position:

"It's through my mental faculties, however, that I can distinguish reason from imagination."

Reason . . . imagination . . . The words he thought he was speaking in hushed tones bounded back from the echoing vaults. He became dizzy. He waited for Maître Jacques's answer as for something to lean on. Maître Jacques seemed to whisper in his ear:

"It is the Mind that ought to be controlled by That which knows the Causes, because left to itself, it cannot judge without comparing, without dealing in duality. The Mind is the serpent of the Genesis, the *Dualist* that separates Adam-Eve so that they can look at themselves."

"But aren't you, by speaking to me about this duality, taking part in it yourself?"

"I, Maître Jacques, am he who, in you, knows duality without ever having left his Unity. That is why I am the state in which you can take refuge to watch your mental function without letting yourself be lured by its dialectical conclusions."

"Our scientific formulations do not prepare us in any way to enter into contact with a state of being that is not rationally explainable," objected the doctor.

"Hasn't modern science discovered manifestations of energy that were ignored in the preceding century? You credit science, however, by your passionate interest in it. Nonetheless, these discoveries are much less important for the realization of the *total* Man—your final aim—than the knowledge of the various states of being he is composed of."

"How would I know them? I have only a vague notion of a soul that is supposedly immortal. Scientifically, I ignore the relationship of this soul with a moral sense that is without doubt my conscience. These notions are mere words that establish no precise relationship between my feelings, for example, and my often contradictory desires."

"That is the very relationship that must be pinpointed. The only certainty that you have considered until now is the existence of your mortal being, which includes, of course, your rational intelligence, since these faculties depend on your perishable brain. I shall no doubt shock you in naming this entity *Automaton*, because it believes itself free and conscious."

These last words jolted Thomas, who until this moment was listening to the resonance of these words within himself.

"Do not rebel, Thomas, or you will break the connection. See me as an aspect of yourself that you do not know.

"Without me you are a mere Automaton, since your decisions depend on both your organic state and your psychic state, as well as the tyrannical forces of habit, heredity, and the education and instruction you've received.

"Under the influence of these multiple impulses, your human persona is as defenseless as it is, for the most part, unconscious."

"Do you mean to say that my will is not dictated by any effective free will whatsoever?"

"Free will exists only if it is conscious of the forces that determine what it decides. Otherwise it is under the influence of impulses whose origins it cannot detect.

"However, the 'self' constituted by your Automaton has many faces, according to the role your organism plays in your material, emotional, social, or intellectual life. These faces expose different 'selves,' which are always changing according to age and circumstances. Their goals interlock, modified by thousands of external influences. In the middle of these multiple, transitory selves, can you honestly tell me that there exists within you a sovereign Self sufficiently conscious of its various impulses to make an enlightened choice according to *its own rules of conduct, which are equally enlightened?*"

"First of all," said Thomas, "I think that a 'sovereign Self' would imply continual watchfulness and discernment with regard to the various changing impulses that beset it. Moreover, its sovereignty is not effective unless it has clearly determined a general goal for itself—a goal to which all its decisions must be subordinated."

"Your answer is correct and clearly defines the essential conditions for free will."

"Maybe so," countered Jean Thomas, "but it's a powerful blow to our freedom of action, because these conditions seem to make it possible for only a very small number of men to be guided by such free will."

"It is not free will that guides them. It is the essential goal of the sovereign Self that makes the *choice* of their decisions possible. Free will is the fruit of this."

"I'm trying to understand you, Maître Jacques, but I cannot detect, among the numerous, changing 'selves' you speak of, a *stable* self conscious enough of the other selves to subordinate them to its goal."

"Do not be impatient, Jean Thomas; the complicated situation that you are analyzing is the everyday experience, which makes you suffer because you don't understand it. This stable Self that is capable of coordinating your impulses is the one that is speaking to you at this moment. It is stable because it is a part of your immortal Being. It is the Permanent Witness to all your experiences. Its goal is to achieve that which motivated your entry into this earthly humanity."

"What you say assumes the preexistence of this Witness, and therefore the possibility of his survival. Why should I now accept what I have always disavowed?"

"Today your reason is me, Jean Thomas. I am the presence of your stable Self, which is witness to its reality by the very fact that you hear me and that I am able to unveil what was hidden to you."

"Haven't I always heard you?"

"I have tried often to communicate with you, but your arguments rebuffed me, since I am a state of being that is different from your scientific reason, and which you refuse to enter into. My visits did, however, awaken your inner *disquiet.*"

"If I could only locate this disquiet!"

"Your disquiet is the suffering that comes from the incapacity of your reason to understand the ineffable state of your immortal being. You would not be suffering if there were no other possibility within you. Your cerebral intelligence allows you to *look at yourself* but is unable to go beyond *demonstration.* But the foreknowledge of a state that is superior to demonstration allows you to go beyond it.

"Your foreknowledge is the calling of your immortal soul."

"The soul is an irrational concept."

"It is linked to the rational by the fact that it is one of the Numbers emanating from the Divine Totality.

"Each soul is a Number-entity whose characteristics distinguish it from other Soul-entities. Being an emanation of Absolute Divinity, it also bears the aspect of the Universal. These two aspects manifest themselves during an incarnation, as the dual Witnesses of a single entity.

"Their manifestation, however, is of a spiritual order, a state of consciousness superior to that of the human animal. And this, pragmatic Thomas, is your zone of disquiet. It will continue to be so as long as you have not recognized my role as intermediary.

"Yes, Thomas. I am an intermediary to the extent that you no longer know who is speaking now. You or me? . . . or me in you?"

"What do I know?" murmured Thomas. "Without you I would have ignored what you've taught me. But who is it in me that is able to accept this? And what is your goal? Maître Jacques, if you *are* conscious and immortal, what do you need me for? Why do you remain attached to my mortal self?"

"Because you are the subject I have chosen through which to know the human. If you accept me, I am your immortality. Let me enlighten your understanding of this:

"The characteristic aspect of a Soul-entity (its Permanent Witness) is that it is conscious only of itself. However, the goal of its incarnation is to expand this consciousness through the existence of man, whose innate consciousness summarizes all those consciousnesses that are inferior to it. I am the expression of your Permanent Witness. It is I who imprinted my mark within you at the time of your birth. I am your true tendencies. The other aspect of your soul, your Spiritual Witness, is pure, unspecified Divine Light participating in the Universal Consciousness."

"If that's the case," said Thomas, "then how can it belong to me as an individual?"

"It hardly belongs to you at all, and lives within you only if your desire effectively attracts it. Like me, it can leave you forever."

"How can I desire what I do not know?"

"If you are hearing me, your disquiet is the path of your desire. Dare to accept the absurd fact of 'listening to silence.'"

"Will I be able to attain this state with my current mentality?"

"Have you not yet understood that I am the intermediary who can make the revelation of silence intelligible to you? Maître Jacques, the voice of the Permanent Witness, is that very intermediary between your understanding and your discursive reason. No wonder you were intrigued by him.[1] He is the key to your problem. To know him is to awaken from the sleep in which the human Automatons—even the most intelligent ones—lie buried and suffer their destiny as fate. You will acquire the possibility of an effective free will if you remain awakened and become constantly conscious."

"So be it," said Thomas. "Let's admit this possibility, since you have already won me over to certain points in the discussion of strictly opposing concepts. But what shocks me is that I'm conversing with a speaker to whom I am unable to attribute physical reality."

"Have you never talked to yourself when your reason put forth its arguments against the impulses of your heart or your ambition? That is a true inner dialogue, and if it deals with a passionate love conflict, your imagination colors it even more. Why then refuse the same reality with regard to our discussions?"

"Because the projection of your image makes me fear I'm hallucinating."

"What do you know of such matters? If this image is the authentic symbol of a real Principle that justifies itself by the value of what it represents, it could also be the evocation of a form conceived by the sages, whose lucid consciousness understood the role and the function of this Principle in the mysteries of Nature."

"But how can I evoke what someone else has conceived? Maître Jacques, answer me."

"The world of the intuition is a more subtle state than that of thought. The transmission of thought, however, is a recognized fact. If you can already admit this, you can also admit the same transmission for intuitive

1. See page 4.

perceptions. So what does it matter if my answers come from an 'exterior' wisdom or from within you?

"Maître Jacques answers all those who call him, but the majority of men ignore him."

A divergent thought intervened, breaking Thomas's continuous attention. It was then that the symbol of Maître Jacques dissolved into an image he had registered in his mind from childhood: an angel and a devil were tormenting a poor old man, each trying to lead him in its own direction. Freed by this distraction, Thomas's imagination started to wander, mixing belief with superstition, symbol with fantasy, and mocking fundamental judgments such as "good" and "bad." It evoked legendary temptations and produced the image of Mephistopheles and Faust, leading his rationalizations instinctively to take revenge against the attention he had been giving to the suggestions of Maître Jacques.

"That's the very kind of fiction I must watch out for. It's easy to invent under the pretext of initiation! Hold on to your common sense, Jean Thomas. Humanity has been able to arrive at the age of reason and must not take these fairy tales seriously!"

Why this reaction that suddenly jarred him with revolt? Whom was he revolting against? Against the idea of Maître Jacques? Self-reproach forced him to look at himself. An impression of respect that he had never before felt prevented him from poking fun at his mysterious adviser. Where did this respect originate? What was the source of his reproach? *Who* was revolting? Against whom?

With an almost painful effort he was made to feel the discord between his everyday mentality, nourished by superimposed notions, and a certain state of quietude that was something like that of a half-suffocated man who finds himself revived by an environment that suits him.

Jean Thomas wanted to discuss the matter but was up against the impossibility of disrupting this quietude—or should we say, this consciousness?—that would not allow itself to be shaken.

This was a new feeling for him, because he clearly knew that this "consciousness" did not need the force of argument to validate itself. It *was*.

The scientist was planning to analyze this phenomenon, but it was an unsuitable moment to do so, because the faithful were starting to arrive for evening mass.

Jean Thomas stood up, not knowing whether to be angry or congratulate himself.

3
Maître Jacques versus Pierre du Coignet

Thomas offered no resistance when Jean again returned to Notre Dame. Thomas was even able to concoct an argument that legitimated his curiosity: "someone" had answered his questions with explanations that were directed to Jean. The problem for Thomas was not yet resolved, however. Who was this "someone"? Maître Jacques? A totally irrational answer to the problem!

Nonetheless, he had to admit that he, the intelligence of reason, had until then known nothing about the direction Maître Jacques was taking. At least he had never scrutinized the parts of it that could be verified. But what about the other statements that did not fit in with any of his hypotheses? Where did they come from? No matter! His curiosity wanted to push the experiment further, and a new hypothesis was always possible.

"Possible, but very dangerous in terms of continuing the dialogue! Go on alone, if you are able, Thomas! *I am*, and have no need of your faith."

Jean Thomas, who was daydreaming under a ray of light streaming through a stained-glass window, was awakened by this reproach. He looked around him in vain for Maître Jacques. Apparently he was alone.

He did not try to deny the disappointment he felt. He felt a great emptiness, the absence of that which had brought him to life since his adventure had begun. Feeling lost, he tried to clarify his situation. He was distracted from this by the arrival of a stranger who sat down beside him.

The man was an artist. His hair was white and he wore a black cape. His sketch pad lay in his lap. He made himself comfortable and started working on a sketch that had already been partially drawn. He took no notice of his neighbor.

Jean Thomas was annoyed by the inopportune company and started to get up. The artist stopped him.

"Please don't let the presence of a dreamer disturb you," he whispered. "I suppose you come here to meditate or to pray. Why should the conjurings of an artist disrupt the meditations of a seeker? So many men used to come here in the days when people knew how to seek, and they created an atmosphere that was beneficial to the understanding of the symbols."

"It seems to me that symbolism is the outmoded teaching device of another era."

"Don't you believe it, young man. The sages who knew the secrets of Nature had to teach them by means of concrete symbols in order to force the seeker to find, by means of analogy, the vital relationships that join together all the manifestations of Being. It is the most direct way of discovering the *vital* logic that governs our universe. I myself am in favor of what is *concrete*, and I want Mother Nature to demonstrate proofs of what she teaches me!"

"I couldn't agree more. But can you find this concreteness in symbols?"

"I mean that I search for the concrete in symbols until I have understood the natural functions that these symbols represent."

"Your artistic temperament must lead you into fantasy from time to time."

"I do not confuse the study of real symbols with the artistic expression of my personal impressions. It might be possible for me to find a fleeting portrait of my state of being in this expression, which for me is only a personal interest in externalization."

Jean Thomas looked at the designer's strange sketch with curiosity.

"Do you mind if I ask whether your sketch is based on a statue in this cathedral?"

"It was at first, but that's no longer the case. It's an evocation, of sorts. It's the evocation of my patron."

"May I ask your name?"

"I am Pierre—the surname is unimportant. I was baptized 'Maître Pierre' in the Latin Quarter."

"Oh, I get it. You're sketching your patron saint—Saint Peter."

"Not at all. That one is the patron of the Popes. Mine isn't such a big shot. Come with me and I'll show you where his sculpture stood before an unfortunate fanaticism led to the destruction or mutilation of many of these masterpieces."

The artist guided Thomas to the site of the rood-loft.

"Over there, near the corner of the chancel, the symbol of my patron was sculpted into the stone. My patron's name is Maître Pierre du Coignet, Maître Pierre of the corner, the cornerstone of the edifice, the primitive matter upon which the world is based. As you can clearly see, my patron is far from being a saint, but without him the keys of Saint Peter would be useless. First it was necessary to have something to open."

Jean Thomas listened in silence. His companion asked him to sit down, then chose two sketches from his sketchbook.

"Here we have his first symbol—a statue without forms, a mass of rough stone with angular folds. It's a mass without a face that's waiting for that which will give him his face."

Jean Thomas did not understand and shook his head.

"Wait just a moment. You still haven't seen everything."

The artist took the other sketch, which represented the bust of a devil that grew out of the stone and seemed to be supporting it. The devil had horns and an enormous mouth stained with patches of wax and smoke that appeared as filthy as it did hideous.

"What's that? Did you invent that monstrosity?"

"Absolutely not. I reproduced an image that was well known to the faithful of Notre Dame during the Middle Ages. It was in Maître Pierre's mouth that they would extinguish their candles."

"And that man is your patron?"

"That is one of his faces."

"Wonderful! But I'd still like to understand what it symbolizes."

"Satan is the celestial fire that has fallen into matter. It can be extinguished by matter or resuscitated by it, if its Luciferian aspect dominates and becomes living light, which then animates matter and can even refine it."

"You speak like the old medieval writers. . . ."

"This is how people used to discourse under the vaults of Notre Dame when the seekers assembled together under the guidance of the wisest of men. In those days, they were free to speak about the Spirit as the animating force for all that exists, and positive people such as myself were not foolish enough to presume that destructive energy, artificially liberated, was the same as the energy of the Spirit, which is life-giving and a part of all things."

"What are you saying? You are neither positive nor concrete."

"That's not true. If I speak of the devil, it is because I look around at the men whose mouths extinguish all light, the men who deny the mystery in Nature, the gluttonous, the avaricious, and all that which in myself is solidly linked to the earth. It is because of my consciousness that I have another face as well. It is the face of Pierre, who is more knowledgeable

in the ways of men than in the ways of heaven,'[1] but who all the same
could transform the rough stone of himself into a cubic stone, a firmly
established base suitable for a king to reign on."

"This language is too mysterious for me. Can't you name things for
what they are? Who is the king?"

"You must seek the king as I do, in everything that exists. It is the seed
of the grain of wheat that nourishes itself from the substance that
surrounds it, but which will transform this nourishment into an entire
wheat field as it multiplies. It is the yeast that transforms the dough into
a leaven of its own nature. With animals that live in packs, it is the
animal who is most conscious of its responsibilities as leader of the herd
that would have instinctively selected him.

"If I apply this principle to human beings, I would say that our royalty
should be the supreme, indestructible life-core, more conscious than in
the other kingdoms and capable of transmuting all the functions of its
individuality into living consciousnesses that are responsible for the
harmony of the whole, as are the different members of a kingdom of
bees."

"Your positivism bases itself on Nature, Maître Pierre. But the consciousness upon which you base the mechanics of this royalty is still an
abstraction."

"Is the consciousness of the plant-eating animal that refuses to eat
poisonous plants an abstraction? The consciousness of the sparrow that
builds her nest like an architect schooled in the laws of resistance to jolts
and storms—is that an abstraction? Is the consciousness of roots that go
directly to the point of water an abstraction? In that case, everything in
Nature would be an abstraction, my friend, because everything obeys the
impulse of the vital seed, which pursues its goal to the limit of its
possibilities according to its species. And that is what man is no longer
willing or able to do."

"But if your patron, Maître Pierre, is also the Satan who is holding up
the edifice, how can man's superior goal, if indeed it does exist, be
achieved in spite of such a diabolical opposing force?"

"Do you think that the gold found in mines was always 'gold'? Can you
be unaware of the passion that this mineral must have gone through
to gestate the Satanic fire of its first seed, then to reject or consume all
that was not the substance gold? The royalty of gold consists in the
integral purity of the elements that compose it, and that's what makes it
inalterable.

"That is how I see the progressive formation of our suprahuman
embryo.

1. Mark 8:33.

"I am neither a scientist nor a theoretician, but I am conscious of being, through my body, the ore that gestates my king."

"You're a poet."

"No, I am an artist who seeks to decipher the symbol through the image."

"The symbol is an image."

"No, the symbol is the expression of vital functions. Therein lies my positivism."

"I suppose you must know all the sculptures of this cathedral."

"It's a great book whose authors were wise men. The advantage of this book is to give to each one what he is capable of receiving, and nothing beyond that."

"It's necessary to know how to decipher it, and I would like to learn in your company."

"I can only teach you what I myself have understood. If someday we meet again here, it means that there's a favorable combination of circumstances. . . . Go with God, or with the devil, whichever you wish, my friend!"

Jean Thomas stood there perplexed, listening to the ironic laughter of the departing artist.

Shadows descended on this place of silence, obliterating time and forms, liberating the dream that the day had stifled.

Shadows of past experiences, rumors of thoughts, must I welcome you or must I transcend you?

Are the flickering candles marching in a procession toward Maître Pierre du Coignet?

The chiming of a bell evokes the convent. . . . *Sonnez les matines!* *Frère Jacques, dormez-vous?*

Frère Jacques . . . Maître Jacques . . . What distance separates dream from reality?

Brother Jacques, are you sleeping? . . . Dr. Thomas, are you dreaming?

The hushed sounds of discussion arose from the direction of the choir stalls. Two silhouettes broke away and became clearer as they approached Jean Thomas.

Maître Jacques—for it was no other—was sharply reprimanding his companion:

"Pierre du Coignet, it is your own fault if that young man saw only a rather disgusting image of you. Why didn't you introduce yourself?"

"It wouldn't have served any purpose! He was too busy contradicting my godson, Maître Pierre, and he was doing it with a good deal of impertinence, too."

"Didn't I hear it? That's why I didn't appear. Why should a man so imbued with his science be given an argument that he would attribute to his tiny brain?"

"If it were up to me, Pierre du Coignet, master of infernal fire, I would do it without a moment's hesitation! I'd tell him what I know about the forces of matter and get him to increase his knowledge tenfold and unleash my power."

"You did do it, Satan! You did! Who was he working for in the first place when he split matter apart?

"You're the one who breathed into him the pride of becoming a creator. What have you made of him? A destroyer of the forces of harmony that support the world! Have you taught him the secret of Life?"

"That is not my domain. Besides, if you heard my godson speak, you were able to verify that he's seeking the key to it."

"I know," said Maître Jacques. "He does listen to me sometimes, and his discernment has made him mistrustful of your destructive aspect. But who knows if he will always be able to resist you? You are the eternal deceiver, and you develop man's faculty of denial so that you can enslave him to you even more."

"Careful, now! Maître Jacques, I must interrupt you here. Would affirmation be possible without negation?"

"Infernal dwarf, the world that you are constantly forging is obviously based on division, opposition, and contradiction."

"You haven't gone far enough: I am the power that separates, and provokes the desire for reunification. That, my friend, is love. So ask the men that you 'live within' if they would want my extermination."

"That is because you have an advantage over men: in the hell that you've created, that's their only consolation!"

"Let's skip the sermon, Maître Jacques. You know very well that everything has two sides, even the paradise they dream about."

"And you, Satan, know that you are a liar, because if there is perpetual duality in the paradisiacal state, it's not a viable duality, since there, separation does not exist."

"Man doesn't know it, because he's been chased out of that state. Where's the need to tell him that? You yourself are subject to the law of contradiction when you argue this."

"No doubt about it," said Maître Jacques, "since I am the intermediary between these learned animals and their spiritual soul."

"What a strange job you have! And tell me, aren't you obliged to participate more or less in their stormy passions?"

"I know what you're driving at, Satan. In this regard you have no power over me. My immaterial state cannot be bothered by their corporeal passions. However, it can come to pass that their ambitions correspond to the goal of my incarnation. . . . Well, then, I would obviously allow myself to go along with it."

This avowal was met with a burst of sarcastic laughter:

"Poor Jacques. You've fallen into your own trap. Good for you. I'll remember that when the time comes."

"You devil! It's up to me to remember it so that I can be on the lookout. What pleasure do you take in preventing men from raising themselves up toward the Light? Isn't it enough that you keep them imprisoned in matter?"

"You're getting a bit confused, Maître Jacques. According to you, am I Fire, or the matter that keeps the fire imprisoned?"

"Matter exists only through the incarnation of this Fire, of the Spirit. It's obvious that you can't be one of them without being the other, but there again you are the 'negator.' By imprisoning the Spirit, incarnation becomes the great negation."

"Really?" retorted Pierre du Coignet. "It seems to me that I've heard it said that Incarnation was the great gift of God. Then maybe it's me, Satan, that you should feel sorry for: who, therefore, is responsible for incarnation? If I have adopted an infernal character through this incarceration of fire inside matter, then I am the victim of God!"

"What you are, in any case, is sophistry incarnate, because if by God you mean the potential Power immanent to the world of Causes, who therefore provoked its creative activity, is not *the desire to exist* the infernal tendency by which you are characterized?"

"So be it! Let's admit that this impulse is the determining factor in all creation, and you will recognize that all of Nature eagerly follows this example! From the smallest cell to the spermatozoon, what a point-to-point race it is for fecundation!

"I wonder why you so stubbornly focus on my negative aspect, while you have in this cathedral other images of my evolution.

"And I am first of all Peter. . . ."

"Yes, I know: 'Thou art Peter, and upon this rock . . .'; but I wonder if you would continue to keep the Light under a bushel even if you had the keys. After all, are you certain that you haven't betrayed the great Light that established you as its foundation?"

"It's through my faith that I was chosen!"

"Faith with flaws! Why did you have doubts while you walked on the water? Why the three disavowals before the crowing of the cock?"

"My martyrdom was my great affirmation."

"Your upside-down martyrdom, the inverse of your Master's! That's really the symbol of contradiction!

"Don't defend yourself, Maître Pierre; I'll answer my own accusations.

It's not your doubt that I blame: the resistance of the stone activates the gestation of the Fire."

"My throne is Faith!"

"Your throne is *belief*. Faith is the power that merges the throne with the King. Faith dissolves dogma."

"You speak like a heretic."

"Heresy is the result of dogma. He who possesses the keys has no need of dogma. Otherwise, it means he's lost the keys. If you still possess them, Maître Pierre, what difference does it make?

"Your role, as well as mine, is that of witness. You are the witness of the Redeemer, as I am the witness for each man's immortal being. I do know how difficult a role it is!

"Guardian of the keys, you are the intermediary between Divine Power and the body of the Church—the pastors and the faithful who are more or less unconscious of their initial goal. Likewise, I am the intermediary between the spiritual soul and the Automaton with little consciousness. I know what trouble the dialecticians of the mind cause me. I know the tricks of their sophists to prevent the individual from finding his own Light.

"Poor Me! Poor You, Maître Pierre! It's hard to have a world in conflict to govern when the watchword used to be *simplicity*!"

"Simplicity! Simplicity! That's easy to say for a hermit who governs no one but himself! But when it comes down to managing the affairs of the Lower World and harmonizing them with those of the Upper World, you might as well try to marry the sky with the earth. It's a problem that can't be resolved!"

"That's exactly what must be done, Maître Pierre. Have you thus forgotten how to use your keys?"

"So why don't you do it, pretentious character! Do it, if you can!"

"I can do it because it's my role in Nature to transmute the fire that divides into the life-giving Fire and, from you who are stone, to make the Rock of truth. But would you accept that? I doubt it, because you would have to sacrifice your earthly prerogatives to spiritual Power. Do you have enough faith to achieve this?"

"How dare you speak to me in that way, you who are neither Light nor divine Power?"

"No, but I am the *means*, the precursor of Light."

"Oh, is that so? Well, then, go ahead. I defy you to prove your power!"

As they spoke Pierre and Jacques, who had been walking through the large nave, had arrived in front of the holy-water basin. Dumbfounded, Jean Thomas watched Maître Jacques punch Maître Pierre and precipitate him into the holy-water basin, which was transformed into an enormous shell. A great shout was heard. . . . The water started to crackle, and Jean Thomas found himself alone with Maître Jacques. He hardly dared to speak. He drew near to touch the mysterious water with his own fingers, and while he contemplated it, he thought he saw the body of Pierre melt into that of Jacques like salt dissolving in water. . . .

He stood erect, crazed with anger:

"Enough is enough, Maître Jacques! I can't go on allowing myself to be blanketed about by these insane mirages."

"What is insane, my friend, is your rebellion against the teaching of a mystery of Nature. When men the likes of Pythagoras, Solon, and Thales had themselves initiated into the mysteries of the Temple at Eleusis or at Heliopolis, do you think that they were being taught a bunch of boring tales? What's crazy is for you to believe only in your chemical formulas, which were never able to transform your food into chyle, which in turn is transmuted *into your own nature*. Just try to convert this chyle into distinguishable marrow and this marrow into the subtle energy without which your organs and your vessels would not be able to function!

"You categorize each notion in chemistry, in physics, or in anatomy without seeking in the laws of analogy the understanding of prime functions that make the universe one harmonious body.

"If you listened to my dialogue with Pierre, you were able to ascertain that when I spoke of one thing I was evoking another thing that to your mind was not at all related."

"Well, I was there, and I heard everything."

Maître Jacques smiled. "I guessed as much. It would have been difficult to avoid it, unless you weren't paying attention."

"The toughest thing was to admit—" began Thomas.

"To admit that you would have been making a mistake in not listening. You see, we do understand each other."

"It's *you* whom I don't understand, Maître Jacques. I don't understand your nature and your role!"

"Better to say my 'roles,' because the same 'function' acts in different areas."

"For goodness' sake, explain what you're talking about!"

"So be it. I am the great pilgrim of the Spirit in Nature, the one who must overthrow[2] material form and make it subtle by transforming the fire that divides into the life-giving Fire. Just as I am unifying your innate consciousness and your Spiritual Consciousness. I do the same thing in Nature, where I am the carrier of Spirit.

"Jacques is the living shell of everything that becomes, the subtle shell

2. Genesis 25; 26:9. Jacob = the Overthrower.

through which the material body of a thing crystallizes and which preserves its *essential form*. I am speaking as much of you as of the grain, the
cloud, and the metal that is formed and transformed by him. Do you now
understand the symbol of Saint James the Greater?"[3]

"The scalloped shell that one finds on the ancient coat of the pilgrim?"

"Exactly. This shell is the symbol of the secret water that contains
everything and in which the star of the Magi was reflected. The sages of
the Middle Ages related this shell to Mercury-Hermes, who is known in
Egypt as Thoth. It is said that Thoth is the master of the secret water.

"Note also that Mercury was thought to be the intermediary of the
gods, the great voyager, who establishes a constant relationship between
the Principal Functions and their earthly manifestations. Compare the
symbols and you will verify that they belong to the same function."

"Why all these mysteries?"

"For the reason symbolized in the myth of Prometheus, who paid with
his life for having stolen fire from heaven. For me, it seems to be a very
contemporary myth. The sages of ancient China and ancient Egypt used
only symbols whose reading required a 'consciousness of values' to teach
the secrets of nature. This prevented men from misusing these secrets.
The method of symbolism is wonderful for developing this consciousness.
You would profit from the experience."

"Why did you speak of the contemporary world as a 'world of conflict'
when you were talking to Maître Pierre?"

"Because conflict is Pierre's tragedy. It is the conflict between the
affirmation of *being* and its negation, which is incarnation. Incarnation is
the momentary and thus limiting definition of this conflict. This definition is the *Way* and is conditioned by a particular harmony of the
incarnation. It is the Way that dictates how the being who will be
embodied behaves. It is therefore the particular Way of each Permanent
Witness.

"This Way also controls all the deviations in behavior—the types of
behavior that do not conform to this rule of conduct, which is *imposed
because it is chosen* by the being who is going to be embodied."

"How can a being make this choice?"

"Always through the law of *affinity*, that which corresponds to his
essential qualities."

"Could you specify those elements between which conflict exists?"

"It exists between the conscious being who wants to follow this Way
and the 'personal' impulses that tend to lead him astray. As long as a man

3. St Jacques de Compostelle is the French name for the Apostle James the
Greater. (Ed. note)

has not become conscious of his Permanent Witness, conflict does not exist, since he only suffers the impulses of his Automaton.

"It is only when the Permanent Witness is able to make itself heard that the conflict arises. This is what has now happened in your own case.

"Contemporary humanity is going through a similar phase. The considerable progress that thought has made in scientific research, on the one hand, and the anguish that results from ignoring the goals of existence, on the other hand, create a feeling of instability and uncertainty in sincere researchers. This is caused by the discrepancy between their mental powers and their lack of experience in self-knowledge.

"This suffering on the part of the elite—which the masses also suffer through unconscious solidarity—creates a general unbalance with its accompanying procession of tragedies, crimes, and suicides that are characteristic of these *uncertain* times.

"However, in many cases it would be sufficient to change this incoherent fighting into a fruitful conflict, by simply pointing out the goal and the value of existence.

"Do you want to try, Jean Thomas? France is in a pitiful state!"

"What can I do?"

"Welcome me willingly within you. Then you will also be able to call upon me in others.

"Do you want to try, Jean Thomas?"

Jean Thomas closed his eyes and smiled. "Why not? . . ."

4

The Atelier of
Maître Dominique

That evening, Jean Thomas arrived at the cathedral to find Maître
Pierre busily sketching a devil from the scene of the Judgment. He walked
over to him and, remembering that the artist did not even know his
name, introduced himself and expressed his desire to know what he
thought about these diabolical representations.

"I am hoping that the combination of circumstances is favorable
tonight," he added with a certain irony.

"It is, as far as the hour is concerned, since I'm here," replied Maître
Pierre teasingly. "But in terms of place, I'd rather you came with me to
our Atelier. You are expected."

Jean Thomas was surprised. He hesitated, then let himself be escorted
by the artist, who took him by the arm and quickly led him away.

"This Atelier is a port of salvation. All those who are seeking a life raft
find shelter here, whether they are rich or poor, knights or villagers.
Follow me! Isn't my patron a 'fisher of men'?"

Jean Thomas followed him, speechless, and allowed himself to be
pulled up seven flights of stairs. He saw the artist ring the doorbell and
open a door without waiting: he entered.

The small foyer was set up like the porch of a church: from the vaulted
ceiling hung a low-lit lamp. Two heavy doors indicated two entranceways:
on the left was a holy-water basin carried by a hideous demon; on the right
was an angel holding out an enormous beer mug.

"Which do you prefer, Dr. Thomas, to drink or to pray?"

Saying this, the artist lifted the right-hand door, and Thomas entered
the Atelier.

The space that Thomas entered was more like a tavern than an atelier from what he could discern in the darkness: heavy beams on the ceiling, light oak paneling, wood chairs and stools around wine barrels that served as tables, rustic lamps that gave out a yellowish light, and, toward the back of the room, the bread bin, the wine barrels, and sausages and hams hanging from the beams.

A man with a pipe in his mouth and a glass in his hand was waiting for them. He seemed to be part of the decor. He stood up to greet the visitors.

Maître Pierre introduced him:

"This is Dominique, sculptor, keeper of this den, decorator and contractor for Heaven and Hell. Dominique, I've brought you a sinner to rescue. His name is Jean Thomas, doctor and scientist to the point you'd want to go nuts. Dominique, do your job."

Dominique held out his hand. "First of all, let us rescue the body. If I'm not mistaken, this poor fellow needs some reassuring. With my friend as rescuer, it's not at all surprising. Sit yourself down, sir, and let's have something to eat first. Then you can visit our atelier at your leisure."

Jean Thomas turned to watch the strong hands of the sculptor as he prepared the meal with items from the bread bin and the meats hanging from the ceiling. He noticed how different this man's face was from the cold, scheming face of Maître Pierre. Dominique's features were very pronounced: passionate, deep-set eyes, a beard whose shape accentuated his hardy jaw and sensual but controlled lips. Everything about this man reflected serene balance, a sense of life, of form and of precise gestures.

As he poured the Rhine wine into the goblets, the sculptor watched his guest hesitate before his meal. Maître Pierre provided the impetus by digging into his plate.

"Come on, now, Thomas, relax! Do you think that the learned discourses whispered in the cathedral bring out what's at the bottom of a man's heart? If it's true that Truth can be found at the bottom of the well, I guess the well is the abyss of an animal's entrails."

"Visit the inside of the earth," murmured Dominique; "that's what the old sages advise."

"Yes, but for me," said Pierre, "it's man whose confession I want to hear. I have so little belief in his desire for Truth that I only count on the blissful compliance of the beast or on some great fear to obtain the 'moment of truth.'"

Thomas spoke his mind:

"Count me out, Maître Pierre: the beast in me is dominated by my reason, and you'll have a hard time getting a surprise confession from it. Is that why I was expected here?"

Dominique looked at Pierre with pity.

"You might be an artist, but you don't have much tact, my friend! Be assured, Jean Thomas, that we haven't set a trap for you. You are welcome just like all the other seekers who want to sort out the failings and virtues of the human condition. It doesn't take long to understand that your analyses, your statistics, and your logical deductions are guided by cold reason. But this reason has not been able to perceive the subtle strings we use to manipulate all our marionettes. . . .

"Reason, like speech, is a double-edged blade. When it's used in the service of wisdom, it provokes truly vital reactions and leads to man's understanding of the universe. When used by an imperfect science or for personal goals (whether by men or nations), it provokes opposition, ambition, and the need for control by violence. In your opinion, what were the most glorious and beneficial periods for humanity?"

Thomas thought for a moment.

"I'm reluctant to mention those periods of great conquest that were periods of cruelty as well. The incredible progress that has been made by current science seems to me worthy of this qualification, despite everything."

"I know what you mean when you say 'despite everything.' It's been a great period for the development of our mental powers, the most spectacular of which is the science of destruction. This mental progress, however, is confined to such a small number of technicians and scientists that teaching has become scarcer and more superficial than it was before our generation. But let's look at contemporary life."

"Hurrah for this life of child criminals, multiple suicides, despair on every rung of the ladder, because people can't tell the difference between the High and the Low, Good and Evil," shouted Maître Pierre derisively.

"Stop your sermonizing, Maître Pierre, or Dr. Thomas will leave us."

"The fact is," said Thomas, "that no sermon has ever converted anyone. On the contrary, it provokes a man to conceal his tricks and to put on a mask of kindness. . . ."

"The mask of his idealized Self," agreed Dominique as he sucked on his pipe with conviction. "That's why I claim that the beneficial periods of humanity were those in which the sages directed the trends that governed men by taking into account the laws of reaction, by accepting diversity, but avoiding opposition, by awakening consciousness through an appeal to discernment. Nothing paralyzes discernment more than conformity and the cataloging of sins."

"That's for sure, just as the risk of blasphemy awakens the sense of the sacred," said Maître Pierre. "And you, Doctor? Since you are starting to doubt the wisdom of the builders of Notre Dame, would you accept the sight of a donkey with a bishop's cap and episcopal robes leading a procession there? You think that's revolting, and yet it used to be an annual tradition in those days. It was authorized by the clergy, who knew that the public's acceptance of the event unleashed their instincts and prevented hidden rebellion against ecclesiastical authority."

"There's even more to it than that," said Dominique. "Doctor, do you understand the magical effect of contrast, which goes against all rational argument? *Imposed* respect or faith gets no further than the cerebral will which accepts it, but profound consciousness is moved only by the *thrust* that makes it experience what is untouchable, and therefore sacred, in the subjects that one pretends to profane."

"Quite true," said Jean Thomas. "I've never thought about these things from that angle."

"It's the *vital* angle, my friend."

"Well done, my friend," said Maître Pierre. "I'm going to show you another angle. Turn around, Doctor, and look closely at the sculptures in the stalls against this wall. They are authentic copies of the stalls that existed in the choirs of diverse chapels and monastaries.

"The arm rests and the miserere[1] are, as you can see, decorated with sculptures that have nothing to do with religion. Here you have students with bare behinds being whipped with rods; over there, two obscene devils are leading away a man who's been damned; on this one, there's a cabaret scene; farther over, there's the naked body of a dishonest merchant woman being carried on the shoulder of a dancing devil; in other places there are drinking scenes and scenes of lewdness."

Jean Thomas looked and made no attempt to hide his astonishment:

"What does this filth have to do with religion?"

Maître Pierre went on without answering him:

"Now consider this: the miserere decorated with this sculpture was used as a support for worshipers who had to maintain an upright position during long intonings, and especially during attendance at the flagellation that the penitents had to endure during the entire length of the Fifty-first Psalm, the Miserere.

"Enter the stall, Doctor, and take the place of the monk who watches the flagellation."

Thomas was curious. He obeyed and stood leaning slightly against the miserere, as Maître Pierre lowered the lights and lifted the cover of a chest. The chant of the Miserere echoed solemnly and lugubriously.

Thomas wanted to speak, but Maître Pierre silenced him:

1. Miserere: the underside of the tilt-up seat in a choir stall, made of triangular-shaped wood.

"Be quiet and listen! Evoke . . . evoke. . . ."

Thomas obeyed and conjured up the experience of anguish like his companions in the neighboring stalls.

The funeral stanzas of the Miserere evoked pain, fear, and pity: "Have mercy upon me, O God, have mercy!" The humming of the organ suggested the repetition of the lamentation: *Miserere . . . miserere . . . miserere . . .*

. . . And the cadences of the straps lashing the slumping shoulders . . . and the stifled moans of the penitents:

"*Miserere, miserere!* . . .

". . . For I acknowledge my transgressions: and my sin is ever before me. . . .

"*Miserere, miserere!* . . .

"Against thee, thee only, have I sinned, and done this evil in thy sight. . . .

"*Miserere*, O God, *miserere!* . . .

"Behold, I was shapen in iniquity; and in sin did my mother conceive me.

"*Miserere*, O God, *miserere!*"

The muffled tolling of a bell marks the fleeting moment with its inexorable sound. . . .

"*Miserere!* . . . *miserere . . . miserere*, O God! . . ."

A great sigh punctuated the end of the Fifty-first Psalm, and Jean Thomas brutally rebelled, crying out:

"Now it's my turn to say 'Let's drink'! I refuse fear and I refuse pity! If the consciousness I possess as a man is to awaken, it will be through life and not through the terror of devils and other such artificial fabrications of the mind desperate for control!"

"Well, well!" sneered Maître Pierre. "Do you see what the effects of contrast are? I'll willingly drink to your rebellion, Thomas!"

Dominique intervened:

"No, we will not drink any more. Your job is finished, Maître Pierre, so stop sneering. Men's suffering is a stimulant for you, but today you'll have to find something else to excite you. I'm going to show Thomas around our studio."

He pulled open a curtain. The diffused light revealed the decor of the Atelier and projected the shadows of the sculptures, which created a moonlit atmosphere in the blue light.

Now it could be seen: the Tavern occupied the far end of a long room with a sloping ceiling. At a certain distance from the opposite wall, columns joined by Gothic arcades gave the studio the aspect of a church. Along the wall behind the columns was a gallery bristling with monstrous chimeras and devils, which seemed to be watching everything that was going on in the studio. Horned birds and winged devils perching atop the columns threatened to swoop down.

Grotesque masks were scattered about the Atelier. A jester was shaking his bauble in front of a choir desk. A crowned donkey sat majestically on a throne.

Without describing a thing, Dominique led Thomas to the other side of this long nave that was divided from the sculptor's studio by a low partition. During the day this enclave was lit by the light of a stained-glass window. At night the light was more diffuse. The atmosphere lent itself to work and to contemplation.

"I do the actual sculpture on the ground floor," explained Dominique. "This is my studio for dreaming and for preparing clay models."

Dominique showed Thomas some interesting models. Some of them were more like rough drafts of sketches, but others showed some of Rodin's audacity. Thomas was so taken by the power of these concepts that he remained silent. He observed the work and the face of the artist, his deep eyes, the dignity about him which was unable to conceal his zest for life.

He asked to see the nave once again, and the sculptor showed him the sketches and drawings by Maître Pierre, which were more or less inspired by Bosch and Brueghel, reproductions of whose work lined the walls. It was like being in a zoo as they visited all the demons, which seemed to eye the humans from their positions in the gallery.

Jean Thomas was surprised at the "lunar" coloration that was intentionally given to this setting.

Dominique replied:

"I gave this space the light that best suited the chimeras that inhabit it. It's a lunar atmosphere from the phantom astral world, outside of which they don't exist. Why does good common sense say that phantoms show themselves only at night? Why do people pray at night in Christian liturgy for the 'phantoms of the night' to be chased away? However, you're still too much of a scientist to listen to such things."

Thomas looked at the sculptor with curiosity.

"No doubt it's you who created these baroque monsters.

Dominique smiled. "Yes, it is I who sculpted them, but they are reproductions of subjects that already exist in churches and cloisters."

"What has your healthy and majestic work have in common with this burlesque phantasmagoria?"

"It makes my work possible. It's always a matter of the magic of contrasts. Let's rest here for a moment between the two and look at the world 'in truth.'"

"Is it possible to look 'in truth'?"

"Yes, if one doesn't do so with prejudice, with fear, or with one's own personal preferences."

"I'm not afraid of anything."

"How little you know yourself, my friend. Let yourself relive for a moment the scene of the Miserere: your pale face, your emotion, and your rebellion betrayed you. The chanting, the word, and the rhythm, when applied at the right moment, act upon the *vulnerable parts* of one's being. All that is deeply buried—certain memories or certain tendencies—regardless of the extent to which a human being denies them, can surface unexpectedly. You've got to admit that the obscene images on the choir stalls awakened in you a feeling of disgust. In contrast to this, the chanting of the Miserere produced an emotional reaction that overcame you in spite of yourself. Your not having recognized such a powerful instinct caused you to rebel. You thought that you were beyond such instincts. Don't regret this, but instead rejoice that you were able to face a moment of truth."

Jean Thomas sat with his eyes closed, struggling with himself. The sculptor's voice vibrated with intense emotion:

"Do not run away from this instant, Jean Thomas. In each life one arrives at important crossroads. . . . I, Jacques Dominique, am calling you to life."

"Are you still there, Jacques? . . . I'm glad. Instruct me, and I will listen to you."

The mood became very relaxed. The sculptor took him by the arm.

"Come, let's go look at our monsters.

"Look at this horned devil who seems to contemplate with gravity the crowd of humans standing there beneath his place at the top of Notre Dame's gallery. For him, it is the Lower World."

"Why do you refer to it as the Lower World? Man is superior through his intelligence."

"Man is inferior to that which dominates him. The powers of instinct, which are referred to as demons, are all too often the masters of human beings, precisely because they are unable to recognize them. The fact that animals are dominated by their instincts is in keeping with their nature, and the universal Harmony is not at all disrupted. But when man becomes the unconscious slave to these instincts, it is monstrous. Thus the caricatures that you see reproduced here are quite justified. This world of chimeras is the representation of the instinctive emotions and the fear that make our planet a veritable Hell on Earth."

"That's pretty depressing! Don't you see anywhere in this lower world a paradise sheltered from these troubles?"

"Of course! In the hearts of certain children, in those whose pure devotion allows them to give of themselves without making judgments of good or evil, and above all in those rare human beings who have recognized this hell and through confident effort have *consciously* gone beyond it. But you're not quite there yet, and you're no longer a child. Therefore, learn to know your enemies: these chimeras."

"You say that they represent fears and bad instincts?"

"It's not a matter of good or bad. The forces of instinct are the expression of essential functions (cosmic functions). Incarnated in animals, they are neither good nor bad, but inherent to their nature. Within each species they operate accordingly. Only man has the power—and therefore the responsibility—to control the extent to which he comes under their influence, if he doesn't want to descend to the level of an animal. The emotions that result from this can be put to good use, as you know from what you have experienced today. We'll talk about this again.

"Fears, on the other hand, are *always* harmful. You must unmask them in order to destroy them.

"Since we've been talking about Hell, take a look at this sketch for *The Last Judgment* by Brueghel, with the infernal monster snatching up all the damned in his mouth. The large portal of Notre Dame also represents the monstrous demons that crush all those poor souls who are damned 'for eternity'! These images and the descriptions of the punishments that await men have terrorized the believer for centuries without obliterating his troubles, and what's worse, without obliterating the hypocrisy of the 'repressed.'

"If 'free thought' has diminished credulity with regard to these diabolical henchmen, the fear of Hell still hovers above to get the 'sinners' to seek refuge in the confessional."

"The fear of punishment can bend the backs of men under a yoke," replied Thomas. "But no yoke and no law will ever awaken the sense of responsibility in my consciousness. Isn't that what's most important?"

"You've touched on a valid point, Thomas. You might add to that the sense of human dignity. As a matter of fact, during the Middle Ages, the Church took the initiative in instilling a sense of honor and hierarchy of nobility by creating knighthood."

"Then why did they also vilify and brutalize men with the threat of punishment?"

"It has to do with the misuse of the play of contrasts: on the one hand they were offering glory and honor on earth and *everlasting* paradise, and on the other hand they were offering damnation without hope and everlasting torment!

"Where is the error, Thomas?"

After long reflection, the doctor answered:

"I would situate the error in the discrepancy between the stakes involved and the brevity of the player's life, which is much too short for him to learn the rules of the game."

"That's right, Thomas, insofar as the rule of the game is the awakening of consciousness. But consciousness is more than the rule; it is the goal. But no one ever speaks about this goal. . . ."

"Why not?"

"Because if man becomes conscious and 'knowing,' he understands that good is only relative, he knows the inexorable law that governs the consequences of his acts, becomes his own confessor, no longer fears the threat of Hell or the loss of paradise, but believes in the Spirit and waits for enlightenment."

Pierre's sarcastic laughter, coming from the corner where he was crouching, attracted Thomas's attention.

"Well, my dear Doctor, if you haven't understood the reason for this silence by now . . ."

"Yes," retorted Dominique, "but we've dwelled long enough on this subject for today. We're just starting to get acquainted."

"That's all well and good," said Maître Pierre, "but since you've mentioned Hell and Paradise, you could have spoken about the middle ground: what are you going to do about Purgatory?"

"Ah, yes, of course!" Dominique laughed. "I forgot that it interests you! I see so little difference between this Purgatory and our actual existence that I was wary of repeating myself. Well, now, Thomas, let's take a closer look at this world of fears, desires, and regrets. Let's look at our chimeras.

"Take a look at this old owl with his hooked nose, menacing stare, and siren's tail, the gatekeeper of evening and morning who provokes fear and trembling with his howls.

"Look at the dung beetle that carries its treasure-filled house on its back: the sculptor gave him a disturbing head with an avaricious and mistrustful stare, like the look of someone who is afraid of 'losing' something he has, someone he loves. . . .

"What about this pig with a priest's head who is covering his eyes so he won't see the devil perched on his shoulders?

"Here's the monstrous raven with a man's feet and behind. He's threatening us with his beak. And over there, adjacent to the gallery, a perfect example of a 'fearsome' devil who's breathing down on us with his monstrous snout.

"And what about these chimeras with human heads who express every aspect of fear? Do you recognize them? The fear of death that dances before it . . . the fear of 'what will people say?' . . . the fear of credulity . . . the fear of remorse, the fear of the invisible world . . .

"Fear is a cancer that eats into our emotional being and makes us vulnerable to harmful influences."

"But we can experience fear through conscious doubts," retorted Thomas.

"Like what, for example? The fear of sin? That's a subject we give special attention to. Today, let's be content to look at it only from a psychological point of view: If I got used to a continual vigilance that made my consciousness a mirror reflecting all my actions, gestures, and intentions, I would feel *responsible* and would be the sole judge of my behavior, because my current consciousness is the measure of this responsibility. Thus, the only sin I still have to fear is that of the hypocrisy of my judgment. However, this hypocrisy takes the form of apology, another kind of chimera that blinds us, just like this sneering devil who is blindfolding this woman by appealing to her vanity under the pretext of charity. If my guard is up and I repel the temptation, not in order to obey the law but to obey the voice of my spiritual being, then I do not experience fear, because *I know that I will know* what I must do.

"Take notice of the fact that the same holds true for distinguishing superstition from faith—that is, certitude."

"Are all these chimeras and demons real or not?"

"The *forms* we attribute to them were created by the human mind and imagination. They subsist in the emotional (phantom or astral) world in which all these images are inscribed. In this way they can affect our body with emotions of which our shadow is composed, and go on to obsess it after our earthly existence. This domination disappears to the extent that consciousness is enlightened. But even if these forms are nonexistent in relation to the reality of the spiritual state, the cosmic forces that they 'clothe' do exist, because they are the more or less altered manifestation of true cosmic functions."

"Then I wonder why you have populated your atelier with all these uncouth monsters," said Jean Thomas.

"For the same reason that the cathedrals (which their builders intended as temples of teaching) have given them the place they occupy in the earthly world. They have no more influence on conscious men. Those who are ignorant must learn how to unmask them in order to become conscious."

"I don't see any of the gargoyles from Notre Dame here."

"Nor are there dragons or composite animals who symbolize realities of another order. If you're interested, we'll study them when the time is right."

"I must admit that I'm still shocked by the donkey in the bishop's cap who's seated on the episcopal throne, and by the jester dancing in front of the choir desk. Is it a gross satire or a disdain for Church ritual?"

"It's neither of those; otherwise the Church would not have continued to authorize the feast of the donkey or the feast of fools inside the cathedral. The costumes, rituals, and liturgy were established by sages who knew the magical value of forms, gestures, and words when they are put into the service of the cosmic laws of the Creation and the communion of mortal man with what is Immortal and Divine. Great hermetic science is at the basis for all the revelations. You skeptical materialists can doubt these realities, but the very fact that you are scandalized by their apparent profanation is the justification for their existence. Your disquiet witnesses a certain sense of the sacred without which this 'profanation' would have left you indifferent."

"If I believe in the 'sacred,' I've certainly never been aware of it!"

"That's right! Any means used to awaken the consciousness is good. The most devout of people are blasphemous when they profane the Virgin with the crudest of swear words. Is it deliberate? No. It's the instinctive search for a thrust of sentiment that, by contrast, stirs up respect. If anything is to be feared, it is *mediocrity*, the paleness that stifles the consciousness through habit, and prevents it from awakening.

"What are the causes for the suicides, the unmotivated crimes, and the desperate acts that disgrace our times? You can be sure that above all it's *desecration*. Since rational intelligence claims it can explain everything, does that mean there are no mysteries in Nature, that nothing is sacred, that there's nothing to hope for beyond our human condition? 'Profit,' then, is the only goal left: thus there is class struggle and fighting between nations to extract the greatest possible advantages out of domination."

"This might hold true for the majority of people," retorted Jean, "but I protest this in the name of a small group of selfless people who, behind the scenes, are scientifically, physiologically, and socially seeking to pave the way for a better life for future generations."

"Hope! High hopes! Why, and on what basis, would tomorrow be any better than today? Man is not benefiting from his own experience, and in the eyes of the universe he's responsible for the 'present moment' and for his own actions with regard to his contemporaries."

"What do you think we are lacking?"

"The knowledge of what there is to adore."

"Inventing that could only be worse for us!"

"There's nothing to invent: we live from 'That' and for 'That.'"

"Again you're talking about being religious."

"No, I am referring to man's knowledge. The error of science is to make us believe that our rational intelligence is our supreme superiority. It's not the first time that such a crisis has occurred, and each time it has given rise to horrible destruction.

"Human destiny goes far beyond this pitiful existence. I am talking not about haphazard paradises, but about a state of consciousness that allows each 'present moment' to collect the knowledge of why man is here on Earth, and to participate in the 'superior life' of the universe. Great beings (who were here long before we were) proved that this is possible through their own realization."

"And what was the result?"

"A Wisdom that enabled them to guide their contemporaries in a life that was *in harmony with their possibilities*. Even more, a Knowledge that we can draw upon today for certain *vital* sciences which are beyond our reach."

"How?"

"With the confidence in man's possibility to surpass himself, and with the intensive cultivation of his consciousness."

"That sounds as if it must lead to a highly inflated ego."

"Not at all! An inflated ego is not something that needs to be taught. Listen to this."

Dominique chose a record.

"I'm telling you in advance that I haven't invented any of this. It's the recording of a worldly conversation, and only the useless parts have been cut.

The record spoke:

I myself am terrified by the number of accidents.
I myself am surprised that there aren't even more.
I myself don't understand our government.
I myself would issue an immediate decree!
I myself, my dear, am always right.
I myself say: "Your book, Master, is a revelation!"
I myself adore it! I adore your hero.
I myself am thinking of Balzac: he's inferior to you!
I myself see you becoming a member of the Academy.
I myself am not chasing after acclaim.
I myself am allergic to strawberries.
And *I* to castor oil.
If *I* were the pope . . .
I myself don't believe in Fatima.

I myself am not ready to pronounce my opinion.
I myself am certain that they're going to canonize him.
I myself am unable to sleep alone in bed.
I myself think that Einstein was really something!
I myself find that Brother X has beautiful hands. I adore his sermons!
I myself find that life is unbearable without money!
As *I* always say, a man is a walking corpse if he has no money!
I myself don't have to keep an eye on my weight. I've got a model's waist.
I myself am only interested in charitable deeds.
I myself choose my protégés judiciously!
I myself think Dior is a genius.
I myself can't stand listening to Wagner anymore.
I myself adore the cha-cha-cha.
I myself see the advent of nuclear war.
I just happen to have some inside information, but it's hush-hush!

The record ended. Jean Thomas shrugged.

"That's quite a litany of I-myself!"

"Yes, my friend, but we're so used to it that we don't even see the odious ridiculousness of it. Evoke the *danse macabre* of all these me's clouded over with their little personal goals and allowing themselves to be pushed around by their instinctive forces, and you'll see that all of them take on the figure of devils or 'well-intentioned' angels: philanthropic or egotistical ambitions, devotion or disharmony with regard to the destiny of others or of themselves, religious arguments over dogma that has been modified a hundred times, crimes in the name of human as well as divine love! . . .

"Watch this procession of opinions march by, and you'll see each spectator sticking on a label of Bad or Good according to his *opinion*. Opinions! Opinions! When they used to credit the king's jester with uttering certain truths when he unleashed his mind, weren't they less crazy than we are today when we take all these contradictions, unfounded opinions, interchangeable beliefs, and unfounded skepticisms so seriously?"

Jean Thomas, his head in his hands, was deeply troubled. After a long silence he lifted his head. Both reproach and prayer appeared on his face.

"Don't overwhelm me, Dominique. If you see clearly through all this chaos, I myself am used to considering it as the normal condition of existence. Do you have a remedy to suggest?"

Dominique looked kindly upon him.

"I'm neither prophet nor messiah, my friend, but I'm humble enough to believe that our scientific intelligence has perhaps lessons to learn from the sages who offered solutions to the vital problems that distress us."

"But isn't looking backward a regression?"

"I'm not talking about the conditions of life that change from one period to the next. There are laws of Harmony that men have periodically been taught, then neglected, according to the openness or the closedness of the *Intelligence of the Heart*. The knowledge of these laws reveals the role of man and the goal of his existence—*an invariable goal*—as well as the stage at which our contemporary humanity is situated.

"The means of attaining this goal *vary according to the 'stage'*: thus it is necessary that each period adapt in terms of mode and language. That is very important to know, since that is what can shed light on your chaos. Once the goal is clarified, despair has no more reason to exist, because current existence then presents itself as the level on an ascending path which ends with the realization of the Total Man (the suprahuman realm), in whom opposition and contradiction no longer exist.

"Of what importance are the incidents along the path?"

"Dominique," murmured Thomas, "I think that I have no choice in the matter: will you be my Master?"

Dominique burst out laughing.

"For lack of someone better? You are right, because you will find your Master among men who have understood, today this one, tomorrow another. Light is communicated through beings who are seeking . . . on the right path, of course!"

5
Breaking the
"Barrier of Possibility"

When Thomas returned home a little before midnight, Anna was there waiting up for him.

"What are you doing up at this hour, Sister Anne? Is something wrong?"

"A pilot friend of yours is waiting outside on your balcony."

"What friend?" Thomas rushed out with a shout of joy:

"Jean-Jacques, old boy! It's been a long time! It's great to see you again!"

The pilot hugged his friend.

"Yeah, I've come to ask you for a survivor's welcome."

"What happened?"

"I've just returned from a mission that I thought was going to be my last."

"Did you have an accident?"

"As I was landing. First my radio stopped working, for no apparent reason. The rain had turned into a fine drizzle and the cockpit was covered with fog, which made visibility increasingly tough. I made a first pass at three hundred meters at slow speed to see the direction of the wind-sock that indicated the runway. There it was, clearly visible, the bottom hanging along the length of the mast which indicated roughly: weak wind, runway oh-five. I prepared to land accordingly, but visibility was almost zero and I didn't cut the throttle until I reached the runway. My plane, which usually glided like an iron over an ironing board, took a while to reach ground. It finally touched. . . . I braked, but the rain had dampened the brakes and they didn't work. Despite all my efforts I felt myself being slowly carried toward the ditch that surrounded the runway just past the safety zone.

"Crash! At sixty kilometers an hour I pass through, head over heels. Unhurt, I jumped from the plane, pressed against the tail wing, and straightened it out. The starter wasn't working, so I jammed the brakes and tried to get the motor started manually. It turned over three times, coughed, and with a horrible explosion the whole thing went up in flames: I barely had time to jump back! We later learned that the carburetor had cracked from the shock that occurred when the plane had nosedived: the wind-sock, drenched with rain, had indicated the wrong direction."

"What an experience!"

"Ah, well, it's just one of the many. . . ."

"Have you seen your commanding officers?"

"We did what was necessary for the verifications. The rest can wait until tomorrow. Can you put me up for the night?"

It was Anna who answered. "Of course, I've already prepared your room. And here's the welcome you requested."

Jean-Jacques was thrilled: "What a fine late-night supper you've prepared! I was right to tell them at the airport that I had private matters to attend to: you!

"Are you alone here in Paris?"

"Yes. Over the past ten years my family has shed its leaves all over . . . and beyond. I am alone, strangely alone."

"Not anymore, since I am here."

"So I see, but I'm talking about another kind of solitude."

Supper was served in front of the open window in the glow of candlelight, upon the pilot's request. As he ate, he contemplated the dark Paris sky with emotion.

"It's true that the sky over a particular place reflects the space beneath. Will I still feel the same about this reflection?"

"How melancholy you seem. Where's that old jolly fellow I used to know?"

"Oh, he's still there, but perhaps he's changed his pace. I'll tell you, old chap: living in the constant company of danger sharpens the claws."

"Perilous missions?"

"Special missions that I'm not at liberty to speak about."

"Still in airplanes?"

"As a rule, yes, but with intermediaries, and always with the un-expected. It's a bit like abandoning yourself to Providence."

"Under the circumstances, wouldn't Providence be the fantasies of your commanding officers?"

"Do you believe that? When a commander who's conscious of his role as a human being, which is just as hard for him as for anyone else, takes on the responsibility for watching over the security of his country, and sometimes for avoiding catastrophic cataclysms, do you think that this commander allows himself to experience fantasies?"

"What I meant were fantasies of daring whose consequences he is not always able to measure."

"A commander who's worthy of this title—and there are men like this in the secret service—don't have much choice except between different rash deeds, for the simple reason that the *basic* destiny of nations—as of men—involves developments that cannot be predicted, because we are not wise enough to get to the roots of such developments. To understand the direction and the 'will' of the branches, you've got to study the roots of the tree. The Chinese have a saying that in order to estimate the consequences of an act, one must envision its repercussions up to seven times seven."

"Do the commanders you know have such powers of deduction?"

"It has nothing to do with logical deduction. In any event, this logic cannot be accurate unless one knows the nature of the tree's seed, which is carried out by the tendencies and the 'will' of the roots that sustain it."

"How can you speak of the 'will' of a vegetable?"

"Because plant life is truly a manifestation of will. The root is its first expression and its first resting place. It's the root that fixes its fluidity in the earth, and the root will run in the direction of the water, or toward those elements it needs to sustain itself. If you look for the roots of a nation in this same spirit, you'll notice that the nature of the fruits it will bear cannot be changed. You can't change its branches either. They are the expression of its behavior."

"But this nation of people could be transplanted."

"In that case the people would take on the characteristics of the place to which their roots would have to adapt. I use the word *adapt* because the essential nature of the roots would remain. However, the consciousness of these differences in nature and of the possibilities of adaptation is lacking in the conquerors and politicians who claim they lead people according to the laws, rhythms, or religions to which they are unable to adapt themselves. They make twisted trees out of these people, who are constantly trying to stand according to their natural tendencies."

"But don't these 'special missions' that you collaborate in serve the purposes of these imprudent politicians?"

"You could even use the word *disharmonious* to describe them. They're obviously working toward the goal conceived by these politicians. But frequently their secret leaders, who are more experienced in psychological warfare with the reactions of their enemies, apply themselves to the task of tempering the catastrophic results of ill-timed decisions. Can you understand the instances of conscience that we must submit to without discussion?"

"It must be even more difficult since you have no choice in the matter but to obey."

"Necessarily so, and for me the most difficult circumstance is to have to sacrifice the individual."

"And yet you remain faithful to your position."

"I don't know if I'm going to stay. I'm so obsessed with the problem of human life that it's becoming unbearable."

"You find the same thing everywhere, even the most religious peoples in the world—Hindus, Chinese, and Japanese—sacrifice the alleged enemy without a trace of pity."

"I think there is a difference in terms of the peoples you've mentioned," said Jean-Jacques. "I think many of these people have an excuse that we Westerners lack: they believe in reincarnation. For them each existence is a passage, an experience that is perpetuated in future incarnations. In this case, death is not the definitive end to the unique existence during which man prepares to achieve his goal and his 'realization.' For them, killing is not the annihilation and definitive spiritual loss of a man."

"Does that mean you believe all this?"

"I've done a lot of traveling. I've seen the faith the Chinese have in the reincarnation of their ancestors. I've seen the faith of the Japanese in the act of hara-kiri, through which they achieve consciousness of honor for their next reincarnation. I've seen the faith of an Indo-Chinese thief who asks to be decapitated in order to experience the horror of stealing and liberate himself from this tendency in his next existence.

"All these peoples believe in immanent justice which will repay human acts with their own consequences. This is made possible through a succession of existences that allow them to benefit from acquired experience, even if their cerebral consciousness is not involved."

"But how can a man who's reincarnated profit from acquired experience if cerebral memory is annihilated by death?" objected Thomas.

"As to forgetfulness, I asked a very wise Hindu about what was represented in the Greek myth of the river Lethe, in which the dead were supposedly immersed to lose the memory of their existence. He told me: 'It's the symbol of an intermediate state between the mental state and the more subtle state which follows. It's already spiritual since the mental waves break there like waves against the shore.' In other words, cerebral memory is effaced by the rhythm of waves that don't correspond to it.

"But this Hindu explained to me that our ethereal body conserves our emotional impressions for our 'purgatory,' alas! However, it also is the registered experience that allows the reincarnated being to enlarge his consciousness and 'subconsciously' benefit from it by altering his consequent behavior.

"In believing this, one no longer is outraged by the seeming injustice of unmerited suffering or by the impunity of criminal or dishonest acts that people benefit from, nor by catastrophes that deprive their victims of the existence they need in order to evolve. All these injustices could be blamed on Providence if man had only one existence to achieve what is called Eternal Salvation or . . . eternal damnation."

"This obviously needs thinking about," said Thomas with a sigh.

"After seeing things from this point of view, I asked myself how we can kill a man in cold blood, casting him into what, *according to our religion*, could be eternal death, since we don't believe in reincarnation."

"I'm astonished to find you've changed your mind to such an extent. You're not the joyous impenitent unbeliever I once knew!"

"Living with death, and the necessity of killing out of 'duty' that's accepted, awakened in me a consciousness whose very existence I had ignored. And once that happens, old buddy, it's under your skin to stay. There's no getting rid of it!

"When you spend so much time flying up there, you get a more precise notion of how scanty the Earth is. And that's also what makes me understand the importance of having roots, this power that holds us to the Earth."

"The force of gravity?"

"It's not gravity I'm thinking of, but that which attracts our material bodies toward this material Earth."

"The inevitable effect of gravity is what does it."

"That's true under normal conditions, but the man who knows how to incorporate his spiritual being into his physical being can minimalize this servitude, first by increasing the force of his subtle elements, then by revitalizing the 'cruder' elements. In certain cases of extreme experience (which have been carefully controlled and verified in India and Tibet), he can even levitate. It's been confirmed that many Western mystics have been able to achieve this."

"Even if this sort of thing does exist, it's extremely rare," retorted Thomas.

"Obviously so, but the fact that it's possible confirms that the spiritualization of being can weaken man's attraction for matter and develop his affinity for more subtle states, states of which he already bears the seed.

Many confirmed miracles are nothing other than the application of this disposition which can modify certain aspects of the material by diminishing the cohesion of its composite elements or by harmonizing all that is disharmonious. It is this that causes wounded flesh to heal.''

"Are you telling me that now you believe in miracles?"

"On the contrary, I believe that we've got the wrong notion of what a miracle is. We generally attribute it to a Divine Power, or more precisely a Divine Being, who intervenes on behalf of the believer. I don't know enough about it to be sure whether or not this is justified, but I have understood that a lot of so-called miracles result from supernatural action—in the sense that laws which defy those physical and rational laws are brought into play. This action is the application of human possibilities that normally remain undeveloped."

"By Jove! You're going beyond our rational thought processes, but let's leave this aside for the moment: it demands verification."

Thomas interrupted his remark to think about his own mysterious vision, which also went beyond rational concepts. False modesty prevented him from confiding this to his friend, and he diverted the man's attention to hide his distress:

"Without being indiscreet, Jean-Jacques, can you tell me what all your travels and observations of human behavior have taught you, and if you've been able to come to any interesting conclusions with regard to different nations and their mutual relations?"

"In terms of the peace prospects for our little ball of earth, I'm not optimistic! That's because it comes down to a chaotic conflict between the overall interests of humanity and the egotistical interests of entire peoples, who, like individuals, are all blinded by their own self-interest.

"This blindness frightens me even more than the threat of nuclear weapons, because the causes of this conflict go right to the vital points of human society; they run the gamut from racial bitterness to spiritual dissatisfaction via all the inherent miseries of a disordered economy. All you have to do, Thomas, is look around you to see a capsule image of the global situation: political squabbling, discord between the numerous parties, the infinite number of opinions, the large number of group movements that are groping for methods of 'initiation'! This multiplicity is due to the ignorance of *essential realities*, and it opens the door to anarchy, which obscures all consciousness."

"You're no doubt right, Jean-Jacques, but do you really believe there's a possibility of remedying this chaotic state?"

"Unfortunately, that's outside the realm of my expertise, but I do believe that every available means must be used to alert reasonable men to the danger of superficial opinions and the fact that dangerous opponents, who have gathered their strength through a clearly defined goal, are waiting in ambush."

"Your hopes are a bit utopian, somewhat like those of a man who would like to stop a storm by shouting!"

"Utopian? Maybe it's only a matter of politics. But aren't you sensitive to the anguished cry of our contemporaries? It's the scream of men who feel the current of this madness, the haze of *uncertainty* or their loss of the ability to discern the goal of their existence. Uncertainty gives rise to incoherence, in which notions of the Divine and Providence are negated by the triumph of evil, by misery and injustice with no *apparent* motive."

"Did you find this same sort of distress among the peoples of the East?"

"No, because their religion responds to this by showing them the immanent justice in *karma*, which is the consequential effect of successive lives. I found that they believed in the supra-evolution of a human through communion with the Divine.

"I also found political and racial strife that we Westerners have sometimes provoked. And I discovered that they had their own vices, which, before we arrived on the scene, hurt only them. We added our own vices to theirs, in addition to *envy* for what they call our 'civilization.' This envy now threatens us, and we have to defend ourselves against it: it's a wretched situation."

"And it's all due to the lack of insight and the ignorance of our heads of state!"

"That's right, old friend, an ignorance of the nature and qualities of each race and each nation. Above all, it's their ignorance of the cyclical movement of world history and the subsequent consequences in the evolution of human beings.

"This ignorance is a serious matter. Take the white man's claim of superiority over all the other races in the world. They have to justify their claim with the knowledge of man's higher destiny and the spiritual elements that are necessary to achieve it. However, we Westerners are inferior to the Easterners with respect to this knowledge—in both theory and *practice*. The Easterners know it, and this lessens us in their eyes beyond belief."

"Are you sure of what you're saying?"

"Totally sure. I've observed it in India, in China, and in Japan (despite a certain religious decadence brought about by westernization). They know it, and for us this represents a danger far greater than their military advancement. Moreover, despite their giving in to materialistic influences, they've still kept the sense of individual nobility, something that we've prostituted through democratization. Under the pretext of 'equality' we've wrought the loss of qualitative values upon ourselves and advocated it for others. We've placed the importance on utilitarian values, leveling everything off into mediocrity."

"I've got to agree with you on that," said Thomas. "Nonetheless, will you admit that the suppressive caste systems in the East were governed by the same sort of principles?"

"The East, like the West, is subject to the rhythm of our times. Adapting to this rhythm necessarily brings about certain changes. The *way* in which these changes are made has destroyed harmony instead of allowing it to adapt to the social and spiritual necessities of the times. Aren't we Westerners partly responsible for this, as well as for the disdain with which we looked upon the culture of black peoples when we wanted to 'civilize' them? The only thing we're able to replace the heritage of nobility with is vulgarization."

"Just a minute here! The nobility of caste was its own source of destruction, through the decadence and abuse of its privileges."

"That's true. But the main cause of this decadence was above all the loss of the Knowledge that the first banners of chivalry bore witness to. The second cause was the transmission of titles and privileges *through heredity.*"

"Here, I'll have you notice, Jean-Jacques, that the principle of heredity can be justified by the need for a suitable education, and a bloodline that 'remains noble' through prohibiting its members to join professions that are not noble, such as commerce and certain uncouth trades."

"It would be justified if the transmission of Knowledge maintained the effective value of Nobility. However, Knowledge cannot be transmitted through heredity. It's conditioned by the awakening of consciousness and the intuitive qualities of the seeker.

"However, you must understand, Thomas, that this acquiring of Wisdom is *always individual.*"

"If I understand you correctly, does this mean that a fixed 'nobility' would be made up of an elite selected on the basis of *quality?*"

"That's how ancient China and ancient Egypt understood it and practiced it."

"How is it possible to achieve this in our current period, when society tends toward an equality of mediocrity?"

"We're in the midst of a conflict between two divergent tendencies. There's the sense of 'collectivity,' on the one hand, which wants to equalize intellectual as well as material values by the sharing of rights and duties without regard to the degree each individual has evolved. On the other hand there's a vulgar manifestation of individualism which expresses itself in inconsiderate and ungainly rebellion, in art as well as in opinions. It also expresses itself in the need to stand up to criticism through scandal or through originality.

"It's curious, though, that these contradictory tendencies correspond to two states of consciousness that divide our contemporaries. The New Testament—like other Traditions—describes these states as the Many and the Few: the Many strive toward a goal of earthly existence dictated by cerebral intelligence, whereas the Few aspire to the suprahuman realm by means of the Intelligence of the Heart."

"I never would have thought that these two categories could be so clearly defined."

"I'm not concerned with intermediate groupings. What I'm looking at are the two governing impulses that characterize the aspirations of these two categories.

"In one sense, the Few correspond to an elite that has been chosen for its spiritual aspirations and for its noble behavior, attributes that make Knowledge accessible. These Few would not find joy in the kind of gratifications that the Many are looking for. In another sense, this group has the right to act and behave freely, which is necessary for the increase of consciousness.

"Contrary to this, the Many want a better state of well-being and more earthly pleasures, with equality of laws and social obligations. This is what they need to guarantee their security, because they would not accept the selflessness and the rigor of conscience that goes with the quest of the Few, and which are more severe than any laws!

"The understanding of this difference would provide the solution to the conflict. Each one of the two categories would be accorded the advantages it wants. Likewise, the laws and the learning possibilities corresponding to their respective qualities would be justly accorded."

"What you're asking for would demand a government of Wise Men!"

"That's true, but ancient China, India, and Egypt have proved that this is possible, so it's not just a utopian notion. It is such a notion, alas, in our world, given the way it's organized, because *know-how* has replaced *Knowledge*, religious rivalries have replaced the unchanging teaching of Wisdom based on the great laws of Harmony, and individual interests dominate all of international politics.

"A will for independence breaths in each country, and the leaders of these countries are thinking only about how they can better their chances of survival at the expense of other countries. Needless to say, these two tendencies are incompatible with the attainment of international understanding."

"Obviously, the problem won't be solved as long as the appetites of

some are opposed to the independence of others. That's what characterizes the ongoing history of conquest and rebellion, but in our times this
conflict has reached epidemic proportions: one after another, people are
awakening to demand their rights, just like vipers who suddenly stand
erect to threaten passers-by!"

"'Like vipers' is a good way of putting it," admitted the pilot, "because
words like 'nationalism' and 'independence' have been spurted out like
venom by deliberate agitators who want only to serve themselves. These
slogans are used to give certain powers the leverage they need to 'liberate'
a people. Once this happens, they impose themselves on the people for
so-called reasons of protection. These slogans have been a war cry to
the common people, who have allowed themselves to be swept into the
spirit of anarchy and revolt. These slogans provide an excellent pretext
for them to express their resentment, which is based on an inferiority
complex."

"Possibly, said Thomas, "but in certain cases this inferiority complex
seems justified by a very real incapacity for self-government; it could be
because of jealousy between leaders or between tribes, or the lack of
ability to organize the economic or technical machinery."

"This kind of inferiority demands the reinstatement of a balance,
which itself will always be temporary: the weakest are obliged to accept
the help of the strongest, even if it's to free themselves from bondage.
But as long as egoism governs the world, the price to be paid for this help
becomes just another form of bondage for the countries that one is
claiming to liberate."

"Why is it that these countries can't see the shadow of the new iron
hand that awaits them?"

"Because they're blinded by mercantile interests. The people allow
themselves to be manipulated by politics based on shameless bargaining.
The humanitarian ideals that appear to help the cause of national claims
serve as pretexts for the powers that want to control the world, and who
have the financial resources and the means of destruction as their essential
weapons to accomplish this."

"If our era seems truly opposed to colonialist principles, it's hard for
me to see the opportunity for imperialist ambitions in all this," said
Thomas.

"Colonization has no more reason to exist, since the massive network
of rapid communication has already more or less equalized the peoples of
our planet. A nation has the right to colonize a people when it brings
them the qualities and the knowledge that can only be acquired by being
governed, formed, and 'educated' by it. From the moment this people
attains the level of the colonizer, it can legitimately demand to govern

autonomously. The colonizing nation can then expect an *association* of interests instead of *domination*, as payment for the advantages that the people have acquired. The newly acquired individualism of the people makes this unacceptable."

"I get what you're saying, Jean-Jacques, but that's just one more reason to be surprised by these imperialist thrusts which are so contrary to our times."

"It's no longer a matter of colonization, but of domination, which is being played out on an enormous scale!" retorted Jean-Jacques.

"Numerous large-scale trends of social or spiritual idealism, which are more or less bolstered by repressive forces, are trying to compel recognition as the World Government. We're dealing with the same problem of small-scale colonization: the right to govern belongs to superiority through quality. What determines this superiority in terms of our humanity, if not the degree to which the consciousness is awakened, and the ascending march toward a suprahuman state that is spiritual in nature?

"This ascending march—which corresponds to the highest point of view and goal of religions which are striving to be revealed—is the program proposed by evangelical doctrine for those who, while being *in* this world, are not *of* this world.

"This program is diametrically opposed to the methods of domination utilized by 'this world,' which are based on financial superiority, the means for destruction, the violation of consciousness in favor of ideals imposed by the dominating power."

"I understand what you're getting at," said Thomas. "You're trying to evaluate the legitimacy of imperialist ambition according to the quality of its impact."

"According to how the program it proposes corresponds to the degree of humanity's evolution and the needs that result from this. These needs, however, correspond to two different aspirations: one wants the continuation of existence on Earth while the other wants to go beyond the conditions of earthly existence, which it experiences as bondage.

"The same imperialist power is not able to manage these two categories unless it is led by sages who are able to understand the difference between the needs of the masses and the aspirations of the elite."

"I'm starting to catch sight of the seriousness of the problem," said Thomas, "because it's clear that each power that wants to dominate the world addresses itself to the masses. Regardless of which one eventually achieves its ambition, it means that the aspirations of the elite will be stifled."

"It's inevitable," acquiesced the pilot. "This elite could counter arbitrary dogmatism with real Knowledge, while dogmatism, in *imposing* a belief, prevents the awakening of consciousness and of the Intelligence of the Heart."

Thomas sighed. "The situation is tragic for those who want to acquire 'certitude' through their personal quest.

"This brings to mind words from the Gospel, which intrigued me because they were addressed to the Scholars of the Law, who at that time had sole authority over the interpretation of the religious texts that referred to the Messiah: 'Woe unto you, lawyers! for ye have taken away the key of Knowledge: ye entered not in yourselves, and them that were entering in ye hindered.'"[1]

The pilot smiled as he listened to his friend.

"Since you're quoting from the Gospel, here are words that add to those you've cited: 'But the hour cometh, and now is, when the true worshipers shall worship the Father in spirit and in truth: for the Father seeketh such to worship him. God is spirit: and they that worship him must worship him in spirit and in truth.'[2]

"Take note of the fact that these were the words of Jesus spoke to a woman of the Samaritans, a tribe that was repudiated by the Judaic scholars at the Temple of Jerusalem."

"Indeed, that is strange," admitted Thomas.

"Take note, as well, that the Samaritans accepted the mission of Jesus because of this teaching, while the theologians of Jerusalem became his enemies."

"Why give this message to a woman who was obviously not a theologian?"

"Perhaps for that very reason," suggested the pilot. "But weren't you struck by the words 'The hour cometh, and now is . . .'? Curiously enough, these words specify the New Age which characterizes the appearance of the Messiah: the Age of Pisces, the new zodiacal sign, which will give to Christ's disciples the symbol of the fish!"

"Very interesting indeed," acknowledged Thomas: "the New Age, the new symbol, and the new teaching. But this message was also calling for a new direction, because it attached more importance to the Spirit and less to the letter of the law. Truth became more important than . . . what is the word used to express the opposite of Truth?"

"Go back to the preceding phrase: 'Ye worship ye know not what: we [the disciples of Christ] know what we worship. . . .'

"In other words, until then people *adhered* to a faith commanded by

1. Luke 11:52
2. John 4:23–24

law; henceforth, it's necessary to *know* that which one worships. Knowledge replaces belief. Isn't Knowledge the consciousness of what is real, outside of forms, theories, hypotheses, and sensorial and cerebral illusions? Isn't that what 'worship in spirit and in truth' means?"

"I'm tempted to agree with you, although I've never given much thought to these things. I must say that I'm quite impressed by the opportunity this teaching 'in spirit and in truth' provides for these chaotic times of rationalism, materialism, and exclusive dogmatism."

"Times are once again on the verge of a new precessional sign, since we're about to enter the Age of Aquarius," continued Thomas enthusiastically. "If I had the spirit of the apostolate, I'd cry out like Jonah in public places: 'Woe unto them who have lost the keys of knowledge and who prevent others from entering!'"

"Bravo!" exclaimed the pilot, laughing. "But I think you're getting punchy from lack of sleep, old boy. Jonah only predicted the destruction of Nineveh (an appropriate reference, though). Let's end the discussion with this eloquent touch, which is rather astonishing to hear from a scientist known for his unabashed positivism! To what do we owe this sudden interest in the word of the Gospel and the keys to Knowledge?"

Thomas shrugged his shoulders, trying to avoid the question, but Jean-Jacques's curiosity gave him cause for hesitation.

"It's too long to explain," he groaned, pretending to look for a cigarette. "Certain fortuitous coincidences have forced me to revise some of my materialistic concepts, and the problem of the possibility of intuitive perception came up. Even when fact obliged me to admit it, it still didn't show me how to consciously acquire the use of this faculty, or even how to modify my way of seeing. It's all very well and good to be opened up to another 'point of view,' but you just can't make a tabula rasa of deeply rooted notions and habits that have been acquired through atavism and education! How can those of us who are molded by this mentality retrace our steps?"

The pilot shook his head, smiling, and lit up a cigarette.

"What do you do to retrace your steps?" he repeated dreamily. "You can't imagine how well you've put it. I've got to admit that I didn't think it was possible, and this thrust me into unbearable torment. However, an important experience led me to believe otherwise.

"Do you know what it means to 'break the sound barrier'? It's a colorful way of describing the critical moment at which the airplane attains the identical speed of a sound wave.

"This speed varies according to the altitude: on the ground it amounts to 1,225 kilometers an hour, whereas at an altitude of 10,000 meters it's only 1,060 kilometers an hour. Regardless of the altitude, the moment it's attained is always dangerous, if you are unable to move quickly beyond it. Here's why: sound produces a sort of wave which is a state of vibration that is different from heat or light waves. That's common knowledge. However, as long as the plane is moving at a speed less than that of sound, it's moving *behind* the wave. If the plane attains the exact speed, it enters into conflict with it. This conflict produces violent disturbances in the matter and structure of the plane, which was built to evolve in the same 'world' as sound, but at a slower speed than that at which sound is translated, and therefore it does not attain this state of vibration.

"If the plane is able to go beyond the speed of sound, it again finds a peaceful zone because *there is no more sound*. It's traveling faster than a sound wave. Therefore, there is no longer a conflict."

"I get it," said Thomas. "The critical instant is therefore the passage beyond, despite the resistance of the plane."

"That's right, and this moment is very moving, because all the elements of the craft are jolted, since the plane is undergoing an effect of distortion with frightening vibrations. It starts to tremble like a panicking animal. The first attempts to break the sound barrier—whether voluntary or involuntarily—caused many fatal accidents. In certain cases the dislocation caused the plane to explode. Finally there was a pilot who, having understood that it involved passing into a 'state' different from the one the craft had been conditioned for, had the courage to act against the normal way of maneuvering. He went beyond the critical point as soon as he hit the speed of sound, and the craft once again became peaceful and docile, having broken through the sound barrier.

"Listening to my buddies tell the story of what is now an easy thing to do, I got passionately interested in trying it myself. I was duly instructed and forewarned about the way the craft would react and to how the pilot had to behave. I went about it with cold-blooded preparation so that I wouldn't make a mistake.

"The actual experience was really rough on my nerves, because it's disturbing to feel your plane tremble and buck like a terrified horse. But the real test was to be conscious of the extraordinary phenomenon that called for the reversal of the controls in order to outrun this dangerous race. I thus had to react *in the opposite way* from what one normally does.

"The peace and calm that followed this reversal were much more upsetting than the instant of danger. I was anxious to get back down to the ground in order to get hold of myself, and to contemplate this spiritual event, which for me had been the real experience.

"When I got back to the ground I felt like shouting: 'I'll be! I had no idea it was so simple!' Thomas, have you understood the importance of this symbol which suddenly lightened my path? No? You haven't understood. Let me try to explain.

"What keeps us from reaching the superior World that the spiritual powers as well as the subtle states of our immortal being belong to? It's precisely the distance between this spiritual state (or mode of being) and our physical or mental state. You can even compare this to the different vibratory states that our physical body and our mental faculties and functions are conditioned by.

"There are no tricks to passing from one state to the other: the mind cannot gain access to intuitive knowledge, whose perceptions are no longer conditioned by our 'three dimensions.'

"Having been conceived by our intuitive sense, knowledge can then be communicated to our cerebral intelligence, just like the pilot who was able to understand this phenomenon of going beyond and then adjust his maneuvers accordingly. But this passage into a different vibratory state demands a maneuver that is not only different from but opposite to normal behavior."

Thomas was intent on his friend's passionate delivery:

"It's this inverse action that intrigues me."

"This 'reversal' was the revealing spark for me. Follow me attentively: we cannot attain the state of intuitive knowledge by bringing our cerebral faculties into play; they register and assemble notions, ideas, and thoughts that are mental 'vibrations.' Knowledge is the entry into a different state, on a level at which personal thoughts are replaced with *realities*: living connections, the interplay of Harmony and functions of a universal nature that are the causal world of the phenomenal world that we know.

"We can penetrate this causal world only through the state within us that corresponds to it, through subtle senses or faculties that have the same order of vibrations. Do you follow what I'm saying?"

"I'm beginning to see what you're getting at, but I have no idea how to get there."

"Break the Barrier of Possibility:[3] reverse the controls! Instead of trying to understand through thought, remain silent. "Listen" from within in order to go beyond the mental vibrations. You see, nature refuses excess. If you force it to go beyond itself, you'll break through the veil that will allow you to enter a superior state. But if you try to force the passage with the usual mental means, the machine will jolt and inevitably be thrown out of gear."

"And you succeeded?"

3. See Chapter 18, page 300.

"Having understood this, I tried to put it to use. What I had caught sight of from *patient* meditation, I applied to my cerebral machine. I allowed it to register without letting it intervene.

"That's the whole of it. And I've learned more since that day than during all my complicated studies."

Thomas somberly observed his friend.

"I see that your long absence has matured you and profoundly marked you. Are you aware that this maturity has been engraved on your features, giving them the assured expression of 'one who knows'?"

"You're exaggerating, old friend! My consciousness has awakened to the human condition and to the goal of existence, but I know what's missing: knowledge of the foundations that allow us to distinguish the real from the relative."

"I envy your knowing what it is that you're missing."

"Until that day my only master had been life. But then life took on the responsibility of informing me about it. Now I aspire to a more precise teaching.

"What's become of you over the past ten years?"

"I'm a doctor, working at a laboratory."

"I see: sedentary and without adventure."

"I never sought adventure, but it found me in spite of myself!"

"That's interesting. Tell me about it."

"Not tonight," pleaded Thomas. "It's all very recent, and I still need to pinch myself to make sure I'm not crazy."

"Why not now? Our experiences have clearly brought us closer. Who knows if you'll still be able to tell me about it tomorrow.

"In the tragic times we live in, I think you've got to be on the lookout for adventure, since it happens to us by chance. I think of adventure as the whistle on a boiler that is about to explode, or, if you prefer, a warning, something inside you that 'knows,' or your high Destiny, which is waiting for you to *awaken* in order to manifest itself.

"Just look at my plane accident this evening: I arrived with the impression that I had a new duty to fulfill. I was hesitant, feeling more like rest than like action . . . but the whistle blew. I knew I couldn't put it off any longer. Tell me about your experience, Jean Thomas. Who knows? Maybe I can be of help."

And so Jean Thomas recounted his "adventure."

They didn't sleep a wink that night.

They had breakfast together on the balcony. The pilot was smiling at his friend's sheepishness.

"What are you ashamed of, you fool? You've been incredibly lucky! How? There are people who spend their entire lives using complicated methods in the search for their own Light, that which allows them to know the reason for their existence and their true destiny. And you are visited by it with one stroke of lightning (or . . . grace?). You hear it, you see the symbol of it, and you're frightened. What are you afraid of?"

"I was afraid of deluding myself."

"Who would accuse you of deluding yourself? The right-minded bourgeois trembling in his shoes when death approaches? The atomic scientist working toward 'world peace'? The fanatical terrorist preaching the happiness of the masses? The moralist who wants prostitution abolished?

"But tell me: when you were a 'well-balanced gentleman' before this experience, did you have any inkling of what your precious Maître Jacques has taught you?"

"None at all."

"As far as I'm concerned, if I hear words that put me in touch with *my Reality*, I couldn't care less if they came from a clown, the dalai lama, the pope, or from the cover of a box of macaroni! I'm just grateful. I listen and I try to provoke the surging feeling from within.

"Don't you see that you must always seize the moment!

"Come on, old man, you've broken your sound barrier despite yourself and not even knowing how you did it. From now on you can do it on purpose."

Thomas was filled with emotion as he looked at his friend. He stood up and squeezed his friend's hands.

"And now I'm going to meet my destiny," he said. "But I'm beginning to think that your 'adventure' has brought me over to your path."

6

The Two Aspects of
Soul and Consciousness

In the intimate atmosphere of his small "Tavern," Dominique was listening to tales of the adventurous voyages of Jean-Jacques, the pilot, whom Thomas had wanted to introduce him to.

Jean-Jacques was now waiting, trying to guess the impressions of the sculptor. But the sculptor was peacefully smoking his pipe and for a while said nothing. Then after a long silence he spoke to Jean Thomas.

"I would like to know," he said, "why you brought me your friend, and why he, trained by his profession to be extremely prudent, could have spoken so openly to me."

Jean Thomas hesitated before answering, seeking the approval of the pilot, who, with a nod of the head, acquiesced.

"You've known me for such a short time," said Thomas. "However, you have so clearly seen through me that I have adopted you as my Master. But now the confidences that my friend and I have exchanged have caused me great confusion. Both of us have realized that a profound change has taken place in us, with this difference: his experience is much more complex, older, and more enriching than mine, which was so brief. Despite that, it's to me that he came to state his 'matter of conscience' and to help clarify it. Jean-Jacques is mistaken about my maturity! But I knew that in my current ignorance there was only one thing to do for him: bring him to you."

"That's not exactly where the problem lies," said the pilot. "I haven't judged my friend, no more than I have judged you, sir. But during the course of my risky adventures, I developed in myself a certain way of sensing things out, and experience has taught me to discern the quality of it. This way of sensing has frequently saved my life and has allowed me never to betray what was confided to me. But I soon understood that this instinct was part of my lower nature, because many animals have this gift as well. Then I tried to understand the nature and the origin of it. And my conclusion was the following: my instinctive impulses warned me about the dangerous or good effects of particular acts or particular involvements, while my reason and all my cerebral knowledge were ignorant of these things. However, these instinctive impressions only concern my physical life and my daily existence, and are still related to animal instinct.

"Therefore, I ask myself why man, being gifted with a superior state of being, and more conscious than the animal, is unable to cultivate perception as intuitive as the instinctive perspicacity, but in a much more subtle area, which would then put him in touch with the psychological state of those like him."

Dominique smiled. He said: "By that do you mean an intuition that is independent of the cerebral faculties?"

"Obviously. For without that it would be mere deduction and not direct perception of the secret tendencies of an individual."

"You've got to be very self-assured in order to be able to discern one from the other!" retorted Dominique.

"Precisely; and the fear of deluding myself at first made me very distrustful for that very reason. But as I continued to experience, I found the way that gave me undeniable results."

"What way was that?"

"Neutrality. I suppressed all judgment and even all hypotheses about the nature of the individual."

"You are to be congratulated, dear sir, but I'm still curious to know how you were able to arrive at something so difficult."

"The practice of my profession, which continually exposes me to multiple dangers, created in me a type of fatality that you might call a gift, or a sacrifice, of my life and of my personal desires through devotion to the cause that I was serving. This was my first apprenticeship in neutrality, or, if you prefer, nonwill."

"However, you had the former goal, to succeed: that's totally opposed to 'nonwill,'" objected Thomas.

"When I acted through *will* to succeed, I often made mistakes, and I noticed that obtaining the *willed* result could be negative in the long run. Therefore, only chance events made my rational logic useless.

"That's when I tried to cultivate an intuition that would allow me to know the vital reactions of my adversaries or of my partners."

"Thus you have learned *silence*, the long meditative silence that is necessary in order for intuition to manifest itself."

"I learned how to keep my mouth shut, to keep my mouth shut and to *listen*."

"You've acquired a treasure, my friend. But since this intuition is the expression of your supranatural conscience, I'm surprised that it sometimes didn't create a conflict with certain of the orders that were coming from your commanding officers."

The pilot sighed and looked at Thomas. "Here we are on dangerous territory again. I want you to know, Maître Dominique, that I have confided my current matter of conscience to no one. I followed my impulse in telling Thomas that which brought me here to you. Can you advise me about the conflict?"

"I think that your immediate problem, my friend, is not a matter of making a decision, but is to clarify the elements which can determine that decision. It's all very well and good to have verified and experimented with intuition, but you still have to know how to discern the value of these impulses in terms of your spiritual destiny.

"However, in order for this to happen, you must learn to distinguish the voice of your *real being* from that of your imagination."

"His problem is exactly the same as mine," interjected Thomas. "I've told my friend about the experience that I related to you the other day in detail. The explanations that you gave me are so new to me that I would be happy to hear you speak more about them."

"It would be more fruitful for you first to talk about your current conclusions," retorted the sculptor.

The doctor asked for a moment's reflection.

"Allow your heart to speak," advised Dominique. "Try to reexperience the emotion of your first contact with your mysterious adviser."

"It was a terrifying shock!" said Thomas. "I was outraged at the presence of 'someone' in me who knew something of which my reason was ignorant. Was it necessary to dissociate my intelligence from another faculty that until then I hadn't even suspected? The knowledge that was revealed to me by this suddenly awakened faculty owed nothing to my rational studies. . . .

"It took me a certain amount of time to admit this evidence. Then I sought to give it a name. It never occurred to me to compare it to my soul, whose existence my materialism doubted, for the divine nature of the soul, as defined by catechism, is incompatible with the possibility of being 'bad and damned'!

"Nor did I think of naming it consciousness, since I knew only the philosophical definition of this word.

"Then, yesterday, Maître Dominique expanded my notion of consciousness by establishing its relationship to the two aspects of my immortal
being—in other words, its Spiritual Witness and its Permanent Witness."

"In this duality of the soul," added Jean-Jacques, "only the names of the
two Witnesses are new, because in the teaching of Ancient Traditions you
can find the same principles as in the early Christian Church, which called
them *Spirit* and *Soul*."

"I never spoke of the duality of the soul," corrected Dominique, "but of
its two aspects, which is something essentially different. I think it is
urgent that I give you a precise explanation of these fundamental *realities*.

"But I'd like you to listen to me with complete nervous and mental
relaxation. Can you do this?"

Jean Thomas and Jean-Jacques enthusiastically consented.

Having taken a moment to gather together his thoughts, Dominique
continued: "Consider each human soul as one of the Number-entities
coming from the Absolute Unity, which contains all of them, since it is
the Divine Totality. However, no two Numbers are strictly identical: each
soul is blessed with the characteristics of its Number, and these characteristics are what make it different from other souls. The traditions that
liken each soul to a star (or to a sun) give us a key that should not be
neglected. A sun is a star that emits its own light, but this visible star is
only the physical body of the spiritual Sun in which it is englobed. The
Egyptian sages called it the eye of Ra, being the globe that is animated by
the indestructible divine Ra and whose luminous rays are perceptible to
our eyes.

"However, these rays are not its only emanations.

"The radiation known to modern physics can allow us to understand
the metaphysical aspects of our 'Sun Soul': The diverse solar radiations
are differentiated by the number of their vibrations, which respectively
give heat, light, ultraviolet rays, and emanations that are more difficult to
perceive and that current science is progressively discovering.

"The sum of these emanations constitutes a vibrating sphere that
encircles the planets of the solar system in which we live. The fact that
we are able to detect individually each one of their manifestations (heat,
light, ultraviolet rays, etc.) proves that these multiple radiations *intersect
each other without blending*. This is due to their various vibratory states
and to the subtle differences that result from them.

"However, despite their diversity, all of these emanations are *part of a
single sun*.

"I wanted to use this image to make you understand the possibility of
two aspects of our mortal soul which constitute one unique entity:

"That which in this entity carries the characteristics of its Number is its Permanent Witness, which imprints its signature on the newborn; whereas that which is divine essence (pure eternal light, which is impersonal and nonspecific) is its Spiritual Witness, what early Christian doctrine called 'spirit.' The word *Witness* is justified because these two aspects of your immortal soul are the two witnesses of your Number-entity."

"Could you please explain to us the line of demarcation between differentiation and unity in these two 'immortal states' with regard to the relationship between these two Witnesses?"

"The demarcation between the Permanent Witness and the Spiritual Witness is explained by the difference between *existence* and *Being*. Note that the Permanent Witness (although spiritual, and despite the latent and impassive presence of the Spiritual Witness) is what makes us experience our existence. Human consciousness has the faculty to distinguish this difference. I will explain it to you."

"I understand the double error that must be avoided," said Jean-Jacques. "On the one hand, the notion of two souls, and on the other hand, the affirmation of a unique soul without discerning its two aspects. However, it's important to recognize them if their roles are different."

"Take note that this difference disappears when a man realizes their unification," answered Dominique. "The Permanent Witness's goal in incarnation is to enrich itself from the consciousness of earthly creatures, of which human beings are the summit and the summary.

"Where does one situate the animal soul, which according to Moses was carried in the blood?" interjected the pilot.

"It's a state of animation that is less subtle than the immortal soul which has been accorded to man. (Since you've quoted Moses, he also says that God breathed the soul into Adam.) For every creature who is part of dualized Nature, it's the animal soul that is impregnated by the *consciousness of the species*. This specification separates it from the universal light, which renders the human soul sacred.

"We carry this animal soul in our blood, and this is what links us to the animals."

"That's all very interesting, but what bothers me is not being able to perceive the intermediary state between my animal being and my immortal being," said the doctor. "And yet it must exist *since I'm bothered by it* . . . otherwise could my problem just be a simple mental game?"

"You're right, Thomas. An intermediary state exists, and I've already mentioned it when I spoke of Human Consciousness. I'll try to define it for you, but I want you to open your inner ear if you want my *explanation* to evoke in you the vital meaning that my words might betray. . . .

"At the two poles of consciousness that humanity has, we find the inferior stage of the consciousness of the species innate in the human animal; then, at the higher level, that of the two Witnesses.

"Between these two states of consciousness is an intermediary state, which is the result of our human experience. This consciousness belongs to all creatures that inhabit the Earth regardless of whether it is innate or conditioned through education or through the psychic reactions of the Automaton. It exists independently of the Permanent Witness, which (when it is present) can be in agreement or disagreement with it.

"This Human Consciousness is superior to that of animals (even the most evolved) since man has the ability to look *at himself* and through his faculty of comparison[1] is able to distinguish between good and bad. This possibility of choice makes him subject to the divine laws of Harmony. In common language, it's a matter of the immanent justice of 'natural law,' which will make him pay for his transgressions through karmic repercussions.

"It's to this Human Consciousness that you can apply the popular term 'good soul' or 'bad soul'. It goes back to the Automaton, in which it inscribes the impressions that result from its experiences."

"Would this Human Consciousness be the intermediary state in which my impressions and daily struggles are expressed (with the exception of the intervention of my two Witnesses)?" suggested the doctor. "In other words, would it be what classic psychology calls the psyche?"

"You could express it that way, but we'll come back to it."[2]

"Is this consciousness the synthesis of my human experience, from which stems the cowardly mistrust and protection against antagonistic forces? (I'm speaking for my own personal case): it's what I call the bourgeois morality, which is opportunistic and utilitarian, and it's against all innovation that could go beyond it.

"With this mediocrity in my background, I find myself so handicapped that I have no idea how I can get out of it!"

"I think that your comprehension of Human Consciousness is a bit too simplistic," said Dominique. "Allow me to go into it at greater length.[3]

"First of all, it involves the innate instinctive consciousness from which flows the Consciousness of the species. This is the heritage of every creature, but the mind obscures it.

"Then comes the conventional moral sense, which you have badly

---

1. R. A. Schwaller de Lubicz: through the faculty of *negation* (see *The Temple of Man*).
2. See Chapter 18.
3. See Chapter 10, page 153–154ff.

defined. It's the sense that creates artificial faith through fear of sin and of punishment.

"But it can also include a less egotistical sentiment (admitted or not): a certain religious sense, be it innate or acquired, through dissatisfaction with the inferior human state. This creates the impulse of faith, which is the aspiration toward what is immortal and Divine. It is the highest degree of Human Consciousness, the closest to the spiritual state of the Permanent Witness. Religions are necessary in order to develop this, or if not religions, a mystical ideal (regardless of what the object is), which awakens an individual who has been deprived of the sense of the sacred. It must at least awaken in him the desire to go beyond his mediocrity."

"Scientific progress has rerouted this desire to 'go beyond' to the profit of our cerebral faculties. It has given us the illusion of the possibility of unlimited mental progress."

"It's for you to decide, Thomas, whether this desire is sufficient for you to fulfill yourself."

"I've got to admit, Maître Dominique, that certain things that Maître Jacques said spoke to unavowed impulses in me. But I would like to be able to pinpoint the source of these secret impulses. The imprecise term of the unconscious no longer corresponds to a positive reality for me."

"Your Human Consciousness is this positive reality, Thomas. It's these underlying impulses that harbored it, and thanks to them you were able to *listen* to what your Permanent Witness, Maître Jacques, was saying to you.

"*Reality is simple*, and becomes perceptible to him who dares to refuse complexity."

"It seems to me that the complexity of our psychoanalytic psychology comes from the absence of a 'fixed point,'" said Thomas, "since all the elements of the Automaton—psychic as well as physical—are subject to continual variation, and are destroyed through death."

"What do you mean by 'fixed point,' Thomas?"

"Our survival element. The dual aspect of our immortal soul."

"Do not confuse survival and immortality, dear doctor. Our Human Consciousness survives our earthly existence, but for an undetermined time because it has the character of perpetuity immanent to *the creature from which it proceeds*. But it does not have the immortality (hence infinity) of our Spiritual Entity, which is of divine essence."

"Does this mean the Human Consciousness would be the only thing to survive the dead man if these two Witnesses have abandoned him?" continued Thomas.

"This is true, if he has lost his soul," replied Dominique. "Consciousness subsists in his emotional (astral) body, and constitutes the pitiful state of disincarnate being deprived of a soul. Such beings are called 'human larvae.'"[4]

"Reduced to that state, can the dead person still reincarnate?" asked the pilot.

"When that happens, I pity the poor man who results from it," answered Dominique. "He is a disinherited being who has lost his spiritual destiny."

"Such cases could explain the sad condition of certain degenerate beings who are evil-minded because they are abnormally amoral, and whose reason for existing we are unable to understand," suggested Jean-Jacques.

"Or what about the seemingly baseless despair of children who commit suicide or unwarranted criminal acts?" added Thomas.

"That could be," admitted the sculptor. "The frequency of these cases in this 'end of an age' makes this hypothesis even more likely."

"Doesn't the hopeless situation of these poor larvae correspond to what Catholicism calls eternal damnation?" insisted the doctor.

"It would correspond to that if we were talking about cycles instead of eternity. But would you be humble enough to accept the eventuality of Divine Mercy, which would not have informed you of its plans?

"Does my sudden outburst shock you, gentlemen? I wanted to make you aware of the insolence of our mental curiosity when we speak about impenetrable wisdom in terms of human understanding.

"It is useful to bring this to your attention: we are tackling some of the subjects that have caused the bitterest of theological disputes. These disputes were in vain because rational comprehension of what is Divine (hence irrational) can only bring mental satisfaction, which deludes us in our knowledge of Reality.

"Do not misunderstand my intentions. I want you to be aware of the dangers of theological dialectic, which is not to be confused with the teaching of elements that are *knowable in ourselves*, and immediately necessary to our fulfillment.

"What is most important to us is a clear understanding of the role of our Permanent Witness. From this will come the practical understanding of how we behave.

"The Permanent Witness is embodied in the liver, in which it imprints the characteristics of our Number-entity. Hereditary tendencies (transmitted by the paternal seed) are also embodied in the liver. The origins of impulses such as activity, will, fulfillment, and all other good or bad expressions of the personality are also there: control or passivity, modesty

4. See Chapter 12.

or excessive selfishness, pride, ambition, vexation, bitterness and vengeance, as well as courage and aggressiveness.

"All of these tendencies, be they hereditary or astrological, characterize the Automaton, and often come into conflict with the legitimate tendencies of the Permanent Witness, when the latter is able to make itself heard.

"When speaking of its incarnation, I should be more precise and speak of impregnation for this first contact with the newborn. This contact renews itself in the different periods of glandular development, in relationship to the cerebral or sexual functions, and corresponds to an awakening of psychic consciousness.

"In normal cases we are not dealing with someone predestined from his previous incarnation for spiritual realization. These moments of contact with the Permanent Witness are attempts to influence and rectify the impulses of the Automaton. But the integration can only take place progressively and *conditionally*, according to the acquiescence of Human Consciousness, which can either accept it or refuse it.

"This integration is the major task of our existence and therefore depends on our courage in subjecting our Automaton to its rules of conduct. The first necessary effort is to be able to discern their respective impulses."

"How will I be able to acquire this discernment?" asked Thomas, worried.

"By continual watchfulness, my friend. You must always be conscious of the movements in the duel. It's a sport like any other sport, after all! And when you have understood that our immortality is at stake, it's extraordinary to have a defined goal instead of being subjected to perpetual incertitude."

"But isn't there a danger, in this constant return to ourselves, of lapsing into psychoanalysis?"

"You must not confuse watchfulness with introspection," retorted Dominique. "The scrupulous analysis of our reactions is a cerebral game, a dissection of *self*. It is to limit oneself to the fearful world of one's own self and to slam the door shut on intuition.

"Such behavior has nothing to do with the watchfulness of the navigator who peacefully surveys the winds and the contrary currents, and who changes the orientation of the ship according to the indications of the compass.

"Our Permanent Witness is the compass whose magnetic needle is invariably attracted toward the north, toward the pole of spiritual realization. It is upon this continual desire that we must focus our attention, and not on the contrary currents of our 'moods' with their diverging impulses.

"Never become tense: verify and firmly readjust the helm."

"Verify!" repeated the doctor. "Maître Dominique, don't you understand the irony of this simple program for a man incapable of discerning the source of his sentiments, of his multiple worlds, of his psyche, regardless of the name that you give it?"

Jean Thomas, his head in his hands, waited for the answer.

Dominique stuffed his pipe, offered the two men cigarettes, and then questioned the doctor:

"Your current crisis, my friend, lies in your resistance to letting go of scientific theories and psychoanalytic dissections in order to look at the major lines of your vital reactions.

"Can you tell me, *very simply*, where you draw the line between the psychic being and the spiritual state?"

After a few moments of reflection, the doctor answered: "If I want to reconcile my personal knowledge with your teaching, I would say that the psychic being of an individual consists of his animal instincts, his effective emotional, egotistical, or humanitarian tendencies, and his mental preoccupations, as well as the emotional, nervous, organic, and sexual reflexes that result from it. All of this is related to the personal or hereditary tendencies of the Automaton."

"Very good, but how do you distinguish the consciousness of a psychic being the way you define it?"

"It's the innate and acquired consciousness of the Automaton, which I think you have named Human Consciousness. Beyond this consciousness, it seems to me that I would enter directly into the spiritual state immanent to my two Witnesses.

"But then how do I define the intuitive faculty that my "flash of lightning' awakened? A subtle sense? A state of consciousness? Or a function that depends upon a physical organ?"

Dominique looked pensively at Thomas.

"I'll lean on what you know to answer you," he said. "If it had to do with sensorial function, the function of vision, for example, how would you define it? As far as I'm concerned, I would say that it results from the visual faculty that comes from the sense of sight. This renders it effective, thanks to an appropriate physical mediator (an organ or a gland, in this case the eye) activated by specific nerves (in this case the optical nerves).

"We can use this definition to explain intuition, but only by analogy, because intuitive perception takes place in a more subtle way than does physical visual perception.

"Intuition is a function of a state of consciousness resulting from the intuitive faculty, and it's commonly said that it comes from the sixth sense (the sense of intuitive perception). But we've got to have a common understanding of the words:

"Intuition is the identification of the being with a certain state of being. However, that which one calls 'intuitive sense' cannot be compared to any of the five senses, since it is universal and more subtle. You could say that it was stimulated by these senses, or by one of these senses.

"The faculty (or possibility of expression) of intuition has its physical mediator in the pineal gland (the epiphysis), which is itself capable of being stimulated by the senses.

"But there is another intuitive sense. It is the region of the Spiritual Heart, which is the seat of 'understanding' of our Spiritual Witness and of the direct fusion with Being. It is to this that what one calls the 'seventh sense' can be attributed, because it's the most subtle of the senses and can only manifest itself by an unexpressed illumination."

"According to your definition, the two types of intuition that stem from the sixth and seventh senses reveal to us perceptions of a spiritual order," said Thomas. "Does this mean that they're immanent to our immortal Being?"

"Exactly, Thomas, but don't forget that these faculties have been physical springboards: the epiphysis in the middle of the cerebral organs, and the center of the Spiritual Heart, which is next to the spleen. These proximities necessitate constant watchfulness in order not to confuse intuitive perceptions with the rational interpretations of the mind, or with imagination, which is emotionally motivated.[5] Acquiring this discernment is of the utmost importance."

"It's pretty difficult to distinguish," murmured Thomas.

"You'll cultivate the ability through your continuous attention to the impulses of your Maître Jacques. The result is more immediate than you think, from the moment that you honestly accept the certainty of *evidence*."

"The evidence could be an aberration of the imagination."

"The faculty of cerebral imagination depends on cerebral contributions that awaken the memory to certain perceptions, associations of ideas, or impressions. Imagination can have an emotional origin in relationship to the splenic emotional center."

"Psychoanalysis knows how to dissociate these diverse elements, in order to decipher the sources of the impulse: cerebral shocks, atavistic influences, or repressed tendencies."

"I know, my friend, but the error of the psychiatrist and the psychoanalyst is failure to take into account the state of being which is more subtle than cerebral intelligence, and which permits man to look at

5. Of splenic origin. See Chapter 18.

himself *in his relationship to the universe*, and to the *being* of which the universe is the production. His relationship can be *harmonious* or *discordant*. It's *this relationship* that is a spiritual state: that is, a relationship that is not material, but which unites what you call matter and spirit, since it involves a concrete pole—the self that is knowable through our sensorial and cerebral faculties—and an abstract pole, which is Being in itself, which we know only through the spiritual state that is within us.

"The faculty that gives *knowledge* of the spiritual state is intuition, which the highest degree of human consciousness permits us to attain. The misunderstanding of this necessarily causes diagnostic errors, because the psychoanalyst frequently attributes certain pathological phenomena to the psychic, emotional, or cerebral states. However, these phenomena are due to a disharmony between the spiritual impulses of the sick person and the reactions of his lower states.

"The axiom of the Emerald Tablet is as valid for man as it is for the cosmos: 'that which is above is like that which is below, and that which is below is like that which is above.' If you understand Above and Below in their most subtle as well as their most material sense (without putting limits on the most subtle sense), you'll know that between these two states there is no solution by continuity. What do exist are constant relationships of cause and effect whose harmony or disharmony produces balance or imbalance—these circumstances in health or illness."

Jean Thomas shrugged sadly as he looked at his Master.

"Your concept of the human being," he said, "is so simple that it's almost repugnant to the scientific mentality, which is avid for details, for minute documentation and scrupulous experimentation."

"Still, based on analysis and particulars," concluded Dominique, "the doctors of today are fascinated by the human mechanism and refuse to look at the interrelationship of *functions*.

"The multiplicity of effects has made you lose sight of the chain of causes. *Your interest is directed toward disharmony*, because it enriches your complexity. The laws of Harmony are too simple for you. If you looked for their correspondences in the human being, you would reduce illness to a small number of causes . . . as long as you keep in mind the mutual relationships of *all* states that constitute our being."

"What you say makes the synthetic method that you've advocated impossible to practice," retorted the doctor, "because it poses as evidence the existence of abstract states that our concrete science refuses to admit."

"However, dear Doctor, these abstract states have concrete 'relay stations' in our physical bodies. When these relay stations, which are nervous or glandular, are touched, it's possible to awaken the abstract faculty that corresponds to them.

"Take your case, for example:

"Your intuitive sense was awakened when you were almost struck down by lightning! I'm not denying that this awakening was provoked by mental reactions through the revolt of your rational intelligence, and by imaginary reactions through the association of ideas and impressions that have been registered before. Nonetheless, the initial fact is undeniable.

"Besides, it's not unique. Other examples have been medically recognized."[6]

The pilot, who had been attentively observing his friend, intervened in the discussion:

"Actually, it's not the intuitive faculty that is causing your doubt. It's the possibility of confusing your intuition with your imagination."

"Yes, Doctor. Jean-Jacques is right," affirmed Dominique. "But your doubt is coming from incomprehension of the various modes of perception. Theory alone is insufficient: you must learn how to recognize them in yourself. However, each time you have the opportunity to try, you are afraid of losing ground. Your analytic mentality is stubbornly dissecting immaterial states as if you were dissecting physical organs.

"You'll never be able to do it, Thomas, because the immaterial states are not *separated* like boxes or stacked envelopes. They are *differentiated* by the rhythm of their vibrations. They can mutually influence each other without interpenetrating. In other words, one of these states of consciousness cannot be *perceived* by the other states without a mediator, which is Human Consciousness. Your mind, for example, will not *perceive* by itself what your intuition perceives. However, it can receive communication from it through your Human Consciousness, which recorded it."

"I think I'll finally wind up understanding," said Thomas. "But could you clarify the diverse mental attitudes? By that I mean the different philosophies."

"I'm not too fond of that type of explanation," groaned the sculptor as he relit his pipe. "but let's try. . . .

"The classical modern philosopher who understands the mind as the movements and operations in the realm of thought, often makes this concept synonymous with consciousness. This notion is acceptable if it is related to cerebral consciousness, in other words, to the mental faculty that enables one to verify one's own perceptions, concepts, and deductions.

"You know this as well as I do. The clarifications that you're requesting

6. "The Wise Man of Naples." See Chapter 7.

are related no doubt to interpretations of Eastern psychospiritual teaching, or those things which derive from it. However, it's very risky to establish an exact relationship between their terminology and ours. Hinduism reduces the aspects of the various stages of Being, which doesn't create the same inconvenience for the Hindu as it does for our analytic mentality. The Hindus' profound sense of self-unity spares them from a common error of Western interpreters, who separate the states of consciousness like so many stacked envelopes.

"The knowledge through experimentation that the intensive practice of yoga meditation makes possible, becomes an erroneous schematic concept in terms of our rational comprehension.

"To avoid the danger of our cerebral way of thinking (innate and cultivated), we need to go back to extreme simplicity, as much for meditation as for the consideration of psychospiritual states.

"All the translators are in agreement in identifying the Hindu term *manas*, the mind, which receives and reflects our association of ideas and elaborates our thoughts. Its activity depends on our cerebral faculties, which are annihilated by the death of the brain. The concepts that result from this can be reflected in our Human Consciousness, if it is receptive to them.[7]

"On the one hand, Human Consciousness corresponds to *antakarana*, and on the other hand, to *ahankara*, or individual consciousness, which is directly related to *manas*.

"Teachings derived from Hinduism mention a more subtle state, called supramental, or higher mind, or higher *manas*. The last term corresponds to the immortal consciousness of the Permanent Witness. The higher mind can be the source of certain perceptions of Reason, in its most highly accepted form considered as *the faculty of forming concepts*. This aspect of Reason is thus Comprehension, which is inspired by the Permanent Witness."

"Isn't this Reason, then, the highest degree of Human Consciousness?" asked Jean Thomas.

"Didn't I say that it was directly linked to the mind? It's through the mind that knowledge which is conceived through the intuitive faculty can be communicated to rational intelligence.

"You'll understand why the mind must be used only to *verify* intuition, then to oversee the testing of it. If you allow rational intelligence to uphold the argument of your hypothetical knowledge, during the *gestation process of intuition*, you no longer have any guarantee of the real

7. See Chapter 10.

quality of the intuition, and are taking the risk of giving birth to a monster."

With a sigh of relief, Thomas showed that he understood.

"I confess that my tyrannical mind is satisfied with these explanations which pinpoint notions identified by different names," he said.

"I could," said Dominique, "establish the same relationship within the various traditions, but I don't want to dwell on the subject. I see no point in superimposing terminologies that can only complicate *that which henceforth must be simplified*.

"A single goal is of importance to us: to conceive the *relativity* of mental perceptions in relationship to the *reality* of knowledge acquired through intuitive understanding, or through the comprehension of that which our Spiritual Being unveils to us."

"Is there a difference between the modes of inspiration of our two Witnesses?" asked Jean-Jacques.

"There is no difference in the case of a total communion with our Spiritual Being. But what we have known in this ecstatic union can be ignored by our cerebral consciousness.

"Except for this exceptional case of unification, the mode of inspiration of the Spiritual Witness is an illumination of the Intelligence of the Heart, which infuses a state of beatitude or of certitude that is not necessarily explicit. If some knowledge results from it, sooner or later, it will make itself felt through *evidence*, rather than through expressed comprehension. It's important to know this in order not to deny such *evidence* because you are unable to explain it.

"On the contrary, the intuition that emanates from our Permanent Witness becomes intelligible through our highest Human Consciousness and can become, through its intermediary, comprehensible to our discursive reason."

"Human Consciousness is the relationship between what is perceptible and what is not perceptible to the *mind*," insisted the doctor.

"Exactly," agreed Dominique. "It is the intermediary between our intelligent Automaton and our Permanent Witness, just as this Witness is the intermediary between Human Consciousness and the Spiritual Witness. That's why it belongs uniquely to human beings, for whom it is the Individual Consciousness."

"To sum it up," concluded the pilot, "it has a very important role in the success or failure of our fulfillment!"

"I'm happy that you've understood," said Dominique approvingly. "You might even say that Human Consciousness is responsible for this. Human Consciousness yields to or resists our egotism. It repels or attracts our two Witnesses.

"It is the instrument of experience of our Permanent Witness, and it is that which undergoes, after death, the karmic consequences of our behavior. Lack of understanding on the part of Human Consciousness makes the synthesis of our different states of being inconceivable. However, it is this synthesis which we must never lose sight of if we want to learn how to manage harmoniously the elements that constitute our human egg."

Thomas's stubborn frown made the sculptor smile, and Thomas asked him why he was smiling. "I understand the image of the egg for the fetus," said Thomas, "but the accomplished man has already hatched out of it, I think."

"Do you take yourself for an 'accomplished man'?" retorted Dominique with a laugh. "The human egg is not an image. It represents the totality of man's multiple bodies or states of being which, for many earthly men, has not yet even incarnated its seed of immortality.

"Therefore, meditate on the human egg, my knowledgeable biologist. . . ."

Jean-Jacques was extremely thoughtful. Inside himself he was establishing the tally sheet of what he had just heard. He warmly thanked Dominique as he stood up to leave.

"The precious teaching that you have just given us," he said, "demands to be deepened, and that will take time. Will you allow me to return when I have been able to draw positive conclusions for myself in order to direct my behavior?"

Dominique smiled. "You know the formula," he answered. "Knock and the door will be opened to you. . . . However, don't be in too much of a hurry to draw a conclusion, because it's easy to confuse the voice of Maître Jacques with the fallacious advice of the Automaton. This discernment demands a certain apprenticeship—but isn't this place a workshop?"

7

Vice, Virtue, and Art

Jean Thomas, left to himself, felt the need to classify these recent events. His work was no longer able to absorb him entirely. Should he go back to Notre Dame? He hesitated, as if intimidated by the eventual meeting with Maître Jacques, whom he didn't dare situate in a definitive way. The teaching of Dominique had reversed the situation. He was somewhat ashamed of his faint-heartedness, and he had difficulty believing in the "irrational" wonder that had awakened his consciousness.

He threw himself into his work, but he was able to see that his research was following a new direction. His curiosity was no longer satisfied by details of phenomena. Could there really be a harmony that would situate these phenomena as foreseeable effects: the effects of *functions* of a universal organism?

He noticed that this question, which until this day had irritated him, now stimulated his interest, despite his current inability to answer it. What was the importance of this inability? Didn't he have two solid friends to support it: Jacques-Dominique and Jean-Jacques? The jester in him reappeared: "Never two without three. . . . Poor Thomas, must you give way to Maître Jacques?"

For the first time he had the courage to laugh about that which was for him shameful. It was joyous laughter, the laughter of a child watching the farces of a Punch and Judy show: "After all, I was Punch, with my silly fear of being ridiculous, with my fear of the devil and of 'the well-thinking gentleman'! Now I will have the courage to rid myself of my fetters! . . . Wait a minute! What would remain of the puppet? His bat. But then who would hold the strings of the bat?"

He searched, and hesitated . . . and suddenly, in a burst of laughter, the truth appeared to him: He would still be the hand that manipulated the puppet! He almost fell to his knees: "Maître Jacques! Of course! The conscious old fellow whom nobody sees, but who manipulates the strings that push us here and there, because he 'knows the way.' . . ."

Was it possible to be that blind? . . .

Thomas was no longer laughing, but in his enthusiasm, he believed he had become twenty years younger. Wasn't becoming younger seeing a new way that one had previously searched for painfully in the darkness?

It was certain. He would not go to the cathedral that night. He would go to express his joy to his *living* Master! He would present to him a different Thomas: a conscious Thomas who was as sure of his reason as of his gestures, and who would make Maître Jacques speak at will!

He rapidly made his way back to the Atelier. This time there was something new in his life: a serene clarity wherein he could situate his position of the previous night and this memorable day without ambiguity. He would have no more scruples and fears of hallucination. He would no longer suffer the chimera of Dominique. What pleasure he would have in mocking these devils and their grimacing expressions!

He arrived at the Atelier. The sculptor received him cordially and asked him to come in. But the devils were no longer there. . . .

Astonished, Jean Thomas looked around at the new decor. On the stiff curtains hanging from column to column were engravings of religious paintings—primitive paintings, and those of the Renaissance, of Giotto, della Francesca, and Fra Angelico. There were Madonnas and angels. Before the Holy See, there was a beautifully illuminated Mass book on a pulpit. At the feet of a black Virgin was a spray of lilies, which contrasted with the ebony of the statue.

"What a change in atmosphere!" exclaimed Jean Thomas.

"I don't like routine," said the sculptor. "You've got to know how to create a suitable environment according to what you want to obtain."

"This one is curiously suited to what I want to talk to you about: Beauty, Candor, Light! Today I experienced a beautiful Light. . . . But first I must speak to you about Maître Jacques."

"Is it really necessary?" said the sculptor, smiling, "He's an old friend for those who have learned to consult him within themselves."

"All right," said Thomas, crestfallen. "But I still have something to tell you. Until now I've been a fool. In wanting to explain everything rationally, I have stifled certain intuitions within me whose value I now perceive. Under the pretext of scientific honesty, I only wanted to recognize the human being by cataloging elements of classical anatomy, physiology, and psychoanalysis.

"This morning however, I understood, recognized, and experienced the existence of an inexplicable consciousness which *knew*, and which taught me (under the strange guise of Maître Jacques) things that until then I had ignored. Surely you have heard of the case—an authentic one—of a man who, after a trauma to the neck, suddenly became clairvoyant, knowing the past or secret lives of people around him, and other things that were totally unknown to him, because his mind or brain had never been able to record them.[1] Is what's happening to me a similar phenomenon?"

"In your case it is a similar phenomenon, but in a more subtle way, with more extended possibilities. But if you want to believe me, my friend, don't exteriorize the enthusiasm of your beautiful experience. Incubate your joy in silence, so you don't anger your reason, which is still on the alert.

"Believe me when I tell you to remain calm and patient so that you don't lose your treasure. You still don't know the strange games of *reaction*. Consciousness is like a mirror of limpid water. If you agitate it, you will be surprised that you can no longer find your face in it."

Jean Thomas did not answer, but in the moment of peace that followed, he had no need for words.

This discussion was interrupted by the arrival of Maître Pierre, who was accompanied by a tall, beautiful woman of sober elegance, whose perfect contours could have tempted a sculptor. The woman looked rapidly and distrustfully around the studio, trying to gauge her hosts by the works on exhibit, whose subject matter obviously received her approval. She moved forward. Maître Pierre led her toward his friends.

"Madam, allow me to introduce you to the sculptor Dominique, and to Dr. Thomas, a medical biologist.

"My friends, I've brought you a friendly penitent who was coming out of confessional. In order to respect the anonymity of my admirer, while also rendering homage to her beauty as well as to her virtue, I'd like to introduce you to the noble Mary Magdalene."

"It's a charming euphemism, no doubt," said the woman, choking a bit. "Of course I venerate the penitent Magdalene, but we two haven't taken the same road in search of the Lord."

"All roads lead to Rome, madam," said Maître Pierre cunningly.

1. The true story of "The Wise Man of Naples."

The woman shrugged and spoke to the two men:

"Gentlemen, allow me to introduce myself: Madam Angelica Delatour. Pleased to make your acquaintance."

Dominique leaned over toward the Holy See.

"The only comfortable chair in the workshop: please sit down, madam. Do you smoke?"

"I have never smoked, sir, but smoke will not bother me. You were saying, Maître Pierre, that you wanted to introduce me to an eminent theologian."

"I did not deceive you, madam. My friend, Maître Dominique, did his thesis in theology."

"Is that so? I'm delighted."

"It is true that since that time he's been duly converted!"

The woman frowned.

"I beg your pardon, sir."

The sculptor looked at Maître Pierre severely.

"I don't appreciate that kind of joke, my friend. Excuse him, madam. He's an old familiar of Montparnasse. . . ."

"Why not of Saint-Germain-des-Prés," mumbled the sketcher. "Madam, I don't dance to rock 'n' roll, and I don't get drunk with perverts!"

Dominique intervened: "Madam, if you'd be so kind as to tell me the reason we are honored with your visit?"

"Here are the facts, sir: Indeed, I was coming out of confession. I had been kneeling down behind your friend to complete my penance. However, I must confess that I allowed myself to be distracted by the beautiful sketches that were spread out in front of me. I was beguiled, among other things, by the ravishing face of an angel, and I expressed to him my desire to get a closer look at it. He brought me here."

"It wasn't an angel, madam," retorted Maître Pierre. "It was a Crazy Virgin from a cathedral in Strasbourg."

"That's impossible! How could the sculptor have chosen as his subject such a beguiling face?"

"Don't you think vice is often more beguiling than virtue?" retorted Dominique. "Besides, what is virtue if not the triumph over what could have been vice?"

"You're too polite, my friend," chided Maître Pierre. "I would go as far as to say that vice is the pedestal of virtue."

In answer to the horrified gasp of Dame Angelica, Dominique explained:

"Understand me, madam. Our body of flesh is interwoven with sensitive and sensorial nerves that demand only to be agents of sensual pleasures. If you throw in our imaginations, our thoughts, and all the egotistical tendencies of our psychic being, you'll have to admit that our physical, emotional, and intelligent animal is a rich field for the instinctive impulses that the Catholic Church calls the seven deadly sins. You'll notice that there are seven virtues that oppose these seven sins. With regard to virtue, theology lists only three. These are referred to as the three theological virtues, because they deal with states of spiritual consciousness: Faith, with is knowledge through the Intelligence of the Heart; Hope, which is the patient gestation of that which was conceived through Faith; and Charity, which is love in the sense of uniting our spiritual being with the Universal Soul, which annihilates all egotism. It's in this way that they are theological. They are of a divine nature because they are suprahuman."

"That's a meaning that I had never caught sight of," said Jean Thomas. "That's worth looking into!"

"I don't want to continue on this subject," Dominique went on, "but we have to give the real idea of virtue its proper place, because what people commonly call virtue is moral behavior opposed to capital sins as well as their substitutes."

"Your definition of faith," retorted Dame Angelica, "is different from mine. My own knowledge is the faith that I accord to the dogmas of the Church."

"Madam, your allegiance and your *belief* are through obedience, or through a comprehension, rarely integral, that depends on your will and your cerebral intelligence."

"I won't argue with that, sir, because I refuse anything that doesn't touch upon my belief. As for virtue, I claim that one can be naturally virtuous, or become so through virtuous acts."

"Let's agree on one thing, madam: each child, by the mere fact of being born, carries with him original sin; in other words, the dualization and the tendency to dualize everything: me *and* you, or, if you wish, me *and* God. As long as he doesn't experience God in himself, as long as he does not feel all of humanity within him, there will be an incompatability of interest between him and that which he considers as being outside of him. Is that not the route of egotism, of envy, or greed, and of possessive tendencies? Have some fun unmasking the various sins in this light. You'll perhaps realize that we are getting closer here to the root."

"To listen to you, sir, one would think that no man on earth is virtuous."

"What I mean to say, madam, is that all men, through their dualistic nature, have in them the root of that which you call 'sins.' But don't you think the sculptors of the cathedrals were of the same opinion when, on the pedestals supporting the figures of saints, they portrayed grimacing characters with vicious or diabolical faces? Shouldn't one conclude that sanctity is the fruit of combat, or rather of the *transmutation* of these natural tendencies into supernatural forces?"

"I know, I know: Satan spends his time tempting the virtuous man. There will always be good men and evil men, believers and disbelievers, Good on one side, Bad on the other."

Dominique smiled.

"You're not very well disposed to metaphysical discussion, madam. I'll therefore limit myself to quoting the words of Mephistopheles to Goethe's Faust, who asked him to define satanic nature. Listen to the answer, because it demands reflection:

"'I am that Force which always wants evil and which, doing evil, provokes good.'"

Dame Angelica rebelled:

"These insidious words are totally amoral!"

"No, madam: they are immoral, which is different. That which is unconscious is *amoral*, because it doesn't have the sense of what's Real and what is relative, and therefore is unable to judge that which serves the cause of one *or* the other. Mephistopheles' immorality is conscious and lucid, and expresses a profound truth: the inexorable law of reaction.

"*Imposed* virtue provokes the reaction of stifled instincts. The temptations of the saints are a perfect example of this."

"Does that mean you are advocating the abolition of moral laws?"

"No, madam. If I had something to advocate, it would be above all the knowledge of the goal of existence, then the true knowledge of our instinctive impulses, and their harmony or disharmony with our final goal. Finally, I would advocate the choice in the directives that can lead us toward this goal."

"The liberty you are according to the individual is dangerous!"

"Indeed, this all assumes the awakening of his consciousness, but it is also a means of provoking this awakening. Since this 'self-knowledge' is a personal effort, it obviously can't exclude the *indispensable moral rules* that work for the order of society.

"The only thing I want to bring to your attention is that the observance of imposed laws, and the fear of their sanctions, does not awaken in man a sense of his responsibility in the face of his immortal destiny and that of humanity, of which he is a part, as would his own discernment of that which adds to or detracts from the fulfillment of this high destiny. However, it's the absence of discernment that motivates the reactions of the instincts which have been suffocated by law or by *imposed* virtue."

"I'm afraid, sir, that I've shocked you with my accusation of amorality, or immorality, as you say."

"Not at all, madam, because amorality is an absence of consciousness. As for immorality, I think it's often caused (in men who are more or less conscious) by an obscure need to experience their own reaction. This reaction, being a search for consciousness, makes it very difficult for men to judge that which you call sin.

"But it is obviously *I* who am shocking you, dear madam . . . and I am very uphappy about this. Can't we speak of more pleasant subjects?"

"With pleasure! It would be wonderful to hear you speak of virtue."

Jean Thomas exchanged a disappointed smile with Dominique, who sighed:

"So be it, since you insist!

"For example, take Charity: in what way would you apply Charity to the practice of Good?"

Dame Angelica smiled condescendingly.

"The answer is too easy. I think that, according to one's means, the Christian must distribute a reasonable percentage of his income as alms."

"The Gospel is more demanding than you, dear madam: Christ attributes the merit to the bestowal of what is *necessary*, and not that which is superfluous.

"Ah, if you take an extreme case . . ."

"Yes, I know. Excess is closer to vice than to virtue, correct? But I thought that charity was synonymous with love."

"That depends on the meaning that you give it, dear sir. Well-guided charity must be certain that its alms are used well and justly attributed."

"And what are your criteria for judging this?"

"I know how to judge men, sir. I am the adviser to the committee for good works in my parish. I don't let myself be fooled."

"I congratulate you, madam. And no doubt there, too, you don't admit the excesses of charity."

"What are you getting at? If the finances of the government were as balanced as my distributions, everyone in the world would have something to eat."

"And would they have what was needed to be happy?"

"What is happiness, if not moderation and obeying the law?"

"Do you read the Bible, madam?"

"It's the book at my bedside, sir. . . ."

"I understand. But didn't Christ add something? 'A new commandment I give unto you, that ye love one another.'"

"Absolutely, but do you expect me to love criminals?"

"What about women who steal bread for their children? Or prostitutes, or unbelievers?"

"I embrace them in my prayers, and I thank God that I don't resemble them."

"I am not worthy of approaching you, madam, because I am a sinner."

"No doubt you slander yourself, or are you a repentant sinner?"

"I'm going to shock you, madam: the only thing I repent for is the lack of love."

"In what sense do you mean that?"

"In almost every sense."

"Except for . . . ?"

"In the excess of love that I hope for, the only thing I exclude is sensual love, that is, love based on sensorial pleasures, including all the aesthetic forms of pleasure, as well as animal jealousy, which is an agent of sensuality."

"I refuse to listen to these remarks, sir. Purity, which is the most beautiful garb of woman, will not allow itself to be touched by subjects that could soil it, As for me, I look in all the things that surround me for purity and beauty. I cultivate beauty!"

"What is beauty? That which is pleasing to your eyes, your ears, and your taste, which is no doubt very cultivated?"

"I love beauty for itself. It exists. Boileau said: only what is true is beautiful. . . ."

"Then you must think that the spider and the foaming slug are beautiful as well. These animals are true. So is the praying mantis who eats her husband after she has witnessed his love for her."

"Your mind has an evil bent, Maître Dominique! I would never have believed it, seeing the delicate choice of paintings that decorate your studio. I would have been delighted if you'd shown them to me. But now I've already stayed too long: my charitable activities await me."

The sculptor was about to rise and show his guest out when Maître Pierre caught his attention: as he was listening to their discussion, the silent artist had sketched a portrait of the woman. She noticed this.

"What are you doing, sir?"

"Your face, madam, is the perfect type for rigorous Virtue, which scrupulously measures its own merit. Do not be offended if the artist couldn't resist immortalizing the traits of such a rare model. . . . Your name suits you perfectly: Dame Angelica—that name is a poem!"

"Madam Angelica Delatour, if you please."

"Let me idealize it! Dame Angelica, the woman of virtue and beauty, armored like Saint Michael against the demon of temptation. . . . What am I saying? Excuse me: I am certain that temptation would never dare to touch you!"

"Sir, I beg your pardon. . . ."

"No, really? Am I exaggerating? Chastity, for example . . ."

"Sir! I won't allow you to—"

"Assuredly, madam, I would never allow myself to doubt it for a moment! I would put only these lilies in the background of the painting, and moreover, I would paint the petals pure white so that even the horrible idea of sexuality will not occur! Don't move, madam. I am almost finished."

Dominique had an opportune coughing fit. He stood up in response to Thomas's terrified expression. The poor doctor, who was obviously exasperated, expressed his desire to leave. Dominique prevented him from doing so. Seeing this, the woman said good-bye to her hosts and left, accompanied by Maître Pierre.

With a malicious smile on his lips, the sculptor looked at Jean Thomas, who was walking back and forth like an angry tiger in his cage.

"Would you like a cigarette, Thomas? Come into the Tavern to quench your anger."

"A change of atmosphere is exactly what I need! I've had enough of candor, pure angels, and virtuous women for one night! I'm glad those two left."

"You mean Pierre and the saintly woman? I wonder which horrified you the most: the cynicism of our friend or the virtue of Dame Angelica?"

"You know as well as I do!" exclaimed the doctor. "I don't understand how you were able to accept this inane discussion with a woman who is frozen in her halo of purity!"

"And why should I have demolished that halo? Saints like her are absolutely dependent on it! In Ascona, a man was walking entirely naked and carrying his tall frame in dignity in order not to disturb his 'aura.' Ah! You are laughing. That's better. Now drink some of this excellent Traminer and perhaps you'll find Truth at the bottom of your glass. . . ."

"Do you mean you don't approve of my judgment, Maître Dominique?"

"I neither approve nor disapprove. I simply find you inexperienced. What's there to judge? Good or bad? You're falling into the trap. It's amusing to see your dual reaction. During your last visit you were disgusted with my devils and my chimeras, which perhaps facilitated your acceptance of what is Real: that which does not allow itself to become sophisticated. Today you come back and find a decor that corresponds to your state of mind: candor, Light, beauty—at least that's what you assumed. Which of the two decors responds to truth? You'll also notice that Dame Angelica immediately took the same direction as you."

Thomas was furious and tried to defend himself, but Dominique would not allow it.

"Let me finish. What would have happened if our saintly woman hadn't given you indigestion from 'purity'? You would have allowed yourself to be equally cradled in my sentimental imagery, which you'd instinctively use to dress crude reality. Before you came here, this Reality had, for an instant, illuminated you. You can't play games with what is real, my friend. We're so unused to coming into contact with it that, before long, we deform it by accommodating it to our old habits."

"You have a way of seeing through my reactions that leaves me a bit disconcerted. Once again you've shown me an unexpected point of view. However, I must object that this time the game was not so simple: what you call the cynicism of Maître Pierre, which is sometimes a rather crude cynicism, jolted me because he is your friend. When I heard his opposing point of view, I was repelled, even though it corresponded to my point of view. How can you accept this constant contradiction?"

"Why not?" retorted Dominique. "It takes all kinds to make a world. And the more the experience of this world is concentrated, the less time we'll lose, if we know how to profit from it. The dualism of Maître Pierre is a true living symbol.

"Do you really think that a man can be 'all good' or 'all bad'? Our error is to want to categorize virtues as well as sins."

"But how can I form my judgment?"

"There's only one way: *get rid of it!* Another thing is the discernment of our own impulses. This is possible because we have within ourselves all the necessary elements to discern the mechanics of these impulses. But to apply this judgment to others whose profound mechanics we are ignorant of—that's another matter."

"Yes, I recognize how insolent it is to judge," said Thomas.

"It's worse than insolent. It's deadly! To judge someone is to take upon oneself the responsibility and the consequences of the hidden effects of the judgment. But here, as in nuclear science, we are playing the sorcerer's apprentice, and we provoke the reaction of forces that we know nothing about."

"You trouble me a bit, Dominique, because it is difficult to remain passive when witnessing evil acts."

"I said nothing of the sort! If you can avoid them, act according to your conscience. But with regard to bringing judgment to the degree of guilt, it's wrong to do so when it's not your responsibility.

"On the other hand, it's extremely instructive and very interesting to *observe*, even insofar as it's only to study the game of human reactions, *by learning how to remain indifferent*. No one will be able to help others effectively if he is unable to see their errors without suffering the consequence of them.

"Moreover, notice that this impersonal attitude is eminently favorable for the cultivation of discernment. The discernment of 'values,' be they real or relative, is as important as artistic discernment."

Thomas violently interrupted Dominique:

"Let's speak about the artistic sense! I have the impression that I'm seriously lacking in that area. I've tried in vain to get rid of all my personal prejudices. I feel that I'm actually incapable of discerning error from reality in modern art!"

"Go on, Doctor. This subject interests me," said the sculptor as he passed him a cigarette. "I'd like to hear your thoughts on it."

"Until now," continued Thomas, "I thought that art was the perfection of craftsmanship. But today I see all sorts of paintings, sculptures, and poetry made from elements that are unrelated, and people call this 'great art.' What am I to think about all this? Is it an aberration or is it a willful disorder?"

"Your uncertainty doesn't surprise me," answered Dominique.

"To understand these tendencies, you have to realize that the scientific progress of the twentieth century represents a kind of epistemological landslide. Consciousness has been broadened. Part of humanity is starting to experience a state of being that is hidden in the object or by the object, which until now made itself felt as a finality. This opening of conscious-ness toward a 'beyond' or a 'within' of the concrete form can be found in all areas, but even more so in art, which offers the most immediate possibilities of experience. The rebellion started, however, with the Dadaists, who were iconoclasts, and it has been continued in the form of a somewhat disorganized quest for a new path.

"It could be said that 'Art must be artificial.' Recently, a surrealist was speaking about 'the tunnel of matter.' Matter becomes an obstacle to vision or hints at a sort of hidden Fire animating the universe. This can be extended to the mathematical principle of uncertainty in nuclear physics, which recognizes that it is impossible to define time and space simultaneously, since this simultaneity is 'the object' in question.

"Today it's a matter of awakening a sense that we could call mystical. It isn't a primitive mysticism, but it's the logical outcome of primitive mysticism, in which the tangible object is only an evocative symbol of a specific function. This function is the creative activity of an abstract state."

"That's a curious affirmation!" said Thomas. "Isn't mysticism irrational, something that logic denies?"

"Didn't you scientists logically invent irrationality in order to balance your equations? You're playing with even more scandalous irrationalities than, for example, that of the notion of God. But let me go on with what I was saying.

"As a consequence of this perception, which is still obscure, of a lack of unity between the phenomenon and its causes, the poet denies the logical relationship between the images he evokes. The musician is looking for harmony among disharmonious elements and the magic of rhythm. The painter is looking for volume through cubism, through the defiance of the laws of gravity, through the dream expressed in landscape, through superimposition and the disruption of images, through the harmony between patches of color, and through abstractions that express feelings. Ever since the genius Rodin made a head of Balzac come to life by digging into clay earth with his fists and with a hatchet, the sculptor has been modeling space into the distorted forms of 'astral dreams.'"

"According to what you say, Maître Dominique, it seems there is a disdain for matter, a revolt against form."

"Not at all, dear friend. These artists don't disdain matter. On the contrary, they love it. They observe it, and above all they experience it, in order to enter into the object instead of looking at it from the outside. Thus, it's quite natural to see certain of them looking for the object of their expression in the symbolism of the traditional religious figures, thus denying the corporality of the forms. They are shaping the form in emptiness.

"You see, Thomas, matter oppresses the artist. Historicism contradicts the real or mystical vision of esoteric or inner life, for which the object appears as the mere symbol. It's the spiritual crisis of this ending of an era."

The doctor listened, as he nodded his head dubiously.

"Aren't you just being idealistic in according this artistic rigmarole such profound meaning?"

"I realize," said the sculptor, "that many artists sacrifice to what they think is 'fashion,' but some of them really suffer in trying to find that which cannot be expressed in a state of being of which they are certain; their only error is wanting to find, in the *distortion of form*, the evocation of their new consciousness of what is real."

"Then according to you," said Thomas, "the most clairvoyant members of humanity are trying to express themselves in a language for which they still lack the words."

"Indeed. This new language lacks words, but I think that by trying to get at the problem from the wrong side the Western World is looking for what's impossible.

"As for me, I remain faithful to the teaching of the Wisdom of the Pharaohs: It is clear that all abstract painting, for example, is the result of an evocation for which a positive fact has served as the seed. If you separate the seed from the evocation of which it is the symbol, you're leaving the door opened to all the fantasies of a mind that obeys the emotions and memories characteristic of moments that are as unstable and variable as atmospheric influences that act upon emotions and upon the associations of ideas.

"Evocation by the 'symbol-fact' belongs to intuitive vision, which loses all its value when it in turn becomes concrete. Abstract art is valid only if the image (in painting, sculpture, music, or poetry) maintains the thematic seed in the atmosphere that is evoked. Thus, it necessarily remains united with this seed (through its lines, its color, its rhythm, its emotion)."

"But isn't the expression of this vision what one calls 'artistic creation'?"

"Could you tell me what you mean by creation?"

"I attribute the same meaning to the word *creation* that Marcelin Berthelot gave to it in affirming that science (in this case, chemistry) could create matter that nature was unable to make."

"Dear friend, aren't you confusing *creating* with *forming*?

"To take the elements offered by nature in decomposing bodies in order to form other bodies artificially is not *creating* but transforming and forming. This word has been vulgarized, as have many others in our day; thus the seamstress who invents a new style allows herself to present it as her 'creation.'

"However, to create is to render that which is Spirit (in other words, intangible) tangible and corporeal. Only the causal abstraction that we designate as God can 'create.'"

"Art is something else. For example, the Hermetic philosophers of the Middle Ages called their work 'art'; it was work in the image of Nature, but went beyond the power and the works of this Nature. To render a thought tangible, or an imagination tangible, is not to 'create' in the absolute sense of the word, because this thought or this imagination is necessarily formed from notions given to us through facts. New ways of assimilating these facts are new forms, not new creations. *Evocation that leads from the abstract to the concrete, from what is undefined to what is finite, is going in the wrong direction.*

"A sketch or an ensemble of patches of color (black or colored) is something else again. You're not dealing with evocations, with emotions, or with personal 'visions,' but with a *graphology* that tells about the personality of the artist himself. But isn't the true signature of the artist's being found as much in the Pharaonic works, which strictly adhered to definite rules, as in master artists throughout all phases of Western civilization?

"Abstract modern art, the art of our times, is the child of the technological deviation taken by science which goes all the way back to Babylonia and Greece. It's a deviation that ancient Egypt carefully avoided, knowing that abstraction in general brings about a descent, a search for the concrete, while the concrete, as symbol, elevates one toward an intuitive vision, much as the high vaults in our cathedrals draw our gaze to the heights. It's from up above that all Life and all Good come, both literally and figuratively.

"The science and art of our times reveal nothing to us about the essence of our being, whereas Pharaonic art or hieratical art teaches us Knowledge. This is transmitted only through fact and experience, and neither the spoken nor the written word can ever teach it to us effectively."

Dominique started to relight his pipe, and waited for the doctor's reaction.

"I think I'm starting to understand what you're saying: the work of art must not bring a vision down toward the concrete, but must call upon sentiments or intuitions that are supranatural. Then how would you define art?"

"A question like that shows your ignorance of the subject," retorted the sculptor, smiling. "It's as difficult to define art simply as it is to define mysticism simply. There's a technical aspect to art and a state of being of the artist, just as there is a dogmatic aspect to mysticism and a state of being of the individual.

"Let's leave this technical side alone for a moment and look at the state of being that characterizes the artist. If we separate the means of expression from that which desires to be expressed, we find a similar state of being in the artist and in the mystic: a communion between man and object, possible only when the duality—or, more accurately, that which makes duality—is eliminated. This communion demands a suppression of the mental, a refusal to separate the object from a sensation or an internal vision. In other words, it's the intuitive knowledge that the artist has that's the object. In order to be more than a mere copyist, the artist must have 'lived' the object. Once this is established, art must not be the mere copy or imitation of Nature. In its purest sense, art is a vision that goes beyond Nature, which for the artist is a mere symbol that evokes an abstraction.

"It is then that the transcription of the vision begins. And it is as fragile as the transcription of the ecstatic vision of the mystic. It's not so much the finished work that makes the masterpiece, but rather what there is in this work which is unconsciously expressed through the personal gesture. Most of the time it is the sketch which most surely reveals the state of the artist's soul. Classical laws, with their rigidity and their finiteness, kill the spontaneous gesture that expresses the intimate life, passion, anger, love, despair, or hope of the sensitive man."

"In that case," asked Jean Thomas, "doesn't so-called 'primitive painting' best correspond to what we call a true work of art?"

"Indeed," said the sculptor, "but conventionalism has reduced the art of the primitives to a purely decorative function. Despite that, as a *whole*, the artistic expression of an era is significant in terms of the mentality and the intellectual tendencies of the era, as long as one disregards the individual artist and sees only the whole of artistic expression, including architecture.

"In this instance, we're dealing with a document and no longer with a work of art. It's a book that tells a story of the thought and the 'state of the soul' of a people and of a period. Moreover, it's the only way to transmit to another period, which has a different mentality, the imponderable impulse of life from a time gone by."

"In brief," resumed the doctor, "whatever the artistic work of a period happens to be, it has a reason for being, which is to express the great problems of life from the point of view of its own civilization. But it's necessary that the whole work be considered, and not the personality of one artist.

"Likewise, can't we perceive the vision of the artist in a current work of art? What I mean is the 'inner' life of the artist."

"Certainly," agreed Dominique, "but when the artist describes himself and speaks of his own sentiments (as writers and poets often do), these works have true value only if the character and his behavior contain within them a universal character. Thus, Shakespeare, Molière, Goethe, and Balzac, among others, have produced works that have created immortal types.

"There is a style expressive of the thought and aspirations of an era, and there is the 'great communion' of the artist with the object, symbol of his revelation."

"This justifies the affirmation that one must never discuss a work of art: it is sufficient that it pleases one or doesn't please one. Thus, it's no more than a subjective judgment, which obviously can be discussed."

"Indeed, dear friend, the aestheticians may say that a work of art can please, and please simply for no particular reason. This is a personal point of view, a fleeting and sensual value. I think that a work of art must speak to something beyond all sensuality, and address itself to supernatural aspiration. To sum it up, it must create an inexpressible rational evocation, a *feeling* of certitude without material proof. Moreover, I'm convinced that this also exists, unconsciously, in the especially sensitive aesthetician when he describes as beautiful something which satisfies the need for harmony. And isn't it the very mysterious and supernatural

Harmony that governs the world and creates within us, starting with a concrete fact, this harmonious call, just like sound that becomes musical? That's the best way I know to describe how I understand art in its purest sense.

"Some write, others paint or sculpt or sing, and all of them are trying to bring back to two-dimensional form a vision that in reality is spatial. But the Great Architect of the world expresses everything in three dimensions, and our human architects are the only artists who throughout time have been able to speak of simultaneity. Others have had to split up the complementary component parts.

"The monuments devoted to faith, during the enlightened stages of human history, are without doubt the highest and the most certain works of art.[2]"

Thomas was dreamily turning his empty glass between his fingers. Dominique watched him cunningly

"Well, Doctor, what do you see at the bottom of your glass?"

"A star is engraved at the bottom. Is it a symbol?"

"Perhaps it's the star of the Magi, which leads the seeker to the cradle of truth. . . ."

2. The discourse on art included in this chapter was given by R. A. Schwaller de Lubicz.

8

The Circus

Jean-Jacques had followed the advice of Maître Dominique: after having patiently recalled his teaching of the two aspects of the soul, he had returned to the Atelier to check his deductions. Jean Thomas didn't have to be persuaded to accompany him. Dominique let the pilot go over what he had recorded, and was content to observe his reactions.

A little bit disappointed by this silence, Jean-Jacques tried to question him.

"What you have retained," said the sculptor at last, "is a correct theory, but you're lumping Human Consciousness into a block. This prevents you from distinguishing the various modes of its expression."

"We haven't really delved into the meaning of consciousness," said Jean-Jacques. "Could we do that now?"

"That's exactly what we won't do," retorted Dominique. "The vital sense of consciousness must be *experienced* before being *understood*. At least that's the method that I practice. I would be satisfied if I could experimentally awaken in you its different aspects.

"What's most urgent is that you learn to decipher the aspects of Human Consciousness that can establish contact with your Permanent Witness. However, it's not theory that's going to teach you. Let me choose the time and the place that are most favorable. Let's meet tomorrow: I'll expect you for dinner. Leave your evening open, and don't jump to any conclusions about what will result from it.

The two friends were on time for the meeting. But Dominique replaced the expected dinner with a stroll along the banks of the Seine, amused to see the reactions of Thomas and his friend, whose worried face was far from expressing the invulnerability that he had boasted of.

"We'll eat later on," declared the sculptor with a detached air. "It's good to fast before partaking in highly spiritual exercises."

And in the presence of his intrigued friends, he started to evoke the turbulent and passionate past to which this old neighborhood had been witness to for several centuries. Finally, having sufficiently tried their patience, he hailed a cab.

"It's time to leave," he said. "Let's go."

And giving instructions to the driver in a low voice, he got into the cab with the two friends.

No one spoke during the ride. The cab stopped in front of the Winter Circus. Dominique paid no heed to the astonishment of his companions and led them into the circus.

"How old are you?" he asked the pilot.

"As of tonight, I'm forty years old."

"You'll be forty years old tomorrow. Tonight you're six years old. You say that you've learned how to listen? Today you are going to learn how to look. Then I will invite you to dinner. We'll have a quiet table, and two friends will come and join us. Pay attention to the spectacle. The circus is a wonderful lesson.

"The circus is a tiny world that 'rolls' like our planet. Although it has Paris as its home, the circus does not betray tradition: it is also 'itinerant,' and its troupes travel all around the world. Nothing is ever fixed. There are no attachments. That's already quite an advantage over our 'bourgeois sense,' which is so fixated on its propriety.

"The circus is round like the earth, and its cloth-covered roof is the roof of the world in the same way that the African tribes thought of their thatched roof.

"The circular ring is subject, *in all circuses*, to a rigorously defined dimension of thirteen meters in diameter."

"I was unaware of that rule," said the pilot. "But I understand that it allows the itinerant troupes to find an identical work space wherever they go."

"But I've seen gigantic circuses that were longer than they were wide," said Thomas.

"Then they are hippodromes, but the ring in the center of the standard arena always keeps the same dimensions. The great Barnum and Bailey circus has three rings that make up the entire length of the enclosure.

"The circus is set up in a curious way. The audience encircles the stage and the actors, who become the center which animates the public.

"Take a look at these spectators. Some of them have come here to laugh: they are the children. Others have come here to be frightened, and perhaps to see an accident. Some have come to appreciate the work of the artists. And finally, there are those poor people who have come just to 'pass the time' and criticize. Isn't this our whole world in miniature?"

"No," answered Thomas. "Two essential motivating forces are missing: earning money and being admired."

"That concerns the actors," answered the sculptor. "Vanity is always purified through the awareness of artifice. In shedding their tinsel and finery, the actors also rid themselves of illusions. As for the love of money, do you realize the unbelievable effort, the continual work, and very often the danger that's represented by each act! And there's always the uncertainty of tomorrow.

"The circus is a hard school, and many of the spectators could learn a lesson from it. But the spectators are of little importance. Today the circus is going to teach you the true sense of the big words that you use without understanding what they are founded upon: consciousness, presence of mind, humor. . . .

"The show is about to begin! Here come the citizens of the circus. The floor acrobats, the tumblers, the tightrope walkers, and the humble gymnasts who spend their free time in continual rehearsal. I assure you they don't have any time to play around!

"The tightrope walker who's following them is already at a superior level. Do you see the cross-sticks that support the wire at the two extremities? On one of them there is a pennant, or a sighting mark, which a tightrope walker must never lose sight of, because he must never look at his dangerous path. Only the goal must guide his steps. What an example, gentlemen! That's an image *never to be forgotten!*

"Watch carefully. Now you will see the illustration of a beautiful mastery of consciousness."

At the very top of the circus, under the soffits, the trapeze artists were beginning their extraordinary acrobatics.

"They are the virtuosos of the flying trapeze," said Dominique, "totally aware that each of their exercises can endanger their lives with the slightest show of weakness."

They throw themselves into emptiness without the protection of the net, and perform perilous jumps by passing from one trapeze to the next. They multiply the difficulties for the pleasure of it. The orchestra was silent, thus intensifying the anguishing moment of the feat. Two trapeze artists threw themselves toward each other at an incredible distance, and managed two somersaults with a difficult jump that made them lose sight of each other. Nonetheless, each had to grasp the other in the emptiness at the very instant when the fall seemed inevitable. The tent broke into applause.

"The public is happy," murmured the sculptor. "They've gotten their money's worth."

"What surprises me," said Thomas, "is how these trapeze artists, *losing sight of their partner* in the double somersaults and the double jumps, find the exact point where they've got to hook up with each other. What is it in them that sees? What is it in them that 'feels'?"

"I can answer that," said the pilot. "You could say that consciousness externalizes itself, extending the hands or the feet like sensitive antennae."

"That's it," answered Dominique. "But do you realize the concentration that is necessary? Above all, *it must never be cerebral*. It must *animate* the 'acting' members of an autonomous consciousness, which is enough to compensate for any mental errors in judging the distance."

Jean Thomas admired the physical beauty of the trapeze artists. They had no excessive muscle (which athletes are so proud of!). Their proportions were harmonious and absolutely flexible, giving the impression of such perfect mastery that they seemed to swim through the air with the same ease that they could have swum through water.

"What handsome men!" said the pilot. "I'll bet that they have plenty of love affairs!"

"You're mistaken," said the sculptor. "I know them. They are sober and chaste, despite the mountains of passionate letters they have to throw into the fire without ever answering.

"To my surprise, they quoted an old proverb that has become a slogan for their trade: 'If you want to save your neck, never work with wine or with women.' It's an ascetic experience that, like other such experiences, allows the practitioner to develop great sensibility. They are afraid of women, and justly so, because women are often the cause of atrocious jealousies, which sometimes lead to crimes of passion."

"However, there are women trapeze artists."

"The directors of the circus are obliged to accept them in order to attract the male public. But for the most daring of acts on the flying trapeze (which is considered the nobility of the profession), a man wants another man for a partner. This often leads to beautiful friendships (which are also always chaste), where the stronger helps the weaker and where the weak ones venerate the strong one without the slightest jealousy.

"I'm telling you that the circus is a small world that has the advantage of developing a sense of independence and sacrifice, and many of the exercises develop the neutrality that favors the awakening of consciousness.

A prelude to marshal music announced the entrance of a group of magnificent horses.

"Watch these gentlemen of the Cavalry advance. You know that the word *cabala* comes from the word for horse, and that the banners of the knights were hermetic emblems.

"The heraldic colors and symbols were the expression of the degree of knowledge and of individual qualities specific to the particular nature of the knight.

"The horse was a part of the horseman, considered in his animal humanity, but the armor and the emblem represented the qualities of the noble being who was to mount and surmount the animal. That's why it's not humiliating for the horse to serve as a mount for man.

"The symbolism of the ancients places the horse in relationship to the vertebrae of man, which carry the fire of the marrow—"

"The marrow," interrupted Thomas, "terminates with a frayed end called 'the horses tail.'"

"Does this mean that the horse is a symbol of fire?" asked Jean-Jacques.

"It's also the animal of Poseidon," answered Dominique. "Think of the horses of Neptune. Moreover, you know that the horse is *born in water* because the mother brings it into the world enveloped in a pocket filled with water. She then tears this pocket with her teeth, and the colt comes out glistening wet."

Attention was drawn to a Spanish horse with an admirable gait.

"They have a sense of rhythm and a taste for ceremony," said Thomas.

"The horse has qualities that men pride themselves on without realizing that these are still faculties of an animal nature. The horse is courageous in combat. In competition (racing or polo) you see the powers unleashed by ambition. But the horse respects life and will never touch the fallen horseman. He is faithful to his master."

"He is also jealous!"

"Certainly! Those are animal sentiments that man should not envy! On the other hand, we can learn from the horse that which our mind has stifled in us: the instinct for danger. This instinct allows it to feel the mood of the horseman."

"But horses also have mental faculties, and a remarkable memory, too," retorted Thomas.

"I'm telling you," confirmed Dominique, "that these faculties are still part of our automaton and our mortal brain.

"But tonight we're here to *observe*. Put yourself into the skin of the different actors. Try to experience their difficulties and to discern the consciousness behind their efforts.

"Here's an amazing juggler who stands up and lies down in the most extraordinary postures. He must follow the balls and other objects at the same time that they move in front of him, behind him, and in all directions. His eyes are not sufficient to do this. How can he be certain of the constantly moving situation of these objects, which are crisscrossing each other?"

"It's his extraordinary power of concentration," said Jean-Jacques.

"If you wish, insofar as he's not distracted. But it's actually the 'exteriorization' of his consciousness that *encircles* all the objects that he manipulates, as if he were a part of them. The Japanese are surprisingly adept at this type of meditation."

"You call this meditation?" exclaimed Thomas.

"Definitely, since it's extending psychological consciousness beyond the material body, with a total disregard for the mental.

"Archery, in the old Chinese tradition, was considered the preeminent noble art because it demands the *conscious* application of perfect harmony and of the *merging* of the archer with his arrow and with the sighted goal.

"It is said that the archers must *go to the heart of ritual rules*: inwardly a correct attitude of the soul, outwardly a correct attitude of the body. The gestures must be so perfect that the arrow, when it leaves, must give the exact note (controlled by the bow), and then it must touch the heart of the target even if the archer isn't looking at it!

"That's a good example of exteriorized consciousness, in which no nervousness, fear, or other personal sentiment can prevent the merging of the archer with his arrow and with his target. For the sages of old, such , behavior was proof of true nobility."

"That's quite a lesson for our mediocrity!" said Jean-Jacques. "It's high time we started to train ourselves in this mastery, if we don't want to lose face in the eyes of the descendants of such wisdom!"

At that moment a crowd of turbulent clowns invaded the ring and were chased by the circus rider from the preceding act. They announced the entrance of the famous clown Claque and his partner, Jocrisse.

While the latter was amusing the public with his silly gestures and active mimicry, Claque, in his startling costume, with his hands behind his back, was gravely surveying the ring and examining the public from behind enormous glasses. With his finger, he started to count the spectators. He stopped, looked around at the ground around him, and started to count again.

The equestrian called out:

"What are you looking for, Mr. Claque?"

As he continued with his mimicry, Claque answered, grimacing:

"Me? I'm looking for my reputation."

"You've lost your reputation?"

"And it's your fault, of course. You told me: 'You better make the spectators laugh or you'll lose your reputation.' I can't do that, Mr. What's-Your-Name."

"My name is not Mr. What's-Your-Name."

"I can't do that, Mr. Whachamacallit. First you have to tell me how many English people and how many French people there are in the room."

"You need to know that?"

"Of course! I gotta know how many I have to laugh for in French, and how many I have to laugh for in English."

"But it's not you that has to laugh. It's the spectators!"

"You don't understand anything. If I don't laugh, they're going to cry. I want to my reputation back!"

"You're incorrigible, Claque: there are Belgians and Americans and Germans, too."

The clown started to whimper:

"I can't do it! I can't laugh in all those languages."

The equestrian moved toward him:

"Mr. Claque, I'm going to get angry. Now, go do your act!"

"No, don't get impatient. I've got an idea: I'm going to bring over a friend who laughs in all the languages of the entire world. Jocrisse, hurry up! Bring me Aristophanes."

And Jocrisse came back, leading by the bridle a rather reluctant donkey. Claque took an enormous carrot out of his pocket.

"Listen, Aristophanes, you'll have your carrot if you get me back my reputation. You laugh in my place, Aristophanes: one! two! one! two!"

The clown took the donkey's tail in both his hands and pulled it in rhythm to his counting. The donkey started to bray desperately with a series of convulsive heehaws! Claque, pulling the tail with conviction, shouted in order to make himself heard above the roaring laughter:

"Come on, Europe, come on! Bray and laugh in all the languages you want!"

Hee and haws rose up into the highest rafters. The laughter became contagious, and Claque was encouraging it:

"Bravo! Laugh!"

While the room was screaming, braying, and laughing, the clown calmly started to eat the carrot. Frenetic applause burst out. Then Claque approached the donkey, hugged him, and sent him away crestfallen:

"Go on, old boy, you've done a good job! For your troubles, I'll leave you my reputation!"

There were all different degrees of laughter: innocent, credulous, and intelligent. All applauded the departure of Claque, who soberly left, eating his carrot.

Dominique said nothing. He observed his friends, whose laughter seemed to have extinguished the dialectic. Now that the first part of the show was over, each of them had understood that the goal of the spectacle was something more than simple distraction.

During intermission, the wild animal cage was set up, and six Bengali tigers and one panther were let in. The animal tamer, whip in hand, watched silently as the animals entered. The atmosphere was stormy, and it made the cats aggressive. There was a concert of roaring outside the ring, as well as inside the ring, which made the public even more nervous than the animals.

Everything was going fine until the last exercise. The animal tamer was putting a panther and a tiger through their performance, while the other five tigers were ordered to lean against the bars of the cage in a semicircle behind him. There was a thunderous cloudburst, and the cats began to get agitated. At the riskiest moment of the exercise, when the trainer was preparing a mock fight with the tiger, two cats behind him left the side of the cage and moved toward him, menacingly.

Their master, without turning his head, lifted his left hand and called out the names of the unruly cats. That was sufficient. The tamer, finishing the exercise, received the enthusiastic applause of the public.

While they were transferring the animals back to their cages, Thomas and the pilot confessed their emotions.

"What surprises me," said Thomas, "is the sharpness of the man's senses. Even with his back turned, he knew which ones were disobedient."

"How can you still be surprised by that?" retorted Dominique. "The tamer who didn't feel, with his eyes closed, what his animals felt, would one day be their victim.

"But look—now the king enters."

A magnificent lion came into the cage. His enormous mane gave him a royal presence. Majestic and arrogant, he approached his waiting master, roaring. Man and beast confronted each other eye to eye for several instants. The lion was obviously giving in. The trainer relaxed the atmosphere by running his hand through the lion's heavy mane.

"You're pretty nervous tonight, my friend! Come on, Goliath, it's useless to be nasty. You know very well that you must give in."

The tame animal docilely obeyed and executed the usual exercises. Then came a small Savoyard bear, which hobbled forward on its hind legs. It had a bib around its neck, like a baby, and was looking distrustfully toward the lion, which seemed amused by its fear.

The animal tamer made fun of it:

"Come on, Martin, say hello to your king. Stop trembling. People will think that you're chicken! Come on, give him something to eat!"

The poor beast, trembling with terror, approached the lion, and on the insistent commands of the tamer, put the bottle into his mouth. The beast, who usually condescended to this humiliation, reacted violently and spat the bottle out with a horrifying roar.

"Listen to the fear of the public," murmured Dominique, "and you'll realize the coolness of the trainer."

The trainer signaled a helper to get the frightened little bear out of the ring. The trainer then stood in front of the raging lion and spoke to him like to a child he was trying to calm.

"Yes, I know," he said as he caressed the lion. "It's embarrassing for a great king, but you're my friend. You are my friend, arent' you? Prove it, then, and be nice. Open your mouth. Open! You see, I have confidence in you!"

The lion's roars were calmed, and his heavy breathing subsided. Finally, he opened his big mouth before the tense audience and let the tamer put his head into it and then remove it without incident.

While they took apart the wild animal cage, the pilot and Thomas exchanged impressions.

"Do you know," said the sculptor, "that one of the greatest dangers is the nervous panic of spectators? During a storm, like the one we're having today, this could affect the animals."

"I willingly believe it," said the pilot. "But I wonder what the reactions of the spectators would be in the event that there was a tragic incident."

"Some sixty years ago such an accident occurred. It involved a famous animal trainer, Bidel. Bidel was putting a lion through his stunts despite the fact that he was suffering from gout. Bidel knocked his foot against a double-edged harpoon and lost his balance. He fell flat on his face. An enormous scream issued forth from the crowd. A horrified silence followed. The trainer, handicapped by his bandaged leg, decided that it was better to remain motionless, like an inoffensive cadaver. The lion, crouched against the bars of the cage, watched him attentively. Suddenly, the lion came to attention, got to its feet, and step by step, approached the tamer like a distrustful cat. Then the lion made up his mind. Putting a paw on the shoulder of the prone man, he started to tear apart the man's clothes, and then ripped the flesh from his shoulder and neck.

"From the moment the lion started to approach, the public had started to scream with horror. Men and women rushed around the cage.[1] The women were knocking over the men in order not to miss a thing! It's clear that their screams were not made to appease the beast.

"The tragedy was brought to an end when two men, armed with picks, entered the cage and pushed the lion into the neighboring cage.

"Then the spectators looked on with stupefaction as the great Bidel stood up, despite his bleeding shoulder, and confronted the beast, which was retreating into its cage."

"The spectators applauded, of course," concluded Jean Thomas, disheartened.

"Thanks for the applause!" cried the pilot. "How shameful for human beings to exhibit such sadism!"

"What is most shameful," retorted Dominique, "is for us to delude ourselves about our inferior nature without having confronted our secret tendencies. It's under the surprise of a shock that man reveals his animal instincts, which conventional morality has so carefully masked. On the one hand, it's hypocrisy, and on the other hand, it's respect for convention that keeps us from affirming our faith in our immortal being.

"Humanity is not beautiful when it delights in vulgarity, my friends. However, vulgarity is *unconsciousness* and satisfaction with *mediocrity*.

"We can leave now. The final procession is of no interest to us. Let's go and eat. The beasts are about to be fed! I hope that your beasts haven't tormented you too much during this imposed fast. Don't protest; each of us carries the animal within himself. What's important is to know who leads whom. . . ."

They found a friendly, quiet corner in a restaurant. They had hardly started to order wine and look at the menu when the two invited guests arrived. The sculptor introduced them to his companions and smiled at their astonishment:

"I think you recognize the animal tamer that you applauded. As for my other friend, he's the master of laughter whose real name is—"

"Please, let me be known by the name that my friends, the children,

1. It was a double-tiered cage that had been placed upon a long vehicle.

know me by," said the clown with alacrity. "I am Claque, gentlemen, and I'm not at all ashamed of it."

Thomas and the pilot reacted warmly and expressed their new interest in this circus world, which the public only knew by its appearances.

"It's a fascinating life," said the tamer. "It's almost the antithesis of the bourgeois mentality. While bourgeois mentality bases its existence on the 'civility' of man, on property, and on security, we, as companions of the road (even though we use modern transport), are liberated from the chains that attach us to one place. Our only property consists of the faculties and the aspect of the mastery that we have been able to develop *individually*. As for our security, it is constantly threatened by the occupational hazards that can disable us."

"Then what motivates your interest and what attaches you to your profession?" asked Thomas.

"It's above all the sense of *freedom*, as opposed to the fear of losing what one is attached to. You can't imagine how wonderful it is to go to sleep at night putting your trust in destiny, with no other care except that of perfecting tomorrow what was acquired today. And then, there's the mystique of the road (a little like the gypsies): the road! Our path is constantly changing, and leads us into unexpected circumstances. The only fixed roof we have is the stars. The only will is that of the demiurge who is the director of the circus we are temporarily working with."

"However, you don't say that you're not worried about tomorrow!" said the pilot.

"That's just what we can't allow ourselves. If we do, we'll lose our coolness, the calmness of nerve that is indispensable to the 'noble' categories of the circus: the trapeze artists, for example, as well as the jugglers and the animal tamers.

"The floor acrobats, however, think only of perfecting themselves to attain a higher level. I'm not talking about the great clown, who is a very rare being because of his deep psychology."

"However, you can escape the inherent vices of the actor," objected the pilot.

"Footlooseness, for example?" said the clown. "Well, it's amusing to note that our wandering life shields us from it by the very fact that the public is continually changing: they laugh, they admire us, they applaud . . . and we pass on and are forgotten

"Even with the best circus artists, the admiration of the spectators is tinged with a kind of pity for these 'wanderers' who live on the fringes of bourgeois society. It's as if they resented us for being able to escape the chains of convention that keep them bound."

"I understand you very well," exclaimed Dominique. "You have chosen freedom! What's more, you've escaped the intrigue and the false notoriety of the stars who have been sanctified by Hollywood."

"And what about jealousy?" asked Jean Thomas. "Doesn't it ever take its toll among you?"

"Very rarely," answered the clown, "unless love and women come into it. And even in those cases, the indispensable discipline needed in our work saves us from such adventures.

"Through force of circumstances, a hierarchy of *quality* is established in our small world: the degree of risk in the acts, and the quality of mastery that is demanded because of it, have created a category of artists, somewhat like a ladder of nobility. And this exists without bitterness or unhealthy envy because if the floor acrobats dream of arriving at the apotheosis of the flying trapeze artist, they also know what price they have to pay to do it: chastity and soberness. Thus, the hierarchy of the circus establishes itself through quality."

"The quality of acquired consciousness," confirmed Dominique.

"What a wonderful example," exclaimed the pilot with enthusiasm. "And for you, a tamer of wild beasts, what an exercise of mastery it must be!"

"Training," answered the tamer, "demands a perfect presence of mind and the perfect comprehension of the nature of the animal and its individual character.

"A wise animal tamer will never undertake the training of a beast without having observed at length its behavior, tastes, particular faults, and reactions. Only then, and without warning, will he enter into the cage; he must impose himself upon the beast suddenly. From the very first the beast must be aware of its master, and from that moment on, not one instance of weakness is permitted."

"Does the beast rebel at being made to do stunts?"

"It will accept it if the trainer is careful in the beginning to ask of it only that which it would like to do if it were free. The lion, for example, likes to jump. He even likes to jump over fire. But his degree of nobility manifests itself in his repugnance of slavery. For the elephant, this repugnance is so great that you must take infinite precautions to make it accept what you want it to do. At first, you must surround it with two other elephants, called monitors, and even then, if the trainer has not waited the necessary time before harnessing the elephant, it's possible that the poor beast will collapse during the first effort and die suddenly from a 'broken heart.' That's the expression used by the natives, who are very much aware of the elephant's sensitivity.

"However, if nobility is conditioned according to the degree of consciousness, the elephant is, more than any other animal, the most noble of earthly creatures. There are abundant examples of this."

"What is most difficult about taming man-eating animals?" asked Thomas.

"It is to tame oneself, dear sir, because you must replace thought with sensation, and fear with total confidence.

"It's necessary to be in communication or, even more important, in constant communion with the animal, not only with the one that's working, but also with the others waiting in the cage. The animal tamer who is unaware of the impulses of those he turns his back on, will sooner or later be their victim."

"It's always a matter of exteriorizing consciousness," said the sculptor.

"Do you believe that the beast is waiting for that moment of inattentiveness in order to avenge itself?" asked the pilot.

"That could be the case for the animal that is trained by terror, an unhealthy and unjust method. But above all, a man must inspire in his beasts the confidence in his loyalty, which is only possible if the man is master enough of himself to have that confidence, and to impose this certitude on the beast."

"I admire your courage, and the discipline that such mastery requires," said Thomas.

"Courage and discipline are still 'natural' qualities," declared Dominique. "But that which goes beyond the human animal is the *conscious wakefulness of intuitive consciousness*, which has allowed our friend to make his beasts experience the superiority of his being a man. This is not done by force, but by a state of consciousness in the face of which their animal instinct can only give in."

The animal tamer looked at Dominique with touched recognition.

"You have elevated me in my own eyes, dear sir. If I were only worthy of this praise. I would have almost attained the goal of my existence."

Dominique looked at Thomas and to the pilot for an answer:

"What do you think? Have I exaggerated in speaking of the conscious acquisition of mastery?"

The animal tamer, embarrassed, called on the clown to change the subject:

"Come on, Claque, how about showing off a little of your genius to save my modesty. Claque, gentlemen, is much more gifted at these things than I am. The human animals that he 'puts into a cage' with his humor are difficult to master, in a way that is different from my beasts."

The clown shook his head.

"Hmm! If you knew the source of my humor, you might call it misanthropy, although in truth it's more like a great pity for humanity."

Thomas looked at him cunningly.

"If you go to the bottom of such pity, wouldn't you find an element of vanity?" he said.

"Most likely I would, Thomas, if I didn't include myself in this humanity," answered Claque.

"All that's childishness," retorted Dominique. "Your humor is the fruit of a lucid consciousness of the unbelievable possibilities of man, and the stupid way he's used these possibilities."

"That's right, dear friend. The true clown is the expression of this consciousness of ridiculousness."

"It would be wonderful if that were the case," recognized the pilot. "But the clowns who do this knowingly must be the exceptions."

"The majority who practice it are traditionally schooled."

"Wasn't Pierrot the first clown?" asked Thomas.

"No. The naive and sentimental Pierrot belonged to Italian pantomime. The burlesque clown and the monkeylike acrobat are imports that are half-English and half-American (mostly in terms of their imitation of blacks). They were the *minstrels* and the best of them are still the *buffoon* and his partner, the straight man. The Shakespearean clown is still the lout who is always being knocked out, and who has become our Jocrisse. The burlesque English and Irish clowns are big drinkers, and brought to their spectacle what was comic about their drunkenness. The English clown brought with him 'eccentric' comedy, which resulted from an exacerbated sense of the blues, which was carried to the point of systematic and calculated craziness."

"But you, too, use craziness, and the unexpected," said Thomas.

"Of course. The unexpected is the essential weapon of the psychological clown. Laughter is produced by the shock that results from the gap in the audience's attention, thought, or feeling. I'll give you an example.

"Call our waiter, and tell him (as if you were confiding to him) that I'm a very famous person, and ask him to guess my profession."

The waiter, flattered by this "confidential secret," took on an air of importance as he observed the face of this "well-known gentleman."

"Didn't I wait on you, sir, at a dinner of diplomats?"

"No, my friend, you've made a mistake."

"Then you are a Hollywood star!"

"No, I don't make movies."

"Excuse me, sir. Would you be a famous surgeon?"

"Not that either."

"What am I saying? Of course your're the famous reporter—"

"No, I don't do any reporting."

"Then you must be a nuclear physicist!"

"No, I'm not, thank God!"

"I'm terribly sorry, sir, I really don't know. What are you?"

Claque said in a cavernous voice:

"I am Ca-tho-lic."

An outburst of laughter drew the attention of the other people in the restaurant. The waiter gulped.

"Ah! That's a hard one to swallow! What a great joke! Now I see: You're a cl— a comic artist!"

"Say it, my boy: I'm a clown, and you are an excellent audience. Thank you, young man. Let me shake your hand."

The maître d' was coming over to find out the reason for the disruption. Dominique ordered some champagne and the maître d' went away without inquiring further.

"There you have it!" said the clown. "The old joke always works. The effect of the unexpected never misses. Attract the attention, thought, or feelings toward one direction where the audience is waiting for a logical conclusion, and then suddenly break the expected link by creating a gap or a change in the object upon which the attention is focused. It's an illogical shock whose ridiculousness provokes a spasm of laughter in which the audience finds compensation."

"Extremely interesting," said the pilot. "But you must know other ways to provoke laughter, so that you can vary your effect."

"The true clown has to have a whole barrelful of laughs! First of all, there's the vulgar laughter that you frequently find in uneducated peasants who get excited at sexual or scatological allusions. A step above is laughter as response to commonplaces: jokes about the mother-in-law or the cuckold. Laughter that is provoked by mockery is more interesting. It's an obscure feeling of revenge against mundane hypocrisy and imposed amiability."

"Freeing people from repressed ideas? Say, that's something that should be put to use," said the pilot. "Such little games of ridicule should be introduced into the salons to offset the underhanded criticism of malicious 'friends.'"

"Try it," answered Claque. "But it would be too honest to have much success!

"Luckily, there is compensation in candid laughter, the laughter of children and simple people who don't look at evil. This laughter is the expression of their confidence in life and the goodness of people. . . . Poor humble folk! For them the costume of the clown is sufficient proof that he's the jolly man who is going to amuse them and who will never make them cry.

"And understand me well: that laughter is paradise on earth for the philosophical clown with the melancholy smile. It's the only clarity without underhanded shadows. Little children know it, and they love it. Clowns like Footit and Chocolat have distracted so many sick children from their suffering!

"Next we have the naive or credulous laughter of the 'willing audience,' which allows itself to fall into the traps laid for it by the buffoon or the clown. They need to shake with laughter and lay in a bit of gaiety. That public is the middle public. They're not very demanding in terms of how the clown proceeds. They are the man who has come to forget his daily worry and who is grateful to the clown, whose accomplice he becomes by pretending to ignore the 'tricks.' The clown likes him as well, and knows how to reach him.

"At the pole opposite to children is the more subtle pole where dialecticians sit. This group is made up of 'serious people' who reflect, or who 'want their money's worth.' There are very few clowns who know how to touch this group, because they must be taken by surprise, by unexpected gaps, or by a lack of logic that is astute enough to disconcert them."

"That's pretty high psychology, my dear Claque," said the pilot. "And it seems to me that very few clowns are cultivated enough to apply it."

"That's right," answered Claque, "but the fault also lies in contemporary mentality. The man of today is humiliated by mystery and claims to have an answer for everything. Even a little boy of six years old, in front of a magician, refuses to accept the illusion and wants to find out what the trick is. He refuses to dream—and his parents, who are very proud of him, will one day be surprised to see him disillusioned and committing insane acts!"

"I'm happy to know you, my dear Claque," said Jean-Jacques. "Now I understand the depth and wisdom of your lucidity, and I congratulate you for knowing how to overcome your melancholy in order to provoke laughter in those of us who are 'enchained.'"

Dominique addressed the pilot:

"Just a moment, dear sir: I'm sure you have misunderstood the melancholy that you attribute to our friend. Insofar as it exists, it must be, in my opinion, the reflection of a feeling of solitude experienced by a lucid being in the midst of the human species.

"However, the human species of which we have spoken tonight must not be considered in general terms.

"There are only five of us here, a small human pentagon, of which each element represents a search for mastery. But what does mastery mean if not the successive awakening of the various consciousness that are asleep within us, despite the resistance of the menagerie that each one of us represents?

"From the earthworm, which is the most primitive organism, to the monkey, which imitates man just as our monkey mind would like to imitate the Creator, through the jackal, which digests in its stomach, and the dog-faced baboon, which symbolizes the respiratory system, and the serpent of fire in our vertebrae, we must recognize in each of our organs the incarnation of a functional consciousness. Man must become the trainer of his consciousness if he wants to be worthy of the title 'king of Creation.'"

The trainer was ecstatic.

"That's something I had never thought of before, and explains the cause of human power over animals!"

"My exposition is incomplete," said Dominique. "I haven't used other examples, such as the animal that governs the liver, or the human animal, because consciousness of the higher self has its seat on one of the twelve areas of the liver. That's why bilious anger overshadows this consciousness and puts you, the tamers, in an inferior position to the beast, which feels it."

"How right you are, sir! Anger, along with fear, is our greatest danger."

"Every morning, man should visit his menagerie and give to each one of his organs the impression that it is commanded by the consciousness of each function."

"But that's what we do as tamers. Whether we feel good or bad, every morning we must come in contact with our animals to experience, in a friendly but firm way, their submission."

"That's all very fine for you," said Jean-Jacques, "but what about the other members of our pentagon? What kind of experiments should we practice?"

"It has nothing to do with experimenting. It has to do with realization," replied the sculptor. "It's a continual training of our animal Automaton, including our monkey mind, which we must make a dutiful secretary to our intuitive faculties. The trainer must be our conscious self. (I'm speaking here of our mortal consciousness.)

"But haven't we philosophized enough for one night?"

"No," retorted the clown, "because you are stopping at a tragic moment: the moment when this conscious self becomes conscious of the unconsciousness of men, and finds itself in conflict with their judgment."

"That's at the center of your concept, isn't it, my dear Claque?"

"Yes, it is, and I would be very happy if you knew how to resolve it."

"I see only one way," answered the sculptor soberly. "A certain super-egotism which concentrates our personal effort on widening and unifying our consciousness, and whose result is the realization of Total Man, who is immortal. Such a man is a shining sun, with more power to better other men than any discourse or sermon.

"I would like us to empty our glasses now, in communion with our pentagon, which gives to each of us the serene joy of no longer being alone in confronting the 'human beast.'"

"Thank you, Dominique," said Jean Thomas, expressing the general feeling. "And thanks to you circus artists for having given us, through your example, an unforgettable lesson!"

9

The Family and the Couple

"What's going on, dear friend? Why this urgent call?" said Dominique
to Jean Thomas, who was waiting for him in the airport restaurant.

"Excuse me," said Thomas, "for abusing your generosity, but again I find
myself in a difficult situation that I am unable to resolve alone. I came to
Orly to accompany my friend Francis Dutheil, who is going to take a
plane to Bombay. I apologize for making the rendezvous in such a
busy place, which is, no doubt, unfavorable for a serious discussion,
but I had no choice, and it is urgent."

"Don't apologize. I like the atmosphere of these airports, where so
many voyagers are living out their little dramas of change, whether they
are arriving or leaving, and what it involves in terms of the unknown, of
hope or abandonment. This is a crossroads in which the emotion of uncertainty and the game of destiny inspire me."

"Well, I'm glad about that," said Thomas, "because it is indeed a
crossroads that you will have to deal with. I asked my friend to finish up
his errands so we could have two or three hours before he leaves.

"Francis Dutheil is a remarkable young man. His judgment is impartial,
and his behavior is straightforward, in business affairs as well as in the
difficulties of his daily life. He sees the problems of existence as a series
of experiences that he calls the 'maturation of consciousness.'"

"That's fine," agreed Dominique, obviously interested. "What's important is to know how he deals with them."

"When he has something to resolve, he (in his own words), 'balances
it.' On the one hand, he looks at its utilitarian or rational aspects. On the
other hand, he tries to see the good or bad effects in terms of attaining his

higher goal. For Dutheil, the balance would always lean toward the attainment of his goal."

"Very good, but I'd like to know what this goal is."

"How can I translate it? The finality of the human being, says my friend, cannot limit itself to the fulfillment of cerebral consciousness, the consciousness of a rational intelligence, regardless of how strong it is. Neither can any faculty that belongs to his normal body be of use in fulfilling this. My ambition, he says, is to find that which is *indestructible*, to attain a state of consciousness that is nourished by my experiences and that survives this miserable existence, whose sole excuse is merely to make this possible.

"That's the way he says it, and not without bitterness. He considers the human condition to be a state of intolerable mediocrity. This is even more painful for him because his inner conviction has alerted him to a higher destiny whose possibilities lie within him."

"Your friend sounds interesting. Why is he going to India?"

"On a business trip. He's got a very successful company, which is now managed by his associate."

"His religion?"

"A nonpracticing Catholic."

"Is he single?"

"He's married and has three children between the ages of eleven and seventeen."

"What does he expect from me?"

"I think he finds himself at a crossroads where his indecision over a choice of orientation could become dramatic. Try to get him to talk about it himself. Here he is."

A stream of passengers entered the restaurant. The energetic and straightforward allure of the man who was approaching them made Dominique like him. Dominique looked at the caring seriousness of his expression. His forehead indicated a clear intelligence.

Thomas introduced them and suggested he leave them alone to talk.

"We'll have lunch together," declared the traveler. "I have no secrets to hide from you, Thomas, and it's the example of your transformation that made me decide to ask your master for advice."

"Will you be spending much time in India?" asked the sculptor as he sat down opposite Dutheil.

"I don't know, because it all depends upon our discussion, dear sir. My business requires only a month, but I would like to take advantage of the trip for my personal quest, which could go on for quite a while—indefinitely."

Dominique scrutinized the man's face. He sought the answer within himself, but he asked the man a question.

"Are you breaking chains? Or are you jumping into the unknown?"

"Perhaps both," answered Dutheil seriously. "Allow me to tell you about my situation.

"Until today my life was devoted to my social duties: to ensure the future of my wife and children. This goal has been attained, and now I find myself not knowing what to do next. I don't see any other way to continue in the same path, and this stupid existence of mine has no relationship to a deep aspiration that oppresses me."

"Can you define this aspiration?"

"I would rather explain it in terms of its frustration: the failure to attain a higher goal, which I can imagine without being able to put my finger on it."

"Your friend told me, however, that you were looking for the attainment of that which is indestructible in you."

"Exactly, I am unable to believe that the current condition of man is his final destiny."

"You're right, because the animal-human kingdom which has attained the stage of the mentally accomplished man only attains finality in exceptional cases. This finality is the suprahuman. However, this last stage involves the awakening of man's intuitive and spiritual consciousness, and the mastery of his animality and his cerebral consciousness.

"It's the realization of the *Total Man*, and the attainment of his immortality. This realization is the goal of his earthly incarnation."

"So I was not mistaken. That's what I instinctively felt."

"It's better to use the word *intuitive*, because this foreknowledge is a warning, an unveiling of your indestructible consciousness, which makes you superior to your intelligent animal being."

"I think I understand you, Maître Dominique, and it's a great relief for me to hear you affirm this possibility. But it's hard to believe that nothing in our formation has prepared us for this higher destiny."

"The Heavenly Kingdom," replied Dominique, "interpreted as a paradise inaccessible before death, has obscured for us the reality of the suprahuman realm, which is a state of Consciousness, an integration of our immortal being which is attainable in this existence."

"Understanding this possibility is of the greatest importance," said Dutheil, "because if the promise of paradise is just bait for virture and for obedience to religious laws, it doesn't teach us how to develop the subtle faculties that give us access to the suprahuman realm. How can I come into contact with my Spiritual Consciousness?"

"It is within you," confirmed Dominique. "All you have to do is to awaken it."

"But how? Calling upon the Holy Spirit through prayer doesn't seem very helpful."

"That's because we imagine that the Spirit is outside of us. Spirit is *within us*, but our mind and our dispersed lives prevent it from illuminating us."

"So be it," conceded Dutheil, "but what we are taught in the West tells us nothing about the soul. What happens is that we inevitably confuse 'good intentions,' suggested by conventional morality, with the calling and reproaches of our secret voice, possibly our immortal Consciousness, which we don't allow to manifest in us!"

"Oh, I know that," said Dominique, sighing. "This ignorance is the great misery of our chaotic times."

"You know it," retorted Dutheil, "but this ignorance can lead to disaster. Do you know *that*, Maître Dominique? Do you know how much despair results from this aspiration which can't be satisfied, because the immortal being from which it emanates is unknown to the human being who carries it?"

"It seems that this unknown being is not unknown to you, Monsieur Dutheil. Why don't you know where to turn?"

"I feel like the bird that senses its wings growing but doesn't yet know how to use them to fly, but with this difference: the bird *knows* that it has its parents there to teach it, while I, a modern man, materially and intellectually rich, remain a prisoner in the nest of routine, for lack of someone to teach me to fly.

"That's why I have decided to look in India for the help that I have not been able to find here."

"Of course," agreed Dominique. "The existence of psychospiritual states is obvious for Easterners, who have experienced different aspects of yoga. Meditation is so natural to them that even children practice it.

"But do you think that our Western temperament, our hectic way of life, our exacerbated mind can accommodate itself to practices that demand total liberation from these chains?

"Many attempts made by swamis in France, in England, and in America have all too often proved that the Eastern method applied to Westerners doesn't have good results. Western education emphasizes mental activity, thus creating the danger of confusion between psychic and spiritual states, because the discernment of these diverse states demands a long and carefully controlled preparation. Otherwise, cerebral or nervous accidents, imbalance, or upset may occur, not to mention undesirable astral manifestations as well."

Jean Thomas looked at his friend with a nod of approval. Dominique continued:

"You see, dear sir, each era had its Wise Men, the initiators who provided formulas and methods applied to the particular faculties that were developed in the people for whom they had come. It is not wise to transpose these methods inopportunely.

"Do you intend to experiment with them in the East?"

Dutheil answered, hesitating:

"At first, I just want to look around for what answers my aspiration. Is your opinion based on experience, Maître Dominique?"

"Definitely," affirmed the sculptor. "*I never speak of that which I don't know*, in fact as in theory."

"Then I must take your advice into consideration. But my problem is more complex, because the question of family is at stake. My wife is now only the mother of my children for me. She has raised them with devotion, but according to the formulas and habits of a previous generation, which provoke mistrust and often rebellion in modern youth.

"Each of my children is a little egocentric character who forms his or her opinions, judgments, and decisions from a pragmatic point of view in which I see no trace of an altruistic ideal. You could call their behavior a compromise between unavoidable concessions to scholastic, familial, and even religious discipline, and a fierce defense of their 'dignity,' which resists everything that could contradict the secret impulses of their little egotistical selves."

"Your judgment is harsh," said Jean Thomas.

"Unfortunately, it's accurate in the majority of cases," retorted Dominique. "Premature mental development, aggravated by the recent precocity in puberty, gives modern children the illusion of cocksure free will."

"They no longer know how to *play*," said Dutheil. "They mistrust the innocent, *unselfish* game that has no goal except childish amusement, laughter, and relaxation, like that of the cat, which plays for no reason. They need competition and pragmatic goals. My daughter, who has just turned eleven, thinks only of being first in her class, of being 'the strongest,' and of pressing on with her education. My younger son, thirteen years old, talks only about cars, speed, and sports competition. My older son, seventeen years old, dreams about the atomic techniques of the Americans. It's useless to try to guide their reading habits: haunted by radio and television, they absorb predigested opinions and nourish themselves on popularized, simplistic notions. What they call the right to independence is the freedom to cast a shadow over their consciousness!"

"Can't you show them the dangers in this vulgarization?" asked Thomas.

"My poor friend, I'd be treated as uncomprehending and backward!"

"You *are* backward in a certain sense," quipped Dominique. "You are backward in your ignorance of the causes of this state of affairs. It's yourself that you have to educate first. Then you will know how to awaken their consciousness to the realities that will make you, in their eyes, no longer backward but a comprehending and *competent* precursor."

"How can I, if I myself am torn apart by my own uncertainty? I am overwhelmed by the individuality of my children. Each of them exhibits an assurance in behavior that could delude me about maturity."

"This maturity isn't necessarily illusory, dear sir. The course of time and of stages is currently accelerating, like a wave that is being precipitated before it breaks. Look at the rapidity of scientific progress: from year to year the pace increases at a disquieting rhythm. It's disquieting because our discernment (or consciousness of what is Real) has not developed in proportion to our cerebral consciousness.

"It's the rhythm of an era that we're experiencing—the accelerated rhythm of the end of an age, which our children are entering into fully, while we, vaguely worried, are trying to postpone it!"

"Do you see another solution?"

"Certainly. You can't go *against* the rhythm of an age, and it's useless to rebel against it. But it is also deadly to undergo it unconsciously, or to resign oneself to it through impotent fatalism. It's necessary to recognize it and to look for an impetus in this rhythm that will enable you to go beyond it.

"I'm convinced there are a certain number of children who are able to understand this language, if only one could awaken in them the consciousness of and the desire (I was about to say ambition) for their higher humanity."

"That doesn't seem uniformly possible," reflected Dutheil. "In the case of my children, I see very clear differences among the children of a similar family; you could even call it two opposing currents."

"That's true," answered Dominique. "There are two inverse tendencies that correspond respectively to two different states of spiritual evolution, or, if you prefer, to two different states of consciousness that classify being into two categories that the Gospel and all the sages call the Many and the Few. These two categories cannot be treated in the same way. They do not understand the same language. Those who are part of the Many want animal and mental satisfaction. The others, the Few, aspire to a higher state. However, you can't begrudge those of the Many who don't have the possibilities for the goals that the Few have. But must you sacrifice one because of the inability of the other?"

"Obviously not. But what you are talking about demands a clear vision of contradictory elements. Could you define them for us?"

"The familial situation," explained Dominique, "is the same as that of nations and of societies. The two opposing tendencies are individualism and collectivism.

"Individualism is provoked by the inner impulse of our Immortal Consciousness, which pushes our human consciousness to blossom through the *free experience* of its humanity. Theoretically, this holds true only for those elite beings who are capable of this realization. However, many others feel it as well, through contagion, and through the impetus of the rhythm of the times.

"The collectivist tendency, which you can also call egalitarianism of rights and duties, dominates the Many. It makes them envious and jealous toward those who are superior to them.

"This doesn't mean that the masses renounce individualism, which they translate in terms of rebellion, multiple opinions, and egotistical demands. This incoherent mixture characterizes current nations and societies which are part of the Many.

"If you apply this to the family, you'll see that the same drama is taking place. And don't say that this is always the case. This struggle between the two tendencies—which throughout history has manifested itself sporadically according to the evolution of people and of individuals—is crystallized today by two clearly defined thrusts. These thrusts are irresistible because they are unconscious of their cause and are thus very difficult to put back into their proper place.

"Can you draw any conclusions about your family from this exposition?"

"If I understand you," answered Dutheil, "there is no immediate solution, because it will take a long time to cultivate in my children the notion of their situation in our current world. And, above all, it would take a long time to inspire their confidence in my understanding of their individual situations.

"As for my wife, there's no possible link between her conventional and pragmatic directives and my spiritual quest. We can continue to live side by side in order to keep a home for our children, as long as we limit our contact to the problems of everyday life.

"And I'm not the only one in this painful predicament. What's become of the family of the past?"

"The wheel has turned, my friend," answered Dominique. "Since the time of the cult of ancestors, whose reincarnation ancient China awaited, so many stages of humanity have been attained that now the family is broken apart through antagonism, age, opinions, or unavowed vices. Even in families that are apparently united, there are as many diverse concepts as there are chairs around the table. Each one keeps his own secret aspirations, whether they're banal or profound. The individual is alone in his intimacy, and will remain so more and more because the time has come for individual realization.

"*It's no longer a matter of perpetuating oneself through one's descendants*, at least for those who aspire to the Higher Kingdom, or for whom the earth is a country of exile. Everyone is 'sucked up by his own desire,' and the goal that he sets for himself orients the path he takes."

Dutheil was listening with his head in his hands. . . .

The airport was alive with activity. A hallucinatory impression was given off by the stream of travelers of different races and countries, scattered abroad by airplanes whose speed obliterated time and space. . . .

"Just look at how the suppression of distances accentuates the acuteness of individual problems," murmured Thomas. "All the personal questions are evoked at this crossroads where so many destinies intersect. Try to experience these diverse emotional currents, in which each individual (who is undergoing them unconsciously) finds something to nourish his own worries. . . ."

Over the loudspeaker came the announcement for passengers to board a flight to New York.

The occupants of the neighboring table suddenly stood up. A woman was crying and saying farewell to her husband, who was obviously embarrassed. Her son was impatient to leave. He listened with one ear to her last-minute advice, while a little boy played with a new toy, the latest gift from his father.

"The family!" Dominique sighed. "Where is the element of cohesion for this group with dissimilar interests?"

"Doesn't the home, which used to be sacred, have meaning anymore?" asked Dutheil.

"The vital sense of the home, my friend, is the hearth. Today, what fire could unify the personalities of a family with its warmth? The patriarchal life concentrated on a common ideal? That's an old cliché that has been relegated to the attic with the old clothes of another period. What about the radiance of conjugal love? Small indeed is the percentage of couples who are united by *real* love, independent of carnal appetites and purified of the spirit of possessiveness, where the two partners, in their own fulfillment, are seeking to unite what has been separated."

"Dear sir!" exclaimed Dutheil. "With those criteria for conjugal affection, the number of couples who are truly united must indeed be very limited!"

"It's not I who is setting up these criteria," retorted Dominique. "It's the severity of the times: the end of an age, I'm telling you. *Only he who fulfills his essential destiny will be able to maintain cohesiveness.* All that which is deviant, falsified, and conventional is coming apart and degenerating into incoherent elements. And it's this merciless severity that explains the failure of efforts toward family unity, social unity, or international unity."

"That's all very well, Maître Dominique, but if the love a couple must share, according to your definition, is independent of carnal appetites, must sexual relationships be eliminated?"

"*I never said that!* But first let's get things straight: what kind of couple and what kind of love are you speaking about? All couples who are passionately in love are ready to swear that their love and their union are eternal, and they do this without even considering the number of their previous loves!

"I am saying that *real* love must not be dependent on carnal appetites, in the sense that it must *go beyond them.* And this is true because sexual love is not a unifying element but an element of dualization.

"Above all, we must understand each other with respect to the meaning and the goal of conjugal union.

"The immortal being of each individual is an *entity*, which you can understand as being one of the Numbers emanating from the One.

"*That* which in this Soul-entity carries the characteristics of its Number will imprint its signature on the newborn child and will be his Permanent Witness, while *that* which is the *nonspecified spirit* will be his Spiritual Witness. However, this Soul-entity cannot be referred to as androgynous, since, 'created in the image of the Creator,' it has no sex, but it carries, in a potential state, the two principles, the active and the passive, which in the physical body become the two sexes: male and female.

"When a human being is born, the Permanent Witness will be characterized by the sex of this newborn, and the Spiritual Witness will consequently be its complementary aspect.

"This doesn't mean that this Soul-entity has been doubled into two beings: one a man and the other a woman. For *each human being* the two sexes are represented by the two aspects of its global soul. The Spiritual Witness is the true wife of the male being and the true husband of the female being. In other words, it becomes its own spiritual complement. Its Permanent Witness must be reunited with it."

"This would explain the name 'bride of Christ' given to the Catholic nun, wouldn't it?" asked Jean Thomas.

"Yes, in a certain sense, since the Christ that we must form within ourselves[1] is the unification of the divine with that which has become humanized.

"But we don't have enough time to develop the subject adequately because our friend Dutheil is not familiar with either the idea or the name of the two aspects of the soul."

Dutheil was listening to Dominique with anguished surprise:

"Do you realize what confusion your explanation has thrown me into?"

---

1. Cf. Galatians 4:19.

"Is it really confusion?" asked Dominique.

"To be more precise, let's call it astonishment. If the situation between men and women is really as you describe, the search for spiritual unification, which certain people who are in love dream about, is an illusion that prevents them from realizing this unification *each for himself or herself*."

"That's right, Maître Dominique. It's an obstacle because the satisfaction of sentimental love suffocates the desire for union with one's own spiritual complement."

"Isn't it true, however, that the *effective* union and reciprocal fidelity of a couple are the inherent conditions of a respectable marriage?"

"These things are very necessary," affirmed Dominique. "Marriage is an *association* in which, ideally, the two participants would be united by a profound affinity of goals and tendencies, an affinity that is physical as well as affective. This allows them a communion in their identical quest for the realization of their family goals, social goals, and, if possible, their spiritual goals.

"The error is to misunderstand the nature and duration of the conjugal union and to imagine that it involves our immortal beings beyond earthly existence. Proof of this is that one of the spouses can remarry after the death of the other.[2] The Gospel confirms this reality when it says that there is no marriage between people who have reached the Heavenly Kingdom.[3]

"The only spiritual unification, which is therefore the only *real* unification, can happen only between the two complementary aspects of the same Entity. But a human couple *can be bound by affinities during and even after earthly existence* through a common aspiration toward a higher state of being. This conjugal association can help them spiritually if there are no mistakes made through falsely interpreting their 'union' and thereby wandering far from their own *individual* unification.

"It's sexuality that, in incarnation, marks the separation of the two aspects of the Immortal Entity. Therefore, it's sex that becomes the obstacle to its reunification."

"For what reason?" asked Dutheil.

"Because sexual union gives one the illusion of true union. However, it's only the accentuation of duality, since it's only momentary and the two sexes find themselves once again separate and once again slaves of this attraction. However, the obstacle to individual reunification is not the sexual act, but the illusion one has about its value for unification.

"In order to remedy this, it would be necessary to willingly become

2. 1 Corinthians 7:39.
3. Mark 12:25.

conscious of the fact that *submitting* to sexual appetites keeps man on the animal level of the human realm, whereas liberation from this servitude attaches him to the suprahuman realm. By 'liberation,' I don't mean the elimination of sexual relations, but a certain behavior that places them in the service of spiritual evolution.

"The two spouses can help each other respectively to attain this result, if, of a common accord, they practice an eroticism that has neither a sentimental nor an aesthetic motive. These motives would blind their consciousness with regard to the animality of sexual passion."

"I don't understand how the aesthetic and the sentimental can be an obstacle," said Dutheil.

"Come on, now! Brutal desire for the opposite sex is one thing; the fantasy of sensual joy that physical charms might promise is another. And the sentimental idealization of a love based on imaginary qualities which are maintained through the *worship* of memory or through minor attachments that prevent the couple from every going beyond their lower humanity is something else again.

"Whether they're true or illusory, these motives of sexual desire hide or disguise the animal function that provokes them.

"Man calls his desire 'love,' regardless of what the motives of this attraction are, but the more passionate he is, the more he provokes possessive impulses. What results from this is jealousy and therefore egotism. The candidate for the suprahuman realm must liberate himself from these things."

"What a fiercely cruel criticism for the majority of men who don't conceive of love in any other way!" exlaimed Thomas.

"What are you asking me for," retorted Dominique: "the law of the Many, or, on the contrary, the behavior necessary to go beyond our human animality?"

"It's the latter behavior that interests me," affirmed Dutheil, "because it's the first time that I'm able to glimpse the error in our comprehension of love. Could you tell me more about the character of a love that contributes to the higher goal of the human couple?"

"It is love 'in truth,' answered Dominique. "It is impersonal love in the sense that it seeks *neither to possess nor to be possessed*, but to commune with one's 'companion of experience' in an identical aspiration toward the suprahuman state.

"To attain this goal, sexual attraction can be an efficient means when it sheds itself of all possessive impulses, and when it refuses to allow artificial aesthetic or affective reasons to disguise its animal character.

"If man and woman agree in the search for this liberation, the means of excitement will be very different from the usual means of seduction.

The latter will be advantageously replaced by the erotic shock caused by the contradiction between animal passion and the call of our spiritual being."

"If only I could understand the process of this shock." Dutheil sighed.

"You can understand it," answered Dominique, "if you first consider the difference in the process of being 'in heat' in man and in animals. The animal undergoes periods of heat imposed by Nature. Man goes beyond this natural impulse through his faculty to provoke it through his imagination.

"Now, to incite this imagination, each person instinctively calls upon material that is particularly susceptible to exciting his sexual desire. This choice reveals the motivating force (conscious or unconscious) of his erotic reactions, and this force denotes the quality of his aspirations.

"The lowest motives are the animal need for the opposite sex, and the exclusive quest for sensual pleasure, whose satisfaction leads to servitude to the dictates of desire, which easily becomes a major necessity.

"But you must understand that this obedience to *pleasure* and to *need* is not to be confused with *eroticism*, which is a kind of science of the provocation of desire.

"Pleasure and need are part of the animal realm, while eroticism addresses itself to one or the other of the aspects of consciousness that it awakens by an emotive shock. The nature of the shock varies according to the individual, because each person will address himself to a particular subconscious disposition that is particular to him. This awakening will exacerbate his sexual desire.

"This disposition can be the muted revolt of inhibition, or a need to compensate (as in masochism, for example, which compensates for an apparent autocratic personality), or the desire to *go beyond one's lower nature by provoking the shame of being subjected to animal sexuality.* This desire to *go beyond* is the only effective motive force through which eroticism can become the means to liberation."

"I understand your grievances against sentimental excuses that prevent one from experiencing this reaction . . . but it would be' difficult to explain that to a couple who are in love and who are exalting their sexual joy through the imagination of reciprocal complementation."

"You've also got to realize, my friend, that this is addressed only to those rare candidates for the suprahuman realm. It's for them that it's necessary to *indicate a human means of attaining the suprahuman.*

"However, this means is not efficient unless it is understood in its *reality*. Realize that the call for sexual complementation is only a transposition, a reflection of the spiritual call toward the complementation of the two aspects of the soul for the reunification of its Entity. But the physical form of this call can only be surpassed by the shock to the highest Human Consciousness, which finds itself jolted by the animality of sexual passion. This jolt of consciousness, instead of being negated or minimized by different subterfuges, must be admitted and willfully experienced until it inspires the desire to know a superior state of joy."

"To sum it up, is this jolt, which is the Light, desirable?" asked Dutheil.

"Indeed it is," confirmed Dominique. "But the man whose goal is not this Light refuses it. The male who satisfies his desire does not experience this shock, if he embellishes the brutal fact with sentimental recognition for the woman whom he has 'possessed,' while the acknowledgment without *excuses* of this animal submission is a humiliation for the conscious being aware of his superior destiny.

"It's in order to obtain this result that the two partners in a couple can collaborate effectively. But this possibility is conditioned by the mutual comprehension of the role of the woman, because she can be either a help or an obstacle, according to her inner disposition. Sexually and sensually, the woman is the object of masculine attraction. The function of procreation which results is, in the human world, the 'redemption' of this animal aspect. Outside of this function her role is to inspire love, to intensify life through the exaltation of desire. But this role can be positive or negative according to the quality of the love, the life, and the desire that it provokes.

"Her animal femininity incites the male to idealize her sex and her physical attributes, in order to capture the interest of the male by appealing to his sensuality.

"Her spiritual femininity would instead provoke the eroticism of the man who would 'use' the *female* without idealizing the facts, in order to provoke, through the reaction of his consciousness, the desire to liberate himself from it.

"Then the woman can play her most elevated role: the role of a catalyst who evokes love outside of her personality.

"It's evident," added the sculptor, "that this effort of transcendence is accessible only to the Few. But can you imagine a suprahuman love that can unite the couple arriving at such a state of consciousness? It will not be unification itself (which can only be accomplished individually), but a union of affinity, which can survive this existence and which can make of two individual beings who have realized themselves, two inseparable companions. . . ."

The expressions of the doctor and his friend were understandably full of emotion.

"That's an unexpected solution to the problem of the couple," said

Thomas, "and is worth experimenting with. But what will happen if only one of the spouses wants to apply this behavior?"

"He can apply it despite his partner," answered Dominique. "Nothing is stopping him from looking into himself for the motive force of his desire in a liberating eroticism.

"The liberating motive force is the desire for the shock that illuminates consciousness. It's the breaking of an egotistical impulse: sensual satisfaction, jealousy, possessiveness. . . ."

"I wonder if you would still propose this process as a concession to human weakness, and if your hindsight wouldn't be to incite one to chastity as the ideal means?" insinuated Thomas.

"Chastity, my dear friend, is not a means but a goal. When it is imposed, it often produces negative repression. It's not through violence that one reaches true chastity, which is the serene state obtained through surpassing our animal nature. But this serene state is only stable if one finds it, by the liberation of sensual and sexual demands, a transcendent joy sufficiently intense to render these lower pleasures uninteresting."

"The dissatisfaction with lower pleasures," murmured Thomas dreamily.

"Indeed, a dissatisfaction," agreed Dominique. "Happy is he who doesn't look for fulfillment through artificial means!"

"Obviously, it would be a refusal to answer the call of Light," concluded Dutheil. "But tell me, Maître Dominique: the foundation of a home has another aspect we haven't spoken about—the procreation of children."

"Toward what goal? The continuation of a name, of a race, or a family line? I repeat that he who has a goal for the collectivity loses his interest in the elite, in which each member aspires *individually* to the suprahuman kingdom, through the liberation of his earthly chains."

"You still must recognize," insisted Dutheil, "that, admitted or not, the intimate wish of the father of a family is to perpetuate himself in his children."

"This is the spiritual era," answered Dominique gravely, "*for those who want to go beyond Earth and the human animal*: first of all, because these people must liberate themselves from all their atavistic tendencies so they can realize the essential tendencies of their own entity. It's 'spiritual individualism' that is the first step toward higher realization.

"The second reason is that the desire to *perpetuate oneself on Earth* is a cult of the 'person,' which ties people to the inferior condition and to the routines of earthly existence. And this path is obviously opposed to the path that ascends toward the suprahuman realm.

"The problem of procreation presents itself differently according to the goal and the state of consciousness of the parents. *That which I have just said concerns only the Few.*

"Moreover, if we are speaking from a more general point of view, and if we consider the current situation of the inhabitants of our Earth, the overproduction of human beings seems to be condemned by the catastrophic effects of overpopulation."

"Definitely" exclaimed Thomas. "Just look at how many countries are pushed toward war because they have too many people!"

"Not only that," continued Dominique, "but couldn't you say that the Earth and people are multiplying cataclysms and causes of accidents in direct proportion to this excess?

"I could add some more profound reasons, which we won't go into at the moment.

"However, if you think that one of the goals of marriage is to give bodies to the souls that want to incarnate themselves, we will be in agreement on this point, if the parents are aware of their moral disposition and of their spiritual influence in conception, and of the influence of the mother during pregnancy, which she should be able to guide consciously.

"We will agree, if one continues to raise the child in the spirit of his own time and not in terms of times past.

"We will agree, if one helps him develop his own *true tendencies*, without suffocating them in family routine.

"And finally, we'll agree, if one teaches him to listen to the voice of *his own consciousness*."

"It's a libertarian individualism that you're advocating, Maître Dominique!"

"You haven't understood me, dear sir. It's the *school of consciousness*, guided by the *consciousness of the parents*. What leads you into error is your old conception of the autocratic family, from whose yoke modern children are trying to break free. They do this instinctively, because they no longer find the appropriate guidelines in terms of the rhythm of our times."

"To sum it up," said Dutheil, "the family no longer has the same meaning as it used to."

"Look what's happened to the family in our Western world: Russia has destroyed its privacy, America has exacerbated the independence of women and pushed the children to the point of insolence. In an increasingly rapid way, European youth are in turn emancipating themselves. It's useless to blame egotism or amorality, which are the secondary effects of a fundamental cause: the unconsciousness of the rhythm of the age, which pushes one toward individualism."

"Individualism whose goal, according to you, would be the realization of a conscious man in his totality?" inquired Dutheil.

"Not according to me, dear sir, but according to all Wise Ones who have situated this goal as the finality of our earthly humanity."

"Is the cause of our ills our ignorance of this dramatic situation?" asked Dutheil.

"Definitely. Ignorance of the true human makeup, from which stems inappropriate instruction and education."

"What can be done to remedy this?"

"Dare to speak of the superior destiny of man, not in terms of a beyond, which, to certain people, could seem hazardous, but in terms of *this existence*. Alert our contemporaries to the danger of habits and prejudice. Give to conventions their relative value. Shake up the doldrum of consciousness. Awaken, awaken, *awaken beings individually*."

"But how can the family adapt itself to the spiritual demands of our time?"

"The family, my dear Dutheil, is a collectivity in which those who are of the Many must help each other, but must leave all the freedom to the Few to experiment with what is necessary to awaken consciousness. Then there would be no persecution or dissension."

"This would require the discernment of an enlightened man in each home."

"Obviously," agreed Dominique. "And the rarity of these cases is the cause of so many family conflicts. It's always a matter of ignorance!

"But my answer was directed toward your family situation, and your conclusion is the same as mine: the need for a conscious presence to orient each one toward the fulfillment of his or her true aspirations. I say 'true' because nothing must be forced, be it the will to continue on Earth or the desire for liberation.

"As for your wife or your children, each one, in being incarnated, has brought with him *his Path*, which is relative to his degree of evolution. It's possible that he ignores it or that it will not manifest itself until later on. It's there where your watchfulness is necessary in order to provide insight at the right moment. But this watchfulness must not express itself in terms of surveillance. That would prevent the child from showing you his true tendency, and would inhibit your own realization as well.

"In normal cases, it's the mother, or the understanding governess, and *carefully chosen teachers* who must ensure daily watchfulness. I'm convinced that your too-frequent intervention would counterbalance the weight of the advice that you should reserve for important circumstances. Oh, I know that today the father's role demands impartiality and uncommon sacrifice! But isn't it true that you're not asking me for the advice of middle-class morality?"

"This role would also demand the knowledge of fundamental reality," retorted Dutheil. "What are, for example, the essential notions that one must inculcate in one's children?"

"First of all, *the real constitution of the human being*, which implies the relationship between the immortal being and the Divine Power from which it emanates. Then, *the sense of responsibility*, the consciousness of which elevates them on the ladder of humanity."

"Would they be able to understand that?"

"More than you think, because the child loves something that bolsters him in his own eyes, and that gives him a role to play.

"But it's almost time for you to leave, and your decision still seems uncertain."

"I don't know what to do. Help me, Maître Dominique, because my own realization seems incompatible with my paternal duty."

"I don't think so, my friend, if you know how to situate the two elements of the problem precisely. To fulfill your duty as educator in an equitable way would first demand that you yourself become conscious of certain realities. But nothing is stopping you from finding here in France that which you wanted to look for in the East. Nonetheless, your trip is a good opportunity to come into contact with the atmosphere and methods of competent Hindu Masters."

"That was what I intended," said Dutheil. "But I don't see the value of it, if I don't remain under their guidance."

"On the contrary," said Dominique. "It would be very useful for you to know, or at least to approach, this Hindu teaching which tempts you. Then you can go on your way with full knowledge of the facts. But it seems to me that three months should be enough, if you know how to question, listen, and verify the affinity or the incompatibility of their methods with your possibilities."

"I only hope I am capable of discerning this."

"We'll talk about it when you come back. Above all, you've got to throw away your habits in order to be receptive to some words of Truth. You've got to learn how to see reality from different points of view. But be wise enough to go there without any preconceived ideas, like a beggar of Light who knows that he is poor enough to ask for food."

Dutheil, visibly relieved, accepted this solution.

"I'll follow your advice. But then will you allow me to come back and give you an account of what I've been able to get from it?"

"Of course, dear friend. And I think you'll be able to guide yourself with more lucidity."

Over the loudspeaker came the call for passengers going to Cairo, Beirut, and Bombay.

"See you in three months!" affirmed Dutheil as he joyously thanked Dominique. "You can count on me for that rendezvous."

* * *

Dominique and Thomas watched the travelers leave.

"How poignant the moment of choice of a direction is!" murmured Jean Thomas. "I only wish I could have helped light his way!"

"It's only a preliminary choice," answered the sculptor. "All I did was clarify the elements of the problem, but it's the loyalty of his quest that allows my words to speak within him. He did the right thing, for the Present Moment, the right gesture at the right moment. That's right, he's obeying his true destiny."

"But is what's to follow already inscribed in his act?"

"His *current* path is inscribed in this direction. We'll see what follows when he comes back. No one can predict the moment when his own Light will give him his own Law."

"It's true that when he gets back his family problems will begin."

"He'll solve them easily after he has acquired these supranatural faculties of discernment."

"In what sense is this discernment supranatural?"

"In the sense that it goes beyond rational comprehension, and he'll know how to distinguish it from the voice of the Heart; in other words, from Supranatural Consciousness."

"Does that mean discernment is the voice of this consciousness?"

"Exactly, and one is able to discern it unquestioningly. But do you really think that this is a suitable place to be trying it out?" concluded Dominique, laughing.

"Undoubtedly not," admitted Thomas. "But since it evokes familial conflicts, could you answer this question for me: how can one direct, in one and the same family, totally different people with different tendencies and goals?"

"Well, if it were up to me, my friend, I would first try to distinguish those who manifest the tendency of the Many from those who are predestined to be among the Few.

"Having thus lit my lantern, I would individually guide the latter towards the Consciousness of Self, as I am doing with you. But, at the same time I would try to inculcate in them altruism. I'd do this by showing them that if they have the liberty of consciousness and the superior goals of the elite, they also have the duties and responsibilities with regard to their less gifted brothers. This involves goodness, sacrifice, and comprehensible indulgence, which are the compensatory elements of a superiority that they must never take advantage of.

"With regard to the Many, I would speak to them more or less this way: The family is a *natural* group whose harmony demands the respect for natural ties (blood and honor of the family name), and a solidarity that is as far removed from tyranny as it is from egotism. Regardless of what your personal taste and opinions are, they must never create dissension: the liberty of some must guarantee the liberty of others. When this is said and done, choose the path and work that suit you best. Cultivate your intellectual faculties and your personal gifts according to your preferences, be they scientific, mechanical, technical, or artistic, without ever forgetting, however, that we are still unadvanced in each of these areas, in terms of what could be. Regardless of the work that you choose, never stop at the level of mediocrity. Cultivate the ambition each day to go beyond what you have acquired the previous day."

"What are you saying?" exlaimed Thomas. "You're encouraging mental culture and mechanistic science!"

"Why not, if this corresponds to the possibilities of those I am speaking to? Those in this existence who are unable to attain the higher kingdom, must be directed toward the best means to benefit from their own tendencies by cultivating their innate gifts, but at the same time pushing them to the limits of their possibilities.

"Don't forget, Thomas, that nature refuses excess. To go beyond one's normal possibility is the best way of attaining the supranatural."

"Bravo!" exclaimed Thomas joyously. "I've found you again, Maître Dominique! For a moment I was afraid you were regressing. . . ."

"Is that what you thought!" retorted the sculptor. "So you were already afraid of losing your trampoline! And now, old friend, you can stay here at the crossroads if you wish, but I'm going back to the Atelier."

Dominique didn't return alone to the Atelier. The insistent way in which Thomas was looking at the sculptor made him aware that the man had something to get off his chest.

When they got to the studio the disciple took his place at the foot of the Master and accepted a cigarette that was offered.

"I need your help, Maître Dominique," he finally said. "The way you explained the spiritual couple made up of our incarnated Entity upset me more than I can ever tell you. I was astounded by the idea that I carry in myself the complementary principle of my spiritual masculinity— astounded, as if suddenly I found myself unburdened by an obsession that was perhaps just an absurdity."

Embarassed by his Master's smile, Thomas stopped speaking.

"What's bothering you?" asked Dominique. "Don't be afraid to express it. You think I haven't guessed what your problem is?"

"I must confess that the subjection of man to the domination of woman has always revolted me as an attack against my individuality.

"Obviously, as a male, I'm sensitive to their attraction, but it irritates me to be subjected to the 'necessity.' No doubt this feeling has kept me from marrying until now. I've accused myself of being unjust and inconsistent. But I was unable to get rid of my stubborn bitterness with any logical argument.

"Must I consider this aversion to be something abnormal? Besides, it's incoherent, since the desire has never stopped existing."

"You'll find the answer, my dear friend, in the reason for the emotional shock that my explanation caused in you.

"Your abnormality is not a matter of a deviant tendency in your sexuality, but lies in your refusal (abnormal for the majority of men) to find completion in the union of the sexes, which physiologically you do need.

"This problem doesn't exist for human beings who are satisfied with the illusion of this union. But sometimes a man or a woman, even if he or she is ignorant of the true spiritual complement, feels a vague foreknowledge of it, which provokes the nostalgic desire for a love they can't put their finger on. In their sexual life this confused feeling translates itself into the bitterness of dissatisfaction, or into an incompatibility, or a rebellion against the opposite sex—or even into an often premature decision to remain chaste.

"To understand the true motives for this disillusionment, it's necessary to know the existence in one's self of these two complementary aspects: these two Witnesses whose goal is to realize within the person their unification.

"I could only touch upon the subject with Dutheil, who is too ignorant of these things. But for you, it would be good to deepen the consequences of this reality, the misunderstanding of which is the key to your misogynist rebellion.

"You already know," continued Dominique, lighting his pipe, "that our two Witnesses are the two elements of our Soul-entity, whose different names—according to various traditions—always express the Spirit and the soul.

"These two elements of our entity, being spiritual, are asexual, but they behave, in relation to each other, as two complements that (in the image of the Father-Mother from whom they come) can differentiate themselves without abandoning their unity.

"When a newborn child comes into the world, and his two Witnesses differentiate themselves from each other, each one preserves the double potentiality of the total entity: *Activity and Passivity*. But each one manifests only one of the aspects, by the choice of the Permanent Witness.

"Indeed, *it's the Permanent Witness that will always bear the same sexual aspect as the individual*: active-masculine for the man, passive-feminine for the female. It will therefore attract by complementary affinities the opposite aspect of the Spiritual Witness.

"In other words: our mortal personality, with regard to its sex and its essential temperament, is of the same nature as our Permanent Witness. And this is understandable, since it's the Permanent Witness that 'experiences' throughout our human existence. It's the *soul* characterized by its Number-entity, the soul which is more or less humanized according to the success or failure of its incarnation.

"As for the Spiritual Witness, which, in the Soul-entity, is the *Spirit*: it is nonindividualized divine Light, like the universal Spirit of which it is an integral part.

"For each human being, it is his own divinity, but it will manifest the complementary aspect to that of the Permanent Witness. In other words, the divine aspect as opposed to the sexual nature of the individual."

"As a result," concluded Thomas, "does that mean that the masculine Permanent Witness will attract the feminine aspect of his Spiritual Witness?"

"He will attract its divine Passivity," specified Dominique, "in the same way that the woman's Permanent Witness will attract the divine Activity of its Spiritual Witness.

"But you must understand that this Permanent Witness, like the Spiritual Witness, is potentially endowed with these two aspects (Active and Passive), and that it can incarnate itself in the masculine or the feminine nature according to the sex of the being it 'chooses.'

"Therefore, it's possible that, in its successive reincarnations, it sometimes animates a woman and sometimes animates a man. The two aspects are potentially within it."

"That's almost unbelievable," murmured Thomas, amazed.

"Why unbelievable?" protested Dominique. "Doesn't each human body, even physiologically, carry within it the tendencies of both sexes? One of the sexes is developed, and the other is atrophied or just outlined. In any event, isn't it a double possibility? And this is true to such an extent that after puberty a sex change is sometimes done."

"That's a rather rare phenomenon, but it is possible," acknowledged the doctor. "But in such cases, can one assume there's an error or . . . a hesitation in the choice of the Permanent Witness?"

"Puberty," answered Dominique, "corresponds to one of the attempts at integrating our spiritual being. It's possible that during one of these attempts there is a divergence or a disharmony between the Human Consciousness and the destiny that is willed by the Permanent Witness. This divergence can necessitate the experience of the other sex.

"But this exceptional case is useful only in showing you that our visible body (the organic image of our invisible being) proves the possibility of a potential coexistence of the two aspects, masculine-feminine, which we call the androgynous Adam."[4]

"So be it," said Thomas, "but I don't understand the possibility of complementation between the Permanent Witness, which is characterized, and the Spiritual Witness, which has no characterization or individuality."

"It's not possible," answered Dominique. "But the two aspects, Active-Passive, are potentially within it. Don't make the mistake of categorizing, my friend. The spirit is not broken up into parts, and its components are not to be confused with chemical combinations. One or the other aspect of the Spiritual Witness can be attracted, like a magnet, by the complementary aspect of the Permanent Witness.

"It's we ourselves who are the obstacle to this magnetism when the impulses of our Human Consciousness oppose themselves to that of our Immortal Entity. When Human Consciousness has totally identified itself with its Permanent Witness (thus attaining personal nonwill), it unites itself without difficulty with the Spiritual Witness, and thus reconstitutes its primordial entity. But when this happens, it is enriched with the consciousness acquired through this incarnation and by this union."

Thomas listened intently and asked for more specific answers.

"The consequences of such realities," he said, "are worth deep meditation, because they can explain the balance or imbalance of a being in regard to whether he acts in conformity to or in disharmony with his essential nature.

"However, what comes out of this teaching is that the active or passive temperament of an individual would above all be the consequence of this incarnation (male or female). Hereditary or astrological influences can only accentuate or weaken the temperament that's determined by sex.

"But if that's the case, how do you explain the clear deviation in sexual tendencies, as well as the different reactions that result from it?"

"Indeed, it's these reactions that are different for each individual, according to the origin and *cause* of this deviation. If it doesn't come exclusively from a physical malformation,[5] it could be the result of a stifled tendency in the last incarnation, or it could result from the need for an experience of consciousness.

"Unfortunately, the liberation that should be the result of it is often subject to failure through ignorance: the being knows neither spiritual

---

4. This would explain the words in Genesis: "Male and female created He them." It is only when man is materialized (the materialization symbolized by the tree of Good and Evil) that he is divided sexually.
5. This malformation could even be the sign of this indecision.

destiny nor how his immortal being is constituted, and therefore suffers his perversion as inevitable. In some cases he even considers it a liberating evolution from being enslaved to the opposite sex!"

"Couldn't there be another possibility?" insisted the doctor. "Couldn't a man who was strongly inclined toward *Passivity* attract, through an exalted desire for completion, the *Active* aspect of his Spiritual Witness?"

"It is possible," answered Dominique. "It's possible in the case of the religious masochism of the monk who finds his exaltation in the most humiliating Passivity, or in the case of *advertised* Passivity in certain deviants whose motivating force, more ideal than sensual, could instinctively lead them to look within themselves for this union."

"Is that what you would call mystical vice?" insinuated the doctor cunningly. "Could it be vice that is bent on liberating itself from the opposite sex?"

"Be careful! Vice is the opposite of liberation. The abnormality that we are talking about here is a mystical tendency, and doesn't express itself through sexuality. It could be explained by the need to exaggerate this abnormal disposition in order to break through an obstacle by using it to excess.

"You must remember that Passivity, mystically accepted and consciously cultivated, is the most favorable state for conquering the mind and developing intuition. It's going in the opposite direction of mental and sexual activity. But this abnormal impulse, *which comes from an instance of individual consciousness*, could lead this man to find the opening of his intuitive life through the sacrifice of his sexuality. Many artists are indebted to their subtle sensitivity for this acceptance of Passivity! It's obvious that this example has nothing to do with sexual deviants whose motivation is the search for more refined sensuality, a motivation that will in no way lead them to liberation!

"Nor is it an example for you, Thomas, because your personal example is different. Moreover, you aren't 'abnormal' except in your relationship to the mentality of the Many.

"Your aversion to female *domination* is an indication of masculine dependence that does not want to subject itself to the animal law of the jungle, where love is synonymous with jealousy and possessiveness.

"But that doesn't prevent you from continuing to desire the female sex. I explained, in front of Dutheil, how sexual relations can be put to the service of spiritual realization.[6] It's a matter of inner attitude, and the merciless discernment of what motivates us with regard to passion.

"However, above all, it's important to become conscious that the human being, man or woman, when inhabited by his or her Spiritual

6. See page 125.

Entity, is a complete being. You must not see in the couple the two parts of one entity which are able to reunify themselves through sexual union.

"This erroneous concept prevents couples from finding *within themselves* (and each one for himself) the only true union, and moreover prevents them from finding in their marriage the intimate alliance of two beings who are pursuing an identical goal, as opposed to an impossible union."

"The problem," murmured Thomas, "is starting to become clearer. For the first time I can see the reality of an inner union that can, without disillusionment, fulfill my undefinable desire: the Permanent Witness, being masculine in the man, is the true husband of its own Spiritual Witness, if he knows how to attract the feminine aspect.

"Inversely, the Permanent Witness of the woman, being feminine, is the true wife of its Spiritual Witness, if she knows how to attract the masculine aspect."

"*If*, as you say, Thomas. It's this *if* that is useful to clarify: since it's in ourselves that we are waiting for our own complement, it's toward that, toward our Spiritual Witness, that we must direct our desire. It's toward our Spiritual Witness that we must concentrate our love, all the love that a being can experience for the only object capable of fulfilling its desire.

"Every human being experiences the need of *desire*, and is instinctively searching for an emptiness to fill. Each one according to his nature, and according to the goal that he gives to his experience, augments his needs to experience the 'longing' that you would call desire, love, passion, or devotion.

"From the satisfaction or frustration of these desires result pleasure and passing joy or suffering and disillusionment. None of these feelings are unalterable: all of them are transitory, because they can be modified by psychic or physical tendencies or by chance occurrence.

"*The only unalterable elements in us are the two Witnesses of our Immortal Being.* Their presence is conditioned by our watchful interest. If it's not constantly dispersed over many objectives, this interest becomes 'desire,' because the absence of their animation produces an unbearable emptiness if we don't make the mistake of fulfilling it through illusion.

"But desire attracts their presence, and their presence stirs the need to unite oneself to one's divine complement.

"However, in order for this call to be answered, *each human being must attract, like a magnet, his own Spiritual Witness, an attraction that is all the stronger since this being will have developed a nature that is complementary to that of the Spiritual Witness: in man it is his Active nature, in woman it is her Passive nature.*"

"Could you explain this in practical terms?" insisted Thomas.

"It seems to me that it's more in metaphysical terms that I should be explaining it; and then you can deduce for yourself the necessary way of behaving. Make an effort to follow my reasoning.

"If we have a concept of Activity, we necessarily have a concept of Passivity. Nature gives us a living symbol of this double principle, which is active in our humanity:

"Earthly existence depends on two heavenly masses, the sun and the moon.

"If the sun is Activity, the Passive moon is the immanent resistance to Activity.

"If the sun is being in itself, the moon is the mirror of being, the reflector of its light.

"The sun is the male aspect, which emits and impregnates.

"The moon is the female aspect, Passive and receptive.

"The sun is Active, and yet its powers of fecundity depend on its divine Spiritual Sun, which encircles it.

"The physical solar globe is the Active Principle of the Divine Sun, as the Permanent Witness *in man* is the Active Principle of his Spiritual Witness.

"The divine Spiritual Sun is 'the Cause of causes,' which is manifested in the activity of the solar star.

"The moon manifests the Passive Principle of the Cause of causes, as the Permanent Witness of *the woman* manifests the Passive Principle of its Spiritual Witness."

"I understand your insistence on the importance of the principles that characterize the differentiation between the natures of man and woman, because what they must fulfill depends on this comprehension," said Thomas.

"Exactly," answered Dominique, "but it's more than a matter of comprehension. It's a matter of the *initiation* of Human Consciousness into the desire of complementation: because it's this which is responsible for the failure or success of reunification.

"Comprehension can prepare a favorable ground, but only the emotion of the Human Consciousness can awaken in it the thirst for the suprahuman, an insatiable thirst for plenitude that becomes the *desire* capable of attracting its divine complement."

"You're touching a sensitive nerve, Maître Dominique," said Thomas, profoundly troubled. "Now you can be more specific: It's my desire that's listening to you. Show me the way to Union!"

Dominique was watching his disciple dreamily.

"The way to Union," he repeated, smiling. "We were talking about the path of the couple. Let's see if that can take us to where we want to go.

"In the behavior of the couple you must distinguish the disposition of each partner in relationship to his individual realization, on the one hand, and his behavior toward the other partner, on the other hand. Let's summarize the essential points.

"The Permanent Witness of each human being marks in him, according to sex, the rhythm that corresponds to it, be it Active or Passive, and the mode of action of masculinity or of femininity.

"In order to be in accord with the law of Harmony, man must live and think in the active and fecundating rhythm. But his activity must be guided and controlled by his Permanent Witness.

"On the contrary, the woman must live and think in the passive mode. Her body and her mind are disposed to receive the seed and be pregnant with it.

"Through his active nature, man is the procreator in the physical world. He can become the procreator in the realm of knowledge if he calls upon divine conceptive Femininity, the 'Uncreated Wisdom,' which in him is his Spiritual Witness.

"The woman must identify herself with Cosmic Femininity. She is *Nature*, in relationship to the Fecundating Spirit. If she denies her instinctive egocentric tendencies, she can, through her *neutrality*, reflect the Feminine Principle of Uncreated Wisdom, of which her Permanent Witness is the Passive manifestation.

"Then, the active aspect of her Spiritual Witness can take on the role of Fecundating Activity, provoking the receptive activity of her Permanent Witness.

"I've differentiated masculine intuition from feminine intuition to show you the role of each Witness in both cases. Intuition is provoked in man via the inspiration of his Spiritual Witness, then transmitted, in an active mode, by his Permanent Witness to his mental consciousness.

"The expression of this intuition is called knowledge, as opposed to know-how, which is an elaboration of notions conceived by faculties of the mind.

"I distinguish this masculine process from feminine intuition, which is due to the passive character of its Permanent Witness, which inclines it toward being receptive.

"If the woman acquires the necessary neutrality for this receptivity, she can become sensitive to the life-giving forces of Nature. She can widen her maternal sense into disinterested altruism *by becoming conscious of human solidarity.*

"Then she can instigate enthusiasm and the drive toward surpassing oneself. She can be the intermediary between the concept and its realization.

"According to the role she adopts, she is 'she who elevates' or 'she who perverts.' She is either the one who conjures up the life-giving forces or the illusionist, Maya."

"To sum it up," said Thomas, "the source of knowledge is identical in all cases, but the richness and quality of the revelation differ according to the mode and the quality of receptivity."

"That's correct," confirmed Dominique, "but the totality of this revelation always depends upon the neutrality of the person who is receiving it.

"As for the cultural role of man and woman, note that the active role of the priest was, throughout time, the prerogative of man, while the passive role of the 'sibyl' was always attributed to the woman.

"The right to act in the name of Divine Activity has always belonged to the active masculine nature. This holds true for receiving and transmitting powers, whereas feminine passivity, brought to the point of total neutrality, has always belonged more to mediumism.

"In both cases, however, there is the inherent danger of their inferior nature: for the priest it's the sterilizing intervention of the mind; for the sibyl it's astromediumism."

"Doesn't the idealistic imagination of the woman, as well as her subjective point of view, make it very difficult for her to become neutral?" replied Thomas. "She uses appearance and illusion as weapons of seduction, and gets caught in her own trap."

"Well, that's true, dear friend, but also recognize that masculine reaction encourages feminine coquetry, and lends itself to being led into illusion!"

"That's true, Maître Dominique, but woman is full of contradictions, in love as in religion. She idealizes imaginatively, without forgetting, however, the pragmatic point of view, and her sentimentality goes hand in hand with her instinct for practicality."

"This instinct," replied Dominique, "is the consequence of her maternal function. When she conceives, her role is to *give body to or materialize the spirit*. This function is inherent to her lunar nature, and influences her behavior with regard to her attachment to material existence. Material existence is the place in which the spirit is materialized. It also influences her in terms of possessiveness.

"All the instincts that flow from a *natural* function are natural, and must be taken into consideration. This is the norm for our dualistic world. But for those whose goal is to realize their reunification, the law differs and the attitude must change.

"*Concessions to ideals recognized as illusory are compromises that lead to death in mediocrity.*

"Those who want to find their suprahumanity must take a definite stand:

"On the one hand, each must search with ardent desire for his own union with his Spiritual Witness.

"On the other hand, he must, if possible, be in agreement with his partner in order to obtain in parallel the goal desired by each of them.

"If the spouses are mutually considerate of each other only in terms of their human personalities, they will never be able to help each other along this way. Neither will they be able to help each other if illusion extinguishes the desire for individual union, or if this desire founders in the daily deception of reciprocal incomprehension.

"The secret of success is to consider one's partner as the human symbol of one's divine spouse. I say, 'divine' because our Spiritual Witness is our own Divinity. Our partner thus becomes the image of our complementary aspect. Our role toward her (man with regard to woman, for example) consists in consciously conceiving through her the *Essential Femininity* that man unconsciously searches for. This is at the heart of all human love. (*The error would obviously be to transform this consciousness of impersonal reality into sentimental imagination.*) Then what happens? If the woman understands the impersonal love for which her person is the pretext, she can reciprocally find in her spouse the symbol of the Divine Masculine Principle, which, in her Spiritual Witness, is her own complement.

"In other words: each member of a couple must look at the other as the mirror that shows him or her, in its human reflection, the aspect of the Divine that each lacks, in order to be a totality."

"The Divine *aspect* that we're lacking," repeated Thomas. "If this aspect is our own Spiritual Witness, does it mean that our Permanent Witness is therefore our other divine aspect?"

"Certainly, Thomas," said Dominique, "but it's specified and more or less humanized.

"But remember, Thomas, that the behavior we're describing here has nothing to do with the sexual relationships I was speaking to you about earlier."[7]

"I think I've understood, but . . . I'm not married, Maître Dominique."

"*Do I need a woman, Thomas, in order to practice what I speak?*

"For me, Woman is a symbol of *her* whose reality is evoked in me by my desire."

7. See page 125ff.

10

The Marionettes

"What are you looking for, Thomas? Are you aware of what it is? Are you able to discern *who* in you is asking this question? And from whom are you expecting the answer?"

Having returned to his listening post in the silence of Notre Dame, Jean Thomas was going over his reflections. Two months had passed. According to the advice of Dominique, he had gone back into his former milieu: his life at the laboratory, his bachelor's distractions, which had given him a sense of solitude, and the distasteful sense of lost time, the feeling he had surmounted with such difficulty.

"You need a vacation," the sculptor had declared; "You need to take a little time in order to judge the path that you've been traveling. Don't come back to the Atelier. Don't go back to the cathedral. Go back to your old familiar way of life. Then listen within yourself for these echoes. Above all, avoid being enticed by your reactions, which you must verify without any preconceived judgments."

When the two months had passed, Thomas received an invitation from Dominique to have dinner at the Tavern in his Atelier. He was disturbed by this meeting. No doubt his Master's insight already allowed him to know the result of this experience. But this easy solution repelled him, as if he were abandoning his responsibility. He was willing to accept a guide in order to enlighten the obscure areas of a problem, but only after he himself had elaborated on it, as far as his possibility allowed.

However, what could he bring to Dominique tonight? The avowal that he was satisfied? That would still be negative, and he didn't dare draw any constructive conclusion from that. In the face of his inability to put his finger on the cause of his uncertainty, he had given up his afternoon of work, and deliberately returned to Notre Dame without any other admitted reason than the choice of a favorable place for his solitary reflections. But the time was passing without bringing any new solutions. There were only new questions, to which his loyalty demanded answers: "What are you looking for? Come on, Thomas, dare to admit it: what were you hoping to find at Notre Dame?"

After two hours of silence, something happened. His distracted attention made him realize that he was looking for Maître Jacques. Thomas closed his eyes to keep from looking for him in the shadows, not knowing whether he desired or was afraid to see the apparition of the image. He tried to reason with himself: Was he still hoping for what he called an "illusion"? If not, why did he regret its absence? What was he expecting from his visit? To clarify his uncertainty?

Thinking about the time that had elapsed since the last vision of his mysterious Master, he was surprised not to feel his silence as an emptiness. It was true that certain words of Jean-Jacques, as well as the advice of Dominique, had brought him the echoes of an identical teaching. . . .

"Identical with what, Jean Thomas?"

"With the teachings of Maître Jacques."

"And where did the teachings of Maître Jacques come from?"

Thomas hesitated before answering, and suddenly he realized that the thread of the dialogue was renewing itself in him. The only thing that was missing was the vision, in other words, the elements of possible illusion. He became confident, and he listened attentively.

"Give up illusion, Thomas, and keep Presence."

"What Presence?"

"The Presence without form, the Voice with neither tone nor sound. Do not look for proof. Listen to the Silence. Dare to break through your shell, dare to escape from the web of your argument. Without thinking, without willing, open yourself up. Give yourself up, and I will deliver you!"

"Who are you?"

"I am You. Be who I am; know what I know."

The voice stopped formulating . . . the words became proof . . . the silence became Presence.

There is no duration for that which cannot be situated. Each heartbeat rendered the unique and continuing Present Moment perceptible to him. This was the only reality that no longer limited an unknown future and an already nonexistent past. He became the *living consciousness* of this indivisible Presence, whose succession in time and division in space are a transcription of the mind, which is unable to conceive its transitory manifestations synthetically.

Thomas regained ground in his mental consciousness. He tried in vain to fix this ungraspable moment in which he had experienced something of importance. But his stubborn thought bucked before an obstacle, and this resistance suddenly made him aware of the "breaking of the sound barrier."[1]

To go beyond the mental zone, to enter into the intuitive state and *become Knowledge*: empty words, or Reality? Knowledge, Consciousness, the Present Moment: all these words would have only an arbitrary meaning for him—*unless their Reality could be experienced from the other side.*

This idea taking form broke his resistance. This time Thomas willfully put the controls into reverse and, allowing his thoughts to fall into the emptiness, listened to Silence without worrying about the outcome of it all. . . .

And the outcome was very simple, as with all things that happen "in truth." It was a state of calm, free of conflict, because there was no resistance. It was like water without ripples when it becomes transparent because it is calm. And this transparence revealed to Thomas the obvious presence of that which in him *knew*: the source of answers already received, the secret voice, Maître Jacques, the expression of his own "word," the Witness of his living, indestructible being.

And the evidence of this Presence filled him with a force he had never known before: *certainty*.

What a liberation! Now he could talk about responsibility. Now he could accept a Master.

He stood up and, without thinking, moved by an impulse he had long ago forgotten, got on his knees in a gesture of deferential gratitude.

It didn't take long for him to react. False pride brought him quickly to his feet in self-reproach for this concession to an outdated religious act. Standing with arms crossed, Thomas listened to the reproach, realizing within him the revolt of an adversary with whom, until that day, he had identified himself. Weighing his arguments, he understood that this gesture had expressed, despite himself, a new feeling of respect for something he could only name "Presence."

Then the adversary tried to argue with him:

"Where can you situate this Presence? Within you, or outside of you? Which one of the two were you kneeling before?"

1. See Chapter 5.

"You're catching me off guard, Satan. If I situate it within myself, it's before myself that I knelt. If I situate it outside of myself, I made the gesture of the believer before a tabernacle. However, today I know that within me and outside of me, I feel the same Presence!"

"That's just fine," continued the teasing voice. "In that case you can kneel in the street or in your room."

Thomas hesitated a moment.

"I could have, if you didn't stop me from doing so. But your objection made me understand something: the meaning of the 'Temple,' this place where so many prayers, so many emotions, and so many pleas are concentrated. These things no doubt magnetically attract Presence. It's a matter of establishing a communion between all these desires and that which participates in them through being called."

"You speak very well for someone who's been newly converted! But what about all those far or recent echoes which are much less edifying: the gossipers in the vestry, the jealousy of the bigots who whisper calumnies and other scandalous tales that corrupt this atmosphere?"

Thomas smiled as he remembered the arguments he himself had so often invoked.

"No doubt," he murmured, "but now I know that the state of Presence is no more altered by these insanities than the sun's rays are by the odors emanating from a heap of manure."

Thomas then had the impression he was listening to Maître Pierre with his jeering laughter:

"I'll find you again, Thomas, because my arguments were yours. Go with God, or 'with the devil,' as you wish!"

Thomas couldn't help laughing.

"Yes, as I wish; that time you told the truth. But the roles are reversed: today I identify with Maître Jacques, and henceforth you will be the adversary, Pierre du Coignet,[2] because I am taking my allegiance away from you, old jeering Satan!"

Still laughing, Thomas left the Cathedral. He was now in a hurry to find his Master again. He had missed their fruitful meetings during his forced vacation.

The Automaton proposes and Destiny disposes!

When Thomas arrived at the Atelier, he found the sculptor in the midst of putting some last touches on the face of a marionette. Standing next to him, Jean-Jacques was trying to manipulate the strings of other little puppets.

2. See Chapter 3.

"Here's my model!" exclaimed Dominique when he saw Jean Thomas enter. "You've arrived just on time. I needed someone to serve as a model. But what's happened, Doctor? Your expression has changed: you look almost candid. You're smiling. That skeptical frown has disappeared. My word, Thomas, you've been changed into a babe!"

"His nursery days weren't long-lived," said the pilot. "It's been only two months, hasn't it?"

"These two months were very long for me," said Thomas with a sigh. "Above all, they were very boring! As for my change in expression, it didn't happen during this depressing vacation that you so willingly allowed me, Maître Dominique. It happened today!"

"Perhaps it's the fruit of this vacation time," murmured the sculptor as he modeled another face around the neck of his puppet.

"He's got two faces. Is that the way that you see me? Or are you destroying the first face?"

"Let's allow some time before we wipe away the original. Time is the genesis, and in every genesis phases of shadow alternate with phases of light. It's still very interesting to know its two faces.

"Before we go to eat, I'd like you to meet my two marionettes. Do you recognize Maître Pierre?"

Thomas started to laugh at the ambiguous expression on his smiling lips.

"Why didn't you give him a devil's face?"

"I gave him hooked feet," answered Dominique. "Dualism is at his base, but his face is still human, very human, despite the fact that one eye is looking toward hell while the other is drawn to the gates of paradise."

"What a curious character! He'd make an amusing mate for the saintly Angelica, who's so attached to her halo."

"No, there's an abyss between them: consciousness. Don't be mistaken, Maître Pierre knows himself! And that's what makes him interesting. And this pilgrim—do you recognize him as a friend?"

"It's Dutheil," exclaimed Thomas. "Why did you give him an astronomer's telescope to carry?"

"Because he's searching in the clouds for the wellspring that is flowing at his feet."

"Haven't you made a puppet for Jean-Jacques?"

"He wasn't able to," answered the pilot; "he's seen nothing but my back! I've spent all my time unraveling the threads of the marionettes."

"That's what he calls unraveling his consciousness," said Dominique, laughing.

"I'll make his face when he has understood the secret of the strings."

"Is it so important?" asked Thomas, suddenly coming to life.

"We'll talk about it while we eat. Come sample the Tavern's menu."

Jean-Jacques took his friend aside and apologized for having accepted the sculptor's invitation:

"Perhaps I should have left the two of you alone, but Dominique insisted."

"Dominique was right," said Thomas, "because it's to the two of you that I owe the change in my frown."

"May we know the story of this metamorphosis?" asked the pilot, intrigued by the unusual serenity of his friend.

Thomas did not have time to answer. The sculptor, who was standing at the entrance to the Tavern, interrupted:

"We won't know anything before we've sampled my pickled cabbage. Let's not keep it waiting!"

"I agree that this sauerkraut merits all of our attention," Thomas complimented the sculptor; "but without even touching upon serious questions, I'd like to know the reason for your infatuation with the marionettes."

"Do you think it's a frivolous preoccupation?" asked the sculptor as he took from his pocket a small masked clown.

"And what do you call that one?" asked Thomas. "What character is hidden beneath its plaster?"

"There's a mirror under his mask, my friend. It's the mirror that reflects the eccentricities of humans and foresees their reactions . . . if this clown is a wise one."

"Is he man's monkey, then?"

"No. Here's the monkey."

Saying this, Dominique drew from his pocket a puppet with a monkey's head.

"This is the animal imitator of *mechanical* humanity. The clown consciously reflects psychological humanity."

"Are you gathering a whole collection of little puppets?"

"I like to capture the gestures and traits characteristic of a person, the better to examine the motivating forces that he obeys in each phase of his existence.

"Try to imagine a theater of marionettes whose impulses and gestures are controlled by various strings. Be careful: the strings are the agents that make the puppets *react*. It can be a lot of fun! Why don't you try it? You are the operator, and you have to establish your control mechanisms."

"That's easy to say," exclaimed the pilot, "but it's less easy to imagine! My control panel will be more complicated than my plane's because each character has several possible reactions, once he's provoked by the strings!"

Thomas was amused by the idea.

"I think that first we've got to define the essential motivating forces, because we can't multiply our strings ad infinitum."

"These are what I see as the essential ones," said Jean-Jacques:

"First there are impulses that *come from passion*, ranging from valid expressions of it to vicious perversion.

"Then there are the *goals* that each individual has set for his existence, beginning with the *profit motive*, which is proportionate to his needs, or rather his requirements, and continuing with the *ambitions*, and the egotistical impulses that flow from them. And finally there are *ideals*, which are provoked by a selective emulation of artistic, political, humanitarian, and religious doctrines.

"That gives us already a good number of strings!"

"And that's not all," added Thomas. "What about the influences that are imposed on us or that we are constantly affected by: education, obligations, inventions, opinions?"

Dominique smiled as he listened.

"If the strings that you enumerate were the only incitement for your puppet, our humanity would be reduced to a collectivity of automatons, mentally superior to the most intelligent animals, but with a destiny subject to incoherent accidents in a world that is in continual transformation.

"If human destiny involves possibilities that are superior to those of Automatons, I've got to be able to provoke them in my imaginary theater, if this is to be a sketch in keeping with Reality.

"However, three things have to be taken into consideration: the marionette, the stage on which he will evolve, and the setting, or Cosmos, in which this stage is situated.

"Logically, I should first evoke the Cosmos, which all the marionettes are part of. But in practical terms, I wouldn't understand their reactions to the working of the strings if I didn't understand the makeup of my puppets.

"First let's look at the human marionette. It's an Automaton because for the most part it is unconscious of its true motives. Its physical organism apparently functions by a mechanical chain of complicated chemical and energy transformations, which are all interdependent, just like the clogs on a wheel in a closed circuit."

"These essential functions," remarked Thomas, "don't demand the intervention of mental will."

"They are so independent of mental will," confirmed Dominique, "that mental consciousness can be totally ignorant of them, and generally is. But that doesn't mean that their operations are reduced to a simple chemical and mechanical game. The *life* which allows this organism to function is the fruit of continual motion and of the reaction of the functions that are vital to this motion."

"What vital functions are you talking about, Maître Dominique?"

"Those that no mechanics or chemistry could possibly govern. For example: assimilation, the transformation of a substance into vital energy, and in general the submission of each organic function to a Principle Function, of which it is the incarnated consciousness."

"Does that mean that each organ is conscious of itself?"

"Absolutely, as long as you don't confuse this consciousness with mental consciousness: each heart cell 'beats' like the heart because it is the expression of its innate consciousness. It doesn't 'think' it, *it is*. It's the perfect blending of the organ with its Causal Function."

"How humiliating to think that man doesn't realize this marvel!" said Jean-Jacques.

"No more humiliating than that this marionette doesn't know the hand that supports him.

"The majority of gestures that the automaton attributes to Conscious Will are provoked by the motivating force that I call puppet strings, because the Active Will is not conscious of their source."

"If I understand," said Jean-Jacques, "our ignorance of the source gives us the illusion of free will."

"That's correct," answered Dominique, "on the other hand, observing this would be an act of discernment that would make the governing of the controls autonomous."

"Then you must tell us, Maître Dominique, about this consciousness which is able to form our discernment without error."

"Judge for yourself, Thomas: you know that our cerebral consciousness is in contact neither with our innate instinctive consciousness nor with our intuitive state. Only these are able to make us discern Reality from the appearances that our cerebral faculties show us. Those are the two faces of the marionette, Thomas: one disputes and assumes, the other 'blends' and *knows*."

"Enough of this!" exclaimed Thomas, beating his fist on the table and making the others laugh. "It's stupid to keep walking around a truth and it's time we called things by their name! I, Jean Thomas, declare that the only elements of my marionette that are independent of the strings are the two aspects of my immortal being: my Permanent Witness and my Spiritual Witness. These have nothing to do with my doubts, but until today I treated them like the poor parent whom one prefers to ignore so as to have nothing to concede to him.

"Is that clear? And I don't want to hear anything more about these strings!"

Dominique and Jean Jacques laughed so hard at this outburst of turbulent faith that tears ran down their cheeks.

"It's absolutely clear, my friend," said Dominique as he refilled the wineglasses. "But for those who still haven't banged their fists against the table, I'd like to complete my theater. I've only shown you the actors. However, you've also got to consider the stage on which they're evolving and the setting, or Cosmos, as well. How could I do that?

"What man sees of the Cosmos is the Great Clock constituted by the positions of the sun, the moon, the planets, and the constellations relative to that of our planet. What this clock contains is apparently an enormous emptiness. This emptiness is populated by invisible powers, whose hierarchy goes back to the inconceivable initial Ternary, and which, in the descending chain of its successive emanations, give the Principle Functions that are manifested in the functions of nature."

"Organic functions, for example?" asked the pilot.

"Organs are their incarnations, as I just said, but you must understand that these powers are not the strings of the human marionettes: they are the functional causes that have constructed their organism. Likewise, the elements of the Great Clock are the animators and the regulators of their vital functions. All the beings that live on earth are governed by them."

"They are the great stage managers," suggested Jean-Jacques.

"They are, for everything that's under the influence of the alternating pendulum: separation-reunion, repulsion-attraction, contraction-dilation, et cetera. They determine the time of the earth: day, month, year, the cycle of precessions. And all these are subject to vaster cosmic cycles whose influence reverberates in the events of our existence. That's the way we are currently being swept along the accelerated rhythm of the end of the Age of Pisces, which is taking us toward Aquarius."

"We're moving at a faster and faster speed," added Jean-Jacques, "which is unbalancing all these poor marionettes and is making them commit thousands of follies."

"It's the *cause* of this imbalance that interests us," insisted Dominique. "If our contemporaries knew how to distinguish this inevitable cause (the rhythm of this age) from personal motivating forces that their backward mentality is unable to modify in order to adapt to the new rhythm, they wouldn't suffer such distress, *which is due to the great fear of progress demanded by this age.*"

"Science made this progress a reality," exclaimed the pilot, "and with an alarming rapidity!"

"This forward march of science," noted Dominique soberly, "is the work of the mind, which alone has progressed. However, that progress is a trap that slows down our journey toward a higher humanity."

"Take America for example," said Thomas. "It's currently provoking the ambition in its students to *go beyond themselves*, giving them as an ideal model the 'superman,' but in the sense of intellectual and scientific progress, above all applied to electronic techniques."

"That only aggravates the modern error," answered the sculptor. "The transcendence demanded by our final goal is the passage beyond the cerebral. It's a matter of awakening the higher being within us which outlives our mortal intelligence. We must become conscious of the motivating forces that direct us and make automatons of us.

"However, that in us which *knows* the motives behind our impulses is the Permanent Witness, which is not directed by any string whatsoever. Our Human Consciousness can *become conscious* of this when it allows itself to be enlightened by our Permanent Witness."

These words brought a smiling reverie to Thomas's expression. His Master expected this and observed it with interest.

The pilot broke the silence when he asked Dominique:

"If I understand you, the main problem of man is the comprehension of what you call Human Consciousness: that is, the totality of our Individual Consciousness, regardless of whether or not it is enlightened by the Permanent Witness."

"That's right," answered Dominique, "it is the total consciousness of all earthly men, independent of their immortal souls. But this is rarely recognized by men who, either through ignorance or through inattentiveness, only take into account what they can verify with the mind. What is commonly called the 'subconscious' concerns all of those states of consciousness that are not verified by the cerebral faculties."

"I'm a bit upset," retorted the pilot, "by the multiple aspects of this Human Consciousness: I understand the innate consciousness of the newborn and the consciousness acquired through experience of the individual. I understand the functional consciousness of each element of our physical being, that of our psychic being, and even that of our mental consciousness. But I wonder if it's necessary to consider each one of them as one of these 'stages' of the totality? Or am I just getting far off the track in erroneous schematic representation?"

"You need the words to express yourself, my friend, but I'll try to invoke in you the reality of these various states. And this will be none other than the application of the specifically human faculty which is the power to observe oneself. It's the power of Adam to 'name' every creature that is inferior to him, and then to recognize his superiority as man.

"Here's where the consciousness of the human *specimen* stops. There is the possibility, however, to go farther, by the foreknowledge of a state higher than that of mortal nature.

"That in us which answers the call of this foreknowledge is the *highest degree* of Human Consciousness, which then can only go beyond itself through identification with the Divine Consciousness of the Permanent Witness.

"And each one of the intermediary degrees is nothing but the vital consciousness particular to each of our component states which enlarges the Total Consciousness of the individual each time he tries to *recognize* one of them instead of being blindly influenced by it.

"As for the instrinsic nature of Human Consciousness, I think that the least erroneous image is that of a tissue made up of the innate consciousness of each newborn child. This is constantly built upon and modified through multiple impressions of his current existence. I say *impressions*, and not *notions*, because notions are engraved only in the cerebral memory. It is the *impressions produced by* these notions that can affect the fabric of our Consciousness."

"Is this 'fabric' definitive, or can it be modified?"

"One must differentiate what in these various consciousnesses corresponds to the following: On the one hand, realities, whether they are relative because they are momentary actual states, or whether they are absolute because they correspond to the laws and functions of Cosmic Harmony; or, on the other hand, the impressions produced by transitory experiences. We could call these transitory experiences spots on a fabric, spots that can be removed by totally contradictory impressions, or modified by impressions that are more or less different.

"It's the excess of badly defined spots that troubles a consciousness and creates confusion and uncertainty in the behavior of the individual."

"This image of the single fabric is valuable," said Jean-Jacques. "It allows me to better understand the continuity of the Human Consciousness throughout successive existences. Moreover, it eliminates the false idea of the stages, or the tightly enclosed divisions, between the various states of consciousness."

"It's *always the same consciousness*," confirmed Dominique, "which is related to the more or less subtle states of the individual. This consciousness nonetheless doesn't go beyond human possibilities, because then it would become Suprahuman Consciousness; that is, it would be integrated with that of the Permanent Witness."

"Thank you, Maître Dominique. I can hardly dare to ask this other question. . . . I still find it difficult to try to imagine this Individual Consciousness that survives our earthly existence."

"If you need an image," conceded Dominique, "you can represent it to yourself as the conscious form of that which was, on earth, your personality and which reincarnated itself with or without your Permanent Witness according to whether you have kept or lost your Divine Entity."

"How is it that we don't retain the memory of our previous existences?"

"You retain the consciousness that you've acquired from them with the profound tendencies and impulses that are the consequence of them. As for the facts and the images of your personal life, their memory (such as you understand it) disappears with the destruction of the organism, but they are inscribed in the *Akasha*, from which you have separated yourself to enter into the state of Light in order to return to the earthly world."

Jean-Jacques and Thomas were moved by this unhoped-for clarification and ruminated in silence on the consequences.

"He who has tasted profound meditation will understand the value of this teaching," said the pilot finally. "It also explains the forgetfulness (which the Greeks symbolized through by waters of Lethe) . . ."

"The change in vibratory states," murmured Dominique.

". . . and yet the possibility (in certain cases of clairvoyance) of retrieving in the Akasha various facts and images of past experiences."

"The problem of Human Consciousness seems much clearer to me now," said Thomas, "but I still want to insist on the idea of the Permanent Witness, because if it is our only element of autonomous government, it's the Permanent Witness that is the basis of our free will."

"Indeed it is," confirmed the sculptor. "Since it's our permanent and infallible consciousness. Unfortunately, this Witness can be veiled by our mental preoccupations. However, if the silent attention of our human consciousness allows it to enlighten us, we can then have these conclusions *confirmed* by our Mental Consciousness: It's what one calls *becoming conscious of one's consciousness.*

"The practice of this, if it's done with patience, will allow for the *reintegration* of our real being in our automaton, until this Integrated Consciousness totally awakens our marionette, who can then spontaneously manipulate its own strings."

"Perhaps that is the most difficult for our contemporaries to do," sighed Thomas, "because our mental robot really believes that it's the true master of the entire control panel!"

"Of course," exclaimed Jean-Jacques, "and I now understand what Dutheil was talking about when he said 'unravel my strings.' He was talking about my unraveling his consciousness, because that would be discerning the inherent motivating forces of the psyche of the automaton from the exterior influences that bombard us and trap us in an artificial web of obligations. What slaves we are without even being aware of it!"

"I choose liberty," said Thomas joyfully. "But jokes aside, the marionettes have clearly shown me that I am enslaved. There is still one detail that intrigues me. Dominique spoke about the stage where the characters evolve, but he didn't explain its meaning."

"It's quite simple, Thomas," said the sculptor, "it's the *place*: the soil, the country that imposes upon its inhabitants its character and influences their behavior, their way of thinking and expressing themselves and even their personal reactions. It's this influence that creates the group soul of a people, its particular genius and its general qualities."

"This imprint must mark an individual at the expense of his personality," suggested the pilot.

"It does affect his automaton, in the sense that it participates in the collective soul of the country. But this domination loses its power to the extent that man becomes more conscious of his Entity. It's not these exterior influences that are terrible but our unconsciousness, which undergoes them without discernment. It's the same with the influence of the stars."

"Well, we're pretty much obliged to suffer the stars, because we can't escape them."

"That's a mistake. If I have deliberately oriented my way toward my higher destiny, it's this higher destiny that will give the orders, and I will no longer be subjected to Fate."[3]

"Now we're getting into something interesting," said Thomas, "because it's a positive hope to get rid of all these strings."

Dominique shook his head indulgently.

"My dear friend, this desire for independence is honorable, but it's a big task! There was once a very wise man who preached the effective way of destroying the strings at the roots. His name on this earth was Lao-tse, and the means he used was nonwill. But this nonwill is the union of our being with Being. It is its reintegration, in the sense that our totalized Consciousness (from our innate instinctive consciousness to our awakened intuitive Consciousness) directs us completely, without any voluntary effort, and without the need to have it verified by our mental consciousness.

"This is the true nonwill and the attainment of 'the will of the Father' without regard to personal will.

"I'm not quite sure whether or not you are susceptible to this.

". . . Tell me, Thomas, did you like the sauerkraut?"

---

3. Fate: understood here as the destiny determined by astrological influences.

Jean-Jacques laughed heartily as he saw his friend thrown off the track.

"In other words," concluded Thomas, brooding, "you still need to manipulate my strings."

"Not at all, man," replied the pilot. "If I've understood the lesson well, the first thing that you must do is to observe them. You've got to be like the big owl that I captured one night and attached by a cord to the foot of my chair. It didn't revolt, it didn't rebel; at first it just looked at the cord with attention, then it watched at length, eating the food that I put down for it. After four hours of patience and apparent docility, it took advantage of my first absence, figured out how to *undo* the cord, and flew out through the open window."

"Congratulations, Jean-Jacques," exclaimed the sculptor, "you've learned the lesson."

"However, Maître Dominique, I still have a lot of questions to ask: what is one to think of luck?"

Dominique sucked on his pipe in silence.

"Luck," he said finally, "is a hunchbacked puppet, and men are pulling the strings themselves. This character was invented by superstition in order to have someone to blame for circumstances that help or hinder our existence.

"As a matter of fact, the puppet's hump is the abnormal impulse (because it's instinctive and not mental) that makes us do something positive or negative. The roots of this impulse go back very far, but we're so inattentive to them that we don't see where they lead."

"Must one include all fortuitous circumstances in this definition, such as those that keep us from an unforeseen danger, or bring us profit that we logically couldn't have attributed to chance?"

"Luck or chance—whatever you want to call it—has no meaning in the world of causes," said Dominique. "The field of more or less subtle forces, which are the determining forces of circumstances in our existence, are not visible to us, but to deny them for this reason would be very stupid. If we don't perceive the line of forces in it, the play of Numbers or simply of affinities, that doesn't mean they're not constantly acting despite the inability of our logical foreknowledge to apprehend them.

"In order to live in harmony and in peaceful coexistence with these invisible motivating forces, we have no other means than our instinct or our intuition. If they make us (unbeknownst to our reason) do something favorable, we congratulate ourselves for being lucky. If we are stubborn or inattentive, we call our experience bad luck."

"One more important detail," asked Thomas: "does this instinctive or intuitive signal indifferently serve the interests of our Automaton or those of our higher being?"

"It serves the goal that guides us. Or, if you prefer, the god that we serve. If this god is money, ambition, sensuality, or another passion, our instincts will alert us to favorable coincidences in regard to the object on which we are concentrating our attention.

"The case in which one deliberately gives power to one's Conscious Being in order to transcend our human nature is something totally different. Then it's our Being that orients us toward favorable coincidence and our 'luck' obeys our 'will to the Light.'"

The pilot was distractedly watching the smoke from his cigarette. The sculptor respected this silence for a few moments and then questioned him:

"What are you dreaming about, Jean-Jacques?"

"I was imagining your theater in action—the uninterrupted circus of the Great Clock, the colors and influences of the space populated with characters, the movement of their gestures put in action by various forces, the double face represented alternately by the puppet of Thomas, the unrealized movements of my own marionette—and I was surprised to find that all the puppets are shaking with an inner agitation caused by the multiplicity of impulses that provoke them."

"You're right," said Dominique, "we are indeed 'agitated,' and despite that we are asleep because we ignore it. Our existence unfolds like a nightmare from which the only respite is deep sleep.

"But suppose that the Consciousness awakens, and that its Light illumines your marionettes from within: you would suddenly see their attitude change, they would become simplified, certain strings would fall away, others would be guided by an effective free will. Their agitation would then give place to the serenity caused by a unified direction.

"Let's try to test this power out on our own marionette. Try to deliberately pass into this state of attentive silence where you can make contact with your Master of Light."

The two friends agreed without saying a word.

A long silence followed. Then Jean-Jacques murmured:

"I start to get there, but the worries just come back to bother me."

"For my part," said Jean Thomas, "I find the state that I knew when I was at Notre Dame, and that I came here to talk to you about, but the uselessness of my scientific research still comes back to haunt me."

"These troubling interferences are inevitable," said Dominique. "But they will become more and more rare when you have taken firm ground in this serene state *through practice*. Imagine a man who is already used to this intuitive silence: even if he still doesn't bring into play the causal functions of phenomena whose mechanism his reason tries to understand, his mentality will transform itself. He will attempt to 'live them in himself' in order to *know* rather than to *understand*."

"I know as of today that it's possible," said Thomas. "But the misery of our human condition is the domination of the inevitable contingencies of existence."

"Do you think I am not subject to them as you are?" retorted the sculptor. "But when this happens, and I am, as you say, in bad shape, I make my way up the ladder of my desire and go above the clouds that are making me sad, and from the top I look down at the reason for my bad mood. Seen from afar, outside the bilious reactions, they diminish in importance and I can even consider them impersonally, as if they belonged to someone else. Then I weigh them in terms of my *essential goals*, as I can easily distinguish that which I am obliged to undergo from that which I can eliminate."

"Difficult, but possible," agreed the pilot, "and quite interesting!"

"Try the experience," said Dominique. "Your current disturbance, Jean-Jacques, is a state of consciousness that puts into conflict two discordant duties. Practice what I tell you, and I will be surprised if the will to obey the higher destiny doesn't inspire in you the acceptable compromise.

"As for you, Thomas, if your current profession allows you to live, why not use it in order to acquire mental discipline? Because it's a mastery to know how to limit one's rational intelligence to one's professional work, and on all other occasions to put oneself to the task of taking the advice of the Intelligence of the Heart."

Thomas seemed reticent.

"Isn't there a danger of badly confusing these two mentalities?"

"Mastery consists in this discernment," answered Dominique. "The problems posed by rational science must be reasoned out by your mental faculties, if that is your professional duty. But nothing is preventing you from listening from within to the objections of an intuitive vision, which is more synthetic. It's an excellent exercise which you don't have to tell your superiors about. In other words, if I'm speaking of intuitive life, I understand it above all (except for the moments of meditative silence) as a constant *disposition* which demands *watchfulness* rather than action."

"Is it a conscious state of being?" asked Thomas.

"Indeed it is, and its first recompense liberates you from all of these strings.

"Why are laughing, Thomas?"

"Most of all it's because I am so happy that something I needed to be cleared up has been. Then it's also the pleasure of having observed the favorable coincidence of a succulent pickled sauerkraut with a discussion of spiritual philosophy."

The sculptor winked at him maliciously:

"I see! The hunchbacked puppet is executing my will tonight, because the euphoria created by savory pickled sauerkraut, harmonized with Alsatian wine, is familiar to the accommodating silence of the mind. In order to force the attention of the Intelligence of the Heart, it's sometimes good to put our ravenous dog and our mental monkey to sleep in animal bliss."

11

Simplicity

"I'm going to put your insight to a test, my dear Thomas," declared Dominique as he sipped on the coffee that Anna had prepared. "Why do you think I invited myself to dinner in your apartment?"

Thomas looked at his Master, who was smiling.

"No doubt, my insight is already failing, because I should have known there was something behind your desire to come here. I simply assumed that you wanted to see the atmosphere I live in."

"I know the atmosphere already. I was interested in the guardian angel you've got, who has such a rare quality. That's right! It's Anna that I wanted to see at work, in *her* milieu."

"Where did you meet her?"

"You recently sent her to the Atelier to leave a note, and I was so taken by her radiant face that I asked her to come inside. Didn't she tell you?"

"Anna is the soul of discretion, and unless I ask her about something, she won't say a word. She's a curious type, isn't she? I'll bet that as soon as she left, she became a subject for one of your marionettes!"

"You can't make a marionette when there aren't any strings."

"No strings? Is that possible? This time you've got to explain yourself, Maître Dominique."

"I'd like to ask you this, Thomas: haven't you ever looked at Anna? This woman is an anachronism. In our world of complexity she is the incarnation of simplicity."

Thomas, a lost look on his face, murmured: "What is simplicity?"

"It's very hard to define, my friend, and it's almost as difficult to define as *that which Is*. But let's try.

"'Simplicity is a negative quality, in the sense that it's the absence of all foreign elements in the essential nature of the subject. But it also has a positive aspect, because when everything else is put aside, the subject *is*, or expresses, its essential nature: its intrinsic reality.

"This nakedness is so rare that it struck me in the physiognomy of your servant. I thought up an excuse to prolong her visit. Thinking that I was absorbed in reading your message, she wandered around the sculptures that were on display, observing them with surprising interest. When I asked which of them she preferred, she pointed without hesitating to the subjects that had real value."

"That is curious," recognized Thomas, "because she's never had any kind of artistic education."

"It's not surprising at all. She feels the proper lines and the harmonious gestures because her simplicity inculcates in her the sense of Harmony.

"I wanted to pursue the experience, and under the pretext of inviting her into my Tavern, I showed her the sculptures of the miserere on the stalls. She looked at these burlesque images with an amused smile.

"'Why not?' she said. 'This proves that the sculptor has understood people well. After all, it's the rear end that is leaning against the miserere, and the devil is right where he belongs. The monks who came to pray in these stalls must have known it better than anyone, because I guess that it's in order to learn to know themselves that they go to the monastery. Isn't that true, Monsieur Dominique? And if the god they're praying to *is God*, He knows the truth: so you can't talk nonsense to Him!'

"'What nonsense could one possibly tell Him, Anna?' I asked her.

"'There's no lack of it,' she replied: 'good opinions that one has of oneself, with all the baggage of excuses and 'good intentions,' and pious indignation against those who don't practice one's own religion. . . .'

"'What do you think about religion, Anna? Can one speak of God while drinking beer?' I asked, and filled the old mug that she had been admiring.

"'How can I speak of God?' she retorted. 'I don't know Him. I don't know anyone well, except myself. I know that I've got both the angel and the beast in me, and that the two of them are not looking for the same nourishment. If I listened only to the beast, I'd live like an animal. If my beast obeys the angel, it teaches me what my beast doesn't know.'

"'By angel,' I suggested, 'do you mean soul?'

"'Soul or angel, whatever you wish: my eyes don't see him, but my heart knows him and is often looking for his company. I can't doubt him because he shows me the way, like a dog leading a blind person. He's what gives me the desire to kneel, as I would in front of my Master, and he can take me into a world where one no longer dies. So you see, I can't think anything more, because I don't want to start telling tales about what I know nothing about.'

"I approved enthusiastically, but I couldn't resist asking her another question:

"'I understand very well what you are saying, Anna. But if you think of God, what do you call him?' Listen to what she said:

"'Tell me, Monsieur Dominique, how do you say *oui* in English?'

"'You say *yes*.'

"'And in German?'

"'*Ja*.'

"'And in Italian?'

"'You say *si*. And in Arabic you say *aiwa*,' I added, laughing.

"Therefore, in all the languages one thinks the same thing, but one expresses it with a different word. Well, I *think* God, regardless of the name that men give Him. I speak to Him through my angel (or my soul, if you will), as if it were a small image of what God could be life-size! That's all I can do. I'm too ignorant to know more.'

"Such candor took my breath away. I changed the subject to hide my emotion:

"'Anna, what do you do for Dr. Thomas?'

"'I am a servant.'

"'Is your housekeeping work tedious for you?'

"'What difference does it make? It's a job! It's not what one does that has value, but what one learns from it.'

"'Are you happy with your master?'

"'Of course, if he is happy.'

"'And what if he married?'

"'I'd continue to serve, that's all.'

"A serene smile confirmed these words, and there was no need for commentary. I complimented her on her name:

"'Anna is a beautiful name. *Anneau* means *ring*, the cycle of becoming and of returning.'

"'Oh, the doctor is very inventive with my name: Grandmother Ann, Mother Anna, Sister Anne. . . .'

"'Doesn't he ever say "Saint Anne"?'

"'Nothing so silly as that. Sainthood is none of my business.'

"In a burst of laughter, she left me to 'go put the soup on.'"

Dominique was silent and observed his friend, who was silently smoking his pipe.

"I'm amazed," confessed Thomas, "and a little bit ashamed, because I have the impression that I've never *seen* Anna!"

"That's quite probable," agreed Dominique. "We have too much of a tendency to look at others through our own prism, so that we judge them according to a personal interpretation.

"This woman is a very rare example of conscious independence. She doesn't worry about the past, and she doesn't worry about the future. She constantly lives in the Present Moment, without being concerned about other people's opinions and without allowing herself to be troubled by human turpitude. Please tell me: what strings could possibly manipulate her marionette?"

"You're right," acknowledged Thomas. "It's an extraordinary 'nakedness.' How was she able to attain this degree of liberation? Because of her frankness? Or perhaps because of self-sacrifice?"

"Through *simplicity*. However, let's distinguish between innate simplicity and acquired simplicity. Little children have innate simplicity, as long as it is not corrupted by imposing conventional notions and an education that prevents them from listening to their instinctive consciousness. It's these little children that the Gospel speaks of when it affirms that 'their angels' (that is, their souls) 'do always behold the face of the Father which is in heaven.' In other words, the veil of complexities has not yet exiled them from 'paradisiacal simplicity.'"

"But for us who have lost it," said Thomas, "it seems impossible to retrace our steps!"

"It's necessary to reacquire it," answered Dominique, "and there are two ways to do it:

"We can take the honorable attitude, which is to close the door on arguments and on dialectics, on the vanity of 'know-how' and the finding of rational proofs. Then we can learn through silence to listen to the teaching of the Intelligence of the Heart and the impulses that it provokes.

"Or we must let go of opinions and diverse theoretical hypotheses, and try to find the base of knowledge in the traditions that teach with certitude. But we must do this in concentrating our attention exclusively on what is *essential* to the subject in question."

"But I'm obliged by my research to first see all the possible aspects of the question that I'm studying, foresee the objections, and then rely on an accepted opinion. Finally I choose from among the rudiments the elements valuable for erecting my own thesis."

"That's the rational method, dear Doctor. But what I'm speaking about now is a reeducation of thought with the goal of arriving at simplicity.

"Simplicity is the culmination of Knowledge. But it is also true that it's the way of Knowledge, in that the elimination of complexity (in thought, in life, and in feelings) eliminates one of the greatest obstacles to intuitive conception."

"Such simplicity is so opposed to the rhythm of existence and the mentality of our contemporaries that I can hardly imagine the possibility of it."

"It does exist, however, in certain beings whose awakened Consciousness has erased egotistical interests and the cerebral vanity of the lower personality. I'm not even speaking of your servant, because you can object that her case is due to the very favorable conditions of her protected life. To that I would reply that she herself has created her own conditions, because she was free to accept or reject the same opportunities for gossip or distraction that other women of her condition choose."

"That's right," answered Thomas. "And I realize that I have often lacked perspicacity with regard to her.

"But for those who are caught up in their professions and the rhythm of the time, what motive force is strong enough to impose on them a different way of behaving?"

"Try to find out for yourself, Thomas."

Thomas wrinkled his brow and smoked heavily as he meditated.

"I think that this motive could be the hope of clarifying thought, which would allow me to rapidly discern the value of my hypotheses in order to progressively transform the most interesting ones into certainty. This constitutes the most difficult part of my scientific research, and could be a way of allowing my reason to make the necessary sacrifices."

"The definition of this motive force needs to be clarified," retorted Dominique. "According to you, it would be the acquisition of certitude. On what criteria would you base this certitude? Scientific proofs?"

"That would be a secure first way."

"And would this security be assured, since new discoveries could render it invalid?"

"It could still serve as the merciless logic that would allow me to justify my belief through the impossibility of its negation," said Thomas.

"All constructed arguments based on rational deduction or on cerebral imagination can be contradicted by a more subtle argument or by a more ingenious imagination."

"Didn't you tell me that reason should control intuition?"

"First you've got to have intuition, and eventually experimentation, but not rational deduction. Just observe how you're deviating from your initial idea: you proposed the verification of hypotheses in order to find certainty, a certainty whose criteria would still be hypothetical logic!"

"You yourself spoke of verification through experimentation, Maître Dominique."

"Experimentation with what? Intuition? Intuition is the *goal* that you're looking for through simplicity. However, you're looking in the complexity of dialectical logic for an inducement that's strong enough to give you the courage to eliminate your complexity."

"Dominique, your simplistic method would lead me to credulity!"

"You are dodging the issues, skeptical Thomas, just like Maître Pierre."

"What can I offer my rational dialectic in order to win its compliance?"

"That which can seduce it: certainty, as long as your reason is honest and is not satisfied with a compromise. However, it's your *Reality* that must control this certitude.

"Define your problem by establishing its data on the essential basis of the subject: what is in you that is *Real?*"

"I suppose that it's my Intuitive Knowledge?"

"Exactly, because it's the consciousness of your indestructible being. Under what condition can it manifest itself?"

"Under the condition that I eliminate what is obstructing it."

"Now we're talking!" Dominique sighed. "And the obstacle is the complexity of your reasoning, which is getting far from the essential subject, and also the *multiple incidences of the goal* that you envisage.

"Our final goal is simple: the reintegration of our mortal being, which is identical to the awakening of our Total Consciousness.

"The *current goal* must also be simple. It must lead us to simplicity. However, the key to success is the concentration of our energies, our thoughts, and our sentiments on this unique direction. Thus, you must eliminate all useless complexities."

"I could answer that every work of genius was achieved through concentration, even nuclear physics, for example."

"Now it's my turn to answer you, Thomas. The complexity of scholarly thought has directed science in a way opposed to that of vital science, whose law is ultimate simplicity. Therefore, this method has led man to the opposite end of his final goal.

"The fruit of concentration obviously depends on its motivating force and the object to which it is applied. *If our objective is simplicity*, we must force ourselves not to waste our energy on secondary interests or relative values.

"We must learn how to discern the real values that merit concentrated effort, and in this regard we allow ourselves to be distracted much too easily.

"Success demands the courageous elimination of all that is not essential to the goal pursued: the abandonment of interesting subjects or details that are exciting for cerebral curiosity or for scientific acquisition, but whose complexity prevents the simple vision of the subject considered."

"This austere elimination of complexity seems like an impossible thing for an intellectual like me."

"Of course it does," recognized Dominique, "because it goes in the opposite direction from the way you were brought up and educated. Our educational methods are exclusively geared toward the pragmatic goals of our earthly existence. This is done to such great length that the 'final goal' is evoked only by religion, whose teachings are considered by educators as something of secondary importance that 'free thought' turns into a question of *opinions*.

"From the very beginning, this duality of education falsifies the mentality of the child, whose egocentric development is oriented solely toward the utilitarian values of his social existence.

"It's useless to cry over a state of things that, at first sight, can't be changed for the large majority of our contemporaries. It's to avoid these mishaps that certain monastic rules were established. The rigorous discipline of these rules was geared toward obtaining evangelical simplicity. In our times, the efficacy of these rules is debatable for two reasons:

"In the first place, modern man needs to be *instructed* about his real constitution and his individual situation in relation to the critical phase of evolution that humanity is undergoing.

"In the second place, the urgency of his awakening of consciousness seems to demand the free choice of *his goal*, and the experience of the difficulties inherent in the social condition in which his destiny has placed him. This test seems to be more effective for the conscious reversal of his orientation than that of monastic reclusiveness and blind obedience to its discipline, which absolves him from responsibility for his behavior."

"That's a reassuring point," said Thomas. "It justifies the considerable effort needed in changing my way of thinking. Moreover, it satisfies my imperial need for liberty in the pursuit of my essential goal. Perhaps this is still a weakness, but . . ."

"It would be perfectly acceptable," answered Dominique, "if you have the courage to fix the initiation into simplicity as your first objective.

"In order to help you, let's look at this from another point of view.

"There is a tale about the day the disciples of the Buddha asked their Master if he could summarize the *essential* part of his teaching. In response, the Buddha picked a flower and contemplated it in silence. The absence of all commentary made it clear that the flower was, in itself, the *signification* of the essential.

"Let's try to discover it.

"What role does the flower play in the plant that supports it?

"The goal of the plant, from the smallest plant to the largest tree, is to generate the seed for its reproduction. The trunk, the branches, and the stem are the carriers of the vascular system, which allows continuous circulation of its fluids and sap, from the roots to the tip of the stem and its leaves and flowers, and their return within a closed circuit.

"The leaf is the main organ of respiratory exchange.

"The root holds the plant to the nourishing base.

"However, the seed, which is the goal of the entire organism, is part of the secret of the flower, which protects the reproductive organs, which become the matrix of the seed.

"The flower precedes the seed. It reveals the *qualitative image* of the seed in the formation of the grain or fruit. Simple or multiple, it's the seemingly useless corolla that expresses the characteristics of its 'Logos': its Number, its nature, its qualitative color, and the perfume of its essence, which is its soul.

"It's the flower that 'chooses' the Light and the emanation of the sunlight that suits it. And from these rays and the dew that it breathes in, it prepares the quintessence, which will be *the subtle food for that which will be the seed.*

"The bee knows this, but our blind intelligence cannot even see this phenomenon of Nature and remains indifferent to the workings of this innate consciousness, whose choice and call address themselves only to *Quality! That* is the sole work of the flower. Thomas, do you understand?

"The seed, having been conceived, receives its nourishment from the sap and *the body* of the plant and the soil where its root lay. Then the flower disappears, because its role is not earthly. It doesn't generate life, and doesn't worry about its physical continuation.

"The flower is the *face* of the plant's being, a face that carries its signature. It is to the seed what the aura is to the human being.

"The entire body of the plant is earthly and expresses the will of its earthly existence.

"The flower *wants* nothing: *it opens itself up and receives.* It awaits its subtle qualities from Heaven and it *infuses these qualities in what will be* grain or fruit, in the form of vital energies and of taste.

"Thus, it has the role of individualizing the soul. It is the life-giver and, for us, the model of impersonal work that obeys Heaven and expects from it what is essential. It doesn't care about the material fruit."

Thomas savored in silence the vibrating serenity that emanated from these words. He expressed his recognition to Dominique:

"Today you have been my Master," he said. "You knew beyond comprehension how to imprint within me the vital sense of simplicity!

"I would like to add something," said Dominique, smiling; "the last words of the Bodhidharma, the founder of Zen Buddhism: 'When the five-petaled flower opens, the rest follows naturally.'"

12

The Invisible Powers

A new surprise awaited the visitors at Dominique's Atelier: next to the sculptor's studio was a beautiful aquarium, lit by the opaque light from the window at the south end of the Atelier. Goldfish were swimming around aquatic plants. The magnificent red fish were agitating their translucent fins.

Maître Pierre, whose vocation was fantastic visions, had populated this corner of the Atelier with grimacing gargoyles that gave off a greenish light. Floating silhouettes evoked vaporous elves. Salamanders were crawling up the columns, creating a red light. Maître Pierre, dressed in the suit and bonnet of Pierre du Coignet, squatted before a cauldron, heating punch. Even the punch gave off a diabolical light.

Dominique welcomed Jean-Jacques and Jean Thomas and apologized for the strange welcome: "It's not my idea," he said. "Pierre du Coignet is our host tonight for the inauguration of the aquarium. This incorrigible joker takes every opportunity to evoke the world of his dreams."

"Oh, no!" jeered the gnome, mocking Dominique. "Madmen call reality a dream! Come in, come in, gentlemen. Are you afraid? Come and warm yourselves around the flames of my fire . . . and assure yourselves that this is not Hell, but simply the world in the midst of which you're living!"

"Give us a moment to breathe," said Jean-Jacques with a laugh, while Thomas admired the furnishings and the fish in the aquarium.

The sculptor asked them to come and sit down around the cauldron.

"Obey the master of this house," he said. "It's a matter of simple courtesy. After all, even demons have something to teach us."

"Demons!" retorted Maître Pierre as he filled their cups with the scalding beverage. "*Demons* has a bad ring to it! Above all, it's a misunderstood name. Come on, gentlemen, I'll drink to your fire, in the hope that you don't lose your heads . . . although 'losing your head' is sometimes a way of entering into a relationship with characters that cold reason hides from your skeptical eyes."

Thomas interrupted him, protesting: "Are you denouncing reason? You, Maître Pierre?"

"Pierre du Coignet, if you please. But, under the circumstances, Maître Pierre would not have spoken differently. You see, my friends, for once I have the freedom to teach in this Atelier. I will tell you the bare truth, my truth. It's the truth of the Prince with Hooked Feet, who astutely leads the credulous into the disorderly saraband of his infernal ballet. Why that mocking smile, pilot? Why the skepticism, Doctor? Don't you trust me? And with what right? Are you saints? I say you aren't, because if you were, I would have already been tossed into the Holy Water."

He stopped talking and ironically listened to the general laughter, then suddenly interrupted it: "There's no way to make me shut up. Your curiosity is already sharpened too much by the kind of subjects that well-balanced scientists never talk about! Would you dare to question me about them? Dr. Thomas, I'm listening."

Thomas sensed the trap and said nothing. He observed the artifices used by the artist to create this phantasmagorical decor. Sketches, pastels, collages, and clay models evoked a world of sylphs, elves, mermaids, and hobgoblins with ingenious effects of shadows and light that multiplied in the imagination of the spectator.

Thomas analyzed it. Jean-Jacques played the game. With half-closed eyes, he immersed himself in the dream conceived by the designer and tried to evoke what the decor suggested. He sought in vain to provoke in himself a favorable atmosphere. Finally he leaned over to light his cigarette on the flames of the cauldron.

"It's the work of an artist, and not of a magician, that you have created," he said to Pierre du Coignet. "You've forgotten to animate your images, and you're therefore falsifying the tradition that claims Satan (your boss, I believe) is an all-powerful fabricator of illusions."

"I want nothing to do with scientists," retorted Maître Pierre. "It's you who lack imagination. If I showed you the photo of a horse race, your first impulse would be to imagine the horses' movements. But now you're refusing to evoke the world suggested by all these symbols."

"How can we prove that they exist?" asked Thomas, agreeing with Jean-Jacques.

"What proofs do you want? If you've never seen the astral phenomena produced by invisible beings, generally referred to as spirits, at least you can rely on the indisputable observations of those whose skepticism has yielded before the reality of certain phenomena."

"I fully agree," declared Jean-Jacques. "Notwithstanding instances of trickery or suggestion, whether individual or collective, I have witnessed undeniable wonders. In India, Japan, and black Africa, as well as among the devotees of voodoo, I've seen men provoke rainfall or dematerialize fruits or various objects, which then reappeared right before my eyes. Without going so far, I recently had the opportunity to observe and verify an instance of levitation and displacement of furniture and household utensils. There was no trickery involved, and it happened in broad daylight.

"I can also think of almost funny incidents of lightning that I observed with my own eyes: one was in the form of a fireball which fell through the chimney, turned around me, and went out the window. Another was the experience of a peasant from Normandy, who, without being burned, suddenly had his shirt melted and his chest bared by lightning. This took place before my eyes just moments after he had made fun of the so-called fantasies about lightning."

"If I didn't know how undeniably astute you were, I'd never be able to take these elaborate stories seriously," declared Jean Thomas. "But in this last case, you've got to attribute a kind of intelligence or consciousness to lightning that common sense refuses to give it!"

"Common sense consists in not denying what one doesn't know," retorted Maître Pierre.

"I'd like to believe you, if you could only explain the causes of these phenomena," said Thomas.

Jeering, the dwarf threw incense sticks into the coals under his cauldron. "Your scholarly world is so backward when it comes to what is not rational science that the life of the Invisible World is as foreign to you as the science of electronics is to the Eskimos!"

"Can you show us this world, Maître Pierre?"

"As Pierre du Coignet, I am one of the actors in it. My other boss, the one who holds the keys to Paradise, frequents some of the people in Purgatory. But I myself, poor Pierre, can barely navigate between the two worlds. All I can do is give you my personal opinion. This opinion, which might burn you from time to time, nonetheless has the advantage of being confirmed by certain authentic scholars of an authentic tradition."

"It's a good thing we have an authentic critic here to control it!" retorted Jean-Jacques.

Dominique seemed to ignore this last statement, and continued to smoke his pipe in silence.

Maître Pierre got up to put out the lights, then continued his discourse.

"Your curiosity, gentlemen, gives me the power to evoke the Invisible World. You're living in the midst of it like blind disbelievers.

"Look at the water inside this aquarium. Fish are silently speaking to one another in it and nourishing themselves with imperceptible living organisms. Beings formed by subtle substances, which are invisible to us, provide life in this aquarium. Let's call them naiads, or spirits of what we call *water*. These spirits allow the seminal virtue of things to develop within it. This is true regardless of whether it's the water of earth, rain, or dew. These spirits confer their nature upon it and coordinate these qualities. Forget the walls of this aquarium, which separate the water inside from atmospheric water, the humidity that is in and around us. Allow these water spirits to participate in your own lives; they are indispensable to your sustenance.

"Now breathe. You can't do it without introducing the air spirits into your lungs. They surround you just as the elements of fire surround this cauldron.

"You are constantly drawing magnetic forces from the earth you walk on. The earth spirits have formed your flesh and bones, and have infused their qualities in them.

"Nonsense, you say? Nonetheless, you exist only through the cooperation of these elements, whose spirits (the elementals) produce various energy patterns and particular characteristics."

"Do you attribute the miracles and the hoaxes that Jean-Jacques mentioned to these elements?" asked Thomas.

Maître Pierre hesitated before answering. He was disturbed by Dominique's ambiguous smile.

"You're not claiming that—"

"That these immaterial beings, which have no brains, have an intelligence?" continued Maître Pierre. "Is that what you're thinking, Doctor? Nonetheless, the smallest animal acts through the innate consciousness of its species. The spirits that characterize each of our four elements act through it, as if they were its consciousness."

"You say: 'the spirits of *an* element,'" retorted Thomas, "yet you speak of each of these four elements as an individuality. . . ."

"You say 'humanity,'" retorted Maître Pierre, "and yet you attribute to each one of us his own individuality."

"Stop!" intervened Dominique. "You're exaggerating, dear Master. You mustn't confuse the human being, who possesses an individual spiritual soul, with the elemental, whose rudimentary intelligence is *only the participation in the collective consciousness of the spirits of its element*, even if this elementary spirit, clothed in astral form, seems to act individually.

"But we'll come back to this when our learned professor is finished with his discourse. *You must never confuse the plan with reality!*"

"Then let me continue. I'll use one of Maître Dominique's expressions:

'elementary spirits clothed in astral form.' This actually occurs, and that's how they become perceptible."

"Perceptible to our imagination," said Dominique.

"If you insist," conceded Maître Pierre. "Myth has made use of images appropriate to the nature of the elements in order to represent their elementals, known under the names *dwarfs, elves, naiads*, et cetera."

"And that's what you wanted to include in this decor?" asked the pilot.

"The form is of little importance," answered Maître Pierre prudently. "It's their presence that I want to evoke. But the effort is wasted on your incredulity. I hope these spirits play a trick on you to crush your stupidity!"

"And who says they haven't already done so?" murmured Thomas, looking at Jean-Jacques and Dominique.

"You're mistaken, Thomas," answered the sculptor. "Your stroke of lightning should be interpreted as the intervention of your inner Maître Jacques, who thought it most suitable to awaken you with a storm, because it best suited your disposition.

"If that's the case, this is an example of the action of a spiritual entity (which is thus superior to elemental lightning). It's brought into play at a moment determined by your own receptivity."

"That seems clearer," agreed the doctor. "But I want to know the difference between superior spirits and those which Maître Pierre is talking about, because in order to believe in them, I would need to see their manifestations and listen to Pierre du Coignet's specifications."

"Be careful," exclaimed Jean-Jacques. "I doubt that dialectics and curiosity have ever led anyone on the path of truth."

"Cerebral dialectics and curiosity," answered Maître Pierre, "are the irresistible weapons that my master, the all-powerful Satan, uses to take advantage of his right to seduce human souls. This is a right that he acquired."

"If these means succeed in seducing their victims, we must assume the victims have a total lack of knowledge," said the pilot, "because these means have no appeal for those who 'know.'"

"Well said, Jean-Jacques," exclaimed Dominique. "However, since Maître Pierre refers to his boss, I accept his challenge, but only if he speaks seriously. You've been bantering around enough.

"It's between the two of us, Maître Pierre! You define and argue. I will respond. Jean-Jacques and Thomas, you are the ones who are going to be seduced. You have the right to object, to express your opinion—until you have found the path of certitude."

Maître Pierre took his stand:

"I, Pierre du Coignet, say that my boss, the Satanic power of Fire, is the Master of the World, and I'm going to prove it.

"He is the essential Fire incarnated in matter, and, as such, he becomes the cause of all the reactions that are manifestations of *life* on Earth.

"Whether you're sleeping or active, he imposes himself, and obliges you to acknowledge that his presence is at the base of all vital phenomena in the four areas of Nature:

"He's the dragon who holds the treasures of the underworld. He incubates the depths of the earth and makes volcanoes explode.

"He sleeps in flintstone. He engenders metals.

"He makes the thermal waters boil in the pot.

"He sterilizes the sands of the desert.

"He heats your tissues, your entrails, and your seed, and dominates you through your passions.

"He nourishes himself with the illusions of your imagination.

"If he were extinguished, the earth would become cold and all of nature would cease to exist.

"Where does this power come from, gentlemen? From his divine source, the essential principle of *Heat*, Satan, who, in the beginning, was the ruler of the highest Celestial Hierarchy. He descended from the thrones of angels to Hell. He intervened in the government of inferior powers in order to cooperate in the creation of the human world.

"In order to do this, he instructed the archangel Lucifer to attract those souls who had stayed in the heavenly state in order to give life to human creatures. Some refused. Others allowed themselves to be seduced, and thus started the great schism of angels and demons, too. It also started the fall of souls, whose schism (regardless of how much ill we speak of it) was nonetheless a part of the evolutionary work of the world, since from that time on, human souls were in need of a redeeming Savior in order to recover their lost dignity."

"Hogwash!" exclaimed Dominique, to the great relief of his friends, who were listening in astonishment. "First of all, devil's advocate, you've made a fundamental error by situating the beginning in time. The beginning is 'in Principle,' and our intelligence cannot conceive it.

"By borrowing (and distorting) the Manichean doctrine, you make two characters out of Satan and Lucifer, but the *latter* is *the subtle form of Satan*, who orients himself toward Light.

"Finally, you give to Satan one of the highest places in the Celestial Hierarchy without having situated the other categories."

"These are the categories," retorted Maître Pierre: "Seraphim, Cherubim, Thrones, Dominions, Virtues, Powers, Principalities, Archangels, and Angels."

"That's the acknowledged classification," agreed Dominique. "But you left out the nine subdivisions of three fundamental states, which stand in a hierarchy according to their degree of power and subtlety:

"Seraphim, Cherubim, and Thrones are part of the supracelestial spirits. Dominions, Virtues, and Powers cooperate in governing the cosmos. Principalities, Archangels, and Angels are closer to us because of their lesser subtlety. This inferiority makes them the intermediaries between the highest emanations of Absolute Divinity and the beings and things of this lowly world."

"Can you attribute to them a quality of intelligence?" asked Jean Thomas.

"What you understand by intelligence, my dear friend, is so far removed from *the immanent consciousness of the inconceivable state of these Powers (which are an integral part of Harmony and Cosmic Function)* that I'm unable to answer your question."

"What you've just said is an answer!" exclaimed Jean-Jacques.

"So be it," replied Dominique, "on the condition that you immerse yourself in this truth: each being can comprehend in reality only those states for which he has corresponding states in himself.

"That's why you can't teach men 'realities' that go entirely beyond them. You can teach them only through mythological representation and rather artificial terminology."

"That's too bad, because mythological representations give me the impression of a democratization of the Divine!" said Thomas.

"That's true, if you transpose the universal to the plane of the particular and to the human comedy," answered Dominique. "That's why myths must not 'humanize' (as the Greek myths did, for example). Instead, they must anthropomorphize. In other words, in terms of myth, the image of a human being must not represent *a person*, but instead, the Cosmic Function that man summarizes.

"In order to fulfill this role, the image must be the real symbol of all its parts: in its proportions, its forms (normal or abnormal), its gestures, its dress, its appearance, and in the attributes that complete its significance. These attributes, in order to have an initiatic language, must be true symbols, or express the play of Numbers or of geometry."

"What do you mean by *true* symbols?" asked the pilot.

"Every *natural* thing is a real symbol insofar as it expresses the *characteristics* of the functions that have made it what it is.

"That's why hieroglyphics are the most perfect form of initiatic writing, because they use natural symbols."

"That's fine," said Thomas. "But the words that are embodied by this writing must form a universal sacred language. Otherwise, all terminology can be a source of error, depending on the various possible interpretations."

"That's what happens when someone wants to translate an initiatic language without knowing the secret of its Numbers and its keys."

Maître Pierre was getting impatient, and asked his listeners not to stray from the subject under discussion.

"For lack of a sacred language, it's useful to know the categories that various traditions attributed to these invisible beings. For example, in Judeo-Christian theology, there are nine classes of demons. The first were called *false gods*, that is, imitators of gods, whose powers they pretended to possess in order to seduce humans. Then there were the *spirits of falsehood*, makers of false predictions; the *vessels of iniquity*, who inspire evildoing and depravity, as well as schemes and artifice; the *avengers of crimes* (such as the devil Asmodeus); the *magicians*, who seduce through wonders and false miracles; the *powers of air*, spirits of corruption that are active in heat and in storms; the *furies*, who provoke wars, discord, and corruption; the *crime-committers*, spirits of espionage and betrayal; and the *tempters*, who attach themselves to individual humans.

"However, the word *daemon* does not mean 'evil force,' but often signifies intelligent, wise power.

"Evil demons are fallen angels. Good demons constitute the Celestial Hierarchy of which we have already spoken.

"There are four angels in particular who preside over the four winds: *Michael* for the east, *Raphael* for the west, *Gabriel* for the north, *Uriel* for the south; and there are twelve who govern the signs of the zodiac; four powers for the elements; twenty-eight angels of the houses of the moon—"

Dominique interrupted:

"That's enough erudition, Maître Pierre! Otherwise you are going to make it necessary for us to translate the equivalent of all these things in all the traditions!"

"And that will get us far!" exclaimed the pilot sarcastically. "Not only are the names for the multiple beings of the invisible world different, but also the imagination of what they signify. However, this imagination varies according to the antiquity of the people and the degree of consciousness of the individual."

"Your observation is correct," said Dominique. "Revealed traditions were more or less distorted during the successive changes of the ages in political and religious orientation. That's what caused so much upheaval in the formation of nations and individuals.

"That's why, in our time, with the upset that's produced by the new change in rhythm, neither erudition nor scholarly terminology can help us obtain the Knowledge that generates serene certitude.

"The only erudition that can give us the notions needed to avoid errors of the imagination would be the science of Numbers and of Cosmic Harmony, which is divine geometry. This demands the use of intuitive faculties to awaken in oneself the consciousness of Cosmic Functions. That's what I'm trying to prepare you for.

"Before talking about the essential notions you need, to avoid the digressions of the imagination, I'd first like to pursue the theories of Maître Pierre. He enjoys the role of Pierre du Coignet, but he has another boss whose function on earth is to save souls. Let's let him tell us briefly about the condition of man and his goal! Go on, Pierre! Instruct your brothers. We're listening."

Maître Pierre stood up. He was a bit awkward in his role of preacher.

"If I must be satisfied with a few words, the only thing I can do is refer to the teachings of the catechism: 'God is an eternal spirit infinitely perfect, Creator and Master of all things. . . . The most perfect creatures are angels and men. . . . Man is a reasonable creature composed of a soul and a body. . . . This soul is an immortal spirit that God created in His own image.'

"The goal of man, according to this teaching, is to save his soul by obeying the commandments of God and of the Church. If he does this, 'it will go to Heaven, where it will see God forever.'

"'If he has done evil, it will be damned.' In other words, 'it will suffer in Hell with the demons forever.'

"The evil that leads to Hell consists in the sins that the Church calls mortal sins, if they have not been pardoned by absolution.

"If these same sins are pardoned, as well as the venial sins, the soul is led into Purgatory so that it can be purified before rising to Heaven.

"Men are helped by the angels, and are tempted by the demons, who try to pull them into Hell.

"That's the essential teaching of the catechism on the constitution of man, and on the final goal of his earthly existence."

Thomas was taking some notes. He asked to speak:

"I've got a lot of objections:

"If God is *Absolute*, can you define Him as *a* spirit?

"Is it to the same Divine Power, absolute and unknowable, source of Cosmic Harmony, that we must attribute the creation of our dualistic world, this earthly existence where beasts are obliged to kill one another? Is it that Jehovah Who regrets his decisions and Who advises vengeance and the massacre of enemies?

"If the most perfect creatures are angels and men, must we envision the sad prospect of there being no beings superior to our poor earthly humanity on other worlds?

"If the soul was created in the image of God, how can it be so faulty? How can it be bad? How can it be damned?

"Will the 'damned' soul be in Hell forever?

"Does man have only one lifetime to learn how to save his soul?"

Dominique stopped Thomas:

"That's enough," he said. "You're objections are justified, but they go beyond the context of this discussion. I think that, little by little, they'll find answers. Today, in order not to disperse our thoughts, I'll only refute certain essential points.

"Maître Pierre places in opposition to each other two states, which he presents as being absolute: *Heaven and Hell, good and evil, salvation and damnation*. That does not conform to reality."

Maître Pierre protested:

"You yourself, Maître Dominique, teach that in our world everything is plurality: every Quality, like every Power, is in conflict with its opposite."

"No, Maître Pierre, there are no contraries in nature. There are *opposites*, opposed like the two poles of the axis of a sphere, but not contrary. They are two complementary aspects that determine a relativity, which itself is the reality that cerebral intelligence cannot grasp.

"There is neither absolute good nor absolute evil. There is harmony alternating with disharmony. This alternation gives the illusion of definitive good or evil, when the reactional effect necessarily becomes the active cause of a new reaction. While being relative in the real world (except for the Absolute One, which contains all Possibilities), the new reaction will be more or less good or evil, according to whether it is in harmony or disharmony with the final goal of man.

"That's why it's unwise to posit Heaven and Hell as *eternal contraries*. There are subtle or crude gradations within these states, and Satan himself finds his redemption in Lucifer, who is his sublimation into Spiritual Light.

"But we'll have a chance to speak again of Good and Evil, which is too important to be treated superficially.

"Now is a good time to clarify the meaning of Hell and damnation. Hell is the *state opposed* to the Heavenly state, as punishment is opposed to recompense.

"In the French language, the Gospel speaks of Hell in the plural: Christ descended into the hells. This confirms the existence of different forms of separation from the divine state. One also speaks of the seven heavens, like seven states, which get closer and closer to the intrinsic Divinity, the Essential Light and Universal Consciousness, which is inconceivable for our intelligence.

"The word of Christ has confirmed the plurality of these celestial states: 'In my Father's house are many mansions.'[1] Likewise, the substance (immaterial) of each one of these infernal states is all the more crude, according to how close it gets to matter and, since we're dealing with our earth, the closer it gets to our earthly atmosphere.

"It's true, however, that the Spirit incarnates in all the products of nature. But this *involution*, which provokes the effort of Spirit to liberate itself and reascend 'to the right hand of God,' creates a continual state of *revolution*. This state is the continual struggle between opposing principles, which results in the production of phenomena that we, inhabitants of this dualized world, consider natural. No doubt they are natural in that they are the consequences of the functional activity of the universe but we are forgetting that matter's resistance to the liberation of the Spirit provokes discord, breakdowns, and accidental phenomena, which result from this resistance to the harmonious path toward perfection.

"And this is aggravated in human beings, whose cerebral consciousness multiplies the oppositions and the disharmonious gestures, as well as the disorder, injustices, wars, and other cataclysms that we blame on destiny."

"But isn't this succession of contingencies in our earthly existence already an infernal state?"

"That's correct, Thomas! And if you have become conscious of that, you can transpose the same state into the inferior spheres of the Invisible World which is closest to your own. You can catch a glimpse of the awful condition of beings (demons or disincarnate humans) who are playing the same game of rebellion and opposition to Divine Harmony because of the despair of not being able to participate in spiritual redemption."

"That's horrible," murmured Jean-Jacques. "But I want to understand the obstacle that prevents them."

"Regardless of what the particular resistances are," said Dominique, "it seems they can be summarized in this way: the desire *to exist*, the rejection of impersonality, the illusion of creating, and the pride in acting, knowing, and governing beings and things. And I suppose we could add to that the pleasure of destroying or annihilating what one does not possess. I say 'I suppose' because it seems obvious that human passions cannot help reflecting cosmic forces which have deviated from their harmonious objective and which, in this case, lead toward destruction what they should have led toward transmutation.

"However, a different phenomenon is produced in humans, whose ambition and uncontrolled desire for love or power are provoked by the feeling—which is *impotent because it is unconscious*—of the possibilities of a higher order which belongs to the suprahuman realm."

---

1. Moreover, this is suggested in the Catholic canonization of different degrees of sainthood.

"It's ignorance that makes this foreknowledge useless and impotent," said Jean-Jacques with a sigh.

"Not only our ignorance," retorted Thomas violently. "It's this condition of duality that leads us in the direction opposite to our final goal. I understand the rebellion of intelligent beings who have glimpsed the dead end of our infernal situation!"

Maître Pierre burst our laughing, but the severe expression on the sculptor's face made him stop.

Softly, Dominique answered Thomas:

"I'd agree with you, and would understand this revolt, if I didn't know the initiatory aspect of the role as it is devolved on our planet, despite the resulting difficulties for the inhabitants.

"This role is the apprenticeship of the 'conscious self.'"

"The myth of earthly Paradise is correct in that all beings who come into existence on this earth enter into a dualistic world.

"However, it's thanks to this duality that a being can *recognize himself.* This is the means of attaining the reunification of the divided consciousness, and the return to a conscious paradisiacal state."

"I wasn't expecting that," exclaimed Thomas.

"Think about it, Doctor," said Dominique. "For once I'm calling on your logic: all beings in dualized nature have (by the mere fact of their existence) an innate consciousness, but they cannot observe it. Man, who is at the summit of earthly beings, is the only one who possesses the power to mentally project this innate Consciousness outside of himself. This Consciousness becomes the mirror through which he can recognize himself. That's what the intellect does.

"This observation, because it is reflected, is dual, and makes one aware of one's consciousness: *self-consciousness* is the first step on the way toward the return to Unity.

"Consequently, dualization, which is the reason for our fall into mental illusions, also makes it possible for us to consciously reacquire the total consciousness of our anthropocosm."

"I'm astounded by this point of view," confessed Jean Thomas. "It makes our Earth both a gate to Hell for those who are unable to go beyond their mental condition, and the way toward a suprahuman state, which, I suppose, is no less definitive."

"Common sense and the law of Harmony show us that this state must be the beginning of a progressive participation in Light-Consciousness, the degrees of which must be made up of the various 'mansions in the Father's house.'

"In addition, if we understand Light as the spiritual plenitude that involves neither death nor shadow nor 'darkness,' we can, through contrasts, understand the evangelical term 'outer darkness,' in which all those beings who have not been able to free themselves from the dualized condition remain. These are the same beings who are unable to liberate themselves from the thirst for existence, which keeps them in a perpetual state of earthly incarnation."

"Can we assume that there are intermediary worlds, where the human being can perfect himself toward the suprahuman state, but in more favorable conditions than those we have on Earth?" asked Jean-Jacques.

"All the traditions affirm this," answered Dominique, "regardless of whether they're speaking in terms of more perfect stars, on which the more highly evolved man participates in the Knowledge of Cosmic Laws, or in accord with the statement of an authentic Veda: 'There are visible worlds where invisible beings live.'"

Jean-Jacques and Jean Thomas avidly drank in Dominique's words.

"Is it true, as Maître Pierre said, that the soul of man, which is immortal and divine, can be damned?" asked Thomas. "Can it be held forever in Hell?"

"That's impossible," answered Dominique. "Being virtually impersonal and spiritual, man's soul can neither do evil nor be punished or recompensed. But you must understand the meaning of the words. It is here that the comprehension of the immortal being of man becomes indispensable.

"The soul of which I have just spoken is our Spiritual Entity, which does not inhabit our mortal body unless it is attracted by the call of our Human Consciousness[2] and by the submission to its directives. This immortal soul *can never be lost*, but man is *in danger of losing it*, because it can become alienated from him, either temporarily or definitively, if the behavior of a man is opposed to his spiritual destiny.

"The universal and thus nonspecified aspect of this Soul-Entity is its Spiritual Witness. The other aspect, which carries the characteristics of its Number-entity and which is its Permanent Witness, can temporarily deviate from the goal of its incarnation through contamination by personal impulses and tendencies that belong to the intelligent automaton. If it is unable to remain independent from this influence, it finds itself faced with two possibilities after death: either it remains wrapped in the astral form of the dead person, which becomes its support until the things caused by his promiscuity are purified, or it definitively separates itself from them in order to look, with the Spiritual Witness, for another incarnation that will allow it to fulfill its human experience."

2. See Chapter 6.

"Then what survives a definitively abandoned man?" asked Jean-Jacques.

"His 'body of desires': his so-called astral form or phantom form, animated by Human Consciousness. It's the consciousness of his being that is the human Automaton, which maintains the impressions inscribed by its emotional experiences. Add to that the suffering of a being deprived of the Spiritual Presence that has abandoned him, and you will have an idea of the state of these poor residues of humanity referred to as 'larvae,' which are trying to regain contact with the human world to find a semblance of the pleasures that they can no longer satisfy."

Jean-Jacques, who was depressed by this last description, wanted to ask a final question:

"Can you tell me if this last case corresponds to definitive damnation?"

"I can't say, my friend, because no one can know what complications, be they purifications or degradations, can improve or aggravate the state of these poor larvae. What is possible is that they find themselves rehabilitated in a period that in India is called *Manvantara*, and, starting again from zero, they can begin a new destiny. This is the ultimate divine Mercy."

"No doubt it demands an enormous and incalculable amount of time," said Jean-Jacques.

"What is Time?" murmured Dominique.

Maître Pierre returned to his place beside the cauldron. Anguished bitterness tormented his face.

"I feel as if I'm suspended between my lower consciousness and my ignorance of the higher consciousness!" he said. "Lord, have pity on me!"

"That's the only thing to say, my friend," answered Dominique seriously. "Because your Lord is indeed the Mediator, who through the conjunction of what is Divine in humans can bring us back to the Father and initiate us into His Knowledge."

Thomas was the first to break the silence:

"I must confess, Maître Dominique, that I am disturbed about Maître Pierre's evocation of the world of spirits. In the past I would have treated this subject as superstition. Now it throws into confusion all of the teachings for which you have given us the basis."

"You're wise in asking a clarification of this thorny subject," answered Dominique. "Multiple theories have come out of it, owing to arbitrary interpretations that don't take into account the essential laws of the Genesis. Erudition, which consists in comparing various opinions and theological disputes, alienates the seeker from the *simplicity* of Divine Harmony. Man could find the counterparts of this Harmony in himself if he concentrated his efforts on acquiring the one necessary thing: *the continual attraction of Presence, which unites in us the Divine and the human.*

"Without the control of Presence, how do you expect to discern what is real from what your logic or your imagination suggests to you? Don't forget that you can never understand the beings of the Invisible World unless you understand the Cosmic state to which they correspond.

"Only Cosmic states that correspond to what exists in ourselves can become intelligible to us, and we have to become conscious of them.

"It all seems so simple! So obvious. . . ."

"In other words, it's useless to learn about them before we have known them within us," concluded Thomas bitterly.

"No, my friend. It's good to *know that which is not false*, in order to avoid the complications of getting involved in a search where you can only lose yourself.

"Moreover, whether you know it or not, you are in contact with positive forces and negative beings in the Invisible World. Because of this, I shall give you some clear notions that are absolutely necessary in terms of your behavior. It's up to you to believe and to profit from them.

"These essential notions are the following:

"I spoke to you about the disincarnate being whose Permanent Witness is still tied to it for the time necessary for its purification.

"It's deadly, and even criminal, to evoke those beings, to enter into relation with them, or to obtain messages from them. This contact with the earthly atmosphere can only soil them, prolong their suffering, and delay their liberation.

"Beneath them are those who are very inferior because they've been abandoned by their immortal being. They are the human larvae of which we've already spoken.[3] Their emotional animal consciousness gives them the ability to suffer, desire, and regret the emotional aspect of passion that they are unable to satisfy. Their inability to better their condition makes them aggressive and cunning in their attempt to regain contact with men. They delude men by taking the name and the appearance of known characters, or even of spiritual beings (in the form that man attributes to them). They have the ability to imitate and to reproduce themselves through mediums, voices, forms, and thoughts, since they are imprinted in the astral substance.

"These human larvae, having lost their immortal being, are often called 'elementary terrestrials.' You musn't confuse them with psychic embryos (or 'antitypes') of human beings who are waiting for their first birth on Earth and who are unable to make themselves visible to us.

"The class of spirits called elemental, which give life to Fire, Air,

3. See page 182.

Water, and Earth, are different as well. Each one of these four elements, which we need to live, shelters elementals of its own nature. Mythology has represented them according to their essential characteristics.

"This class of spirits never incarnates in the human race. However, our psychic existence is conditioned by the degree of their elementary qualities."

"I never would have thought that the four fundamental elements could have been the source of such widespread and mysterious literature. Through an excess of symbols, we have lost the notion of their reality!" said Jean-Jacques.

"Each of these four elements can be considered under three aspects," said Dominique:

"One, their *fundamental* aspect, which comes immediately from the original Trinity. These are the pure principles of *essential quality*: Hot, Cold, Dry, Humid.

"Two, their *substantial* aspect (not yet materialized), which results from the four-way combination of the four essential qualities.

Fire = Hot-Dry	Water = Cold-Humid
Air = Hot-Humid	Earth = Cold-Dry

"Three, their inferior aspect is the material manifestation of the second aspect and results in the four elements that characterize the state of matter. Each of their essential principles is a power in itelf which we can only know through synthesis."

"By synthesis, do you mean the combination of their four natures?" asked Jean Thomas.

"That's right," said Dominique. "None of our four elements is absolute, because each contains, to a lesser degree, the nature of the other three. It's this synthesis that makes for their materiality.

"However, the elemental spirits that give life to their material aspects are, in each case, the Functional Consciousness of each one of our organs. Just as our organs are able to defend themselves or to compensate for themselves, so does the elemental of each element act and react in its own substance in a way that would indicate a rudimentary intelligence.

"But we can't be deceived by this appearance. The possibility of their voluntary manifestation *doesn't exist*. Whether we're talking about apparently intelligent gestures (such as lightning) or the appearance of gnomes, mermaids, or hobgoblins and the like, there are mental projections—conscious or unconscious—which activate these elementals or clothe them in the forms that our human imagination evokes."

"How can we have such powers of mental projection?" asked Thomas.

"You're still forgetting that man, being the summary of the Universe, has in him the innate Consciousness of the states and kingdoms that preceded him. By awakening this consciousness, and concentrating our attention on it, it's possible to act on these states with our thought, or to project onto them the form that we imagine.

"Also realize that these same elementals, in their various apparitions, such as seances, obey the suggestion or the imagination (which is sometimes unconscious) of the mediums or the believers, and produce visible or tangible phenomena for which they are not responsible."

"Is this also true of the electrical energy that we use in so many ways?" suggested Thomas.

"That's right," answered the sculptor, "but there is a difference. Our will and imagination replace the appliances and the wires.

"You must realize that human beings are not the only ones to have this power over elementals. Invisible beings use it as well, according to their intelligence. For example, human larvae or certain diabolical spirits."

Thomas shrugged and looked worried.

"You're putting my materialism to a hard test, Maître Dominique! But you must realize that my skepticism is solidly based because of the trickeries of charlatanism and the foolishness of superstition. How can one discern potential realities in all this phantasmagoria?"

"By forgetting images and starting with things that are accessible to your reason," answered Dominique.

"I realize that Maître Pierre has chosen the opposite method. The test is conclusive: erudition based on the imagination and on terminology that ignores symbolic value can furnish knowledge, but it throws intuition off the track. However, it's the intuitive faculty that allows us to distinguish imaginative illusion from reality.

"The principal obstacle is the confusion created by false erudition.

"If we're talking about beings who constitute the Invisible World (invisible to our present visual faculties), your inability to meditate prevents you from conceiving their reality without unconsciously comparing them to earthly beings that surround you.

"To avoid this fundamental error, it would be wise to start by replacing the notion of *beings* with the notions of *states*. This term would allow you to lean on the positive reality that you know."

Dominique looked at Thomas, who was listening with full attention. Dominique continued:

"The most comprehensive meaning of the word *state* deals with states of matter: solids, liquids, and gases—terms that distinguish the qualities inherent in each one. We can also cite qualities that are more subtle than gaseous states, such as states of energy and light.

"The progression of subtlety can engender powerful properties that are unknown to science because they attain a spiritual state that the scientist's investigations are unable to penetrate. Whether we call this state the Spiritual World, the world of the soul or of living consciousness, or give it the names of angels, gods, or heavens, it will still be the various states of being that emanate from the Absolute Spirit."

"Is it true that each of these states can only be defined by its Qualities?" asked the pilot.

"Yes," agreed Dominique. "But we must conclude that we define Quality by the effects we attribute to it."

"Alas! We always seem to wind up back on Earth," said Jean-Jacques. "I guess we're obliged to if we want to use our reason to grasp notions that go far beyond it."

"If we come back to where we started (states of matter), we regain contact with the four elements," said Thomas; "and in order to rise to the summit by following this thread, we must consider their spirits or elementals, which we can only define in terms of their Qualities. . . . I think I've understood, Dominique: everything fits if I base all of the states on the notion of *Quality*!"

Dominique congratulated Thomas:

"That's fine, my friend, but you must be precise. The Quality of Consciousness of these elementals is extremely rudimentary in relationship to all the 'states,' or spirits of the Invisible World.

"Your materialism makes it all the more difficult for you to accept the idea of Celestial Hierarchies and diabolical powers. Let's put these images aside for a moment and look at the subject in metaphysical terms.

"If we consider Spirit-Activity, we'll say that it can only be the *Cause* because it contains in itself its own Resistance.

"This Resistance will react as long as it has not incarnated (absorbed) the Activity of the Cause. If it is unable to do this, it will substitute *opposition* between Causal Activity and *Resistant* Reaction. This opposition to the Cause is called Evil, and religious myth calls it the Fall.

"However, if the Causal Activity is absorbed by Resistance, there will be no more *opposing* Reaction. Therefore, there will be no Evil.

"If Resistance is able to react in the direction of Causal Activity, *it will be salvation*."

Dominique fell silent, and then continued:

"According to wisdom, those are the measures of Becoming and of the movement toward Return.

"And if we return to myth, we understand why Lucifer is the salvation of Satan."

"Please continue," Thomas begged timidly when the sculptor stopped to relight his pipe.

"I will, but don't get angry, Doctor, if in order to continue, I must return to images.

"In speaking of Harmony or Disharmony you will understand that it's a matter of Reaction to the Action of the Spirit, according to whether it is in *conformity with* or in *opposition to* it. This will provide you with the basis of seeing the real meaning of celestial or infernal states.

"Let's say that what is true for the four elements is necessarily true for the spirits that are part of the Hierarchy of Powers, and consequently, 'as above, so below' for the spirits of infernal states.

"If the three aspects of the four elements are differentiated by their degree of subtlety and integrity in terms of Quality, it will also be the degree of sublimity and integrity of the spirit that will differentiate the nine Powers of the Celestial Hierarchy.

"If we're speaking of crude consciousness in terms of the spirits of the elements, we will be speaking about the Intelligence (or Consciousness) of the Laws of Harmony for the Superior Powers, which are the forces that govern the cosmos. We can call them Seraphim, Cherubim, Thrones, Dominions, or whatever you please, but that will add nothing to your knowledge of these realities if you have not been able to awaken them in your Consciousness.

"What more could you do, my friends?"

"And what more could we hope for, Maître Dominique?" added Jean-Jacques, emotionally following his inner vision.

"I could leave you in peace with this evocation," continued Dominique. "But you still must be wary of the reaction of alternation, which would make you fall back into the traps of complexity, even more so, now that you have touched upon certain truths. If I let you go now, you'll come back one of these days to ask me about demons or about the 'reality' of the entities which have 'revealed' to you, through a moving table or a clairvoyant medium, the secret of your past lives or a message from a loved one, or the means of attaining so-called initiation!

"The first way of eliminating all errors on the subject is to clarify your thinking about demons.

"In French, the word *demon* is synonymous with the devil and satanic force. In my opinion, it does more harm than good to discuss the various theological and occult opinions about the nature and diversity of demons.

"If we go back to our metaphysical principle and consider the various orders of Celestial Powers as the harmonious development of Causal Action, we shall understand that they are classed in terms of how they emanate from the One, from the strongest and most direct to the least subtle and closest to earthly Nature. The angelic spirits are closest to earthly Nature. Because of this proximity, they are the immediate intermediaries between humanity and the Celestial and Divine Worlds.

"Then, we can also understand states of 'opposition,' or infernal states, which are part of Disharmony because their resistance *reacts in opposi-tion to* the Causal Action of the Spirit. This is characteristic of the demons whose prototypes were named Satan by biblical theology.

"What are commonly called 'demons' relate to the forces of opposition which are the closest to us. They describe the tendencies in us that prevent spiritual realization. These tendencies are the personalization of the same tendencies in dualistic Nature: the tendency to perpetuate form and appearances, the tendency toward multiplicity, toward disorder in individual will, toward violence, toward possessiveness, et cetera.

"What links us to them are the tendencies that we have not been able to transcend. It's important to understand this, because the fact that we tolerate this consciously makes us solidly responsible: if we feel hatred, for example, it aggravates the power of hate that influences the human collectivity.

"In this way you can understand, without phantasmagoria, our rela-tionship to the 'demons' (or the forces of opposition) that are the closest to us. The less subtle their nature, the closer they are to our nature, and the easier it is for them to immerse themselves in our psychic impulses. Because they cannot incarnate as human entities, they act on our emo-tional states and on our inferior mind, which their own state allows them to participate in.

"The power that they gain in this way is a kind of compensation for these lost spiritual powers. In order to accumulate power, they gladly abet the weaknesses of humans so as to make us the companions of their misfortune after our death.

"Their power over men is explained through their capacity for cunning, illusion, and subterfuge, which allows them (by using the elementals) to produce apparitions and other miraculous phenomena. They can even usurp the names and popular images of certain spiritual entities to delude believers with false teachings or predictions."

"Do you attribute the spirit messages and materializations to these imposters?"

"Those are the greatest dangers," answered Dominique. "I cannot emphasize enough the banefulness of evocations and messages from the 'beyond,' especially when people participate in these things in good faith. From the *physical* point of view, astral influence (even with spiritual pretentions) has disastrous effects on the solar plexus, the blood, and the spleen, because it exposes them to a dangerous necrosis which could become cancerous.

"From the *psychic* point of view, their relationship to beings of the astral world gives them power over the humans who attract them. This power continues even after earthly existence.

"From the spiritual point of view, the *greatest mistake* of mediumistic seances is the attempt to make contact with disincarnate beings. Luckily, most of the results obtained are due to shameful trickery. However, if one unfortunately obtains a genuine evocation of a dead person whose Permanent Witness is not yet liberated from earthly attraction, the fact of calling him back into our atmosphere causes him useless suffering, and contaminations that hold back his liberation."

"Can spiritual entities also manifest themselves in these evocations?" asked the pilot.

"Your common sense should be able to answer that for you, my friend. Besides the disincarnate beings that it is criminal to evoke, think about what categories of spirits are used in the usual mediumistic seances:

"On the one hand, the poor human larvae who produce illusory manifestations or personifications; on the other hand, the diabolical spirits who are agents of miraculous phenomena.

"How in the world can a spiritual entity be attracted into such an unhealthy milieu of phantasms, and manifest itself in a psychic atmosphere that is incompatible with its own spiritual state? Moreover, what criteria would the people present have for discerning the reality of its message from the lies of the spirits of falsehood?"

Thomas, visibly impressed, interrupted Dominique:

"These bleak perspectives unnerve my skepticism, which I thought was invulnerable," he said. "Your earlier explanations gave me a reassuring impression of reality. But I confess that I'm surprised to feel myself troubled by a subject I have always treated as superstition."

Dominique listened to Thomas with an understanding smile.

"I am happy for you," he said. "This proves that your intuition 'heard' what I was trying to transmit to you.

"The feeling you speak of has its purpose, for your new comprehension puts you face to face with a danger that could compromise your intuitive awakening, if you misunderstood its importance.

"Do not forget that credulity doesn't mean recognizing a danger that really exists. It means putting confidence in deceptive communications with a world that can only *ape* spiritual realities.

"Never forget that no contact is possible between the spiritual state and the imaginative and mental astral state. The only way you can communicate with a cosmic state is through its corresponding state in yourself. You can only penetrate the spiritual world with your consciousness of the spiritual, and to get there *you must liberate yourself from all astral and mental interferences.*

"Remember the old saying 'Birds of a feather flock together.' I would add to this astute saying that we attract only the forces or qualities that correspond to something we have in ourselves.

"It's not necessary to know the names of the spiritual or diabolical powers, but we should know the essential law that governs our relationship to them and their power over humans.

"If this *simple* concept is not enough for you, it's up to you to satisfy your mental curiosity by consulting the numerous occult or theological manuals, but—"

"But it's certain that we'd have much to lose and nothing to gain from it!" interrupted Jean-Jacques. "It seems to me that if we meditate on this discussion, we'll be able to discern the 'one necessary thing.'"

Maître Pierre was crouching in front of his cauldron. He seemed deep in reflection.

Jean-Jacques and Jean Thomas lit up cigarettes, hoping for a conclusion to the discussions of the evening.

Dominique watched them, listening in himself to the reactions of each of them.

"My friends," he said, "I allowed Maître Pierre to compose this inoffensive and childish decor because I wanted to intervene in the debate that would ensue from it.

"Dogmatic dialectics is a cerebral sport that produces more experts in the world of opposition than in the Divine World! It's normal for Pierre du Coignet to enjoy this, because he's in his element.

"However, when he spoke on behalf of his other patron, we could have hoped to hear another voice: that of the spiritual pole, which has the power to absorb opposition if it possesses the key to the words of Truth. This key opens the lock of all the traditions, without argument or subterfuge.

"Instead, we heard sterile formulas, whose major argument is eternal damnation for 'guilty souls': souls 'in the image of God'!

"Where is the key to truth, Maître Pierre?"

Maître Pierre replied timidly:

"There isn't *one* key, but *two*, Maître Dominique."

"Obviously: one key opens and the other closes. Opening and closing refer only to that which has a dual aspect, hence to what is part of Nature. But to claim that this power can also be applied to Divinity would be to affirm two eternities: one heavenly and the other infernal. However, this would still be acceptable if we understood that the 'end of the world' as the beginning of another one. If this is the case, there is more than one life: the existence of any one being is *multiple*."

"Then the world is cyclical, and that could last forever," said Maître Pierre.

"Yes," answered Dominique. "But only until it's reabsorbed by that which caused damnation."

A profound sigh was Maître Pierre's only response.
The silence continued. . . .

Dominique suddenly stood up. He put down his pipe and threw some incense into the coals.

Standing with his arms crossed, and measuring his words, he said:

"What I have just said was a response to the conflict in which Maître Pierre is caught.

"Jean Thomas and Jean-Jacques, I invite you to abandon this conflict with me; for there is only a conflict if we accept the dualistic position between the concept of what is Real in ourselves and the consideration of an illusory World evoked by hypothetical knowledge and our imagination.

"Our long discussion on the Celestial Powers and the Infernal Powers is nothing new. Each time a ray of Light has tried to enlighten humanity about the states that go beyond human intelligence, man has tried to explain the inexplicable in multiple ways. The conflict is born of this confusion.

"I reject confusion, and I refuse the conflict that pits error against truth!

"One cannot change error into truth, but one can reject the erroneous means of conceiving Reality. The error lies in wanting to use the mind and imagination to explain states that are inaccessible to them.

"The forces that are opposed to cosmic Harmony are the result of this dualization, and are therefore part of the inherent 'movements' of all that is generated. Their disharmonious aspect is relative and temporary. But when we speak of these unhealthy forces, we are admitting that there is a world that is not our world. We give these forces importance by allowing them to act on us in the same way that we imagine that we can act ourselves.

"However, there aren't many Worlds: there is a Unity from which emanates (in a descending hierarchy) the Principles of everything that 'becomes' through successive generations.

"What does the Fall mean to me, when I can, through Consciousness, rise directly toward the Cause?

"The obstacle to overcome is mental complexity. The brain is only a reflector, and because of this, it dualizes what is actually singular. This provokes us to project outside of ourselves the sentiments, the notions, and the activities which are within us. And this projection makes us imagine a so-called occult world, which is only real insofar as we are unable to master this inferior mind.

"But if, through meditation (regardless of the process), we are able to eliminate this mental illusion, all of these diabolical worlds, this infernal world, this world that is crawling around us, will evaporate like smoke, because it's all a mere illusion *for those who can situate themselves in immutable Reality.*"

Thomas, profoundly moved, interrupted his Master:

"What you have just said is a total reversal of the common mentality, and seems to render your former explanation null and void."

"You've understood me, Thomas: *I'm renouncing mental curiosity to 'know' through the certitude of the heart.*

"Aside from certain metaphysical principles,[4] this dissertation was only a general weaning out of certain fundamental errors."

"A very necessary weaning out," insisted Jean-Jacques.

"No doubt, dear friend, but I'm demanding even more: I want the direct way through simplicity. Weren't you struck by the insistence of the teachings of the Gospel (like that of the sage Lao-tse) on the essential conditions for entering into the Divine Kingdom: 'submission to the will of the Father' and 'childlike simplicity'?

"If you look at these two precepts 'in Spirit and in Truth,' you will see that the latter is what should be applied first. Get rid of the habits that vulgarize these two words. Replace the word *Father* with the idea of Divine Harmony, and you will be able to translate the expression 'submission to the will of the Father' into 'nonwill.' In other words: non-opposition to Destiny which obeys Harmony, and even *nonopposition to all activity directed against you*, regardless of whether it's intellectual, emotional, or physical; because all action engenders a reaction, and it's your opposition to aggressive activity that gives birth to conflict."

"Aren't conflicts the experiences that enlighten our consciousness?" asked Jean-Jacques.

"What you're speaking of is the long path of suffering," Dominique answered gravely. "It's the misuse of the Mind."

"This Mind, which earthly man is saddled with, is an evil gift when it's used to analyze and to divide. This is the error of our times. The Mind must become the instrument of our liberation because Consciousness, acquired through the reflection of the Mind, is the recognition of what is Real in relationship to what is illusion.

"Recognizing this is therefore the means of conceiving the possibility of Redemption."

Jean-Jacques looked at his friend.

"It seems to me," Thomas concluded, "that our Master has just pointed the way to serenity. . . ."

4. See page 187.

13

Remorse

"Which one is the chimera? Which one is the reality? murmured Jean Thomas as he contemplated the silhouette of Maître Pierre and that of a horned devil. Both leaned side by side against the balustrade of one of the towers of Notre Dame. Their somber forms, profiled against the pink sky of the setting sun, looked like the double image of a timid human being with his disturbing phantom.

Jean Thomas approached.

"Excuse me for interrupting this tête-à-tête," he said, taking Maître Pierre's arm. "The extent to which you brought these chimeras to life for me makes me feel that I'm on familiar ground. But don't you think it's time to come back down?"

Maître Pierre mocked his companion by winking.

"What's your hurry? I thought you weren't at all uncomfortable in this intermediary world suspended between the dizzying solitude of the Upper World and the heavy multitude of the Lower World. The day that is ending awakens the owl and peoples this tower with phantoms of stone. You're shivering, Thomas, and I don't think you would like to spend the night here. Don't protest: it's the instinctive fear of confronting powers over which one has no control."

"You're making fun of me, Maître Pierre. I'm not a chicken."

"I'm not making fun of you: I'm trying to light the lantern to show you the corners of your hidden depths. Fear? A brave man recognizes his fear. We have numerous subterfuges to camouflage it—prudence, swagger, boldness, boastfulness—but it's still always fear, fear of the unknown, fear of shadows from the past, anxiety about the future, fear of being

surprised by one's own inferiority. Believe me, fear is as responsible for
heroic gestures as it is for foolish acts. One throws oneself into dangers
imagined by fear because anxiety creates fear, and fear creates danger."

"That's not true in my case, Maître Pierre."

"Come on! The truth is that you're afraid of discovering what is hidden
in your own depths. Lean heavily against this balustrade and look down,
as if you were attracted by the precipice. Try to experience the horror of
the fall as if you were tempted by this suggestion. . . . Be curious, damm
it! Measure the distance you would fall into the emptiness . . . imagine
it! Imagine it!"

"It's not hard to do that," brooded Thomas as he stood up, nauseated.
"As soon as I jumped, I would crash! I'd knock my brains out."

"As you say, materialist! And I'm saying that your emotional consciousness would survive long after your brain, and would make you pay, poor
phantom, for the anguish of the tragic instant that you would never be
able to erase! Ah, you don't like this phantom, do you? It's all very
amusing how men think that they can eliminate it by a shrug of the
shoulders!"

Thomas backed up. He was in a bad mood. Maître Pierre came over and
stood next to him against the wall of the tower.

The darkness was thickening.

All of a sudden, at the opposite end of the balustrade, a somber
silhouette approached, leaned over, and seemed to measure the depth of
emptiness. Its equivocal movements and halting breath, rendered louder
by the surrounding silence, awakened the suspicion of the two unseen
spectators. In tacit agreement they made their way along the wall on
tiptoe. Suddenly, with a rapid movement, the man stepped over the edge
of the balustrade. Maître Pierre got there just in time to catch the man's
pants leg. The man screamed and fought to finish his act, but Thomas,
getting a good grip on him, pulled him back to the edge of the stone. The
desperate man was forcefully pulled back and landed on his two feet
before the two friends, and he allowed himself to be brought back to the
wall. Held fast so that he could not fight, the unknown man looked with
astonishment at his two unexpected saviors.

Maître Pierre's mocking voice disconcerted him even more:

"What kind of acrobatics were you performing? It's a bad time to be
exhibiting oneself! The next time you should put up a poster; two
spectators isn't nearly enough!"

"Leave me alone. It's none of your business!" cried the man. "You
won't keep me from committing suicide, if it's my destiny!"

"Your destiny, my good man, agrees with ours, since it brought us here
to witness your exploits! Besides, it's too late tonight: the spectacle is

over. Let's go down and have something to eat. You can relax and have a beer with us!"

"Get out of my life! You'd be doing me a great favor. You don't have the right to get involved. Do you know what hopeless despair is?"

Maître Pierre held him by force against the wall. Then, on the pretext of lighting a cigarette, he tried to make out the man's face: it was intelligent and anguished. Thomas, who was still firmly holding his wrists, felt his uneven pulse.

Maître Pierre tried to uncover some of the man's secrets:

"Let's look at the reason for this despair. Did you go bankrupt? Are you broke? Are you ruined?"

"I would never kill myself over a question of money."

"Problems of the heart, then? Are you heartbroken?"

"Absolutely not. That would never be a sufficient reason!"

"Well, you've got good sense, dear sir. My old friend Saint Cyprian knew what he was talking about when he said: 'Women lead you into Hell through the door of Heaven.' Speaking of Hell and Paradise, does that mean anything to you?"

The man rebelled:

"You're not a priest, are you? And it's none of your business. I certainly wouldn't go to you if I were going to confess."

Embarrassed, he tried to apologize:

"Excuse me for being rude," he murmured, "but failing like this is even more cruel than succeeding in the act. Everything would be over with now. . . ."

"No, it's then that everything would begin. Because remorse remains on the other side."

The man blushed.

"Remorse! Remorse! How do you know?"

Thomas, extremely embarrassed, looked for an argument to convince the man he was holding captive. He had a brilliant idea:

"In any event, we've got to go back down," he said. "If you commit suicide here, we will be accused of murder. Do you want to expose us to that?"

"That's right," confirmed Maître Pierre. "The sacristan, who knows me, saw us come up here."

While Thomas took the man's arm, Pierre led them toward the stairway. When they got to the first step, he turned around to the desperate man:

"It's useless to try anything. My friend is a black belt in judo, and I am a real live devil. If it's him you're looking for, there's no need to go any farther. What can I do for you?"

"Stop joking, Maître Pierre!" cried Thomas as he carefully descended the stairs.

"He's right to jeer," mumbled the unknown man. "Existence isn't worth any more than that. It's a stupid drama in which the actor doesn't even know the cause or the outcome. We go toward our 'little happiness,' each for his own profit. We become criminals to defend our life: necessity dictates—how can it be any other way? Where is the goal? What is our reason for living? We juggle with words, we are blinded by scientific progress. . . . Go! Defend yourself! It's survival of the fittest! We're thrown into the scuffle like meat for the hounds, and too bad for the poor animal who falls into their teeth! Great, isn't it? Everybody's grabbing to be there at the finish with all the fanfare! How great it would be to nab it! What a triumph for the hunters! What hunter would dare feel remorse at the sight of the silent tears of the poor captured stag? . . . One limits awareness to externals."

A sob of emotion cut short his speech, then turned into sarcastic laughter.

At the bottom of the steps the three men looked at each other, hesitant and embarrassed. But Pierre had understood. He signaled energetically for Thomas to sit their prisoner down until he returned. He left rapidly to find a cab.

Despite his resistance, the desperate man got into the cab and sat between the two friends.

"Where are you taking me? There's no point in my going with you. Sooner or later I'm going to manage to get away from you."

"All right, all right," said Maître Pierre. "If you still insist on jumping, I've got a seventh floor to offer you, with some Rhine wine to put a little of the devil into you. The least you can do is accept a glass of friendship. Here we are."

Solidly surrounded, the man arrived at the entrance to the Atelier. Surprised, Dominique let them in. Maître Pierre introduced the sculptor and Dr. Thomas, then looked at the unknown man, who said nothing. He hesitated an instant and then relented.

"Marcelin Faux-Larron," he mumbled. "You can spell it however you want."

Dominique didn't move. With a penetrating look, he scrutinized the traits of the visitor, whose fearful attitude was not in keeping with his powerful maturity. He held out his hand, and waited for an explanation . . . which didn't come.

"Dear Thomas," said Dominique, "would you please do the honors in the Tavern? We'll join you in just a moment."

With a few words, Pierre filled Dominique in on the situation.

"I'll let you handle it," he finished. "He needs to confess, and I think your arguments are better than mine. I shall be the cupbearer."

Dominique nodded with an air of doubtfulness.

"Let's try," he said with a sigh. "As for you, old boy, just drink and keep quiet! Listen, Pierre," he added, "turn down the lights and put on the record to *Parsifal*."

Dominique stood there alone, lit his pipe, and went into worried meditation.

When he entered the Tavern, the three men were sitting there silently, smoking and drinking an old wine. Dominique sat down next to the guest. The man tried in vain to suppress his emotion. Tears were streaming down his face.

"Which is better," asked Dominique, "the gold of this Rhine wine, or the Harmonies of the Grail?"

"What's a Grail?" murmured the guest.

"The blood of the vine is the Grail," answered the sculptor, "but what do men know of it?"

"And you, what do you know of it?"

"I know of it what the bees know when they gather the pollen to extract the essence. What more could one desire from existence? To allow the essence of each creature to express itself!"

"Beautiful literary image! Have you tried it on humans?"

"It's my turn to ask a question: what do you know about man?" retorted Dominique, offering him a cigarette.

"I know his tricks and the chains that excuse them: egoism, desire for profit, or (what is even worse) condescending charity. Our society is a prison camp where men are chained to each other without hope of ever breaking their chains except at the expense of their companions in infamy . . . for it *is* infamy, regardless of what you think. This society is organized around the power of money, so that the artisan must sacrifice quality for mediocrity in order to survive; the teacher and the doctor are persecuted in their priesthood by egalitarian standards; the clerk, the businessman, and the politician are subjected to the pressing temptation to augment their livelihood with illegal profits."

"Alas!" said Dominique. "I cannot contradict you. But on a ship in danger of sinking, what is the proper behavior for men who are worthy of this name? Obviously, you will answer: 'Save those who can be saved.'"

"You're so right, dear sir, that you've just passed my sentence."

"We'll see about that," answered Dominique. "Do you know the story of the sinking of the *Titanic*? Split apart by icebergs, the ship was condemned. Then the orchestra, in accord with the ship's commander, played with a moving calm: 'Nearer, My God, to Thee!'"

"How many of those passengers, until that night, had ever worried about anything except their pleasure, or their more or less shady business dealings, or their keenly egotistical ambitions? Yet a certain calm came over all of those people, most of whom were going to die: 'What was worth saving' suddenly became tangible in the face of the inevitable. For those who accepted the serenity, it was the reunion of that in them which would survive and the intangible entity that their mortal bodies separated them from. . . ."

The man held his head in his hands, reflecting.

"Listen to me, sir," continued Dominique. "I am neither priest nor minister, nor religious fanatic, but I have good reason to believe in the continuity of life beyond our bodily existence. Even more, I believe in the perpetuity of my consciousness in the Beyond, where the greatest disbeliever among the materialists will have the unpleasant surprise, after death, of realizing his error and rediscovering his remorse. I believe in the repercussion of my actions in a measure and a duration that do not depend on the judgment of men, but *on the reaction of my own conscience*, which can lessen their effects.

"If I'm not mistaken, you are just about in the same situation as those people who were shipwrecked. There is one major difference: they were leaving the Earth at the time marked by their destiny, while you are taking the responsibility for breaking the thread of your destiny. It's an act of free will in the bad sense of the word. That's to say in the negative or opposing sense of the word.

"It's an act of rebellion that the cerebral will takes as its right, owing to ignorance of its relationship to your immortal being.

"True free will is the free impulse of our *knowing consciousness*, which submits our cerebral will to its judgments and decisions. However, these decisions, necessarily wise because they are taken *with full knowledge of the cause*, are able to rectify the deadly consequences of an evil act. Tell me, if you can, how your rational intelligence, limited to your cerebral faculties could direct your decisions 'with full knowledge of the cause': is it able to perceive the deeper motives and subtle influences that determine your actions? Is it able to foresee the repercussions for you and for others?"

The two men looked at each other like two opponents who were sizing up each other's weapons.

"Excuse me, sir," said the unknown man, "but the arguments that you're using to convince me are so new to me that I'm unable to answer you. If there is some truth to what you say, give me some time to get used to it."

"I'm at your disposal, dear sir, but I can assure you that my arguments are not just words of consolation. Nor are they personal hypotheses: *I know the vital laws on which my affirmations are based.*

"But I respect the freedom of others too much to intervene in a drama whose cause is unknown to me. However, the confession of your ignorance authorizes me to ask you a question: *sincerely*, do you still regret the intervention of my friends?"

The man's anguished face betrayed his indecision.

"I don't know," he said finally. "All I can say is that you have cast a doubt on the advisability of the act that I was going to commit. But as far as renouncing it . . ."

At a glance from Dominique, Pierre and Thomas retired to the Atelier. The sculptor respected the prostrate man's silence. With an abrupt movement the man rose and looked Dominique straight in the face.

"Where does this authority that emanates from you come from?" he demanded.

"Let us use the word *certitude* instead of authority. You could also say understanding of the human drama, and the understanding is certain if it is fruit of personal experience."

"Have you ever had the experience of despair, Monsieur Dominique? The experience of absolutely relentless remorse?"

"There is no such thing as absolutely relentless remorse; and I pity the man who has never experienced remorse.

"But this discussion is useless, because I am a stranger to you and I know nothing of you. You must also understand that I'm not trying to impose any conviction on you. You came to me by accident (which no doubt is your destiny). I welcome you as I would welcome a poor man who would die of hunger if he didn't get food. It's not for me to judge the cause of his undoing. I give him what I have, because he is a man like me. Neither would I judge him if he responds, as a beggar did one day, by throwing away the soup that had been offered to him, because it would have spoiled his absinthe!

"The bitterness of your absinthe has inebriated you with a kind of sadistic madness from which you are afraid of awakening. I would understand . . . if the awakening was not inevitable . . . but the awakening of a man who would commit suicide is a *despair without remedy*!"

"That's not the opinion of the Japanese, for whom hara-kiri is a sacred duty."

"That's something different," answered Dominique. "First of all, the Japanese believe in reincarnation. Hara-kiri is a noble and justified goal: to serve his lord and country in expiating a fault, a man can then reincarnate to wipe away the consequences. Sometimes he also practices hara-kiri out of loyalty to his dead leader in order to accompany him to another life. Those are conscious and courageous gestures.

"Moreover, this man accepts *with full knowledge of the cause* the responsibility for the consequences of his act. The relations that he had with his spiritual being during his lifetime will allow him to reincarnate in favorable conditions.

"Admit, dear sir, that the comparison with hara-kiri is rather humiliating for people who commit suicide in ignorance, who take their lives through cowardice in order to escape suffering which they deem intolerable. It's the idiotic gesture of a fool who throws himself into the water in order not to get wet."

"If you're right, the foolishness of the person who commits suicide can be excused by his ignorance."

"Will ignorance prevent this person from waking up? If you're not a coward, it would be good for you to meditate on the despair that would follow this awakening. You had better strengthen your spirit, for there is no way whatsoever of escaping it. Perhaps now you have become accustomed to despair, and this would be a reason to go find it again 'on the other side': if that's the case, dear sir, I won't prevent you. . . ."

With clenched teeth and a defiant look on his face, the man suddenly stood up. Dominique didn't budge. Very pale and trembling, the unhappy man started to leave . . . then returned to the sculptor.

"No doubt you're right," he said. "There is cowardice in my attitude: the fear of suffering and the fear of losing the courage to do away with myself. I owe you an explanation."

Dominique asked him to sit down and refilled his mug.

"First my real name: it's Folaron. I'm going to be fifty years old. I'm a widower with no children. I was at the head of a financial group that underwrites numerous enterprises with different interests. One of them was run by one of my friends, also a widower but with two young children. My own interests lay in a company that was his competitor. One day I had the opportunity to make a bold move that would give my company an absolute monopoly, by putting my competitor into an impossible situation. It would be an unhoped-for fortune for me. For my friend it meant ruin, and the impossibility of honoring his recent contracts and commitments. My only excuse is that I wasn't aware of his debts. Had I been aware of them, I wonder whether I still could have resisted the temptation of this enormous wealth. It would have allowed me to realize certain political ambitions. Today I see the ruthlessness of my egotistical will, and I doubt . . .

"But it's a moot question. The evil has already been accomplished. My friend, who was already beside himself from the death of his wife, went off the deep end and committed suicide."

"Went off the deep end," murmured Dominique. "I'm glad to hear you say that."

"You mustn't confuse my circumstances with his. The despair of a man who has lost his entire means of livelihood and his business reputation is different from the despair caused by the remorse of my heinous crime."

"But didn't you have a duty to fulfill: his children?"

"I provided for their livelihood, but how could I stifle the remorse of an act that no human tribunal will accuse me of?"

"You're evading the question," retorted Dominique. "Do you consider suicide an effective atonement?"

"I consider it an act of equitable justice," answered Folaron: "suicide for suicide, an eye for an eye, a tooth for a tooth."

"The penalty of retaliation is a savage way to pay a debt, for the thirst for vengeance is an impulse of the human animal, and its quenching has two bad effects: first, it engenders hatred and becomes the cause of new acts of violence, because hatred attracts hatred and violence engenders violence. Moreover, it submits the revenger to the inevitability of passionate reactions, which prevent him from going beyond his human animal."

"My case is different," said Folaron, "because it is I who am applying this law of retaliation to myself."

"Then let me pose this problem to you: either you believe in the survival of the soul or you deny it. In the latter case you admit that neither you nor your victim will benefit from the sacrifice. On the contrary, you will only deepen your debt toward your victim by shunning the responsibility that his suicide imposes on you, because you could find a way of minimizing the moral and social damage caused to the orphans by the suicide of their father.

"If, however, you admit the survival of your consciousness, you must also admit the survival of your remorse, with the horrible perspective of never being able to make amends."

Folaron listened intently in silence. He was visibly upset. Little by little his features relaxed. His haggard expression gave way to profound reflection. Dominique respected the struggle that was going on within him.

After a long silence, Folaron could finally express himself with some lucidity:

"I must admit that your arguments have seriously upset me. The least I can do is to thank you for putting up with my brutality," he said. Then, after hesitating, he added: "I think I also must thank the men who saved me."

Dominique smiled.

"Maître Pierre has disappeared," he said, "but I can call the doctor."

Dominique motioned for Thomas to return to the Tavern. Thomas came in and shook the hand that Folaron extended to him, but he evaded his thanks and began to smoke in silence.

"If you have any questions to ask me," said Dominique to Folaron, "you can speak in front of him. His materialism is sufficiently . . . evolved for him not to be scared off by a case of conscience."

"Let's say that he's on the way to being tamed," retorted Thomas, laughing. "In any case, dear sir, here we are, on common ground. My skepticism and my materialism are of a scientific kind. That is, my tendency is always to look for proofs and rational arguments. But I must admit that recent experiences have proved to me the superiority of intuition over reason, and have awakened me to the presence within myself of a being who is more subtle than my mortal self. This is the frontier of my present belief, and I am still surprised by my most recent observations."

"You're far ahead of me!" said Folaron. "My materialism is that of an ignorant man. It's the materialism of a businessman who had never had any other goal in life but his business. My current drama has upset all this."

"His current drama is remorse," explained Dominique, responding to Thomas's unspoken question.

"It's a drama with no solution," murmured Folaron.

"I don't agree," retorted Dominique firmly. "Remorse, on the contrary, is the key to the solution. But once again, I don't want to impose my conviction on you. Do you or don't you authorize me to attack this ignorance which is the true cause of your despair? I want you to answer honestly. It should be the response of your underlying desire, which *refuses* or *agrees* to find a solution."

Dominique stood up and began smoking his pipe with an indifferent air.

After a few moments of reflection, Folaron called back the sculptor, who was moving away:

"I'm ready to listen to you," he declared. "And regardless of what my decision is, I am grateful for your intervention."

"Perfect!" agreed Dominique. "Now we'll try to clarify your dramatic situation, which is caused by the remorse that obsesses you.

"This remorse is complicated by the fact that it has provoked in you problems that you weren't used to reckoning with. We can examine these problems from various points of view.

"If I want to *think simply*, I must first look for the essential nature of the subject: remorse is a burning repentance for an act that our conscience deems unworthy. *Of whom?* To answer 'in truth,' I am obliged to speak of realities that are independent of personal opinions or beliefs. Please listen attentively.

"A man's conscience can be more or less awakened. To the extent that it is awakened, this conscience is the measure of his responsibility. Obviously, this measure is not diminished by a disloyal refusal to recognize it: that would be too easy! But involuntary ignorance that blinds the conscience does diminish responsibility.

"I believe in your loyalty, and that's what I'm addressing myself to in order to make you accept the enlightenment of your conscience.

"According to your point of view, an act can inflict injury; whether to you, to someone else, or to the "established order," including immanent justice, which religion would call God, but which I can define as the Law of Universal Harmony, which cannot be transgressed without engendering other disorders."

Thomas apologized for interrupting:

"I understand this definition better than the idea of 'an offense against God' because God is Absolute Being, hence absolutely impersonal. I'm unable to conceive that any act could inflict injury upon Him or offend Him in any way. Otherwise, you have to admit that it's a personal God, controlling and legislating human acts. However, this is incompatible with the impersonal character of the Universal Principle of Causality, which is the only thing I can conceive as the One Absolute God. Otherwise, I would logically be obliged to admit two gods of differing power and differing views.

"Is my logic faulty, Maître Dominique?"

Dominique began to laugh. "For once I commend it, dear Doctor. But your young theological science is unable to satisfy our new friend, whose ignorance demands a more personal point of view."

Dominique paused to ask Folaron if he would allow him to explain the situation to the doctor. He continued after Folaron agreed:

"In the case of Monsieur Folaron, I must depend on what he knows of himself, that is, the actual conscience that provoked his remorse. This remorse is caused by the egotistical act that drove his friend to suicide."

Then he looked at Folaron:

"What shocked you about the disaster? Was it primarily a sense of your responsibility as a friend, perhaps also of social responsibility? Are you sure that in the financial struggle you didn't cause similar bankruptcies without having any scruples about it? Don't defend yourself: the game of finance is a merciless game, and obviously not a school of altruism and generosity! But your present remorse seems to indicate that a larger sense of solidarity was awakened in you, as well as the responsibilities that flow from this.

"It's important that you recognize this, because the consciousness of our human solidarity already goes beyond the moral sense determined by common law and by the need for social order. If the intensity of your

remorse is the fruit of this, dare to accept it as a light that opens the way
to a higher humanity."

"Don't try to bait me, Maître Dominique. You can't propose an idea
like that to a man who has been crushed by his indignity!"

"You are wrong, sir! To awaken a sleeping consciousness is to take one
step forward on this path. You're letting your guilt over your friend
overshadow you. Let's enlarge upon the problem: Thomas took issue with
the idea that one could believe it possible to offend the invulnerable
Divine Absolute Principle. Okay. But the consciousness that survives your
earthly existence is an integral part of Universal Consciousness. Whether
you name it soul or whatever you wish, it's what makes us superior to the
animal. The soul is our *indestructible worth*, since it is the Immortal
Witness to all our experiences, and our true judge, as well.

"*It is the soul that we offend* by our refusal to listen to it, more so than
by our depravities, because they are the weaknesses inherent in our
inferior state and can, by the shock of remorse, establish a contact with
our conscious soul. That is the goal of its incarnation in our animal
humanity.

"My dear Folaron, are you aware of the stupidity of skepticism, which
gives the name of delusion to the recognition of what constitutes our
human dignity?"

"Can you reconcile the belief in an immortal soul with the elements of
your materialistic science?" asked Folaron, addressing himself to Thomas.

"I have experienced a Consciousness that is independent of my cerebral
consciousness and my sensory faculties," said Thomas. "From this I
inferred the possibility of a state of being superior to that of my mortal
self. That put me just one step away from asking myself whether there
weren't other states of being even more subtle, and even other conscious
intelligences that were totally independent of material form. In all good
faith I could not consider this further step to be nonsense, since modern
science is gradually discovering modes of vibrations and manifestations of
cosmic energy that were previously unknown."

"Let's not get ahead of ourselves," interrupted Dominique. "The immediate problem is the awakening of consciousness. Remorse is the
effective agent of this consciousness, if it is not repressed and doesn't
deviate from the cause that gave rise to it."

"Does that mean we've got to bear it like a ball and chain that we must
drag around forever?"

"*Bear* is not the word," answered Dominique. "It's necessary to 'recognize' it until you can clarify the reproach of your conscience. Then you
must use it like a fire that consumes the roots of the evil that caused it."

"Isn't that what the cathechism calls 'contrition'?" said Jean Thomas.

"If contrition went that deep, absolution would have an effective value! Let's not confuse remorse with regret, repentance, or contrition.

"*Regretting* a fault is the displeasure caused by behavior that can be criticized. Whether this regret is caused by an 'emotional disturbance' or by a rational observation of the consequences of the fault, it doesn't touch the deeper consciousness, and its effect is superficial and fleeting.

"*Repentance* is a self-accusation, with the *intention* of not falling back into old patterns of behavior. It could be a simple cerebral evaluation of the fault, or a reaction, either innate or conventional, of the 'moral sense.' In any event, it would remain an *estimation* that is too superficial to have a powerful erasing effect: otherwise, it would be remorse.

"*Contrition*, according to the way it's defined in the Catholic catechism, is said to be 'perfect' or 'imperfect.' The latter is called 'attrition.' Imperfect contrition is regret of the fault through fear of punishment.

"*Perfect contrition* is 'the sincere regret for the sin because it is an offense against God and caused the death of Jesus Christ.' This contrition thus demands integral faith in this doctrine, and a profound awareness of the offense *made against God* sufficient to create remorse without the intervention of fear of punishment. According to Catholic teaching, 'perfect contrition erases sin, even before absolution, as long as one has the desire to confess.'"

"I'd like to know how many Catholics really experience this *perfect contrition without which absolution is ineffective*, according to the formal vows of the catechism," objected Thomas.

"It's a serious problem," answered Dominique. "It imposes the risky condition of a faith that is often only dogmatic belief, whereas the essential condition would be *to experience in one's consciousness* the fault committed toward our spiritual being (the Divine Soul), from which this fault separates us. This would be true remorse, which this motive makes more accessible to us."

"How do you distinguish remorse from repentance?" asked Folaron.

"*Remorse* is a burning reproach of the conscience, which makes the guilty person *experience* the seriousness of the damage done: whether to someone else, to the established order (the social or universal order—that is, the law of Harmony), or, finally and in any case, to himself through an infraction that jeopardizes his spiritual destiny.

"Even the disbeliever can find in these three instances of remorse an incentive sufficient to awaken in him a sense of responsibility. *But the man who has experienced the Presence of his spiritual being* will naturally be horrified by the faults that could separate him from it.

"Now do you understand the difference between effective remorse and repentance? Repentance is only a mental (therefore superficial) evaluation of guilt, and can only provoke the intention (even though we name it 'resolve') not to repeat past behavior.

"However, we cannot tamper with the tendencies and impulses of our animal being and intellectual being: it makes definite demands, and won't be bullied by 'good intentions.' It gives us a facile sense of respectability, which deceives us about the motivations of our behavior."

"I'm afraid you're right, Maître Dominique," conceded Folaron. "It took this disaster to make me realize the hypocrisy of my respectability."

"Precisely," agreed Dominique. "And I'm convinced that the true cause of your despair was the accusation formulated by your Spiritual Consciousness, whose existence had been hidden from you until then by the excuses of your cerebral consciousness. Confronted with this unexpected judge, you measured the abyss between your suprahuman worth and your pitiful respectability. You couldn't stand it. . . . 'Too late!' rang out like a bell, and you too went off the deep end.

"No more dodging the issue, dear friend: look within and tell me if what I am saying is not the truth."

In a hushed voice Folaron struggled to express himself:

"I'm ashamed of my unconsciousness," he confessed. "You are unveiling a part of myself that I willfully ignored.

"There's no doubt you were right in saying that humiliation was the cause of my despair: the humiliation of a condemnation."

"It's you who are judging remorse as a condemnation," retorted the sculptor. "Don't be blinded by your wounded pride. On the contrary, be aware that remorse is the best agent of purification. *It alone can erase.*"

"I don't understand this possibility of 'erasing,'" objected Folaron. "On the contrary, you said that it's important not to repress remorse."

"I didn't explain myself," acknowledged Dominique. "Erasing a fault can only be effective if we destroy in ourselves the roots of the behavior that caused the fault in the first place.

"Conscious remorse has the all-powerful virtue of destroying these roots, *if it is judiciously cultivated until the moment it inspires in us a definitive horror for the committed fault—that is, when we experience the certainty that it will be impossible for us to repeat it.*

"However, it's not a matter of allowing ourselves to be continually eaten away by this pain: to dwell on remorse for months and for years is a pernicious sickness. It's a matter of the merciless confrontation between our hypocritical excuses and our highest consciousness.

"We must bring into play our highest motives, awaken the vision of our higher possibilities and the enthusiasm for transcending our humanity."

"You've got an extraordinary way of reviving people, Maître Dominique! It makes me want to oblige you to do it!"

"Aren't you satisfied? Too bad for you. I'm going to speak bluntly."

"Hasn't he already done so?" whispered Folaron into Jean Thomas's ear. Thomas smiled as he emptied his glass.

Dominique was not laughing, and his powerful voice resounded in the Tavern:

"Since that's what you want, I'll be precise: it was cowardice that drove you to take your life in order to escape the 'settling of your accounts' with yourself, because suicide would not have settled anything at all. You can annihilate this cowardice if you face the moral bankruptcy of this situation. But this will only happen if you act freely, under the sole impulse of your deepest consciousness.

"Know that you have a companion in you *who knows* what your reason ignores, who can give a goal to your presence on Earth, if only he could become conscious.

"Stop putting a label on your inconsistent opinions: materialism, skepticism, credulity, and I don't know what else. You'd have a hard time justifying them. Have they ever helped you out of a critical situation? It's easier to jump into the abyss than to confront your Immortal Consciousness."

Folaron did not take his eyes off Dominique. A confident smile relaxed his face for the first time. However, he hesitated before asking:

"Do I dare ask you if I will have the opportunity to see you again?"

"I don't know," said the sculptor. "It's up to you. I don't want to influence you. First learn how to feel the presence of your companion, to take him as your adviser . . . then you will have found true liberty."

Dominique stood up. Folaron bowed respectfully before him and apologized for having imposed himself—involuntarily. Dominique smiled as he shook his hand.

"You haven't eaten, Folaron," said Thomas. "Come with me to Orly, where I'm going to meet our friend Dutheil, who's returning from India. You'll have dinner with us when we get back."

Folaron halted in the foyer, intrigued by its two "doors": the angel with the pitcher of beer, and the devil holding up the basin of holy water.[1]

"We could put up a sign," said the doctor: "*Reaction taught here.*"

---

1. See page 33.

14

Brahmanism, Buddhism, Christianity

The lunch that Dominique gave for Dutheil to celebrate his return from India was coming to an end. Jean-Jacques and Jean Thomas, charmed by the picturesque adventures that the traveler recounted with such humor, waited curiously for the story of his more profound impressions. But Dutheil, seduced by the cordiality of his reception, allowed himself to be euphoric and seem little inclined to talk about confidential matters.

He congratulated the sculptor on the calm atmosphere that he had created in the Atelier and the Tavern.

"Must I confess," he added, "that I was worried about returning to the feverish atmosphere of our European life?"

Thomas was surprised.

"I would have thought that the big cities of the republic of India would be just as agitated by now," he said.

"It's very different, Thomas," replied Dutheil. "The streets can be full of disparate vehicles—rickshaws and bicycles and luxurious cars—and a heterogeneous crowd where colorful saris are mixed with the European outfits of Indian students and the jackets of the Brahmans turned functionaries. Indian social life has been complicated by the many customs that they have taken over from the English, but the activity of this swarming multitude can in no way be compared to the mental tension of our European crowds.

"Here at home, men preoccupied with their careers turn their existence into an obsession that stiffens their bearing and limits their horizon. The new constitution of India, which exteriorizes the life of women as well as men, has not destroyed this inner disposition which allows them to remain flexible in their carriage."

Jean-Jacques interrupted Dutheil:

"Your comment on the stiffness of Europeans is very interesting. You relate it to our mania for preoccupation. You could say that the American has understood this problem and is trying to find a remedy for it with relaxation: 'Relax, relax!' has become a slogan with them."

"And they did it," said Thomas, "by observing the injury to the nerves caused by the hurry and mental tension of our overactive life. However, they have not destroyed the cause of this agitation."

"Precisely," continued Dutheil, "and this cause doesn't come into play for the Indians.

"The adaptation of the Indians to our civilization seems to be something superimposed rather than a transformation in the mentality of individuals. The participation in administrative functions, like the instruction necessary for their new activities, has upset their social life, but the materialism of this new direction has not destroyed the fundamental nature of these beings, for whom the action of supranatural powers is still integrated, to varying degrees, in all the acts of their daily life."

"I observed this fact," said Jean-Jacques: "the two mentalities are indeed superimposed on each other, and this gives a hybrid aspect to their behavior, which is disconcerting for us. Similarly, you find a docility toward the laws of the constitution juxtaposed with a libertarian sense that expresses itself through the rather fanciful application of these laws."

Dutheil agreed, laughing:

"Oriental fantasy sometimes involves a picturesque application of laws that is rather troubling for the European, who takes everything seriously."

"What they take seriously," said Jean-Jacques, "are the studies necessary for their new functions, regardless of how different they are from their former concepts. You see, for example, daughters of Brahmans seriously studying the equality of rights for women and men."

"That's where the line is drawn between those who allow themselves to be invaded by this new spirit and the others who, in their private lives, scrupulously respect the laws of old established tradition," said Dutheil. "The same phenomenon can be observed with the castes: although officially abolished, they have multiplied officiously through the fact— according to the opinion of a noted author—that men who had until then been dedicated to a life of meditation, found themselves obliged to work in order to live; this, he said, brought about *ipso facto* the creation of an intermediate caste which stabilized its relations with its neighbors in the other castes—thus giving birth to myriads of intercastes. This is the extraordinary result of a hyperindividualist spirit in contact with a social reality that is more complicated than any other.

"There's another amusing paradox: the author observes that 'India, this metaphysical continent where contradiction flowers, is equally the chosen land of the most virulent racism,' and that the surest way to recognize oneself on the ladder of castes is to 'measure the color of the person to whom one is speaking.'"[1]

"Must one see in that a prejudice that stubbornly insists on maintaining caste privileges, or a psychological judgment on the possibilities of evolution?" asked Thomas.

"In regard to privileges," answered Dutheil, "the rules that isolated the highest caste of Brahmans were more like subjugation to a rigor that was not very enviable."

The sculptor, who had been listening in silence, intervened:

"It's difficult for you, with your rational and pragmatic culture, to understand the culture of a people whose criteria are based on the spiritual goal of their existence.

"The value of these criteria and the reality of their conception varies according to the nobility or mediocrity of the milieu, but on all levels you'll find interpenetration of religious spirit and the most common daily acts. It's not a matter of obeying the dictates of a church (which doesn't exist in India in the way that we understand it), but instead, a unitary concept that does not separate existence and human individuality from the Cause from which they emanate from. 'I am *That*': it's not a belief but a manifest *fact* that molds their behavior, just as their need to eat is a fact. Isn't that true, Jean-Jacques?"

"Your observation, Maître Dominique, seems justified, to the extent that the population of India is filled with concepts of karma, of reincarnation, and their constant relationship to the World of Causes. You mustn't try to comprehend the metaphysical meaning, which remains the domain of those who are devoted to the study of sacred texts, the Vedas. The masses nourish themselves from the permanent contact with the symbols of Invisible Powers, evoked even in the smallest villages by numerous sanctuaries, legends acted out in mime, and ritual gestures. And each man or woman is attracted by the symbolic evocation of the Principle that has its resonance within him or her."

"According to what you say, these Easterners are not subjected as we are to the dictates of imperative religious authority," insisted Jean Thomas.

"If by 'religion,'" answered Dominique, "you mean adherence to a

1. Robert J. Goget, *A travers les sanctuaries de l'Inde* (Paris: Amiot-Dumont, 1951), p. 39.

church outside of which there is no salvation, belief in imposed dogmas under threat of excommunication, compulsory religious practices, and a morality against which transgressions are evaluated in a series of catalogued sins, then Catholicism is the only religion worthy of this name.

"In addition, if you eliminate this severity but preserve the rituals, the evangelical doctrine, and the morality that flows from them, you also include other forms of Christianity, including certain aspects of Protestantism.

"Even with this softening of rules, our Western concept of religion hampers our understanding of the Easterners', which is the individual consciousness of the interdependence of human beings with the Invisible Powers, whose presence they *experience*.

"Their figures of the various aspects of the Divinity represent the hierarchy of Heavenly Principles, of Invisible Forces, and of Cosmic Functions incarnated in Nature, as well as the repercussions of them, which generate human impulses. This consciousness establishes a type of familiarity with these powers that they consider intermediaries between humanity and the Unknowable Absolute Principle.

"Our position is very different with respect to 'personal' God who judges and sanctions our acts and thoughts through the control of a church that presents itself as the indispensible intermediary. This position prevents the Christian from conceiving the *impersonality* of the Absolute Divine Principle, and the great Laws of Harmony which are the expression of what we call 'His Will.'"

"I'm beginning to understand the reactive effect of awakened responsibility through the very fact of freedom of conscience and the absence of obligation," said Thomas.

"However, it seems to me that Hinduism, as well as Buddhism, also has aspects of religious worship such as prayer, ritual, and even certain sacramental acts."

"That's true," agreed Dominique. "To the extent that everything in it is a teaching that is more or less symbolic—or, quite frankly, magical! That is, they put into practice their knowledge of the productive Causes of phenomena. This has nothing to do with sentimental prayers to obtain gifts from God; it's a matter of gestures and mantras that will bring the desired Forces into action."

"In brief, does that mean it's still a teaching?" asked Thomas.

"Certainly. And this teaching, as well as the application of it, is always fundamentally based on the sacred texts of the Veda."

"With regard to the nuances of their interpretation," Dutheil put in, "I have been warned against confusing the rigid Brahman theologians, deeply rooted in casuistics and in the dogmatic interpretation of the 'letter,' with certain Brahmans whose knowledge is based on a life of meditation and a very pure spirituality. I was able to meet with some of the latter. It is in Tibet, in Nepal, that a mystical reality of Buddhism has penetrated Vedantism, and lessened the rigidity of the letter to the benefit of the interpretation of the Spirit. These Brahmans, while fully participating in the new social constitution, have integrally kept the consciousness of their spiritual mission, and are very well placed to estimate the consequences of this hybrid situation.

"They clearly defined to me the elements of progress as a downfall for India that could result from this transformation, whose danger they are trying to minimize."

"Indeed, it does pose a distressing problem," recognized Dominique. "A people whose life is based on profound spiritual roots, and whose traditional knowledge penetrates all the acts of their existence, can keep this imprint intact, despite foreign intrusion and influences. If not, they will become dissociated through abandoning the forces that constitute their soul and their individual genius."

"The sages whom I saw are aware of this double possibility," answered Dutheil. "Listen to their words, which I have faithfully transcribed:

"'Republican India, so eager to change the old ways in order to achieve a higher standard of living, may possibly turn away from ancient traditions and become completely materialistic. Though that state of affairs may last for several centuries, nothing can change the unchanging. India has already known long periods of religious denial, when every belief has been questioned. . . . The vast store of pure wisdom which India keeps hidden will survive all destruction, for some will always choose to devote themselves wholly to fulfilling the Law, without concern for the actuality that binds our lives to the present. A chosen few, especially from our caste (because our traditions incline us in that direction), have always been preserved for this calling. They live in caves or ashrams, alone, or in the world, and their sacrifice is made with full awareness so that others, much later perhaps, may in their turn gain knowledge.'[2]

"And this is the opposite view:

"'How stupid,' said one of them to me, 'to say that India must give the younger generation "characters of steel." Our sons will grow up to be good officials, doctors, and politicians. They will give their wives refrigerators, and their farmers machinery; that is the fashion, but they will forget the relative unimportance of worldly things in comparison with the Higher Aims. One of these days, they will come begging for knowl-

2. Lizelle Reymond, *My Life with a Brahmin Family*, trans. Lucy Norton (Baltimore, Md.: Penguin Books, 1972), p. 58.

edge from those who still sing of the acts of Krishna with a full heart and
perfect simplicity. At the present moment I believe that true knowledge
is thrusting into new levels of consciousness. Evolution will be all the
more stimulated by that.'"[3]

Thomas expressed surprise at this clear-sightedness, unclouded by
sectarianism.

"Certainly these are wise men, who are perfectly aware of the imbalance between two diametrically opposed mentalities," answered Dutheil,
and continued to read:

"'Our fathers,' they say, 'had no refuge from the Western ideas that
intruded in the name of Progress. . . . After they had acquired the
culture, logic, and debating powers of the English, they passed down to us
a strange, half-and-half state of mind, which prevents us from being
consistent towards either of the inherited cultures.'"[4]

"I'd be curious to know what they think of the Western interpretation
of Hindu doctrine," said Thomas.

"That's easy," answered Dutheil. "I've had several interesting responses
in that regard:

"'Western scholars have discovered our sacred writings, arts, and
traditions, but they judge them as inexact sciences by their own standards.
They do not realize the changeableness of our conceptions, nor accept our
attitude towards the fundamentals of life. Nonetheless, for us, our own
natural science of *prakriti*, is an exact one. The Vedic *rishis* (sages)
practiced it in the past, but allowed only initiates to glimpse its essential
principles. It will be for your generation to give a new interpretation of
prakriti that will be understood in the atomic age. The mutability of
forces, energies, and knowledge no longer seems utopian. We live in
troubled times, but already one feels a reawakening of consciousness and,
this time, Western philosophy comes halfway to meet us.'"[5]

"This connection is very interesting, but I can't really see how our
position is related to theirs," said Thomas.

"I can give you the Brahman's answer word for word:

"'It is really very simple,' he said. 'The West starts from the theory that
everything has a beginning and an end, whereas we Orientals believe that
life has neither beginning nor ending, but evolves cyclically, in a process
of continual change. In that unceasing series of transformations we find
our mental stability and our purpose in life. I know that Oriental and

3. Ibid, p. 90.
4. Ibid., pp. 110–111.
5. Ibid., pp. 111–112.

Western points of view are completely opposed; that is why it is so hard for us to understand one another. . . .'"[6]

A moment later he continued:

"'What does Western materialism contain for us? It means not only a search after material benefits, but also attachment to certain intellectual forms and theories, and even to Christian philosophy, which has now passed into history and become a religion. For us, "history" is simply a certain period existing in time, and thus might suggest the false idea of beginnings and endings. Do you realize,' he said to me, 'that Western logic has no truth for us? If you were to ask a Westerner to speak from the premise that time was nonexistent, and that there was a reality differing from his own conception, do you think that he could do so? He would probably find himself incapable, or else might feel as uncomfortable as we do, when we try to give permanent shape to what is either transitory, or has no reality except in the human mind. That is where we both stand.'"[7]

"It's interesting to have the authentic appraisal of a Brahman who is so comprehensive and impersonal," said Dominique.

"The fact is, for the Westerner who is used to judging everything according to his *own* concept, his *own* opinion, in other words according to the projection of *his* thought and *his* sentiment about the subject under consideration, it's almost impossible to assimilate the conception of a Hindu sage, whose consciousness encircles the object instead of looking at it from outside. In other words, the Hindu stays within Unity, while the Westerner dualizes."

"However, to project my thought into the subject that I'm studying is to unite myself with it and not to dualize it," objected Thomas.

"Not at all," said Dominique. "It's to situate the object *in front of you*. You see it according to your sensory and mental vision. This is not 'knowing it' in its reality. And the poverty of your conception manifests itself in the fact that this Brahman *also* understands your mentality, while you do not understand his."

"That's rather annoying for our scientific knowledge," retorted Thomas. "According to this man's words, and according to yours, one could claim that the Easterner, trained in this concept of Unity, could add our scientific knowledge to his intuitive vision, whereas we scientists would have tremendous difficulty in assimilating his Knowledge of Causes."

6. Ibid., p. 111.
7. Ibid., p. 112.

"Congratulations, Thomas. You're speaking like a sage, which proves that *difficult* doesn't mean 'impossible.' However, you are right: opening up to intuitive consciousness is more difficult than opening up to cerebral consciousness. It's on a more subtle level, and above all, it's opposed to prejudice and to dualistic thought.

"In this sense, the religious disposition helps the Easterner, not in the sense of submitting to the laws and dogmas of ecclesiastical authority, but in terms of consciousness of the Unity that connects various levels of the universe and makes all humans more or less one in their progress or their downfall."

"No doubt the Hindu religions—Brahman and Buddhist—are the ones that claim this tendency."

Dominique retorted: "Don't make the mistake of classifying different religious origins and conceptions under the name of Hinduism.

"The Hindu tradition is essentially based on the four books of the Veda: The Rig-Veda, Yajur-Veda, Sama-Veda and Atharva-Veda, whose origin in time is undetermined because their written transcription was preceded by a long oral tradition. This was followed by a traditional line (the *Vansha*) that gave birth to the Upanishads, among other writings.

"Regardless of the analytical or grammatical discussions provoked by 'hair-splitters,' the origin of these ancient texts in direct (Divine) inspiration was never doubted. The texts are the unassailable basis of Hindu teaching, which is called Brahmanic as well as Vedantic."

"There are many versions of Vedantism," said Jean-Jacques. "I suppose that each one corresponds to one of the Brahmanic sects."

"Be careful!" said Dominique. "Don't confuse sects, doctrines, and branches with authentic tradition.

"The original Veda is the formulation of a Revelation which has become the synthetic basis of traditional Hindu Knowledge. It is a cosmological teaching of the primordial Principles conceived in their metaphysical aspect with no intention of moral or mystical preaching.

"The need to draw inferences that could be applied as psychospiritual guidelines first gave birth to the doctrines of Shivaism and Vaishnavism. These are in no way divergences. Like the three aspects of Pharaonic theology, they consider Genesis, then the Becoming of Being in its successive phases, according to the aspect of the Principle that is specifically working in each one of these phases.

"Thus, both the Vaishnava and the Shivaite doctrines (since they are equally genuine) will attract followers according to the religious aspect that is particularly suitable.

"There are also the *darshanas*, distinctions characteristic of the Hindu mentality, which is much less sectarian than ours. These include *six points of view* from which one can study fundamental doctrine. They are called the six *darshanas*:

"The Hyaya is the logical point of view, or if you prefer, the point of view of human understanding.

"The Vaisheshika could be crudely defined as the 'naturalistic' aspect of the cosmological point of view.

"The Samkhya seeks to grasp the degrees of hierarchy in manifest being.

"Following that is Yoga, whose principle goal is to realize in the human being the union of *Purusha* and *Prakriti*. *Purusha* corresponds to the universal Christ principle in Cosmic Man as well as in human beings. *Prakriti* is the universal receptive substance, nonspecified in itself, but whose earthly manifestations are Nature and Woman.

"This is not the time to go into the various schools of Yoga, each of whose methods corresponds to a more or less spiritual goal, nor to speak of the greed for powers of the yogi who practices it."

"I would never have thought that Yoga, being a *method* of spiritual realization, could be one of the points of view of the Vedic teaching," said Jean-Jacques.

"It is both," explained Dominique. "The Hindus know very well that Wisdom cannot be poured into the disciple like liquid into a jar. They know that Knowledge is the conceiving of what is Real, and that this conception demands the elimination of obstacles opposed to it. For them, the student is a field which they prepare by means of adequate mental purification to conceive the esoteric sense of the teaching. It is the fundamental goal of Yoga, in which the subjugation of the Mind is the primary condition required to move toward Union.

"But let us finish with the two last *darshanas*: the Mimamsa and the Vedanta. They are the more metaphysical points of view of the Veda, and rely respectively on the Vedangas and on the Upanishads.

"Now," continued Dominique, "you must understand that I only gave you this very succinct glimpse in order to avoid the error of sectarian and rigid opinion with regard to a doctrine that is a gamut of points of view, accessible to the most diverse branches of scholarship, provided they are exempt from prejudice."

Jean-Jacques and Dutheil enthusiastically agreed. "That was very useful, because we are so used to the combative exclusivity of religious controversy that it's hard for us to imagine such tolerance!" said Thomas.

"It's not tolerance," corrected Dominique. "It's a comprehension of the difference between Knowledge and learning.

"The Eastern Masters give to the student, *according to his particular possibilities*, the necessary elements to dispel his ignorance. If the student aspires to go beyond written teachings, his Master directs him toward a guru who can initiate him into meditation."

"I thought that the Brahman was jealous of his prerogatives in the religious realm," said Thomas.

Jean-Jacques protested: "You mustn't confuse the prerogatives of caste with ecclesiastical authority such as you imagine it in terms of our Western concept of the Church.

"If India has an innate sense of caste, it has an even more innate sense of the individual's freedom to follow the directives of his conscience and also with regard to the responsibility resulting from them."

"That's an acknowledged fact," confirmed Dominique. "The absence of ecclesiastical laws and sanctions doesn't prevent the Hindu from emphasizing the spiritual point of view regarding how one is to conduct one's life."

"Then where does the power of the Brahmans, who are still occupying the major positions, come from?"

"Don't forget that their caste prerogatives also included the rigorous maintenance of ritual and tradition," answered Dominique. "Moreover, they were authorities on the science of the mantra, through which (according to their assertion) they participated in supernatural powers."

"But do they have indisputable authority with regard to the interpretation of the Vedic texts?" asked Thomas.

"It's obvious that the integrity of an interpretation is proportional to the translator's knowledge of the value and the esoteric meaning of the letters and symbols," answered Dominique. "This holds true also for the names attributed to the Cosmic Principles. Without this the original teaching would degenerate into more or less arbitrary interpretations of genuine Revelations."

"Is there a parallel between the Brahmanic and Christian theologies?" asked Thomas.

"They have the same metaphysical basis," answered Dominique: "first of all, the undeniable Unity of the eternal, indefinable Absolute Divine Principle, which the Christians call God and the Hindus call Brahman; second, the trinitarian aspect under which one can consider It. But while this Trinitarian Principle is common to the two religions, there are many differences in the way it is interpreted.

"The Christian Trinity is defined as one God in three Persons: the Father, considered as Creator; the Son as Redeemer; the Holy Spirit, Sanctifier and Consoler.

"The Hindu Trinity (the *Trimurti*) expresses the three aspects or essential Functions of Brahman: Brahma, Vishnu, Shiva.

"The first aspect, Brahma, considered as Creator, is also called in this Function *Ishvara*. However, under this name it 'contains,' so to speak, the *Trimurti*, for Ishvara takes the name of *Vishnu* as Life-Giver and the name *Shiva* as Transformer. And this concept is not far removed from the Christian concept of God the Father, who 'engenders the Son of all Eternity' and whose Holy Spirit is the 'sanctifying' aspect and dispenser of the seven gifts.

"The second aspect, Vishnu, qualified as Protector and Life-Giver, is also named in the Vedas 'the Lord of all activity' and, as such, is considered as the Divine Sun.

The third aspect, Shiva, is called the Destroyer insofar as he is the Master of the great alternation (dissolution, the immanent consequence of creation, which it necessarily resuscitates). Shiva is, for this reason, the Master of Evolution. He is given as many names and symbols as he has essential functions and aspects.

"The first difference in interpretation involves the second person of the Trinity, the Son, and the second aspect of the *Trimurti*, Vishnu.

"According to Christian theology, God the Son is incarnated in Jesus Christ, who is considered the only Son of God the Father. The Hindu religion attributes to Vishnu many incarnations, of which the two essential ones are Lord Krishna and Lord Rama, who are two expressions of the same Divine Principle. To each is attributed several avatars (reincarnations). On this subject, the Bhagavad-Gita has Krishna say these words:

> Whenever spirituality decays and materialism is rampant, . . . I reincarnate Myself. To protect the righteous, to destroy the wicked, and to establish the kingdom of God, I am reborn from age to age.[8]

"As Initiator, Hindu tradition attributes an earthly existence to Krishna. As the second aspect of the *Trimurti*, Krishna (the Cosmic realization of Vishnu is the imperishable, divine being, infinite in relationship to his female aspect, Radha, who represents the 'finite,' which seeks its 'infinite' in conjunction with its divine complement.

"The same principle of Krishna, under the name of *Purusha*, is the divine Cosmic Man, Life-Giver to *Prakriti*, who is Nature.

"Here, as in all Hindu theology, we are dealing with various functions of the same Principle under different names.

8. Bhagavad-Gita 4:7. Translation by Shri Purohit Swami, *The Geeta* (London: Faber and Faber, 1935). The word *age* is a translation of the Sanskrit *Yuga*, one of the four periods of a cosmic cycle. (Editor's note)

"Observe the obvious identity of Krishna with Christ, who, in His universal aspect, is the divine Cosmic Man and who, as Jesus, incarnates the Christ Principle: that is, the unification of the human and the Divine. For man this signifies the unification of the two aspects of his immortal soul."

"Isn't that what Saint Paul meant when he speaks of 'Christ formed in you'?"[9] said Jean-Jacques.

"Precisely," said Dominique, "and it's the sense of Hindu mysticism: to unify Krishna and Radha."

"But you were saying that Radha represents the finite. . . ."

"In relation to the Infinite, which is not determined; for our Permanent Witness is made a specific being by its incarnation, whereas our Spiritual Witness is impersonal and not determined.

"However, the difference between the Hindu and the Christian interpretation of the second aspect of the Trinity lies in the fact that Christian theology particularizes the role of Jesus Christ, whom it makes the Life-Giver of *his* Church, that is, of *Christian* humanity. Moreover, Catholicism denies all divine incarnations other than that of Jesus Christ: the *'only* Son of God,' to whom exclusively it attributes the sole Divine Revelation that it recognizes in human history."

"And the 'salvation' brought by Jesus is conditional upon observance of the rules of the Church and the compulsory practice of them," added Jean-Jacques.

"The Hindu religions have no such exclusivity," confirmed Dutheil. "Even more amazing, they condemn as sin the preaching of their own religion as the best!"

Dominique agreed with this statement. "This position is logical according to their teaching of the universality of a single Reality and its oneness with its multiple manifestations. And it accords with their knowledge of cosmic cycles, and the oneness of the Divine Principle incarnated in each of the phases of human evolution that corresponds to it."

"You haven't spoken of another difference between the two interpretations of the Trinity," said Dutheil to Dominique. "Hinduism attributes to each one of the *Trimurti* a feminine complement: Sarasvati for Brahma, Lakshmi for Vishnu, Parvati for Shiva."

"That's correct," said Dominique. "But these three energies are themselves the aspect of the One *Shakti*, which is the divine Power of Shiva."

"However, I've noticed that none of these feminine principles are mentioned in Christian theology," said Dutheil.

9. Galatians 4:19.

"What about Wisdom," retorted Dominique, "of which it is said 'that she is above all that is'?[10] Nonetheless, you are right: Christianity is silent about the feminine aspects of Divinity."

"Indeed it is, because Mary is the *human* mother of Jesus," agreed Jean-Jacques.

"This subject demands separate consideration,"[11] answered Dominique. "Let us simply realize that there is this important difference that Dutheil has mentioned."

"To sum up," concluded Thomas, "the two religions have an identical basis, but the Hindus have multiplied the divine names that we subsume under the word *God*."

"The obvious goal of the Christian simplification," said Dutheil, "is to strictly maintain a rigorous monotheism."

"Monotheism is no less rigorous for the Hindu theologians," asserted Dominique. "Because of the intermeshing of Qualities and Functions of the three aspects of the *Trimurti*, one can never make an autonomous Divinity out of any of them. But the religious goal of these theologians is to immerse men in the Reality of the Supreme Divinity. However, in order to arrive at this, they replace dogma with the *evocation* of the Divine Presence through its multiple manifestations in the Cosmos and in earthly and human Nature. Dogma addresses itself to the Mind and provokes a complexity of interpretations, whereas evocation addresses itself to the vital emotion and to the Knowledge of the Heart.

"Dogma imposes *belief*. Conscious evocation calls for communion and Faith.

"But you must understand that evocation does not mean imagining a form of autonomous deity, but rather the Divine Presence, of which the believer implores a functional or qualitative aspect toward which he is particularly attracted."

"The Hindu religion allows each believer great liberty in following his natural inclinations and in seeking his spiritual realization in the way that suits him best," remarked Thomas.

"According to his comprehension and the way that corresponds to his current state of consciousness," specified Dominique. "But in all cases only the goal is important, regardless of the name attributed to the Divinity."

"Does that mean they don't have to fear heresy, Maître Dominique?"

"Heresy is created by the legislation of beliefs, Thomas, and this legislation has always created enmity between the Christians of one

10. The Proverbs of Solomon 8:22–23.
11. See *Vierge Cosmique*, chap. 16.

church and those of other churches, each group claiming to be defending the 'true faith.'"

"Until now I have never known religion in this aspect," said Thomas with a sigh. "I was so ignorant of Eastern religions that now I'm trying to grasp only what is *necessary* to know about them."

"That's good, Thomas, and it's also the aim of this discussion to correct your misunderstanding of a tradition that is as real as ours but more explicit."

"I'm beginning to see that. But will I be able to discern whether Buddhism is very different from Brahmanism?"

"There again, you've got to shift your point of view, my friend. Buddhism, in its Principle, was neither a religion nor a philosophy. It was a message. It was the message of Prince Gautama, who had attained the state of Buddha, which indicates the way toward liberation from our earthly bondage and the elimination of our suffering.

"The mission of the Buddha is this exclusive type of quest: to attain Illumination by eliminating the obstacles to it. In practical terms, this means that to be conscious of the causes of suffering is to learn how to eliminate them."

"This is why Buddha saw ignorance as the first of these causes of suffering," specified Dutheil.

"Obviously," said Dominique. "How can you remedy an evil if you are ignorant of its origins?"

"So it's these causes that must be specified," insisted Jean Thomas.

"The best way to summarize them," answered Dominique, "is no doubt the word *covetousness*: covetous desire for all that can tempt our earthly being and attach it to this existence. You might argue that this doctrine is confined to the evangelical doctrine of detachment. That's true, but with this difference: evangelical doctrine depends on practical and moral precepts, which essential Buddhism doesn't worry about at all.

"The position of Buddhism, with regard to individual realization, could translate itself into our Western mentality by an almost Shakespearean point of view: 'to be or not to be.' Integral Buddhism doesn't recognize intermediary realization. This is expressed in the words of Huang Po: 'The Ever-Existent Buddha is not a Buddha who is attained through stages.'"

"But Gautama only attained Illumination after long years of merciless fasts and solitary meditation," objected Jean-Jacques.

"True, but then he denied the method of excessive mortification as inefficient *external* practices," retorted Dominique.

"His doctrine is based on the *impermanence* of the world that we know through our sensory, emotional, and cerebral faculties. The interest that we take in it is the source of illusions, desires, and deception, which cause all our suffering.

"His program is to become conscious of this impermanent world, then to inspire in us personal *compassion* for the suffering of living beings, and *detachment* from all that can excite our personal desires, cultivate our egoism, and keep us from Illumination."

"That's a superhuman program!" exclaimed Jean Thomas. "How did he express it in his doctrine?"

"Gautama Buddha left no written teachings. His conclusions were the fruit of *sudden* Illumination, something like an explosion of Consciousness that no relativity whatsoever could overshadow. Such a *state* was only transmissible through radiance and peace. The Buddha was unable to communicate his Knowledge except in terms of the measure and form that each of his disciples was inclined toward and could participate in.

"Thus, you must not be surprised if the transmission of his doctrines gave birth, after his death, to two different currents of expression. These are called the two Vehicles: the *Hinayana* (the Small Vehicle), which literally transmits the oral teachings of the Buddha, and the *Mahayana* (the Great Vehicle), which interprets the significance of it. The Small Vehicle of these was adapted in Ceylon, Siam, and Indonesia. The Great Vehicle became widespread in Mongolia, China, Japan, and Tibet."

"Numerous Buddhist sects were later formed," added Jean-Jacques. "The direction and the practices of these sects vary according to the rigidity or flexibility with which they apply the essential precepts."

"Above all, these orientations vary according to the tendencies of their followers, be they mystical or theoretical. Some of them are devoted to metaphysical interpretation . . ."

"To the point of getting themselves accused of atheism by the Westerner who doesn't understand," injected Jean-Jacques, laughing.

"Others," continued Dominique, "look to the doctrine for a method of spiritual realization, through meditation, ritual, poverty, the most rigorous vegetarianism, and compassion toward human suffering."

"Is Tibetan Lamaism separate from Buddhism?" added Jean-Jacques.

"It adopted the Mahayana aspect." answered Dominique. "One can often find in it the strong influence of Tantric doctrines, which practice the use of Cosmic energies to activate Consciousness."

"Lamaism gave birth to numerous monastaries," mentioned Jean-Jacques.

"Indeed," agreed Dominique. "And there are three principal sects: the 'Yellow Hats,' who follow the philosophical way and seek realization through meditation on the void; the 'Red Hats,' in the Tantric vein, who depend on magic; and the 'White Hats,' who follow a middle path between the other two."

"In Nepal," said Dutheil, "I found another interesting aspect, in which the Vedic teachings of the Brahmans absorbed the purest aspects of Buddhism. The result seemed to me an extraordinary balance between an acute sense of the positive necessities of modern life and a clear awareness of their relativity."

Dominique looked at Dutheil with amused interest. "You've been quite impressed by a Wisdom that you thought was inaccessible to you."

Dutheil, surprised, looked at the sculptor. "You're articulating exactly what I was unable to express. I found myself with Brahmans of the highest caste who, instead of allowing themselves to leave their class to join the promiscuous spirit of their new social functions, continue to live the inner life—in their own words, 'in the certainty of continuous movement,' situating all things in their relationship to the Principle of primordial life, which is Divine Essence.

"They allow this Essence, which they call the 'Descending Power,' to penetrate their entire being until it transforms even their intelligence, which then ceases to be an obstacle to their intuitive vision."

Dominique leaned forward. "My congratulations, dear sir: you yourself have absorbed something essential."

"This conscious penetration," continued Dutheil, "gives them the serenity of an impersonal position that observes in a detached manner the various reactions of the human self and of the people whom they are obliged to meet."

"Where do they get the courage for such detachment?" asked Thomas.

"What's the matter, old man?" retorted Jean-Jacques. "Didn't you understand our friend's beautiful description?"

"What can I do?" said Thomas. "No doubt I'm still too far away from the right attitude."

"Don't worry," said Dutheil. "I asked myself the same question. I think I can attribute this courage to a certainty that they are so vitally endowed with. It is neither mental understanding nor submission to imposed beliefs, but rather the awareness of participation in Life and in the cosmic Powers. This awareness creates in the Hindus a sense of the nobility of their essential origin and of their spiritual destiny. How else could these men allow themselves to be affected by the ignominy and incoherence of their mortal being, *with which they do not allow themselves to identify*?

"In brief, let's say they are conscious of an interdependence and a continual exchange between our world of phenomenon and the World of Causes."

"You can understand, Thomas," Dominique put in, "that our contemporaries are haunted by this notion of interchange and intercommunication—interurban, intercontinental, interplanetary, so why not interstellar? What does this mean if not an instinctive need to break down limits? It's as if our psychospiritual being experiences an imperious need to go beyond the frontiers imposed by our physical and mental carcass!

"Of course, this impulse is captured and interpreted by our usual agent of comprehension, the Mind, which translates it into a controlled exploration of the physical, chemical, and energy realms that are accessible to it. It is what we might call an attempt to penetrate from the exterior, through the analysis and dissection of controllable elements of energy.

"The *causal* Power of this energy cannot be found through 'mechanistic' analysis, no more than the surgeon can find the soul at the end of his scalpel! However, causal Spirit is the most common as well as the most subtle agent of natural phenomena; but the vital logic of its action is essentially different from the rational logic used by our scientists to explain the formation and transformation of matter.

"The form of matter and its transformation are the phenomenal and perceptible appearance of 'divine geometry,' which, at all levels of being, creates the ideal type before the manifested form. *True* faith is the consciousness of this reality, which can only be known through the 'union' attained in meditative silence."

Dominique fell silent, allowing Thomas to absorb these explanations.

"This is the cause of the opposition between the Eastern and Western mentalities," continued Dominique, lighting his pipe. "More precisely, between the two methods: one is a *study* carried out by the cerebral faculties; the other is not research, but an intercommunication between causal Forces and these same Forces incarnated in the individual—like two waters that interpenetrate when the barrier that separates them is removed."

Dominique's three friends listened silently.

"What can one do?" murmured Thomas.

"Learn how to eliminate the barrier that is preventing intercommunication!"

"I've heard this so often from my Brahmans!" exclaimed Dutheil: "'Stop your thinking machine!'"

"But doesn't the thinking machine of the Vedic theologians function intensely?" objected Thomas.

"That's why the Brahmans whose wisdom I admired considered theologians to be scholars of the 'letter,' and not gurus who lead the way to Illumination!" retorted Dutheil.

"Dutheil, you were lucky to have been received by sages, who know from experience the nature of the conflict we spoke about (do you recall?) during our meeting at Orly Airport: the conflict between our duty toward spiritual realization and the other duties created by our social obligations."

"Of course I remember, Maître Dominique. And I was struck by the similarity between your concept of reality and that of the Brahmans, whose only concern was the continuous vision of 'the one necessary thing.' With them you don't find the polemics, politics, or doctrines that you find in certain circles in India where religious questions get mixed up with the quarrels of the different parties."

"These quarrels are incompatible with the Knowledge of their causes, my friend," retorted Dominique. "Think about the various religious ideas we have discussed today. I had no intention of giving you a course on Hinduism, nor did I hope to convert you to Buddhism!

"What's important is for you to learn how to discern the Universal Reality of each Revelation and the particular character that enables it to adapt to the age and the people whom it must enlighten.

"Man, who is a microcosm of the Universe, gives us a picture of what is happening on Earth and for Humanity. Just as every seven years the cells of our body are renewed, so every seventh year are certain mental, psychic, or spiritual faculties awakened in the human being, the physical repercussion of which is marked by a degree of maturity."

"Seven, fourteen, twenty-one," confirmed Thomas: "the age of reason, puberty, and adulthood. These dates are always approximative and vary according to the individual."

"In fact, whether early or late, they operate around a culminating point," explained the sculptor. "We could say the same of each zodiacal sign, whose influence is prepared or continued before and after the entry of the sun into this sign.

"This same law of rhythms and cycles is at play during the eras of humanity, which are also subject to the influence of our solar system. The conjunction of the two leads to moments of exaltation, which manifest in a spiritual influx corresponding to the maturity of one or another part of humanity. The culminating point of this influx manifests in what we call a Revelation. This Revelation is always the teaching of eternal Wisdom, adapted to the necessities and the tendencies of the human elite for whom it is destined."

"Why do you speak of an elite?" asked Jean-Jacques. "After all, whether we're talking about Hinduism, Buddhism, Judaism, or Christianity, each of these Revelations addressed itself to an entire people."

"By *elite*," answered Dominique, "I do not mean intellectuals or a privileged class, but rather beings who are already prepared by their aspiration to go beyond their egotistical goals in order to receive the influx that is brought to them."

"But you said yourself that the entire Hindu population was penetrated by it; the people of Israel obey Moses; and Christianity would have itself preached to all nations, and addresses itself to the masses. . . ."

"That's true," admitted Dominique, "but note that in every religion born of a Revelation, the pure principle that has survived distortion was initially '*heard*' in its Reality by some of the Master's disciples, who were able to transmit the spiritual influx that had transformed them. After them came the interpreters, the theologians, and the scholars of the Law.

"The masses have always served as the preservers of traditions in the popular aspect that has been imposed on it by legend, custom, and, if needed, the 'taboos' that isolate them from other religions.

"With regard to Christianity—which, socially speaking, seems to lend itself to the masses—hasn't its Messiah declared that he came not for the world, but for those who were not of *this* world? And when he said that the Gospel should be preached to all nations, isn't it obvious that he meant all those in each nation who were outside of the world, all those who were 'called' to the Supra-Human Kingdom?

"What I want to say is this: the pure spirit of a Revelation is always a spiritual ferment, which naturally selects those beings who are predisposed to participate in it 'in spirit and in truth.' And this predisposition is the immortal seed formed in their previous lives, or awakened in their current existence. This is the 'choice' that Saint Paul affirmed when speaking about the 'chosen' ones.

"And on this fixed point of all the Revelations, all the revealed religions come together, despite their multiple interpretations.

"Once you understand this, if you still insist on satisfying your intellectual curiosity, you can delve into all the theologies. Have fun, gentlemen, if that's what you want to do! But please, don't lost sight of the one necessary thing: adapt your quest *to what you need to know in order to calm your thought and find your own Light*."

15

The Compagnons du Devoir

Dr. Thomas and Dutheil were descending from the nave of Notre Dame, thanking Dominique for having shown them the mastery with which the builders had solved certain difficult architectural problems. On exiting the cathedral, they encountered a curious procession taking place outside.

"Bravo!" said the sculptor joyously. "I've shown you masterpieces, and now here are the Master Workers: these are the Compagnons du Devoir,[1] who have come to celebrate their patronal festival."

"What's that?" asked Dutheil. "Is it a religious brotherhood?"

"Not at all. It's the Workmen's Association of the Compagnons du Devoir. They recently acquired this official name so they could be recognized by the government, which has since declared their Public Purpose. In fact, they are descendants of the ancient Compagnonnage du Devoir, and have kept the rule, the rituals, the symbols, and the authentic tradition, as well as the name.

"They are a part of the building trade, but I assure you that these are no ordinary workers."

As the procession passed by, Dominique greeted them respectfully. Thomas and Dutheil watched energetic men passing by two by two, each wearing on his vest a large silk ribbon covered with symbolic signs. Each man carried a cane with a twisted handle.

"That's the cane of the Compagnons," explained Dominique. "The

---

1. Literally, the Companions of Duty, a federation of artisans that dates back to the medieval guilds. (Ed. note)

color of the ribbon indicates their professional rank, and there is nothing childish about it."

In the middle of the procession, some of the men were carrying on their shoulders several models of carpentry and joinery, revealing the mastery of the trade.

"The masterpieces of the Compagnons," said Dominique, "are proof of their knowledge and their technical perfection. The execution of such a masterpiece is mandatory in order to become a Compagnon."

A car decorated with flowers stopped behind the procession. A dignified, smiling woman got out of it and warmly greeted the men who surrounded her.

"This woman plays a very important role," said the sculptor. "She is the 'Mother' of the Compagnons, the only female member of the association. The white ribbon that she wears on her belt symbolizes the virtues demanded of the woman chosen to fulfill this difficult mission."

Thomas and Dutheil, stunned by the nobility of the faces that were passing by, watched the procession go into the Cathedral.

"It's a vision from another era," said Dutheil. "Why do I get the impression of such nobility?"

"It's their ideal," answered the sculptor. "It's a rare thing today to see men who bear witness to a symbolic form of worship and a sense of the sacred. It is so different from the cynicism of the current generation. Isn't it strange to see them affirm, without regard for public opinion, the cult of Duty before a public which speaks of nothing but its 'rights'!"

"It's hard to believe," said Thomas to Dutheil. "Is that really their ideal?"

"It's not only their ideal, it's the absolute law of their behavior," affirmed Dominique. "But let's go back to the Atelier. I will show you the *Journal of the Compagnonnage*, and you'll be able to see for yourselves the strict application of what is stated in it."

"Isn't the Compagnonnage an institution that goes back to the Middle Ages?" asked Dutheil.

"It goes back even farther than that. According to them, their legendary founders were Solomon, Maître Jacques, and Father Soubise. The names of these founders differentiate the three great rituals of the Compagnonnage.

"These rituals, their symbols, and the Rule for each one were codified in accordance with Wisdom. All of this is authenticated by a working knowledge of the laws of geometry, and by the professional secrets of the Master Builders (the Children of Soubise), nicknamed Good Fellows and Passants; the stone chiselers and the Carpenters of Duty and of Liberty, who are the Children of Solomon.

"The Children of Maître Jacques go back to the Grand Masters of the Templars, Jacques de Molay (burned at the stake by Pope Clement V and Philippe le Bel), whose sacrifice in the name of sworn silence affirmed the knowledge of *true* secrets. The Children of Maître Jacques are grouped in different trades: stone chiselers, carpenters, blacksmiths, leathersmiths, et cetera."

"Weren't these the old guilds?" asked Thomas.

"Not at all!" exclaimed Dominique. "Until the French Revolution, the Compagnonnage fervently remained independent from official guilds, which didn't have the same spirit or the same ideal. These official guilds were more or less linked to the Compagnonnage in the same way that our labor unions are linked to industrial capitalism.

"When the Revolution abolished the guilds, the Compagnons regained their freedom of action. Nonetheless, they had to go underground to have their secret meetings (their Hidden Places), but they never discontinued their Tour of France, the trip that every candidate must make in order to become a Compagnon. They stayed several months in every city where there was a Lodge (also called the Mother), and the candidate worked there in the shop. He was housed, nourished, and instructed during the evenings by the Compagnonnage.

"All of this never ceased to exist, although World War II reduced it to only a few hundred actual members. But since 1944 the Compagnons have multiplied, and they now say, with good reason, that they have 'begun the modern adaptation of the most noble institution of work that the world has ever possessed.'"[2]

"I wonder what they can do to transform the mentality of our young people," said Dutheil.

"First, through willing submission to the Rule and to the rituals of their association, and through their respectful attitude toward the Mother, who in each Lodge supervises the candidates and teaches them respect for the established order and for the objects of their trade. The Lodge is very important. Built by the Compagnons, it is always beautiful in its harmonious simplicity and furnished with the comfort necessary to the well-being of the workers. There are private rooms, communal eating rooms, lecture rooms, and study halls as well as ateliers. Everything is arranged to give the working man an impression of individual liberty and the nobility of work."

"Are you telling us a fairy tale, Maître Dominique, or is this true?"

"It's all true, my friend. You'll be able to verify it for yourself. Besides, results prove the efficacity of the method. I assure you that their meals

2. R. Vergez, *La Pendule à Salomon* (Paris: Julliard), p. 33.

are not gloomy occasions! At their feasts and banquets they do justice to the wines of France, and singing is part of their work as well as their pleasure.

"The value of their professional knowledge is judged by their work: the cathedrals and the civil and religious monuments that our country is filled with. Today, as in the Middle Ages, they are still the Master Workers since modern architects turn to the Compagnons for all work that demands the competence and technical perfection of a Master.

"They have always taken first prize in international as well as French contests for Best Worker."

"Are the labor unions often opposed to them?"

"Obviously, for the labor unions are thinking only of their rights, and the Compagnons are thinking only of their duty. Unionism 'creates masses whenever it can, whereas the Compagnonnage continually reveals the individual.'"[3]

"Aren't they disturbed by the modern concepts of construction and the materials used?" asked Dutheil.

"They've adapted to it," answered the sculptor. "They adapt new techniques to those which they preserve. I'll show you some documents. . . ."

When they got back to the Atelier, Dominique showed them some photos of the Masterpieces and the Lodges of the Compagnons. He read them an excerpt from the statutes and summarized the spirit that animated the Association.

"The first qualities that this organization strives for are courage, fidelity (to the Rule and to the Duties), and the discernment of values. The way of acquiring them is as interesting as the results."

"I'd be very interested in knowing it," exclaimed Thomas.

"It's very simple," said Dominique. "First is love of the perfect gesture, which soon becomes *the honor of the Trade* for them; then, the respect for sworn silence, which assures their fidelity to the secrets of the Trade. Each revelation is a reward for progress. Next, the value of essential words which define their program, such as *Duty*, the *Orient*, the *Stroke*, which have old traditional meaning. Then there are the passwords and the words of order, without knowledge of which one cannot be recognized as an authentic Compagnon. The importance of the word is sanctified by a new name given to each Compagnon. It is a name of *Quality*, which is at the same time a portrait and a program, added to the name of the Compagnon's hometown: Parisian the Confident; Nantes

3. *Compagnonnage*, February 1958.

the Faithful; and the like. This new name rejects old links and habits and creates an individuality that corresponds to the particular tendencies of each person.

"The positive way is the supereffort, whose courageous practice leads men to *go beyond themselves*. Do you know what a Compagnon answered his student, a young candidate who was complaining about excessive fatigue? 'Each day you must learn to become less and less tired until the day when you are no longer tired at all.'"

"That's some school!" said Thomas. "And it's so close to what you are teaching us that you even could have invented it."

"Not I, my friend," answered Dominique. "It's the work of ancient Wisdom. But if I had a son, I would send him to the Compagnons to inculcate in him the true sense of nobility. As beautiful as a teaching is, its only value lies in the practice of it."

"All this is quite impressive," said Dutheil. "It's a vision of another era . . . and it's very moving in that it offers the hope of renewal, something to counteract the egotistical drives of our current society. What strikes me is the joyous pride that enlivens the expressions of these working men united by the same ideal."

"Even more beautiful is the fact that this ideal is undamaged by any kind of egoism, even though these workers are strongly individualistic through their freedom of conscience and their beliefs. But this individualism is the will to the ennoblement of man through the development and *surpassing* of his particular qualities."

"This is very close to the formation of the Elite, in the way that you understand it, Maître Dominique."

"Exactly, dear friend, that's why I'm interested in this type of education, which is (physically as well as morally) a school of consciousness. However, what is extraordinary in their method is that intellectual work is reduced to a minimum because the necessary teaching for each trade is communicated *orally* to the apprentices by more advanced Compagnons during the course of an evening, after a day of labor in the shop. These apprentices (or even the perfected Compagnons) come to the same study room or to the atelier to apply what they have received orally."

"They do all of this after a long day's work?"

"It's an essential element for their success: the *increase of effort* freely consented to. This daily lesson of courage, as well as the submission to imposed disciplines, gives the apprentice (according to their own words) 'his formation as a man,' which is the fundamental goal of the Compagnonnage.

"But the practice of the supereffort, whether it's in the quantity of work or in its perfection, has another intention as well. As I've explained to you so many times, Nature does not tolerate excess. The effort that goes beyond the natural possibilities of the worker, or of the researcher, develops in him superior possibilities, and can even awaken his supra-natural faculties, such as intuitive perceptions in the realm of his research.

"Whether you call these strokes of genius, inspiration, or more simply intuition, it's a state of consciousness that *'knows' instead of compre-hending rationally*, a state that no theoretical study can allow one to *experience*."

"But intellectual work is necessary," objected Jean Thomas. "I mean the personal study of what the builder of an edifice, for example, must know. He must know physics, geometry, mathematics, and the special laws particular to each trade."

"The experience of the Compagnons has proved that oral teaching and experiment allow book teaching to be reduced considerably. Oral teaching replaces this advantageously, because theory, which only addresses itself to reason, closes the door to intuition.

"There is still confusion between 'learning' and 'Knowledge,' which makes the Wisdom of this way of education incomprehensible to you! But do you realize that the master carpenters, taught by this method, were the Master Builders of our old Cathedrals? Theoretical architects didn't exist in those times! The Master Builder fulfilled these functions, constructed the model and even the framework of the vault and the arch *with his own hands*, synthesizing his triple knowledge: knowledge of the Symbol, of Measure, and of the Keys, which assured the resistance and balance of the assembled materials.

"It's not without reason that in the hierarchy of the old guilds, the carpenter, as 'possessor of secrets,' predominated. You'll notice that his emblem was the raven."

"Why is there always this idea of transmitting a secret? Is it the revelation of a personal discovery, or of a trade technique given to a student who merited it?"

"There are *real* secrets," answered Dominique. "Those are always related to a *vital* law; that is, they are conditioned at every moment by a phase of genesis, and consequently cannot be taught by fixed formulas.

"The vital functions, like reactions to matter, are subordinated to the play of Cosmic Harmony, which is always in movement, since the Uni-verse is always in a state of transformation and successively undergoes the laws of a continual genesis. This creates an interdependence between the slightest phenomenon of Nature and the energies that are put into play by this cosmic genesis.

"For example, you can't cut a tree that is going to furnish wood for a frame at just any moment whatsoever. Nor can you give a particular remedy at any hour whatsoever, or at any season whatsoever. These examples, among thousands of others, are to allow you to understand a more precise meaning of Harmony, which theologians would refuse to consider, but the knowledge of which allowed the ancient builders to accomplish enduring masterpieces.

"The science of Measure, of Proportions, and of the nature of Number, has nothing to do with our rational mathematics, because these latter have nothing to do with *Causal Functions*, which the Numbers possess as their intrinsic properties.

"Nothing that can be discovered by the intellectual and sensory faculties alone is a true secret, because the sacred sense of a secret is its esoteric (interior) aspect. In other words, it is that which is accessible only to intuitive vision, to the Intelligence of the Heart.

"Take the example of the two 'royal' colors of the stained-glass windows, called 'Chartres blue' and 'Chartres red.' The master glassmaker who had *rediscovered* them was unable to reveal how they were made, not even to his own son. Besides, that's why they only reappear except time to time, in Egypt, in China, then in the Middle Ages. These two colors, which have nothing chemical about them, are real secrets, because they bear witness to the knowledge of certain causal laws of Nature, which reason alone cannot discover.

"Traditional Wisdom is the synthesis of this knowledge, which it transmits through symbols to make it accessible to men who are disposed toward penetrating its true meaning."

"And suppose it were possible to teach this knowledge clearly in terms of its practical application: what would be wrong with divulging it?" asked Dutheil.

"First of all it would be a *deformation*, because man has such confidence in his intellectual comprehension: science refuses to recognize the mystery that veils the creative action of the Spirit. It denies it, and keeps the door to philosophy closed. The scientist wants to explain everything, and in doing so, deforms the law of Harmony, whose initial Cause he misunderstands. As a consequence of this mentality, the secondary laws which the scientist arrives at are oriented by him toward decomposition, which is opposed to the creative intention of Primordial Activity.

"The second danger of this disclosure is the application of destructive power to egotistical goals of domination. I'm speaking not only of atomic weapons, but also of the will to intimidate, which causes the world today to live in an atmosphere of anguish, hatred, and violence, and which has repercussions on the younger generation."

"The result is tangible," exclaimed Dutheil; "uncertainty, amorality, and skepticism, until we come to the *tragic* conclusion, tragic when expressed by young people: 'What's the use?' Is it possible to reverse the situation by teaching men another way of understanding, which would make the meaning of the Symbol and of traditional Knowledge accessible to them?"

"But that's precisely what the Compagnons du Devoir have been able to do in their own domain."

"That's very interesting, but this domain involves working with matter, the work of a manual worker, which cannot be applied to other professions."

"To 'work with one's hands' the material of one's craft is actually the best way of knowing its qualities and reactions. Theoretical studies are unable to give this vital knowledge. Whether he is working with wood, stone, metal, or glass, the material's behavior provides the artisan with a subtle sense of observation, the consciousness and the mastery of the gestures needed to make it obey his will. Concentrated attention develops his intuition, *if the worker pushes the perfection of his work to the extreme*."

"I don't see the relationship between this manual work and intuition," said Jean Thomas.

"You will understand if you can tell me why the archer was considered in China and ancient Egypt to be a proof of wisdom," answered Dominique. "Try to imagine the *quality* of the archer's concentration: he doesn't calculate, he doesn't *want*, he doesn't *think*; he is only 'consciousness.' Consciousness of his hands, of his bow, of his arrow, and of the goal, with which he is united. . . .

"That is the means of *knowing* through the identification of subject with object. If the gesture is experienced that way, it eliminates the distance and the difficulty, gives the arrow or the tool the correct movement and vibration, and subjects matter to the intention of the worker.

"What intellectual study will allow you to obtain this result?"

"It's so strange that I can hardly imagine it," admitted Thomas, sighing.

Dominique was growing impatient. "Make an effort to widen your angle of vision, dammit! The awe one experiences before the Pharaonic monuments at the perfect adjustment of enormous cubes of granite without the use of cement, or the lifting of thirty tons of lintels without the help of machines made for that purpose: yet these builders did it, by seeming to play with the weight of matter or with the hardness of stone. There's the example of our cathedrals as well, where the audacity of certain vaults seems to defy the resistance of the arches, or implies a foreknowledge of their behavior.

"Explain these wonders to me, my friend: scholarly calculations conceived in the office of an architect? That's impossible, Thomas! You must recognize in these phenomena the consciousness of the Master Builder who is one with his work, just as the bird is when it builts its nest.

"Note that when the Compagnon wants to build his masterpiece, he *makes his own tools*, whose secret he then keeps, because they are conceived *by his consciousness of the gestures* that he wants to execute."

Dutheil was stunned. "That's a practical exercise in the awakening of consciousness, Maître Dominique. It's done through positive means, and it doesn't allow one to delude oneself about the results that are obtained."

"That's quite right, Dutheil: there either *is* or *isn't* identification of the worker with the work that he wishes to execute. His masterpiece is his witness.

"However, Thomas, I do understand your objection: the manual worker is excluded from a large number of professions. That's why I hope that each of you will spend some of your free time to work in the school of matter. Aside from that, the example of the Compagnons is valuable for everyone in terms of the qualities that they are trying to cultivate.

"The opening of intuitive perception demands the elimination of the obstacles to it: first the shell formed by our prejudices, atavism, habits, egotistical goals, ambitions, and personal attachments. Why is the Tour of France the test that must be passed in order to become a Compagnon? After a more or less lengthy apprenticeship in a Lodge of Compagnonnage where his work and behavior have been judged acceptable, the apprentice receives his candidate's cane (which is the symbol of the Rule of the Compagnons). Then he must leave behind family, friends, and habits, the atavistic attachments to which limit his point of view. The first step of liberation that leads him into another Lodge is part of the Tour of France: other masters, another milieu which is connected to the first by a single Rule.

"The second stage consists of periodic changes in which the candidate sacrifices the advantage of his new stage to benefit another itinerant. From one change to the next, he becomes conscious, through traveling, of the unity of the goal that links all of these pilgrims, and of their solidarity, which engenders mutual help. Little by little the egotistical point of view is obliterated. There is absolutely no question of jealousy, because the individual's knowledge becomes the common treasure, made available to all those who are disposed to participate in it.

"The final point of the Tour of France will be the competition, for the building of the masterpiece, an individual masterpiece that will become the property of the community. Anonymity shields its author from all vanity, his symbolic signature being the witness to his adherence to the masters who initiated him."

The men who were listening exploded with a burst of admiration:

"How wonderful, Maître Dominique. The Compagnons are not exaggerating when they speak of the formation of men."

"Wait a moment," continued the sculptor. "Do you know the key words that give life to this building? *'To Serve'*! This is no mere phrase. It is the major guiding force of their behavior.

"Can you find a modern organization with an ideal so disinterested as this one? You might be able to name certain religious communities, but they are limited by exclusive dogmatism. The Compagnons can adhere to any religion, so long as each keeps his convictions to himself and abstains from any type of proselytizing. The essential goal of the Compagnonnage is the formation of an Elite through Quality: however, the law of the Elite is freedom of conscience and mutual respect for the experience necessary for individual realization."

"In brief," said Thomas, "you wanted to show us that the qualities developed by the Compagnons are not only due to their manual labor."

"If we get to the root of it, the manual work is their means of experimentation. Professional dexterity is indispensable for them in order to perfect themselves in the consciousness of the essential gesture. But they must also attain intense concentration (which is indispensable in order not to lose anything of their oral teaching), and submit their intelligence to a synthetic vision that constantly unifies the vital and theoretical aspects of the knowledge necessary to their trade.

"In order to attain this, a certain state of being and an inner disposition are necessary. That's why the candidates are given, in addition to their work, certain tasks to accomplish within their Lodge. This could be in the organization of the Lodge or in mutual moral support, in order to awaken a sense of altruism."

Dutheil lit a cigarette to rouse himself from his reverie. Dominique challenged him: "Tell me, Dutheil, can you establish a connection between the Wisdom of the Compagnons du Devoir and the Wisdom of the Brahman that you met?"

"I wanted to tell you about it, Maître Dominique. Listening to you, I realized that it is the same principle applied to different conditions. Both groups are concerned, not with religious doctrine, but with the *formation of man*, who must learn to transcend his mediocrity by transcending his possibilities. Both groups demand cooperation in the creation of an elite which will be the ferment of a superior humanity.

"The rituals of both awaken the consciousness of symbols and the significance of ritual objects: for the Compagnons, it's the cane and the color of the ribbons. Both have the same appreciation of nobility: with the Compagnons, it's the progressive acquisition of consciousness of their gestures; Brahmanic wisdom cites among the essential royal qualities, 'the art of persevering without exhausting oneself, the art of gauging one's efforts in the face of a long and difficult task.'

"For both, Duty doesn't mean submission to arbitrarily imposed obligations, but the observance of the rules inherent in perfecting the trade, and the man himself. The entire family of my Brahmans considered taboos and compulsory acts not as bondage but as a constant reminder of the laws of Harmony. 'You think of them as interfering with the liberty of the individual,' they told me, 'whereas to us, they are measuring-rods by which disciplined men test themselves in ordinary everyday life.'"[4]

"The old Compagnons used to say: 'Burn the shop if the trade bores you, but do not assassinate the work,'"[5] confirmed Dominique.

"You're right, Dutheil," he continued. "This aspect of the Wisdom that you encountered in Nepal can find its application here because it's the indispensable attitude for acquiring the knowledge of oneself, of matter, and of the harmony that governs the universe. What were you looking for in India?"

"It was precisely that. And I confess that I imagined different reasons and different formulas. . . ."

"In other words, what seduces all our idealistic dreamers: the prestigious Hindu Yogas through which Westerners hope to attain illumination?

"You see, Dutheil, I would not rely on the statement of Huang Po that 'the Ever-Existent Buddha is not a Buddha of stages.' I would agree if by this state is meant the total Consciousness of Absolute Reality. But I think ultimate realization demands a preparation that eliminates the obstacles. However, these obstacles are multiplied for Westerners, who have nourished in themselves the worst enemies of the Intelligence of the Heart: the autocratic mind and egotistical preoccupations. Moreover, with the best of intentions to attain this state, how can you pursue a goal that is pure abstraction?

"Quite frankly, Dutheil, do you find yourself attracted by a state which, by virtue of your present understanding, you must imagine as a total annihilation of yourself?

"When one wants to attain a goal, he must love that goal. He must desire it so intensely that it attracts him like a magnet. Contemplatives who find in ecstasy a happiness in which their physical and psychic being have no role can seek this beatitude without experiencing the terror of losing the self. But for you (as for all those who have not been conscious of the intermediary state between the mental world and the world of Pure Spirit), this ecstatic state—indescribable for those who have not experi-

4. Reymond, p. 60. Translation by Lucy Norton.
5. Vergez, p. 128.

enced it—would appear as emptiness: its powerful vibrations would find no echo in your current consciousness, which is obscured by your frightened need to attach yourself to this 'self,' the loss of which would horrify you."

"That's true," admitted Dutheil. "I've understood that we have within us intermediary states that are more subtle than our physical bodies. I've even understood that our Permanent Witness is an intermediary between our psychological consciousness and our absolutely impersonal Spiritual Witness. The association of our Permanent Witness with our mortal self creates a confusion between the impulses of our psychological conscious-ness and the inspiration of our Spiritual Witness. This confusion prevents us from experiencing as a living and indestructible Reality this Conscious Witness, which is, however, our first guarantee of survival."

"What do you think is keeping us from it?"

"Doubt," said Dutheil. "Doubt of the existence of our spiritual being."

"Well, I would say fear," retorted Dominique. "It's the fear that this immortal being, when it has left the body, will no longer be interested in our earthly attachments.

"Try this experiment: attempt to imagine a supernatural world in which the beings who have attained it have to 'worry' (as we do on Earth) about matters that we give so much importance to—matters of the heart, the intellect, social matters, matters of profit, with their emotional consequences, and all the hope and deceptions that are necessarily in-volved. Ridiculous, isn't it? Yet it's the abandoning of all those things which makes us dread death. We're still prisoners of this way of thinking, so it's difficult for us to imagine a state of *higher life*, exempt from all these contingencies!"

"Just a moment Maître Dominique. What you have just said makes me realize the stupidity of our situation. We're complaining about the in-herent miseries of our earthly humanity and are afraid of a state that would liberate us from it! In brief, we live and think like prisoners who would never have known a world other than their prison cell."

"The body is not a prison cell," answered Dominique. "It's a matrix whose role is to generate a subtle and 'glorious' body which is inde-structible because it is immaterial, and which keeps the *essential* char-acteristics (and not personal characteristics) of its Number-entity.

"But no doubt this is not enough for you. It's the continuation of your dear personality that worries you, isn't it?"

Dutheil, embarrassed, hesitated before answering. Dominique started to laugh. "My poor friend, look at the extent to which we are infatuated with our mediocrity!"

"It's curious," remarked Dutheil, "that this uncertainty disappeared when I was with the Brahmans. Could it be because the atmosphere was immersed in the invisible world, which they constantly felt and communicated with?"

"And don't you feel the same way in one of our religious communities, for example?"

"Quite frankly, no, Maître Dominique. These religious communities appear more like a duality: the human being standing before the Divine, which he searches for outside of himself. This attitude corresponds to an aspect of religiosity. Personally, it's in myself that I want to establish the contact, or rather it's my own reality that I want to recognize in widening my consciousness. If I were young, I would perhaps go and work with the Compagnons, because I've understood that their method is a means of widening this consciousness and of acquiring a certain knowledge without letting the mind distort it. It's too late for me!"

"I'd advise you nonetheless to work in an area that would put you in contact with the laws of life in matter: gardening, for example, or glassmaking. It's necessary to learn how to discern nature from artifice.

"Can you tell me why you didn't stay with your Brahmans?

Dutheil gave this serious reflection. Then he answered: "The main reason is that their methods are inaccessible to me in my present mentality. Each one of my words, each of my actions, was judged or interpreted in relationship to a Reality that they never stop thinking about. That makes their life a continual state of meditation, and I am very far from that.

"This doesn't keep them from practicing other forms of meditation. Some of them attain ecstasy, which is an evasion of our rational world. I confess I was tempted by this, but they advised me to follow my own path in the environment where my destiny has placed me."

"They are wise men," answered Dominique. "If we're predisposed to surpass our lower humanity, our destiny situates us in the environment that offers us the opportunity for the necessary experience. However, this experience varies for each individual, the 'way' for each one must be adapted to it, and the person's conditions of existence must also be taken into account.

"The diverse forms of meditation advocated by the Yogis present serious dangers for Westerners: our overactive, agitated, worried life and our nervous centers, which are affected by multiple radiations, make it impractical for us to practice the retention of breath, for we run the risk of cerebral, psychic, or even pulmonary disorders. Although one can attain certain ecstatic states, these are experiences which, for the man bound to the illusions of the mind, are as risky as the artificial paradises sought by drug-users. While we're speaking of this, I would like to know what the Brahmans told you about the yogis."

"They hardly spoke to me about them at all," answered Dutheil, "and yet they showed a touch of malice regarding Europeans and Americans who arrived in India searching for a swami ready to 'initiate' them. I think they were grateful that I didn't insist on asking them for a teaching which demands a rigorous preparatory discipline."

"They're right," agreed Dominique. "The yogi is not a vague mystic who is following a vaguely defined religious goal. It is a *school* for the reintegration of our Immortal Principle in our inferior being.

"The word *yoga*, which means union, link, or identification, expresses simultaneously the goal and the techniques used to attain it. And these techniques are multiple. You already know that the great enemies of this realization are the egotistical impulses of our Automaton and the resistance of the Mind, which does not want to let itself be dethroned. It's a matter of choosing the most efficient method to get rid of them."

"Do you mean the same method used for wild beasts: the gentle method or the ferocious one?" said Thomas, laughing.

"It's a bit like that, although our Automaton is much more complicated than the most savage beasts, because in addition to all its instincts, it is intelligent, and intends to dispute the reality of its Master. Certain yogis, in order to attain the goal, have advocated the 'ferocious' method."

"Are you pulling my leg, Maître Dominique?"

"Dear friend: I'm speaking of Hatha Yoga, which is known as "the Yoga of Power. It consists, at first, of hammering out our animal instincts by severe abstinences and by observances that regulate our inner behavior and control the functions of the physical body and all the vital energies. Then it involves numerous exercises, gestures, postures, breathing, and mental control, which can give the persevering yogi supranormal powers."

"What are some of these abstinences?" asked Thomas, interested.

Dominique, amused, enumerated them: "Abstention from violence, from lying, from theft, from lust, and from the desire of possession."

"After all, that would be acceptable," groaned Thomas as he chewed on his cigarette.

"Who would have believed it?" said the sculptor. "I can imagine you calm, sincere, honest, and almost chaste, as long as you haven't yet found the sister soul of your dreams—but when it comes to possessiveness, well, old chap, that's to be seen. I wouldn't bet on it."

"Seriously, Dominique, if the observances are no more austere than these abstinences, I really don't see any ferocity in them. Besides, many religious Christians are subjected to the same regimens."

"It's a totally different technique, my friend, and a different mentality as well. The Christian mystic distrusts his body as an adversary of the soul, whereas the yogi considers his physical body as the support of the subtle body, which can accumulate spiritual energy and thus become the magnet of the Supreme Self. In other words, its the magnet of our

Spiritual Witness, for it's what must be reintegrated. For the yogi, his body is the field of *indispensable* experiences for finding consciousness."

"It's in vain that the Christian mystic says that his body is the Temple of the Holy Spirit. He still considers it the number one enemy of his 'eternal salvation' and tries to ignore it. The result is often a state of functional anarchy, which gives rise to sickness and imbalance among the various physical, mental, and psychic states, which are too often confused with the spiritual. How many beautiful mystical impulses have been marred by astral visions and illusory phenomena!

"Aren't sexual repression and excessive mortification frequently responsible for this?" asked Jean Thomas.

"Of course," said Dominique. "That's what I call ferocious training. We can manage to suppress our animal passions, but what's the use if our psyche and sentimentality, exacerbated by these brutalities, open the door to astral forces, which are the most dangerous of animals?"

"That's the opinion of the Master yogis," remarked Dutheil. "Yoga, they say, is a school of consciousness in which every discipline must be measured, every reaction (physical or psychic) controlled, or else one exposes oneself to the gravest dangers."

"That's exactly right," said Dominique. "You could even say the same for intensive meditation that is practiced thoughtlessly.

"If I've only spoken to you today about Hatha Yoga, it's because its simplest aspect, which I've crudely sketched, is the basis for other forms of yoga. The other aspects of Hatha Yoga push gestures and postures to the extreme (involving intricate acrobatics). They also push to the extreme the purification of organs, the control of the breath, concentration, and sometimes contemplation that leads to Union—that is, the final ecstasy of samadhi. Moreover, Hatha Yoga is considered the necessary stepping stone which, by eliminating physical obstacles, allows access to the 'royal way,' which is purely spiritual: Raja Yoga.

"I think it would be a needless waste of energy for you to go further into these methods, because they are not practical in modern life."

"Would you allow me to insist on one important point?" asked Dutheil. "In India, I heard them speak of another yoga which seems to me the gentle method: Bhakti Yoga."

"Reintegration through Love," answered Dominique. "It's the way of devotion. Do you think it would suit you?"

Dutheil responded: "Absolutely not. It's not for me. But I thought that Hindu metaphysics must give it a more subtle meaning."

"If you want to 'speak Hindu,' you must differentiate the nuances of the Hindu mentality. To simplify matters, let's discern the popular aspect and the 'cultivated' aspect. People, are atavistically permeated with the contact with invisible forces, a contact that inspires (according to the nature of the individual) deference or devotion, be it fearful or amorously sentimental, for one or another aspect of the Divinity. For example, you find the same sentiments in the Hindu's love for Krishna that you find in religious Catholics for Christ. All the mystical degrees of Love are represented in Bhakti Yoga, even the most abstract, which is the total abnegation of ego to attract in us the Self, a union which excludes all egotistical sentiment, even regarding the spiritual quest."

"I'm very far from that," answered Dutheil. "But what about the Yoga of Knowledge?"

"Jnana Yoga? I'll only speak briefly about that, my friend. It's the path of identification. But we don't need to describe a method of yoga to speak about it: it's the Way of the Heart, the path of knowledge through simplicity, that I've been trying to teach you. But in looking over the different kinds of yogas, don't forget the one that has the most immediate interest for you: Karma Yoga, reintegration through the Way of Action. It can be explained in very few words. It's more an inner disposition than a technique: Karma Yoga first of all considers acts that lead to reintegration as 'good' and those that separate one from this goal as 'bad.' Then its principle is detachment from one's actions and their immediate or apparent results. Each action that is judged good or necessary must be executed with full consciousness and all possible perfection, but in a mood of selflessness and neutrality toward the fruit of this action.

"In practical terms, it's the development of consciousness for its own sake, the perfection of the gesture for its own sake, and obedience to the Law of Harmony. It's the elimination of egotistical goals and of vanity."

"But that's the way of the Compagnons!" exclaimed Jean Thomas.

"That's what I wanted you to realize," answered Dominique. "It's worth the effort to find out about it. Though the Compagnons du Devoir do not depend on religious discipline, they still have the cult of consciousness. Its awakening and its expansion are the goal at which its Rule aims, through ritual and symbol, and through one's "Duty" as a Compagnon. Listen to a definition that was written by one of them:

"'*Consciousness is that which one carries within oneself, which rules from within to without until it has totally enlightened us, and it never leaves us stranded, regardless of the neglect into which one might have allowed it to fall.*'[6] Isn't that beautiful in its simplicity?"

"My compliments," said Thomas. "I would like to be as *conscious of my consciousness* as the author of those lines. Speak to us more about the Compagnons."

6. "Compagnonnage et la question religieuse," by "La Fidelité," in the *Compagnonnage* Journal.

"It's very simple," said Dominique. "They see things 'in truth.' It's not necessary for them to speak of God or of the soul: 'consciousness' says everything. It enlightens, at all the levels of being, the Compagnon who is devoted to the task of cultivating it. Consciousness of the trade, which, through the perfection of gestures, teaches them to feel matter; consciousness of the laws of balance, of Measure and Proportion, which allow them to catch a glimpse of Cosmic Laws; consciousness of their own reactions through the mastery necessary in the practice of the trade; intuitive consciousness awakened by the proponderance of intuition over the mind.

"There are absolutely no mystical illusions in all of that; it's constant watchfulness regarding the gesture that must be attained or the law that must be discovered, in order not to 'betray the Trade.'

"Their only mystical aspect is Fraternity, which is based on their consciousness of human solidarity. It's the sense of the sacred, awakened by their comprehension of ritual and symbol, which is the legacy of knowledge inherited from their ancient traditions. *And this tradition is that of the Master Workers of the Masterpieces of all time*!

"Does my enthusiasm surprise you? But isn't it comforting to find a contemporary example of the most beautiful of mystical systems, one that unifies in its reality all the religious symbols, by preparing the Compagnons (*who will push it to the limit*) for the intuitive Knowledge of the Laws of Genesis and of the great secrets of Nature?"

Dutheil and Jean Thomas were disturbed by Dominique's emotion and were unable to answer him.

The sculptor stood up, snorted, and led them into the Tavern, with its soft light conducive to reverie. He took an old bottle from the shelf.

"This is no ordinary liqueur," he said; "there are extraordinary virtues in old secrets. Savor it with respect."

"What is extraordinary in our time, when science is in the process of discovering everything?"

"Oh no!" retorted Dominique. "Science can only discover that which is comprehensible by syllogistic thought. It turns its back on life. In its haste to make progress and produce in quantity, it makes man a robot. It forces us (in order to exist, in order to take care of ourselves, to eat, and to think) to accept certain given things like *artificial* commodities. And that becomes ordinary for us.

"What is extraordinary, Thomas, is the Wisdom which results from the application of every tradition based on true Knowledge. You recognize the troubles and the imbalance caused by the modern mentality, but you don't dare figure out the source of this misery. Therefore, think. It's necessary to blame the idol of our times: the power of the mind which contemporaries hold in awe and glorify! The rashness of our sorcerer's apprentices who fall into the trap of rational logic is to blame.

"Thomas, Thomas! You, too, are unable to believe, unless you put your hand on disaster! And nonetheless you've received the warning of the Master whom you seem to have somewhat forgotten: Maître Jacques.

"It's easy to evoke him tonight. Haven't you noticed this curious coincidence: in the three traditional groupings of the Compagnons, the third is called the Children of Maître Jacques. However, that's the one that includes a large variety of trades. The Children of Father Soubise are the builders, who are the inheritors of the Christian tradition of the cathedrals. The Children of Solomon are the stonemasons and the carpenters (but these stonemasons were, as in Egypt, masters of geometry).

"The Children of Maître Jacques cite as their authority the Great Master of the Templars, who allowed themselves to be burned at the stake rather than divulge the secrets of their Knowledge. Therefore, they had this Knowledge, and proved it in their works and through their power.

"*What is Maître Jacques? It is the manifest Power of Knowledge.* It is Suprahuman Consciousness, which, when not veiled by our mental pride, shows us the unity of the human structure with the Cosmic structure.

"The Children of Maître Jacques go back to the traditions of the Templars, that is, to the religious symbolism (or mythical symbolism, if you prefer) that was also the major teaching of the Pharaonic Temple.

"What is remarkable is that this symbolism was not distorted, as it frequently is in what one calls today the 'occult sciences.' This is certainly due to their fidelity to this obligation: in each trade, the professional gesture must *participate in transforming the given material*: wood, metal, leather, et cetera. I could also add stained-glass windows, which are no longer spoken of because now the secret principles are almost entirely lost.

"This alliance of *science and consciousness* that the Compagnons seek—and whose dissociation (as one of them said) is, in Rabelais's words, 'the ruin of the soul'[7]—is a splendid symbol of Maître Jacques.

"Our Suprahuman Consciousness is in fact our Maître Jacques, that is, our Permanent Witness, which, through its cooperation with our Human Consciousness, renders Intuition intelligible to us. This Intuition is veiled when our learned reason dissociates itself from Consciousness."

"I have the impression that you have just given us the key to meditation," said Dutheil to Dominique.

"It's a basis for it, dear friend, but you must tell me what you mean by 'meditation,' because the word has numerous interpretations, and there are so many different schools!"

7. Vergez, p. 30.

"It's exactly this complexity which, until now, has repelled me," admitted Dutheil.

"As with many subjects, it's the words that cause confusion," continued Dominique. "That's why I prefer the word *mediation* to the term *meditation*. Roughly speaking, you could say that mediation is an intermediate state between thought and intuition. But this explanation is imperfect because there are various modes of mediation.

"More precisely, meditation is a mediating state between *what* one is trying to know and that *through which* one wants to know. It's the latter that differentiates the quality of meditation. One can meditate intellectually, physically, intuitively, and spiritually.

"Intellectual meditation is the concentration of thought on a chosen subject. As long as it doesn't put into play the cerebral faculties, it's not really meditation. At the opposite extreme, you have spiritual meditation, which is a *union* of human consciousness with the Permanent Witness and the Spiritual Witness. This meditation includes several different levels. The ultimate level is the union of all our being with Being, which is the ecstasy called *samadhi*. The quest for *samadhi* is a real danger for us, because it escapes all control and can expose us to serious imbalance.

"If you have understood the various states of consciousness that I've frequently explained to you,[8] you will also understand that there are several 'mediating states' between the cerebral Mind and the various degrees of intuitive consciousness. To give you a positive example, I'll use the simplest, the one the Compagnons practice *naturally*: all work that consists in transforming a material by 'living with it' in such a way that you can feel its reactions and its possibilities, demands a union of the man with this material. This union awakens *his innate consciousness*, the consciousness of all the states of Nature which preceded the human state and which man carries within him.

"This effort of union is a magnificent type of meditation, which does not lend itself to illusion because its reality is controllable through the work and the professional knowledge that results from it.

"So you can understand why the Compagnons, who have acquired the mastery of this practice, could have succeeded in making masterpieces, and (which is also beautiful) in inventing the appropriate tools whose secrets they carefully guarded.

"In the same way, one must adapt his mediation to what he wishes to attain. In this case, as in all other cases, I will insist on *simplicity*.

"What is our essential goal? It is to become conscious of our entire being. Start with the most tangible: the physical. All our organic functions

8. See Chapter 6.

depend on cosmic functions. Experience them as such, and then, little by little, you will be able to balance them."

"Shouldn't we fear the dangers of introspection?" asked Jean Thomas.

Dominique started to laugh. "You have nothing to fear, Doctor, from the *few instants* of attention that you give every morning to each of your essential organs, so that they *feel themselves watched*. It's the compulsory practice of the animal trainer, who each day visits his beasts to make them experience his authority. Elementary, isn't it? However, it's the most effective way of not subjecting himself to the caprices of his animals.

"It's the same with regard to your emotional reactions, whose best regulator is the act of *daily* faith in your higher destiny."

"Since you're speaking of control, give us a way of obtaining silence of the mind," intervened Dutheil.

Dominique smiled and offered Dutheil a cigarette. "Light it," he said, "and follow its smoke without losing track of it for one instant. . . . Relax, dammit! Want nothing. Don't ask yourself if you're going to succeed. The mind is the most obstinate of animals: if you want to silence it, it's going to rebel. Don't force yourself to eliminate your thoughts. Let them flow without thinking about them: neither violence nor will allow you to obtain inner silence. You will only get there by total relaxation, then by the Mediation of the Heart.[9]

"Mediation of the Heart consists in peacefully concentrating your attention on the region situated between the heart and the solar plexus, because that's the physical seat of the spiritual heart. Little by little, you'll be able to identify it with the Cosmic Heart, which is our source of Life and Light. Allow yourself to be penetrated by its pacifying power. Give it full power to dominate your impulses, and even to control those of your Permanent Witness, whose physical seat is the Liver.

"And now, that's enough for today. This is not the time to go into more detail on the practice of meditation. I'll tell you about it, if you want, in a special session. In the meantime, *think about it.*

"If we were at the circus, I'd take the animal tamer,[10] the trapeze artist, and the juggler as my witnesses. They would show you the possibility of various masteries. But as for explaining them to you, they would say only one word: practice!

"And the musical fanfare would conclude with an enticing march. . . .

"And the wise Compagnons would start to sing.

"Take their example, gentlemen: it's practical mysticism!"

9. Isha Schwaller de Lubicz, *The Opening of the Way* (New York: Inner Traditions, 1981).

10. See Chapter 8.

16

Presence

"I don't understand, Maître Dominique," confessed Thomas, who was trying in vain to classify twelve images around a circle whose center was a shining sun. "How am I to know in which order I must place my characters? What relationship do they have to this other circle, which you have filled with geometrical figures? And what about that one covered with astronomical signs (the zodiac, no doubt)? How can I assemble them?"

"You really lack imagination, my friend! At least one of these characters ought to give you the two principal keys to this puzzle."

"Obviously, I've got to recognize Saint Peter, who carries the keys in one hand and the inverted cross (the head down) in the other. The twelve characters with halos must therefore represent the Apostles: a child could have guessed that! But I don't understand how to make the three circles match in order to find the key to the puzzle. . . ."

"The arrangement of the images should have alerted you. The first thing to notice is that of the twelve Apostles, six are paired, in conformity with the liturgy that celebrates two characters from each of these three groups on the same day. In order to know whether these arrangements are of interest, I displayed the particular missions of the paired apostles, and I obtained this list."

	Celebrated	Particular mission of each
Peter	June 29	Preaches to the *circumsized Jews*
Paul		Preaches to the *Gentiles*

	Celebrated	Particular mission of each
Philip		Offers himself as "intermediary" to the *Gentiles*
	May 1	
James (the Less)		Named by Saint Peter: Bishop of Jerusalem (hence of the *Jews*)
Simon (the Zealot)	October 28	Preaches in the *East*
Judas (known as Thaddeus)		Writes the "Catholic Epistle" for the *West*

"Isn't it curious that each group presents two opposing directives or orientations? However, when this is repeated for the three paired names, it's more than simple chance.

"Another useful observation: if there is a symbolic intention in the figuration of the Apostles, it must be expressed by the instrument of their martyrdom, the instrument by which they can be differentiated. This observation teaches us that three of them were crucified, but that the form of their crosses differs; *Peter*'s cross is like that of Christ but reversed (head downward); The cross of Saint *Andrew* is in the form of an X (two crossing diagonal lines); *Philip*'s cross resembles the symbolic cross of John the Baptist, which has its short horizontal line very high.

"Another similarity between the three crucified men, Andrew, Peter, and Philip, is that, according to the Gospel of John, they were the first three disciples of Christ[1] and came from the same village: Bethsaida."

"I realize that these similarities seem to suggest symbolism, but what were they meant to symbolize?" asked Thomas.

"*Functions*," answered Dominique; "functions that are the agents of Cosmic Harmony, and which have their reverberation in all the vital phenomena of Nature. We find an example of this in the figuration of the principle of John, whose two aspects are celebrated in the two solstices: there is the Saint John of Summer, *John the Baptist* (June 24), and the Saint John of Winter, *John the Evangelist* (December 27).

"John the Evangelist is the 'perfection' of John the Baptist, who is the precursor of Christ. Both of them are celebrated by fire: however, June 24 notes the descent of the sun, whereas December 27 marks the beginning of its reascent.

"All of this is known, but what is commonly not known is that John the Baptist (whose decapitation immediately preceded the public mission of Christ) is replaced after his death in his "function" by Philip, *whose symbol is the cross of John the Baptist*: Philip is chosen as the disciple *at*

---

1. John 1:40–43.

the beginning of the Christic mission, whereas John the Evangelist was present (at Calvary) *at the end*, which specifies the nature of his mission."

Thomas, thinking about the two Saint Johns, asked: "Can it be, then, that the twelve Apostles are related to the twelve signs of the zodiac?"

"In terms of functions, certainly. And you could establish other relationships which would only confirm the value of this symbolism."

"In which realm can it be applied?"

"In all the realms governed by the vital laws of Harmony. After that, you can always discuss the 'errors in dates,' or even the reality of the characters and the historic facts: only one thing is important, and that's the *truth* of the teaching given in the symbolism of the names, the attributes, and the liturgical ritual, which inspired the Master Builders of the initiatory Cathedrals."

"If that is so, must one find correspondences in all authentic Traditions?" asked Thomas.

"Naturally! In the East, as in ancient Egypt, the so-called deities and the *Neter* represent the Cosmic Functions and the Principles of Nature. And the anomalies in the zodiac of Denderah are found in the astronomical symbols of Notre Dame, which illustrates the unity of Knowledge taught by this symbolism."

Thomas was perplexed. "Are you claiming that the realistic statues of the saints and the sentimental imagery of Saint-Sulpice have an initiatory teaching value?"

"Absolutely not," exclaimed Dominique, "because they represent people, and even the Principles of Christ and of the Virgin are represented on a human scale, arousing the emotions of the believers and creating astral imaginings that distance them from Reality.

"The symbolic representations of *Realities* that cannot be expressed rationally are something else—for example, the statue of Saint Nicasius, who is holding his skullcap in his hand.[2] Another example is the crucified 'seraphic Christ,' whose arms and legs are replaced with wings.[3] The details of these two figures confirm their esoteric significance: these images are not intended as portraits."

"The portrait of the Divinity!" scoffed Thomas as he contemplated the three circles, which he was trying, in vain, to superimpose.

"You won't be able to do it," said his Master, "if you don't take into account the functional value of the Numbers that are put into play. Number twelve is the most evident here, and the most eloquent from the reference points given by Nature. But six of our apostles are paired, presenting two opposing tendencies."

2. In the portal of the Cathedral of Reims.
3. On the square of the monastery at Cimiez, near Nice.

"Is it a matter of different functions?"

"Not at all, but each pair makes you notice the duality of aspects within each function."

"If this interpretation is exact, these twelve Apostles must represent three double functions, plus six other simple functions, which brings us back to *nine* functions instead of twelve," concluded Thomas.

"Your reasoning is good," said the sculptor. "Now you've got to find what the Number *nine* corresponds to. There is still the mystery of the three crosses. After that you can attack the symbols of the four Evangelists and have fun solving this: only two (Matthew and John) are Apostles. Do the two other Evangelists (Mark and Luke) enter into our circle? Here, they are curiously linked to the paired group of Peter and Paul, since tradition claims that Mark was the disciple of Peter and Luke the companion of Paul. It's a strange coincidence, isn't it? For once, I'm posing an enigma to try to test your intuition in deciphering the significance of an interesting symbolism. Good luck, Thomas!"

The bell that announced visitors to the Atelier rang, and the sculptor got up.

"Excuse me for coming over without calling," said Dutheil as he greeted Dominique. "I hate to bother you with an incident that you might think is childish."

"What's up, old friend?" said Jean Thomas. "You look very upset."

"I'm somewhat ashamed about it, because my upset is no doubt due to my ignorance," said Dutheil.

"Come in first," said the sculptor as he led his friends into the Tavern. "Take your time in telling us about it so you can clearly explain what's bothering you."

"First you've got to know the origin of the story," said Dutheil. "During my trip to India, I visited an antique shop with a young woman, also a Parisian, for whom I felt a great friendship. Having sold me some old knickknacks, the antique dealer showed us a miniature statue in gold-covered wood, representing Shiva in the form of 'Universal Yogi.' A precious stone decorated his forehead, underneath his characteristic headdress.

"'I have had some rare good fortune today,' said the dealer. 'You would be making a mistake not to take advantage of it: I can guarantee its authenticity.'

"Encouraged by my companion's enthusiasm, I bought it for her as a souvenir of our encounter. 'May it bring you good luck!' I told her as I accompanied her to the ship that would take her back to France.

"I had forgotten the incident until last night, when I received the statuette, which she returned to me with a letter excusing herself for sending it back. Here are the reasons that she gave me: one night during the voyage she had put on a beautiful Hindu costume for a costume ball. She had completed the costume with a turban, on which she had put the statuette. That night she was taken sick with an intense fever, which kept her in bed until they arrived in France. Once she had returned home, she put the Shiva among the other knickknacks without giving it a second thought. But since her return, terrible incidents have been occurring: automobile accidents and family quarrels, which started to worry her. Then her little girl, having taken the statuette to play with, was overcome by an inexplicable fever. 'What else could I do?' she concluded. This souvenir meant a lot to me as a memento of our meeting, but given the strange coincidences, I don't dare keep it. I admit that I wasn't too happy about what I considered to be a stupid superstition. I put my Shiva on a shelf in a suitable setting.

"This morning I was awakened by a very strong odor of something burning, and I saw that the curtain next to the shelf was on fire! I just stopped it in time. Obviously, I found the cause: a short circuit. But you must admit that there are a bit too many 'coincidences' for me not to be somewhat troubled!"

Dominique, a cunning smile on his lips, looked at Dutheil, who took a carefully wrapped package out of his pocket.

'Let's take a look at this culprit!" said the sculptor as he examined the statuette carefully. Thomas, with furrowed brow, tried to guess what his Master was thinking.

Having examined it in every way, Dominique put the effigy of Shiva in front of him. "It must have been a recent cult object. It still bears the odor of spices. . . . What do you think about this story, Doctor?"

Thomas made an embarrassed face. "Rather far-fetched," he grumbled. "How can a knickknack bring bad luck?"

"That depends on where it comes from and on certain circumstances," answered Dominique. "An object can transmit an evil spell for various reasons. But the perfumed incense and the traces of resinous spots that it still has allow me to suspect that it played a role in cult worship."

"That's not sufficient reason," retorted Thomas. "I've seen Hindu vases and idols at friends' houses which were stolen from temples during times of trouble. They never caused any disasters!"

"No doubt it's important to know if they were, or remained, con-secrated," retorted Dominique.

"What do you mean by that?" asked the doctor. "You're not claiming that certain objects taken from a temple or a church could carry evil spells for the unfortunate people who acquire them? The poor antique dealers! There mustn't be very many of them left on this earth!"

"Once again, Thomas, you're joking about something of which you are ignorant. It's too bad: a joke makes a bad lantern for discovering the truth. Do you know the ritual ceremony which they call *puja* in India?"

"I wasn't allowed to attend one," Dutheil intervened, "but the description of it impressed me greatly. A Brahman explained to me that it's a matter of attracting Divine Power, the Shakti, in the figurine or the materials that one wants to consecrate. After having ritually purified them and isolated them in a circle with a red cord, the person who officiated attracted the 'Presence' with the ritual words and gestures of his powerful spiritual call. 'Until the *puja* is finished,' he said, 'please remain in these humble forms.' If all the necessary conditions were observed, the materials and objects that were consecrated then become receptacles of this *Real Presence*, which totally permeates them."

Thomas took advantage of the lesson and listened respectfully. "Could you explain what one means by *Shakti?*"

"It would be difficult to make you understand, Thomas. In order for you to understand me you must be able to refer to certain moving moments that you have experienced in the cathedral.

"Shakti is this undefinable Power that gives life to all that exists. But our feeble brain distorts the notion of her from the moment it tries to determine what she is. Shakti is neither 'thing' nor abstraction. She is Life in the sense of causal animation, but also Movement which engenders life, and fixes this animation in the thing that has incarnated her.

"However, because she is Movement, she arouses a particular reaction in this thing which *limits the Power of the Shakti in making it specific*, because all specification becomes a resistance to the free action of the life-giving Power. That's why Shakti, the very essence of Power, cannot be understood by us in terms of the multiplicity of vital phenomena produced by her manifestation.'

"Why is this Power given a feminine character?" asked Thomas, who was trying very hard to concentrate.

"Think of the word *Wisdom*, of which it is said in the proverbs of Solomon, that she is before anything else.

"In her virtual duality (Shakti-Shiva), Shakti is the *Power* which Shiva possesses; he is the actor who sets her in motion. She is the Movement and the Force of Shiva, through which Shakti is manifested: *Two in One*. And this undissociated duality is what one can call Presence.

"Now, let's put aside the names and the images and try to conceive this reality: Presence . . . Presence that *is* before anything else is both latent and active, both Being and Power."

"Presence," repeated Dutheil: "a great subject for meditation, but it's taking us away from my statuette!"

"On the contrary, it's bringing us back to it," protested Dominique. "The understanding of it gives us a solution to your problem. Shakti working in Nature is a *free, active force*. Its power can be captured and *retained* by the materials and objects that are disposed toward this intention. That's why, in the celebration of the *puja*, one limits the area of its action by encircling with a cord the things that one wants to animate."

"How does man have the power to obtain this animation?" asked Thomas.

"Through mantric words and gestures, and through the intense invocation of the person who is playing the role of officiating priest.

"If this is a real possibility, it's magic!" exclaimed Thomas, scandalized.

"If you call magic the action of moving supranatural Powers, then the *puja* is magic, but of a purely spiritual order, since what it attracts is Divine Power, which will not obey forces opposed to it."

"Does that mean that the act which attracts it is also of a spiritual order?" asked Dutheil.

"Exactly," agreed Dominique. "That's why the inner disposition of the officiator is of capital importance, because all personal, emotional, and mental impulses must be erased for this ceremony, in order to attract divine Presence only. It's the veritable elimination of the ego which must be obtained by this inner purification."

"It's not only interior, but exterior, and in all realms," exclaimed Dutheil. "You've got to see the rigor with which these Brahmans apply it. Ablutions, fastidious washings of the bodily orifices, purifying the breath, and meditative concentration on the various states of being. It's the strict control of states of consciousness. What you've just said, Maître Dominique, makes the importance of these precautions clear to me."

"It's as necessary for the efficacy of such a magistery," insisted Dominique, "as is the intensity of the spiritual call of the officiator."

"But how can you purify the things that are going to be consecrated?" asked Thomas.

"By ritual offerings and appropriate benedictions. You'll also find a reminder of this in the prayers of the mass that precede the consecration.

"When the Brahmans claim that Divine Power obeys them, it's assumed that all the required conditions have been observed. But if this is indeed the case, the Reality and the Presence fixed by the *puja* is such that, to liberate it from its temporary prison, the officiator must, after the ceremony, 'deconsecrate' the objects that have served as receptacles. When the *puja* is finished, these receptacles must be destroyed by immersion, for fear that they might have kept some of this Power."

"What would be the problem, if they did?" asked Thomas.

"The danger of desecration, which could become an evil spell, even if the desecrator was ignorant of its consecration. However, it sometimes happens that the officiator preserves certain objects (a statue, for example) without 'withdrawing' the Presence from them, in order to expose them to the veneration of the faithful. That could be the case with your effigy of Shiva."

"But how could we know?" murmured Dutheil.

"Given these 'coincidences,' wouldn't it be wise to presume it?" suggested the sculptor, who was amused by the distrustful looks of his friends.

"*Seriously*," insisted Thomas, "do you believe that this is possible? Because if we have to attribute the power of an evil spell to every sacred object that is desecrated . . ."

"I was speaking *seriously*," retorted Dominique severely. "Your response, Thomas, proves that you don't understand. Benediction is not consecration. To bless a being or an object is to bestow upon it a beneficial influence whose power and quality are proportional to the person who is bestowing, or to the invocation or mantric formula used, but above all it's proportional to the spiritual power of the person who is giving the blessing. Consecration is even more mysterious. It's the integration and fixation of Real Presence."

"Suppose I ate something into which this Presence is integrated. What would happen?"

"If you admit the reality of this integration, your logic might give you the answer: the Power absorbed by you will be liberated (that is, will disappear) as soon as the matter is destroyed in your stomach. But my consciousness would object that, if you had already realized in yourself the seed of your own Immortal Presence, this seed would serve as a ferment to capture and retain the Spiritual Presence through which it would enrich itself. This would be the true communion."

"That I can admit. But if this state doesn't exist in me, my communion will only be illusory!" exclaimed Thomas. "At least that's what I'm thinking at the moment."

"Good, Thomas, think . . . and keep your mouth shut. This subject has made so much ink and blood run that it should make us circumspect when we're tempted to discuss it lightly."

A heavy silence followed, and the sculptor relit his pipe. "Listen to me," he said gravely. "There are no opinions to express on the Reality of the Spirit: *one knows it in oneself, or one does not know it.* What is Real defends itself against desecration, even if it is blinded by a mental aberration. I'm not speaking here of a 'God' who is judging and condemning the unbeliever. I'm speaking of the evil consequences imminent in the disharmony caused by an opposition between the cerebral consciousness and the Reality of the Spirit.

"Whether it's matter or a figurine in which a magic ritual has fixed the

Presence, and regardless of the religion that practices this ritual, it's extremely insolent for our intellectual vanity to refuse it *at least* a certain deference. It's also stupid! After all, the notion of Presence is accepted by you physiologists on inferior levels of our humanity. It can be identified with the idea of consciousness: a man can be present in body while his Mental Consciousness is momentarily 'absent.'

"There are as many modes of Presence as there are modes (or states) of being: Physical Presence, Mental Presence, Psychic or Astral Presence, Spiritual Presence. The last can be more or less individualized, as is our Permanent Witness. The purest Spiritual Presence can be called Divine Presence. A being inhabited by this Presence can only manifest such Power to the extent of his transparency, that is, his neutrality and his personal nonresistance."

Thomas apologized for interrupting Dominique and said: "In order to be sure I understand you, I'd like to know the exact rational sense of the word *presence*."

"I could answer that it's the opposite of absence, but are you expecting a positive definition? Then let's say that *Presence is the existence of the state of being in a place that is presumably limited.* The limitation by this place is proportional to the subtlety of 'that' which is present. However, the subtlety of a spiritual state can be such that it renders its Presence infinite. Does that mean that this Presence cannot be located in space?

"The presence of atmospheric energy in the body that it penetrates is *also located* in this body, but it's not limited by it, because this body is also surrounded by it. If something is impenetrable to this energy, the thing becomes, by its nonreceptivity, a limitation of the surrounding energy.

"If the surrounding energy is so subtle that it penetrates a body despite its lack of affinity with it, what opposes it in this body will react with resistance. This could create more or less disturbing waves within it.

"The Spirit, being the purest state and the subtlest state of non-manifested Energy, penetrates everything, and its Logos becomes the Logos of this thing *if the latter doesn't oppose it with disharmonious resistance* (that is, that which doesn't conform to the thing's initial goal). The absence of personal resistance is the state of 'innocence,' the neutrality which does not oppose Presence. To better understand this, think about the symbol of the unleavened bread used for the wafer in the Christian mass: the absence of leaven signifies the absence of a specific ferment, allowing the Divine Presence to become the ferment of transmutation.

"*What is this Presence?* In reality, there is only one source of energy: the Spirit. The different aspects in which It manifests can be named: heat, light, electric power, and magnetism (earthly, animal, or human), which are vibratory states perceivable by our physical senses. This Energy-Spirit *when it goes beyond manifestation* can be named Soul, Spirit, Christ Presence, or Shakti: it's always the supreme Energy whose Presence gives life to everything which exists in the universe but which, being captured and fixed, can transcend the quality of that which receives it.

"You must realize that it's not the quality of Energy-Spirit that changes in all of the things that are enlivened, transcended, or perturbed by it: it is the quality of the seed that receives it and the lessening caused by its own specification."

"To conclude your explanation," said Thomas, "must we therefore admit that if the resistances oppose themselves to the beneficial action of Presence, this Presence could produce bad effects because of the disturbances caused by this opposition?"

"This conclusion is correct," agreed Dominique. "It's exactly what Saint Paul affirmed when he threatened those who were indiscriminately eating and drinking the consecrated bread and wine."

"This danger of desecration," remarked Dutheil, "is confirmed by the Brahmans regarding those who would take the food of the *puja* without having venerated its Presence."

"I understand the notion of desecration better," admitted Thomas. "What I found loathsome (for Dutheil's Shiva, for example) was the will of an idol taking its vengeance on the unbeliever."

"What do you mean by *idol*, Thomas?"

"What everyone else means by it, no doubt: a statue that's displayed for the worship of the believers."

"Your definition is a bit simplistic," retorted Dominique. "It might be necessary to distinguish the role attributed to it by those who conceived it. There are two possibilities. One, the *consecrated* statue has fixed the Presence, and in this case, regardless of its form and value (an art object or a piece of pottery), it carries the Power; and this Presence (independently of its form) is what the believers kneel before. Or, in the event that the statue is not consecrated, it's the form that has the initiatory value, if it is the *true* symbol of a Cosmic Principle. Then it's the *Functions* of this Principle that will be represented by its particular attributes. This symbolic teaching, according to the character of the believer who venerates it, will either inspire devotion toward the Power evoked or enlighten his consciousness through the identity of the Divine Function symbolized with that same Function incarnated in man and in Nature.

"Note that there is no intention of idolatry in this double role. That is, there is *no personification* of an Absolute Divinity, which cannot be worshipped as such in its indivisible and impersonal Unity."

"Seen from that angle, wouldn't the religions that we call polytheistic have committed that error?" intervened Thomas.

"The most suspect," answered the sculptor, "would be Greco-Roman mythology, whose figures *humanized the Principles* at the risk of misleading believers about the intention of their initiators. Whereas, for example, an Egyptian Hathor, with its cow's head on a female body, obviously doesn't represent any existing being. Nor does the Hindu Brahma with its four arms and its triple face.

"It's realistic and not symbolic humanization that lends itself to idolatry. And the greatest idolatry of man is the creation of a God in his own image!"

"Is that why the Muslims are scandalized by our statues of Christ, *Son of God*, and by our human figures of the Eternal Father?" said Dutheil.

"*By his humanization without symbols*," corrected Dominique. "Each of the Evangelists, for example, is accompanied by an animal that characterizes him. This symbol of their Function legitimizes this figuration. This was the case in the statuary of the initiatory Cathedrals, where everything was symbolic, Numbers and Proportions, as in the Pharaonic temples."

Thomas, extremely interested, rapidly took in Dominique's answers. Dutheil was contemplating his statuette through his cigarette smoke. "I'm very confused," he said to Dominique. "What should I do with my Shiva, which is 'not an idol'? I'd be tempted to keep it to decipher its symbol. On the other hand, its possible consecration bothers me, and I'm very afraid of not knowing how to venerate it."

Dominique laughed, letting Dutheil stew in his indecision. He looked at Thomas and asked: "What would you do if this object belonged to you, Doctor?"

Thomas lit a cigarette just to do something. The sculptor stood up and took the statuette in his hands and gave it to the doctor, who reddened and instinctively recoiled.

"It's beautiful, isn't it?" insisted Dominique. "Doesn't it tempt you?"

Thomas's troubled silence amused his Master. "Wouldn't you say that the front part of the stone is alive, like an eye that is staring at you? Come on, Doctor. If you are afraid of it, dare to admit it."

Thomas gave in to the cunning expression on the sculptor's face. "To tell you the truth, Maître Dominique, I don't know . . . and that's what gets me angry."

"Such doubt is almost an avowal of belief, my friend. Are you ashamed of being afraid of desecrating it? What's so humiliating about that?"

"I'm not ashamed of faith, but of possible superstition."

Dominique looked at his disciple for a long moment, then said: "If you don't believe that the reality of this object is worthy of respect, then it's your fear that is the superstition. I have no more idea than you do about whether or not it's consecrated. Even if it isn't, it's the obvious symbol of a Reality. *My consciousness of this Reality removes the character of super-stition from my respect.*"

"Very well, give me the object," said Thomas coldly.

Dutheil intervened, lifting the Shiva out of Dominique's hands. "Don't take it, Thomas: your gesture is a bluff, and if I have understood correctly, you might suffer a reaction.

"How can I destroy it, Maître Dominique?"

The sculptor got up to go relight the woodstove that was heating the Atelier. "The fire seems like a suitable burial place," he said, throwing the statue into it.

The gilded wood was easily consumed by the flames while the three men sat smoking in silence.

"The misfortune of the thinking man," said Dominique finally, "is not to be able to dare to search for the motivations behind his beliefs. By 'motivation' I do not mean 'reasoning': belief through argument is a sand castle that other arguments can destroy."

"Belief," suggested Dutheil, "can be encrusted through atavism or through submission to an imposed doctrine. Or else it is a persuasion determined by examining the object of this belief."

"The fault of this method of examination," retorted Dominique, "is that its criteria are based on the mental 'knowledge' that the thinker has confidence in, in order to stay within the limits of reasonable credibility. But how can the mind appreciate these limits, being itself limited by more subtle levels to which it is unable to gain access?"

"I suppose that these more subtle levels are in the realm of faith," said Dutheil.

"Let's put it another way. Faith is a state of inner acquiescence that can lean on the testimony of neither the senses nor reason. Could you tell me what it is, outside of these two witnesses, that can inspire this faith in man?"

Dutheil thought, trying to find an adequate answer. Suddenly Thomas emerged from his silence: "The sense of Presence!" he said with the violence of a guilty man whose confession has been torn from him.

Dutheil, surprised by this explosion, looked at the sculptor, who imposed silence with one gesture. Dominique was "listening" to the silent jubilation of Thomas. . . .

Looking into each other's eyes, Master and disciple measured their mutual comprehension. In a grave voice, the Master concluded: "Could it be that the veil has fallen? If you dare name Presence, you have found *your way*, Jean Thomas."

Without lowering his face, Jean Thomas affirmed: "Maître Jacques."

"Yes, Thomas, Maître Jacques, the universal symbol of our own Truth, the Permanent Witness of your Reality, whose secret name you do not know. . . ."

"The name is of no importance," murmured Thomas, "if I have recognized his presence."

Dominique opened the little woodstove and called to Dutheil: "We'll gather the ashes, and you will go and throw them into the Seine."

17

The Cosmic Virgin

"Are we being indiscreet?" asked Thomas as he brought Dutheil into the Atelier.

The sculptor, singing as he molded the clay, motioned for them to settle themselves in, without stopping his work. Dutheil contemplated him while listening to his beautiful bass voice. The harmony that unified the singing and the gestures of the sculptor was so perfect that one would have thought the clay was animated by the voice.

"That man," murmured Dutheil to his friend, "is a force of Nature."

"But a conscious force," retorted Thomas as he observed the sculptor with respect. "It makes one want to become his apprentice."

"That might be a solution," said Dutheil with a sigh, responding to an inner dream.

With a few strokes of his thumb, the sculptor modified the ball of clay, which was already showing the artist's intention. Then, having contemplated the still-rough shape, he wiped his hands, took a few puffs on his pipe, and came to sit down next to his friends.

"You two are very pensive. . . ."

"We were watching you work," said Thomas. "I was trying to guess what you wanted to do."

"I don't want to do anything, Thomas. I'm molding the earth. I'm allowing it to take form without offering any resistance."

"But isn't the form already conceived in your imagination?"

"Not at all," protested the sculptor. "The form will be the result of the vital function which will have moved my consciousness. This function can express itself in a multitude of forms: this multiplicity disturbs my search for the cause. However, only the cause interests me. To reproduce and imitate are an aping gesture."

"But one can always invent."

"What can one invent that is not already conceived by Nature, or not already composed from parts of things already created? Heterogeneous assemblage creates monstrosities."

"Don't the monstrosities also hold some interest as curious examples of disharmony?" said Thomas.

"There is the vice of the pathologist, dear Doctor!"

"Why not? Can't one conceive the meaning of order through disorder?" Dominique started to laugh.

"In any event," continued Jean Thomas, "it's a fertile source for an artist's fantasy: at least there he can invent."

"It's better to create monsters than not to invent at all." Dominique sighed. "How vain this modern mentality is!

"The role of the procreator has no attraction for me, my friend. On the contrary, I have an unquenchable thirst for indentifying with the cause . . . of everything, of anything; to participate in the life that animates all things, to live with and to experience the play of functions without worrying about the accidents of form . . . without worrying about my personal taste, and without judging or preferring anything."

"Where will that lead?"

"It will lead me back to the Cause, the Active Cause of the functions, *the simple Cause of the Function.* Then everything is simplified, because Nature is only the multiplication of phenomena through the play of functions. That's what interests scientists who are looking for the explanations of phenomena through the analysis of effects. However, what I want to find is the synthesis, and to do it through Simplicity.

"The seed is the synthesis of the specific functions that give birth to the determined plant. In it is the ideal form of the plant, preconceived in the seed, whose germination will only manifest it. For us humans, our seed is the synthesis of all the specified functions of all the seeds of Nature. This is nothing else but the entirety of the stages of man's becoming within Nature. In other words: the work of the sixth day of Genesis.

"This is the moment in which man summarizes the Creation, and would be perfect; and he would have remained that way if he hadn't taken into his own hands a creation in the image of the original dualizing Causal Function. Because it is taken over by a creature, it is no longer creation but procreation. This engenders intellectual knowledge which is only comprehension by comparison, that is, by constant separation and opposition.

"The ultimate effect of this intellectual dialectic is, in its evil aspect, a distancing from Unity. In its *good* aspect, it's a way of becoming aware of the necessity of the single Cause. And this is the moment of reversal, in which the tendency toward the lowest point offers the possibility of rising toward the Source by the eliminating complexity."

"Does that mean that having fallen because of the mind into extreme complexity, I can, by a reversal which would orient my quest toward the study of the *Function*, progressively rise toward extreme Simplicity?"

"That's the progress that I'm attracted to! Do you understand me, Thomas? I refuse to stay bogged down in our phenomenal world, marvelous though it is, as a tangible mirror of what is real. It's like a rebellion of my consciousness which is enshadowed by the complexity of human experience. Now it wants to get rid of it, as a butterfly wants to get rid of its chrysalis. . . ."

"Because each elimination is one step higher," said Thomas, completing his Master's thought. "If I understand correctly, it's climbing up the path of the 'fall' in order to rediscover the Simple Cause, the Cause of Causes that I've been trying so hard to find.

"But what name are you going to give to this Cause? Don't tell me 'God' because my mind would rebel before such an inaccessible absolute. I still need a mirror, or something that Nature offers us the mirror of . . . a Principle, a Power, but it's still too metaphysical."

Dominique listened to his disciple, smiling. "Let's not use the word *mirror* in this case: use the word *symbol* instead. But if you want to find the Cause, look at what cannot be 'the Cause.' Keep looking. . . ."

"You told us that the Cause becomes Cause only because it acts. Does that mean that there is *that* which becomes Cause? That's like drowning in infinity!"

"I'd say it's like drowning in the indefinite. Let's go further: 'the Indefinite Infinite' cannot be specified. Otherwise, there would still be *that* which specifies it. Now, the seed is what specifies. In order for creation to come out of the Infinite, there must be the potentiality of the seed *and* the milieu that can be specified by it. But we were saying that this milieu is Infinity. However, since Infinity would not be such if it were dualized, it is therefore necessary for *that which is potentially seed and that which is milieu to be only one*, containing the double possibility. Thomas, what image would you use to express this incomprehensible state?"

Thomas remained silent.

"Let's look for it together," said Dominique. "The original seminal Power must be universal: there cannot be any particular seed that it does not encompass, or it would not be universal. Let's say that it's an Active

Aspect of the Universal Spirit. This Active Aspect cannot become creator
without the Receptive Aspect, that is to say, the *Milieu* in which it can act.
Now, this Milieu is the uterine aspect of the Spirit, the virginal matrix,
since it's nonspecified. How would you represent it, Thomas?"

"The Cosmic Virgin," suggested Dutheil. "It would be the Cosmic
Virgin who, when the seminal virtue acts in her, becomes the Virgin
Mother of all the traditions."

"Exactly," confirmed the sculptor. "But his expression will remain a
literary image if, with our dualized mind, we are not able to admit the
coexistence of the two aspects of the Absolute State, aspects that are
nondifferentiated as long as they have not become Cause through the
Active Movement of the Seminal Power."

"Wouldn't this movement give us the third element of the Primordial
Trinity?" asked Thomas.

"You could put it that way," agreed Dominique. "It's obviously impossible to express the inexpressible with words that necessarily go back
to notions recorded by our dualized intelligence. Therefore, try to give
yourself something to lean on, in order to clarify what you have understood."

After some hesitation, Thomas said: "The Divine Absolute can be
neither sexual nor dualized. Nor can it be differentiated. It is 'That which
is.' *That* contains all possibilities before their manifestation. *That* therefore contains the possibility to become Cause but will only do so through
Activity.

"The activity of *That* immediately presupposes that which, in That, *is
acted upon*. In other words, Passivity is immanent in this Activity."

Dominique interrupted Thomas: "You've been nuzzling along on this
path for some time, my friend, because you can *experience* Reality, but
you will always be incapable of expressing it. That's why I'd be satisfied
with a symbol offered by Nature to express what is situated 'at the
beginning,' that is, 'in Principle.'

"There is a state of undetermined and passive Substance. By an act that
is an unknowable mystery, this substance provokes its own Reaction,
which becomes the Universal Seed. It's this Reaction which is the Function
immanent in all Nature. It's essential name is *Life*, because Life is the
witness of the Reaction, or rather of the Ternary Unity: Activity-Passivity-
Reaction. This Principle is *apparently* situated outside of Time, Space,
and Manifestation since it is the Cause of them, but in Reality, it is
immanent in that which it 'causes' because the effect is always only a
transformation of its cause.

"This Trinity is only knowable through Reaction, which is the very
Principle of *Function*. Consequently, Reaction-Function is synonymous

with Life. It's in this way that you must understand the vital functions whose multiple names define the various roles of Function-Reaction throughout all Nature.

"But these names will only be 'pronounced' when the synthetic being of Creation (Adam) has recognized them in himself. Adam is the model of the human form. He is animated Unity, not separated in itself, and situated in the center of the Creation as its finality."

"Is that why you call Adam the 'anthropocosm'?" asked Thomas.

"Stop there!" cried Dominique. "Adam is not the anthropocosm, neither in his celestial unity nor in his earthly humanity. But as the finality of the Creation, he is now *going* toward the living realization of anthropocosm, which was potentially contained in the creative Cause."

"I've noticed that in your exposition of the Ternary Unity, you avoided giving the names of the three aspects of the Trinity."

"Who can name them without limiting the Unlimited? Names personify. Do you still want to invent God in your own image?

"I was trying to evoke consciousness of the Function which links the extreme terms of this Ternary Unity. But if you want to awaken the reverberation of its Reality in yourself, you must evoke its symbol: the Holy Spirit.

"Understand this well: Activity in Passivity is the Function that is identical with the Absolute Aspect of the Holy Spirit. This Absolute Aspect has its symbol in the reaction of Passivity, which becomes the *Vital Reaction*. And I say 'symbol' because *this Vital Reaction becomes the sensible Aspect of the Causal Holy Spirit.*"

After a long moment of silent meditation, Dominique smiled at Thomas, who was having a hard time coming out of his reverie. Then he offered a cigarette to Dutheil.

"The Hindu religion," he said, "avoided difficulty in teaching Unity in the Trinity by reducing the nuances of each Function to different names, and by putting together the functions of the Trinitarian Aspect in such a way that it was impossible to define rationally the exact role of each of them."

"It's one way of unifying by apparent complexity," said Dutheil. "This complexity, which is expressed by the multiplication of images, is deceptive for the person who has not deepened his knowledge of metaphysics. However, this complexity has not provoked divergent schisms, as have the theological disputes over the Christian dogma of the Trinity: Should the Holy Spirit be identified as the second or third Person? Does it proceed from the Father? Or from the Father and the Son?

"The ecumenical council of Constantinople decreed that the Spirit

proceeds from the Father, and the Orthodox Church has remained faithful to this dogma. But in the fourth century, the Roman Church decreed
that the Holy Spirit proceeds from the Father and the Son!"

"Let's not bother anymore with these sterile disputes!" exclaimed
Dominique. "They are the sad result of a materialization of abstract
Principles. It's as if one could conceive the Holy-Spirit as *one thing
between two things*! . . . whereas it's a matter of Functions and not of
'things.'

"Haven't you now been able to understand the very simple aspects of
the problem, since you have two points of view: that of the Origin of
Creation and that of the creature?

"And the latter is the symbol of the former."

"I do understand," exclaimed Jean Thomas. "It's again the play of
reversal. And this corrects the error in the meaning I attributed to the
'symbol.'

"This is what I have understood: created man is the finality of earthly
Creation. But the finality of man is to *recognize himself as the symbol of
his Creative Cause*. Doing this, he re-creates in his own consciousness the
living image of his Cause, *in which he realizes himself*.

"Then he becomes the anthropocosm."

Dominique looked at his disciple, seriously moved. "What you have
just expressed is more than comprehension: it is an awakening of your
Reality. But don't let yourself be blinded by the images."

The sculptor saw Dutheil's envious look. "It's easier to enlighten
ignorant incredulity than it is to erase the imagery that veils Reality."

"I realize that," agreed Dutheil. "That's why I'm troubled, when you
pronounce the word *Passivity*, by the multiple representations of the
Cosmic Virgin."

"Let's drop this Cosmic Virgin, if you don't mind. Let's speak about the
Virginity of the Primordial Substance. But above all, don't confuse Substance with Matter. Substance is that which *undergoes* the impulse which
will make of it maternal Matter.

"Virginal Passivity is the aspect of Substance without original form
which has not yet undergone the effect of Activity. This Passivity becomes, in the formed Substance, *Femininity*, symbol of the passive aspect
of the Origin. However, formed Substance, while being the symbol of
Femininity, can no longer be considered in a state of virginity. That's why
physical virginity is only the evocative symbol of the Virginity of Primordial Cosmic Femininity.

"This Reality is called the Cosmic Virgin.

"Therefore, you mustn't make the mistake of attributing the form of
physical virginity to the evocation, which has no form. This is an error
that is too easy to slip into. . . ."

"And one that distorts the Cosmic Reality of the Virgin Mother," added Dutheil.

"It is as inexpressible as the Aspects of the Trinity, of which it is an integral part," said the sculptor.

"It is not expressed in Christian doctrine," said Dutheil.

"You're wrong, dear friend. First of all, certain gnostic texts attribute a feminine character to the Holy Spirit. What we've just said on this subject could enlighten you on this metaphysical concept. On the other hand, can you find a more beautiful expression than the text of 'Wisdom'[1] integrated into the liturgy for the ceremonies of the Virgin? Wisdom is inseparable from the Creative Principle that 'possessed it from the beginning,' with which and in which 'she is Eternal.' Wisdom was and is, in all creation, 'her Worker . . . in the world, her Earth, and among the children of men.'

"Tell me, Dutheil, do you know of a more beautiful expression, as free from deceptive representation? The same text provides the only means of conceiving its Reality: 'May he who is simple enter here!' says Wisdom."

"It's obviously extreme simplicity," recognized Dutheil. "Hindu theology, which I have admired in this sense, attributes to each Principle of the Trinity a complementary feminine aspect that is immanent in it. This *explains* Functions without making the error of personifying them."

"Note that all theologies, being the *explanation* of the states and acts of Divinity, are necessarily adapted to the consciousness and to the mentality of the people. Brahmanism teaches to its disciples a cosmological metaphysics, while its popular mythology attempts to familiarize the human with the manifestations of the Divine, which is evoked through multiple images. But Eastern spirituality maintains an *ideal* character toward that which Westerners would not be able to keep from personifying.

"The teaching of the Egyptian sages was never imposed in a dogmatic way. It took effect above all through a constant education of the mentality. A living symbolism oriented this education toward positive knowledge of the laws of Matter, of Nature, and of the human being's 'becoming' until his realization as Anthropocosm.

"The Temple synthesized the directives of this education, whose theological aspect was reserved for disciples. The people only participated in the external religious manifestations, the processions and the ritual festivals. These festivals were a concrete method of teaching, depicting the role of the *Neter* (that is, the Causal Functions) of the different phases of Genesis, of which the seasonal events were living symbols.

"An elite, its members selected for their personal worth, received

1. *The Proverbs of Solomon*, 8:21, etc.

practical and theoretical instruction conditioned by the astrological nature and the awakening of consciousness of each individual. This awakening of consciousness was enhanced by the perfection demanded in the various trades. Participation in the secrets of each technique, as well as the initiatory teachings, depended on the Masters of the Temple. This minimized the danger of faulty comprehension, and of a negative application of the sacred science."

"This method can indeed explain the perfection in their work and the well-guarded secret of their techniques," said Dutheil. "Moreover, it explains the exceptional continuity of a theology that nothing could distort."[2]

"That's true," confirmed Dominique, "because there were never divergences between theological and cosmographical points of view taught by the sages of Egypt. Each temple developed the theme suitable to the phase of Genesis that it represented, and each period put forth the *Neter* principles that were particularly active in the phase to which it corresponded.[3]

"However, this teaching was strictly controlled by the Temple, whose students received an instruction adapted to their particular tendencies, and in proportion to the awakening of their intuitive faculties. Because it was a matter not of "knowing" but of 'learning how to be aware.'"

"It's a process analogous to that of the Compagnons," suggested the doctor.

"They do have much in common," answered the sculptor, "but the Knowledge of the Egyptian sages extends to all realms. This Knowledge was inscribed in their architecture, in the texts they engraved on the stone of the temples and the steles. But the mode of inscription was such that it demanded an intuitive formation and a linking thread."

"Has what you call the Pharaonic sacred science ever been vulgarized?" asked the doctor.

"You can be sure that if they had made this mistake, the Masters of the Temple would have lost their Knowledge!" affirmed Dominique.

"Their Wisdom had as its objective the awakening of consciousness and the Intelligence of the Heart. Its final goal was the formation of the divine Horus in the Human, but its revelation was the goal of the initiation of the disciples.

"The people were led in the way of Osiris, that is, in the observance of the laws of Nature and in their correspondence to human existence. The

2. See Isha Schwaller de Lubicz, *Her-Bak: Egyptian Initiate* (New York: Inner Traditions, 1979), Commentary V.
3. Ibid.

Divine representations in their worship were limited to those whose functions they could recognize in natural phenomena, for example: Osiris, the *Neter* of the continual renewal of existence, from the seed to the human Osiris who, after his death (under the aegis of Osiris-Sokar), awaited his reincarnation. There was also Amon, the great life-giver and engenderer of all earthly life.

"The expression of the Divine Feminine Principle was also adapted to popular comprehension: Isis, sister and wife of Osiris, virgin mother of Horus,[4] who (according to popular legend) had taught men agriculture and all things that were useful for existence. Mut, the wife of Amon, the Maternal Principle, whose name means 'mother' in the Egyptian language. Maat, *Neter* of Justice. Renenutet, serpent goddess who 'brings up' the sap in the plant and the milk in the nursing mother.

"These examples show us the Osirian tendency in the orientation geared to popular belief. The initiatory instruction reserved for the students of the Temple was something else altogether. This instruction presented the *Neter* as the functional nuances of the single Causal Function, Amon, whose Absolute Divine Principle had no name."

"I'd be curious to know how they could express the inexpressible virginal-feminine aspects of the Origin," said Dutheil.

"In truth, this inexpressible Passive Virginal Aspect of the Origin is symbolized by Nun, the primordial Ocean. Then their theology considers the *double* Active-Passive aspect of each function, which it represents by two complementary masculine-feminine *Neters*. In order to understand their concept of the Feminine Principle, the roles that are attributed to it in this theology must be differentiated:

"In the primordial couple issuing forth from the Unique Atum, we find the two first elementary principles: *Shu*, masculine, and *Tefnut*, Feminine. From this couple comes the two other elementary Principles: the masculine aspect, Earth Principle: *Geb*; and the feminine aspect, Heaven Principle, *Nut*.

"The *Ternary*, which we find in each phase of the Genesis, includes a feminine aspect of each Trinity: Amon, *Mut*, Khonsu; Osiris, *Isis*, Horus; Horus, *Hathor*, Ihi; Ptah, *Sekhmet*, Nefer-Tum.

"The *Quaternary*, which comes from the couple Geb-Nut, is represented by its two antagonistic Principles, agents of all Becoming: Osiris and Seth, with their feminine complements, Isis and Nephtys.

"A fifth Principle, immanent in those of the Quaternary, is the universal *Horus*, who can be compared with the Cosmic Christ (likewise,

4. Isis conceived Horus with the spiritual seed of Osiris. Ibid., Commentary V, section 6.

'Horus in human form' would be identified with the Christ that man must realize in himself).

"In this Primordial Divine World, Horus, eternal and universal, is not the son of Isis: Isis has no other maternal function than that of 'Mother of Existence.' She is the active Passivity, in the sense that she provokes the movement of the Activity that is immanent in her.

"Nephtys (Nebhet) is the negative Passivity, the feminine aspect of Seth, who also is known as Nebhty.

"Now, the Isis type of Femininity plays the same role in the becoming of the being as it does in the Origin, but Egyptian theology diminishes the nuances of its function: Isis, as the seat and *place* of all Activity, whose function she provokes; Nephtys, negative Passivity that provokes destruction; Serket, the contractive power of Sokar, Funereal name of Osiris; Neith, the spiritual virginal aspect of Cosmic Femininity, Causal Power that fixes formed Substance."

"That's the first allusion to Cosmic Virginity," said Dutheil.

"It's not the only expression," retorted Dominique. "And since you still lack the metaphysical sense, you need to make several efforts to differentiate the nuances signified by Neith, Maat, and Hathor."

"Perhaps one can attain it through meditation," suggested the doctor.

"Bravo, Thomas. But you have the hieroglyphics to orient you: in addition to the letters of their names (which already reveal their functions), each of the Principles is represented with the attributes that characterize it.

"Primordial Cosmic Femininity, named Wisdom in the biblical text, carries, in the Egyptian temple, the three names of Maat, Hathor, and Neith. But each one of these names indicates one of the aspects of its function.

"Hathor is (as his name indicates) 'the house of Horus,' that is, of the divine Logos, which, for all eternity, acts in her unformed virginal substance as fecundating Spirit which engenders through her *Ahi.*

"Ahi is the *Reaction* Function of this Trinity, which renders the Logos, Horus, manifest through the *Formed Substance*, which is the mirror of substance without form.

"Hathor, represented with horns as a celestial cow, is the Lunar Principle of nourishing Heaven. Her milk is the Cosmic Substance that sustains all earthly life.

"What is said of Wisdom can be said of Maat, since she is at the same time 'united with her Creator, daughter of Ra, and united with Ra from his beginning'[5]; she is indissociable from Amon-Ra in continual Creation,

5. Ibid.

where she plays the role of the separator of the pure from the impure, because she conserves the true essence of everything and abandons to natural destruction the various wastes."

"Is that why she is the *Neter* of Justice?" asked Dutheil.

"That's true," answered the sculptor. "She is the Universal Consciousness and the Function of discernment for Human Consciousness.

"As for Neith, the Egyptian texts place her essentially as the Cosmic Virgin-Mother: 'A virgin, she gives birth before the birth of anything,' and 'that to which she gives birth' does not differ from that which is realized by Hathor, as by *Maat*.

"These are the particular attributes that indicate the nuances of Function, of which she is the configuration: her hieroglyphic symbols represent two crossed arrows, and the weaver's shuttle. The two arrows evoke the double Cosmic Energy whose crossing provokes the fixation of Substance. The shuttle completes this image.

"But the red crown that is attributed to Neith adds another nuance: whereas the horns of Hathor signify the lunar aspect of the Creative Cosmic Function, the red crown of Neith evokes its solar aspect, as Spiritual Animator.

"However, these four feminine aspects of the Causal Divinity still *belong to the single Primordial Virginal Passivity.*"

"It's interesting," remarked Dutheil, "to rediscover these qualifications of the Cosmic Virgin applied to Mary, Mother of Jesus, in the old Christian liturgy: 'Mother of the Creator,' 'Virgin Mother,' 'Seat of Wisdom,' 'House of Gold,' 'Mirror of Justice.' . . ."

"That's right," answered Dominique, "but this ancient liturgy then used the name of Mary, '*Mother of Jesus Christ the Savior*,' as the human symbol of the Cosmic Virgin Mother, without attributing to Mary (the human mother of Jesus) *her own immaculate conception.* This Dogma (recently promulgated) was revoked as a heresy by the orthodox fathers of the early Church.

"As you must have seen, these epitaphs applied to the Cosmic Virgin were common to the Egyptian and Brahmanic traditions, which never attributed an earthly and historic existence to their symbolic feminine representations."

"No doubt the human images of Mary in Catholicism have fostered this confusion." said Dutheil.

"Certainly," agreed Dominique. "However, one of these images is an exception, the one called 'miraculous.' The Virgin is represented standing on clouds, one foot on the crescent moon; a circle of twelve stars surrounds her; from her extended hand, rays of light are descending. It's a venerable figuration of the Cosmic Virgin, witnessing a true knowledge.

The way she is placed amid the stars of the zodiac, as well as the rays of light emanating from her hands, evokes, without doubt, her role as life-giver, while the crescent specifies the earthly destination of this life-giving force."

"The lunar crescent reminds me of that of the chaste Diana," said Thomas.

"I suppose you mean Diana of Ephesus, whose multiple breasts represent an aspect identical with that of Hathor, the celestial cow?" asked Dutheil.

"It is indeed the nursing function," answered Dominique. "But Diana has two aspects: always the Virgin, she can be white or black like Diana of Ephesus."

Thomas looked eagerly at the sculptor. "Could you answer a question that has always intrigued me, Maître Dominique? What is the meaning of the Black Virgin that they used to place in the crypt in the cathedrals?"

"My dear friend, I hope she will intrigue you enough to reveal to you one day her positive reality," said Dominique. "In the meantime, let's give a bit of our attention to this principle:

"In the beginning there is Substance without form. If it is qualified as 'the Darkness,' it is the beginning of Form."

Thomas, with half-closed eyes, engraved his Master's words in his memory.

Dutheil tried to draw a conclusion. "Does the symbolism of the Virgin therefore have a positive sense in the science of Genesis?" he asked.

"It is the basis of it," said Dominique. "The man who doesn't understand that will never know the mystery of the Origin."

"It's moving to find her in the oldest traditions," said Thomas, "but the Egyptian form of this expression is the most comprehensible for me: perhaps it's because it doesn't separate the concrete from the abstract."

"The Wisdom of the Pharaohs," specified Dominique, "teaches the abstract *through* the concrete, and Divine Harmony through the obvious laws of Nature which are its symbols.

"Note, however, that the physical reality of the symbolism is as undeniable as its metaphysical Reality, or, better yet, it identifies the functions of Nature with their Causal Functions. It involves no fantasy, whether sentimental or imaginative."

"You don't find the devotional aspect either, as in Hinduism and Christianity." added Dutheil.

"The character of ancient Egypt is positive and productive," answered Dominique. "Directives given by her sages relate not to ideal aspirations, but to a mentality and behavior that lead to the realization of the destiny that belongs to one of two categories of individuals. These two categories, which are differentiated by the goal that each gives to earthly existence, are called in the Gospel *the Many* (who are attached to this earthly world) and *the Few* (who aspire to the suprahuman goal). They correspond to the two paths: the Osirian and the Horian.

"Those who followed the Osirian path went, after death, into a state of waiting in the *Dwat*, the intermediary between their earthly existence and their ensuing reincarnation. This *Dwat* included several places (or rather states of consciousness), the lower of which was the astral state, which was a reflection of earthly existence. There, the deceased rediscovered the images and consequences of his human behavior, and had to defend himself against the evil forces, vengeance, hatred, and passions he had evoked by his bad actions."

"Did the fear of this deplorable situation inspire people to embrace a preventive and practical morality?" asked Dutheil.

"Perhaps, although the punishments of our Purgatory hardly seem to deter the vices of our contemporaries!" said Thomas.

"The repercussions of bad deeds in the *Dwat* were of a more realistic order," said Dominique, laughing. "But this *Dwat* included other states of waiting, in which the dead person benefited from a beatitude relative to his awakening of consciousness. And one can speak of consciousness, because the deceased regained contact with the various aspects of his innate consciousness—for example, certain phases of animal conscious-ness, which are abundantly illustrated in the *Book of the Dead*, and which have wrongly been interpreted as metamorphoses. But here again, it's a matter of Osirian evolution.

"From the time of the Pyramid Texts, we find a strict recommendation to abandon this way of earthly rebirth: 'therefore leave your earthly house,' they say, and follow the solar way that 'Horus realizes within the human body.'"

"That's very interesting!" exclaimed Thomas. "Does that mean that the transcendence of the human in the suprahuman was already taught in Egypt?"

"It was the Horian way, the spiritual end of man, revealed to the disciples of the Temple," answered Dominique. "But note that this Horus was no longer the son of Isis-Osiris: he is the Horus who conquers death and dualized Nature, the Horus 'formed in human body by the reunifica-tion of his immortal elements" (*Ba* and *Ka*).[6] For the disciple this was the realization of his own *Neter*, which he knew he could never attain by his own efforts.

6. That is, his Spiritual Witness and his Permanent Witness.

"The *Neter*, which he identified with the functions of his being and of Nature, were objects of knowledge for him, rather than objects of devout entreaty. But isn't identification 'communion'? What is the sense of the sacred if not the discernment of Divine Activity in its multiple manifestations?"

"Does that mean that Herodotus was right when he said that Egyptians were, in the true sense of the word, 'the most religious of men'?" said Dutheil. "Next to them I feel like a pagan!"

"To avoid being one, you'd have to apply the words of Jesus to the woman of Samaria: we must *know what we worship*," answered Dominique. "However, the Absolute is unknowable, but the Divine Cause reveals itself through its universal work. The human being is the summary of Creation. We have to awaken in ourselves the consciousness of this, and if we expand this awareness to the point of suprahuman consciousness, we can know what is Divine in us."

"These words," said Dutheil, "illumine the goal for the man who wants to find in himself his own Light. But it's the way of the Few."

"You're right," agreed Dominique. "And it's clear that religion replaces with devotion the Knowledge which the Many are unable to attain. This is justified if the devotion is based on the possibility of communion with the Divine, *regardless of what the religion is*, and also if it is not conditioned by imposed belief, and if dogmatism does not oppose the awakening of Knowledge."

"That's what Jesus accused the scholars of the Law of," said Thomas.

"And he was justified," affirmed Dominique, "because to force a man to follow a way that doesn't suit him is to alienate him from the Light. He who has a thirst to 'know' in spirit and in truth will be repelled by compulsory belief and devotion. Besides, devotion only works for the one who gives himself up to the quest for knowledge. This person can only worship what he learns to know through the awakening of his consciousness."

"I agree completely," said Thomas. "Without this condition, devotion to me would be artificial sentimentality."

"Note, Thomas, that even without actual Knowledge, it doesn't have to be artificial. Impulsive devotion is a state of prayer in one who intimately believes in the reality of a Divine Power. But then, if his devotion is sincere, his behavior will conform to his faith. And in this case, my friend, you must never attack this faith. . . ."

"Regardless of what the religion is!" added Dutheil, enthusiastically agreeing with Dominique.

"Obviously," continued Dominique, "when I speak of devotion I don't mean prudent submission to religious practices for fear of punishment.

This has nothing to do with the impulsive aspiration toward the Divine, that aspiration which is true devotion.

"But do you realize that devotion is, in reality, the need for complementation? Does that surprise you? Think about it: when your stomach is empty, it expresses its hunger, and you find it natural to furnish it with food. When the mediocrity of your earthly existence creates in you a state of dissatisfaction, if you don't falsely assuage this 'hunger' by artificial means, it provokes a call toward a superior state of being. If you name the state Divine, your aspiration will become *devotion* for the Divinity which can satisfy this hunger.

"If, instead of externalizing your appeal, you evoke the Divine in yourself, it will be your own spiritual state that will respond. And the *joy of plenitude* caused by this Presence will become the object of your devotion. But this devotion will lose its entreating and sentimental character, to become the conscious appeal of your own divine complement.[7]

"In both cases it's the need for complementation caused by the emptiness suffered by your *unfulfilled* human state."

"The emptiness suffered by my *unfulfilled* human state . . ." repeated Jean Thomas slowly. "Oh, let us into this light, Maître Dominique."

"The Kingdom of Heaven is open to the poor of spirit," murmured the sculptor; "that is, to those who are conscious of their 'lack.'"

Dominique then stood up and took the ball of clay in his hands.

7. See Chapter 9.

18
Emotion

Maître Pierre, with furrowed brow, was nervously climbing along the nave of the Atelier. From time to time his solitary work was interrupted with a worried sigh.

The bell at the entrance had rung twice, but no one had heard it. Jean Thomas, accompanied by the pilot and Dutheil, stood at the landing, surprised that no one answered. He checked a piece of paper for the hour of the meeting and tried ringing the bell a third time.

The door then opened and Maître Pierre blocked their passage, asking them coldly: "Who are you?"

Caught off guard by this reception, Jean Thomas protested: "But you know us! Maître Dominique invited us to come."

"Invited or not, you have to answer my question: what do you want?"

Jean-Jacques, sensing a mystery, answered without hesitating: "We've come to beg some words of truth: do you have the right to oppose that?"

"As guardian of the entranceway, I have the right to screen the seeker for sincerity."

Thomas, outraged, retorted angrily: "And what allows you to doubt our sincerity? We are obeying the call that was addressed to us."

"Very well, gentlemen, but you know the saying: 'Many are called, but few know how to enter.'"

The pilot watched Maître Pierre with an amused smile. "It's also said, my friend, that Truth allows itself to be revealed by him who knows how to take it: I've made up my mind." And saying this, he took the 'guardian' by his lapels and turned him around in place in order to let his friends pass.

"What's the meaning of this ridiculous playacting?" grumbled Thomas, venting his ill humor.

"It might not be as ridiculous as you think," retorted the sculptor, who from the entrance to his studio had been observing what was taking place without saying a word. "Not as ridiculous as you think, since Maître Pierre's theatrical sense knew how to provoke in each of you the attitude revealing your inner reactions. Are you so easily disconcerted?"

Without further explanation, the sculptor invited them to come in with a wave of his hand.

Sitting in the studio under the sharp stare of the Master, the three friends felt a bit uncomfortable. Maître Pierre stood a short distance apart from them with the apparent indifference of an actor whose role is finished for the moment.

"What do you expect of me?" said Dominique. "Do you want me to explain this mysterious welcome? I don't have to explain: each one can understand it in observing his own reactions.

"An unexpected shock is always useful to unmask what is sleeping in the depths of our Automaton. The questions asked by the 'Guardian of the entranceway' disgusted Thomas because they posed a condition for access to a teaching which he considered his *right*. Dutheil, who was less impulsive, maintained a state of prudent expectation. Jean-Jacques, who was shrewder, entered into the game—and his response (which was not at all theatrical, as you thought) could be considered that of an initiate. It signaled his attitude in his quest for truth. Undoubtedly you will recognize this allusion to stories describing the old tests of initiation."

"That's what I thought," recognized Dutheil.

"It doesn't matter, my friend: you *thought*, Jean-Jacques *understood* the meaning of the question, and his choice dictated his response."

"Does truth reveal itself, then, through violence?" asked the doctor.

"What is truth?" retorted Dominique. "Regardless of the thing you want to know, its 'truth' is what it is in itself. Therefore, it's independent of subjective judgment. Its veils are woven by our arbitrary interpretations, and their opacity is a function of our attachment to our way of thinking, feeling, and evaluating."

"In short, our vision is falsified by our prejudices," concluded the pilot. "I intend to use my aggressiveness to destroy them."

"That's the inner disposition that your response expressed," said Dominique, "and that's what I gave my approval to. Do you understand, Thomas?

"The question that was asked had a very precise sense: what are you coming to seek here? Esoteric teaching? The solution to problems that are bothering you? Or the indication of a path?

"A path will have no value if it doesn't lead you to the goal that you set for yourself. And this goal must be, for each of you, clearly defined.

"As for your problems, no one can resolve them if they are not clearly exposed in your own minds.

"As for the esotericism of a teaching, it is its *inner* meaning (in the correct sense of the word): that which relates to the essential structure of the subject under consideration, hence to the study of its causes and of their immanent effects. The 'secret' of a teaching may be arbitrary, but its 'esoteric meaning' is real: it is inaccessible to intellectual comprehension, and can only be *evoked* by the intuitive sense.

"You can see, therefore, in all these cases, that what I can give depends, for each one of you, on your mode of receptivity and on the courage to simplify your search by constantly returning to the essential point of the subject. If you remain imbued with prejudices, enamored of learned complexities and multiple hypotheses, you will still understand only the *exoterism* of the teaching.

"The first objective that you must aim for is the discernment of what is real from what is relative, regardless of what you are looking at: the comprehension of a state of being, the validity of a belief or opinion, of a judgment, of knowledge, or of a feeling. It's this discernment 'in truth' which must become your compass to find the best way to your supra-humanity.

"It is to put this compass in your hand that I've called you here today, because the direct way demands a certain temerity. Jean-Jacques understood this; Dutheil is still hesitant, tempted by intermediary methods; Thomas allows himself to be intimidated by the revelation of his own Light. And yet, Thomas, do you believe that having experienced its Presence, you can still refuse it?"

"I would never refuse it consciously, Maître Dominique. But I need guidance so I will no longer allow myself to be blinded—"

Dominique interrupted him: "Be careful, my friend: That's exactly what we have to talk about now. If you interpret 'guidance' as stuffing down your throats lessons, sermons, advice, and even reproaches, that would be allowing your instructor the active part in the work of trans-formation. You would be content with *receiving* and *attempting* to profit from it: that's the way of those who are 'asleep.' They waste their time and energy in multiple fruitless attempts.

"If one wants in this lifetime to integrate his immortal being, he must take it upon himself to abolish the obstacles opposed to it. Guiding you can only consist in making you conscious of things and opportunities that are suitable to the awakening of your consciousness, to the development of your discernment. Destiny often provides you with these opportunities in the form of shocks that can be revealing: you rarely profit from them, owing to ignorance of their value and their origin.

"This is the vital aspect of the Way, a vital aspect without which no teaching will bring you the indispensable balance of your various states of being.

"Until today you have been addressing the essential problems that interest modern man in relation to his personal and social life, taking into account the new conditions into which the precipitous rhythm of this end of an age and the approach of a new age have placed him. I've tried to clarify the situation that flows from this in terms of the individual, according to whether he is part of the masses, that is, of the Many, or part of the elite which obviously constitutes the Few.

"We've touched upon certain Universal Principles to extract from them what is essentially useful for you to know. We have studied the principal problems of the two aspects of the soul, and the various ways of understanding consciousness, purposely escaping all the complexities that would have kept us from the *One Reality*.

"But this is still only a *teaching*, an elaboration of what is necessary in order to clear the Way. We've come to the point where each one of you must find in himself his own Light: this is the obstacle that seekers come up against when they stubbornly insist on *understanding* instead of *experiencing*.

"Each of you is going to bolt at the mention of the word *experience* for fear of deceiving yourselves. Indeed, this fear has some justification, and I would hold myself responsible for your possible errors if I didn't add certain clarifications about your emotional being to the notions previously elucidated. For it is to this emotional being that you must address yourselves if you want to go beyond the limits of your rational comprehension. I know the dangers of it. That's why we must first learn how to discern the causes and effects of emotionality.

"Emotion in its noblest aspect is the reaction of our psychic being to the awakening of a state of consciousness suddenly alerted; the more sudden the awakening, the more intense the reaction. Regardless of the nature of the shock that provoked it, it's interesting to observe it, whether the purpose is to master it or to use it as a vitalizing agent.

"Emotion is always a 'putting into motion': e-motion. What is moved by emotion is a fire. The quality of emotion depends upon the nature of the fire 'moved,' and (which comes back to the same thing) of the state of consciousness awakened. It's up to us to learn how to discern what we must accept or refuse to 'move': this game is part of the *development of consciousness*. However, it's better to risk a profitable conflict than to allow oneself to sink into habitual unconsciousness."

"It seems to me," objected Thomas, "that emotion, by the fact that it overexcites the nerves, causes a loss of vital force."

"Let's be clear about this," retorted Dominique. "What do you understand by 'vital force'? If I'm speaking of fire, I mean the One Energy or Power, which is spiritual, from which the different fires issue forth. In other words, the aspects of our vital force are manifestations of this Cosmic Energy which is individualized in the human being.

"One of these aspects is the nervous force transmitted by the sensory and motor nerves. Another aspect is human animal magnetism, which is, like earthly magnetism, a polarized form of Cosmic Energy.

"The source of our nervous force is subtle energy, whose triple current[1] travels along the vertebral column, but which, because it is already specified in the spinal marrow, only transmits a force limited by this specification.

"Magnetic force, or nervous energy, can be dispensed in pure loss by what we call nervousness, or it can be accumulated by certain processes of concentration. Finally, it can be economized through serenity. But let's not confuse serenity with coldness or apathy.

"You mustn't forget, Thomas, that these two aspects of the vital force differ from Spiritual Power, both in quality and mode of action. Nervous and magnetic forces accumulate and transmit themselves by addition; it's a *quantitative* contribution whose exhaustion terminates action. But Spiritual Power breathes itself in through animation, and acts through the spiritualization of the subject that it animates: It's a *qualitative* contribution that amplifies movement of the Fire already incarnated in the subject. It's the multiplication of energy through inner gestation.

"Consequently, the artificial overworking of the nervous or magnetic forces can result in the temporary increase in our physical vitality, but by *consuming* it more rapidly. The consequence of this overactivity is therefore a wearing away through exhaustion, because it excites without renewing, in contrast with the exaltation of Spiritual Power."

"This answers my question, if I can conclude that emotion, according to the nature of its cause, produces either nervous excitation or spiritual exaltation," said Thomas. "We should therefore be able to discern it according to its effects."

"That would be preferable," conceded Dominique, "but it's not easy to do in such a simplistic way. Is it really so easy to distinguish the character,

---

1. *Ida, Pingala, Shushumna.*

spiritual or psychic, of an emotion? Alas! Many are the believers who mistake sentimental effervescence for mystical ardor. This sentimental effervescence can even be more or less hysterical.

"The error stems from the confusion between the 'emotional shock,' capable of awakening a slumbering consciousness, and the unhealthy state of emotional imagination or sensitive nervousness, nourished by the inner repetition of our multiple impressions: the hunger for satisfactions, or hopes overridden by apprehension, which serve as pretexts for emotional somersaults that bring no vital enrichment whatsoever."

Maître Pierre reacted impetuously: "That doesn't stop this carousel of feelings from being at the bottom of our everyday agitations! We suffer from these things, if we don't know how to master them. However, in order to master them the common mortal has a choice between repression and psychoanalysis."

"Neither one nor the other," retorted the doctor. "If, as I am beginning to see now, it's a matter of becoming conscious of them, it's enough to know how to trace the origin and the effects of this or that insidious disturbance, whether it's affective or stemming from passion. Then one can act, morally or medically, to clear up the organ—or the feeling."

"That's still a negative way of going about it," retorted Dominique. "That's what Maître Pierre calls repression. There is a beneficial way of using emotion, but its practice demands precise knowledge of the relationship between the 'emotional body' and Human Consciousness, and with the physical organism as well. Without this, it's impossible to discern the active or reactive role of each one of the elements in the birth of emotion.

"Above all," continued Dominique, "it's interesting to observe that the organs most strongly affected by emotion are those in which a *qualitative* transformation takes place: in the small intestine, for example, the transformation of chyme into chyle subtilizes and individualizes the nutrients. In other words, it assimilates them into the particular nature of the individual. The locale of this mysterious operation is also a very important center of disturbance. It's the same for the two essential glands, the thyroid and the adrenal glands, and, above all, for the liver and the spleen, which exert considerable influence on transformations of the blood and the humors.

"I could also mention the sex glands (the formation and the 'personification' of the sperm and the ova) in which another passage from the psychic to the physical takes place. Finally, there's the spinal marrow, the ganglia and nervous centers, where a more or less subtle transmutation can occur. This is just for your own information. The roles of these glands involve a domain different from the one we're talking about now.

"Let's first give our attention to the emotional center in relationship to the intestinal function of the first 'individualization.' Located in the abdomen, a little below the navel, it plays a primordial role in the lower stage of emotion. It corresponds to the animal instinct of defense against all that can threaten or oppose the interest of the individual, or upset its normal rhythm: for example, the guard dog that is always on the alert. It has an overriding mistrust, the impetuous reaction against all intrusion.

"The intestines account for our primary impressions of envy, impatience in fulfilling a desire, and sudden stiffening due to fear or worry. It's our gut reaction to unforseen danger, to a hurtful word or act, an upsetting gesture, an emotional or irritating rhythm that, as the popular expression put it, gets us in the guts.

"However, notice that the reaction is expressed by a tensing of the *abdomen*, or even, in the case of surprise, by nervous laughter that shakes up the peritoneum. This type of emotivity must be appeased, because we can't allow the animal to become unbridled."

"Do you have a practical means of appeasement?" asked Thomas timidly. He barely dared to interrupt his Master.

"The simplest way is a certain mode of breathing: after a large and *rapid* inhalation, you slowly and *deeply* exhale, and you wait a few seconds before taking another breath. The instants of 'emptiness' after exhaling briefly produce appeasement."

"I've done that in critical moments," confirmed Jean-Jacques. "The repetition of these exhalations calms the most violent reaction in a matter of minutes."

"This abdominal emotional center is new to me," confessed the doctor. "I was expecting you to talk about the solar plexus."

"That would be a mistake, Thomas. The solar plexus isn't the seat of an emotional source, as are the other organs of transformation. It's a place of *reaction*.

"The solar plexus is the complex center of the entire network of the nervous system, whether perceptible or imperceptible: the sympathetic and parasympathetic systems, and others even more subtle than this. It's a place not of animation, but of the interactions of all these diverse networks, which, because they are close to one another, make this plexus the *reactive* center for multiple nerve currents which are affected by the emotional vibrations produced by the centers that generate emotion. Because these centralized networks reach numerous organs, their interreactions can cause psychological disorders by prolonged emotional agitation."

"How can this be remedied?" asked Jean-Jacques.

"By localizing the emotions. It is necessary to discern the psychic source and its organic seat in order to treat it according to its harmful or life-giving value.

"But how can you expect to do this as long as you confuse the causes with the effects and don't know how to distinquish in yourself that which engenders from that which undergoes the reaction?

"We've begun to clarify these notions by situating the abdominal center at the lower stage of emotion. In the same way we can now examine the pathological effects it has on our various *humors*.

"An emotion produces an expansion or a contracting effect, according to the nature of the sentiment 'moved.' Expansion means it provokes an emission that varies according to the centers affected: tears, urine, emotional diarrhea, cold sweat, or seminal ejaculation.

"The effect of contraction is more dangerous, and produces repression: a reflux of blood, for example, that can suddenly block up an organ. Contracting shock is generally caused by an egotistical reflex which is damaging to self-esteem: it can be an insult, a frustration, or anything that affects the sense of possessiveness."

"What about jealousy, for example?" suggested Thomas.

"Yes—jealousy that is suddenly provoked. But the jealousy that eats away at you insidiously, along with splenic or morbid apprehension, are the latent states that engender all disorders, and are even more dangerous because they are unexpressed."

"It's our unconsciousness of these states that makes them harmful," suggested the doctor. "Once we're alerted, we should be able to master them."

"Don't delude yourself, Thomas. If you want to master this low emotionality through will, the only thing you will do is repress it. At the lower stage, emotion is an animal power to which we remain enslaved if we don't understand the higher stage—that is, the psychic and spiritual incentives of our emotional shocks.

"The hepatic and splenic organs, which are the theater of these conflicts, are for this reason the generating centers of emotion and, at the same time, they are its places of reaction. That's why it can be said that the liver and the spleen are the two pans of our emotional scale.

"You already know that the liver is marked with the imprints of the Permanent Witness[2] which are the characteristic tendencies of our Number-entity, and also of the astrological and atavistic tendencies of the Automaton, at least those involved with the directives or its will and its activities: initiative, courage, inertia, adversity, modesty, or the excess of self-esteem, pride, and ambition.

2. See Chapter 6.

"The other pan of the scale, the spleen, is the seat of healthy or unhealthy emotionality, of sentimentality, and of sensuality. It's the instigator of the artistic sense and the emotional imagination. It is also the physical point of contact with our fluid emotional body, which it influences and whose emotionality it, in turn, accumulates. It engenders humors that elate or depress, according to the excessive or insufficient activity of the adrenal glands, with which it interacts. However, their imbalance engenders morbid splenic reactions such as despair, jealousy, and other distortions of human love."

"Poor us!" said Maître Pierre. "I see that the seven deadly sins are the great instigators of our imbalance. And our 'marvelous organism' designed by the Creator is what's responsible for it, after all!"

"I beg your pardon, dear sir," said Dominique. "The so-called deadly sins are functional powers of the cosmos, without which nothing could live on Earth: it's the personal reactions of each individual that make faults or qualities of them. It's up to you to support your thesis at your convenience. For the moment, we're learning about the mastery of our emotional balance.

"You can already understand that the source of conflicts may be the duality of tendencies which affect the liver."

"Medically speaking," agreed the doctor, "this teaching sheds light on the pathological consequences of this proximity of contradictory influences."

"If you are interested, Thomas, I can add that this conflict is aggravated by the dual character (passive or aggressive) of the hepatic organ. Jupiter is the astrological nature of the liver, and thus serene; but just as in mythology, Mars is engendered by Jupiter, so Martian bile is engendered by the liver. However, bile is in continuous contact with the brain,[3] and the reactions of the two join up with the contrary impulses of the Automaton.

"Moreover, the hepatic organ has the same relationship to the heart as the planet Jupiter has to the sun:[4] the role of a small 'personal' sun, although it's part of the central system (cardiac or solar). Thus, the 'hepatic government' can come into conflict with the 'cardiac government' if it allows the aggressive impulses of the Automaton to dominate.

"As a theme for your meditations, also observe that the Olympian Jupiter is one of the aspects of the Egyptian Amon. In his name *Amon*, he is Western (*Amen.t* signifies the west and the right). He is Eastern in his name *Amon-Ra*, which is his solar nature.

3. See Isha Schwaller de Lubicz, *The Opening of the Way* (New York: Inner Traditions, 1981), p. 103.
4. The liver has twelve functions, like the sun in the zodiac.

"It's easy to establish the relationship: the hepatic region is the west of the human body. Its east is the region of the physical heart and of our spiritual Heart (or Sun)."

"That's what we can call a living symbolism!" exclaimed the doctor.

"You might even add the word *synthetic*," said Dominique. "The living symbolism of the Eastern and Western regions of your body will show you the relationship between your organic functions and your psycho-spiritual states. The relationship between the two 'governments'— cardiac-*solar*, on the one hand, and *hepatic-Jovian-Martian*, on the other hand—illustrates this.

"Likewise, paternal heredity is marked in the liver, just as maternal heredity marks the spleen, especially in emotional matters. *It's the spleen, and not the heart*, which is responsible for these emotions. The heart only undergoes the aftereffects."

"How can an organ be the source of an emotion?" wondered Jean-Jacques.

"You say that the brain is the organic seat of mental faculties. Likewise, the spleen is the organic seat of our emotional faculties. For all practical purposes, it is the heart of the emotional body, in the sense that it is through it that our emotional body attaches itself to our physical body. Thus, it is physically affected by the emotional trouble of which it is the psychic source."

"This explains the influence of these troubles on the hematopoietic functions of the spleen,"[5] observed the doctor.

"You'll discover other consequences if you establish the parallelism between the hepatic region, seat of the Permanent Witness, and the cardiac region (next to the spleen), seat of the Spiritual Witness: the consequent parallelism between the dual influence that engenders the conflicts in the hepatic organ, and the dual influence of the emotions that the spleen can undergo: sentimentality, of which the spleen is the seat, and the emotions resulting from spiritual aspirations.

"The confusion that can result from it in one who is unaware of their twofold origin explains certain psychic problems which can lead to hysteria or to unfortunate aberrations in the spiritual quest.

"The last parallelism is amusing to observe: the spleen (sentimental and splenetic) has the same relationship to the heart that the bile (aggressive and irritable) has to the Jovian liver."

"If I understand," intervened Jean-Jacques, "the main interest of this parallelism is the importance of what you call emotional balance, since

5. In leukemia, for example.

the two essential seats of emotion (the Western liver and the Eastern spleen) each have an organic basis, a psychic motivation, and a spiritual influence."

"Indeed, it's all very interesting," agreed Jean Thomas. "Maître Dominique is opening up new horizons on psychic pathology. Nonetheless, I'm still preplexed about the intimate relationship between the physical, the psychic, and the spiritual. If these three states of being have different modes of vibration, how can they affect each other?"

"Through the intermediary of *Human Consciousness*,"[6] answered Dominique. "It's the individual consciousness of the human, because that's what enters into contact with the three states."

"By what means?" asked Dutheil.

"By our vigilant watchfulness. Don't forget that it is our innate consciousness of all the lower realms, then the consciousness acquired through our humanity, which summarizes them. Finally, it's the inscription of our individual experience, which is enriched according to how much attention we are able to give it.

"Vigilant watchfulness is the only willful act necessary to acquire this. This watchfulness can make us conscious of our organic functions. It gives us control over our psychic impressions and reactions, and if we agree to 'listen,' it allows us to discern our higher aspirations, which attract our two Witnesses."

"If we have such possibilities within us," retorted Thomas, "it's deplorable that we are submitted to this merry-go-round of impulses and sentiments—and that we consider it normal!"

"Our Automaton encourages this," answered Dominique. "It's always concerned with one obsession or another, which it takes as its immediate goal: worry, work, fantasy. Everything becomes a pretext for it not to observe what is happening inside it. If you resign yourself to such slavery, my friends, I have nothing else to add."

They protested in unison, but looked at one another with indecision. . . .

Thomas became the spokesman for his intimidated friends: "You're leaving us up in the air, Maître Dominique, on an unfinished program: you've given us notions (which are new to me) about the various impulsions of emotionality. You've described to us its animal origins and the chaos that results from it. You've given us a glimpse of the vitalizing role of emotion without developing that theme. You've spoken about 'emotional balance' without giving us the means of achieving it. Between the

6. See Chapter 6.

lower stage of our emotional impulses and the stage where the spiritual being comes into play, I must confess that I don't see the steps in between. . . ."

"That's a bit of an exaggeration, Thomas. I'm showing you the swamp into which you're sinking, and on the other hand the firm earth of your suprahuman goals: do you expect me to take the *jump* for you as well?

"I can explain to you why, despite these teachings, you find yourself disoriented: as you have already said yourself, I've given you *notions* which, after long reflection, will allow you to explain your inner dramas. These notions still address themselves to your cerebral comprehension, and not to Human Consciousness, which doesn't register *notions*, but *impressions*.

"However, if I try to make an 'impression' on you, you will become irritated, you'll tense up and resist, afraid of 'losing your footing' if you leave the mental zone. So, although your Human Consciousness can, through its highest aspirations, put you in contact with your Permanent Witness, your rational prudence prevents this contact from taking place by allowing the mind to intercede. And your mind defends itself like a horse before an obstacle. . . .

"And you're looking for the connecting steps!

"But I'm telling you that between the mental and the spiritual *there are no steps.*

"Your Permanent Witness is your *reality.* From time to time it is able to impose itself on you without warning, or you are able to attract it to yourself through your dissatisfaction. But in order to contact it you must *leap* beyond the mental and natural possibilities, to have access to suprahuman possibilities. And this is when emotional shocks take us by surprise, and can allow us to leap over the obstacle through the awakening of unopinionated consciousness."

"It's no longer a surprise if we're able to provoke it in ourselves," replied Dutheil.

"We'll see about that," answered Dominique. "You're forgetting that the man who has decided to rend his veils finds within himself a conscious ally who will know how to take advantage of unexpected opportunities. Isn't that true, Thomas?"

"I did have that experience," recognized the doctor, "and the name of the mirage and the form in which it appeared to me is already an eloquent symbol."

"It's not a mirage," retorted Dominique. "Maître Jacques, is, for each of us, the voice of our Permanent Witness. But in order to hear him, it's necessary to search within *his* temple: *your* own temple. You must know how to withdraw into this secret place of silence to which I have so often referred. You haven't heard it, because deep down you're afraid of this inner solitude where your own light will reveal itself to you.

"The most spectacular experience to occur among you is that of our skeptic Thomas: no doubt it's the shock experienced by his skepticism faced with the brutal awakening of his consciousness that broke his resistance. When will you finally understand that this break is true initiation?"

Dutheil enthusiastically thanked Dominique: "Your warning was necessary. My hesitation in the choice of a path came from my illusions about the true sense of the teaching and of 'initiation.' I am now ready to listen to you."

Dominique leaned forward: "Then let me teach you how to listen to *yourself*. All of our previous discussions have been 'dissertations' to which each of you have voiced objections—that is, you've allowed your minds to argue.

"Today it's Maître Jacques who would like to express himself through me. It's up to you to give him your attention. Then there will be a *mediation* between your Human Consciousness and your Suprahuman Consciousness.

"In order to facilitate this 'heart to heart meditation' for you, I propose that I take you to some place that is favorable for this mediation, a place where the mind will be less indiscreet, if you don't allow yourselves to become discouraged. Would you like to join me? I'm not obliging any-one to follow me: dare to listen to your impulse before accepting or refusing."

Dominique stood before his intrigued friends, waiting for their answer. Jean Thomas, Jean-Jacques, and Dutheil stood up spontaneously. Maître Pierre, after a moment of hesitation, did the same. Their Master led them toward a partition, in which a panel slid aside to reveal a narrow, low door: they had to bend far forward to enter. . . .

The visitors' surprise surpassed all their expectations when they entered, because this round chamber, with no other openings but the door and the air vents, was white and empty from the ceiling, with its diffuse light, to the carpet, on which five large cushions were arranged. The cushions were the only seats in the empty room. Each one sat down, adapting, like Dominique, the posture of the yogi in meditation.

They felt disoriented in this round room. No one felt like talking. Each underwent the neutralizing effect of the impersonal atmosphere. They hardly dared look at each other.

Dominique let this heavy silence weigh on them for a long time. His shrewd glance scrutinized the expressions on the faces of those who were

listening to the silent question, unraveling the impulsions of their emotions.

After the long wait had exhausted their various reactions, the serene
smile of the Master erased the last resistance.

"If you succeed in not situating this place anywhere except in yourselves, you will be well disposed," he said.

"In entering into this state you were disturbed by the total absence of
symbols: emptiness is difficult to bear. . . . However, it's the true sense
of the hermitage. The emptiness is not total, because each of you has
furnished it with tumultuous thoughts, which you are trying to 'interpret'
according to your mentality.

"So how can I, Maître Jacques, reveal myself?

"How can I show through your doubt, Thomas, which is erasing my
image in you? . . . Because I am still *image* for you.

"How can I liberate you from your consciousness, Jean Jacques, since
you still want to judge what you 'must' or 'must not' do, since good and
evil are still within you?

"How can I make you experience naked reality, Dutheil, since you are
still looking for the symbolism that veils it?

"The image is a creation of human thought, 'interpretation': you're
holding on to it so that you don't fall into the Void where your being
without form, liberated from form, is able to make contact with the
Divine.

"Good or evil is, for each man within whom I live, the acceptance or
the refusal, *at each Present Moment*, of his spiritual Necessity, for which
I am the conscious guide.

"The symbol is the expression of an incarnated Cosmic Function. I am
the Function of the Number incarnated in your body, Dutheil. If you
attract me within you, you become my symbol and the living symbol of
the cosmos: why do you need other symbols?"

The Master could be silent: he was disappearing . . . the inexpressible
feeling of a single Presence, particular to each and common to all.

Maître Jacques was revealing himself.

"Where are we?" sighed Maître Pierre.

Dominique smiled. "Perhaps now you will better understand how one
can, without gesture or symbol, calm the infernal dialectic of the mind,
the impatience for understanding, and the mirages of the imagination.
I'm attempting to introduce you into your inner temple, for which this
room can only serve as a waiting room because it is still tinted with your
individual colors. You must learn how to filter them out through denial of

your personal concepts, in order not to distort the Light of Presence. For the Presence which in you *knows* is unable to reveal itself except in proportion to your impersonality.

"Where is the true secret temple?

"Throughout the world there are innumerable temples which are built on symbols. The first and most primitive was a simple stone offering-table, the sacrificial stone, which attracts the Creative Spirit by the gift of the creature.

"The last is defined by Christ when he gave the woman of Samaria the Teaching of the new age: the necessity of 'knowing what one worships' and no longer placing this worship anywhere except 'in spirit and in truth.'

'Knowledge is the fruit of unification, and the unification of what knows with what is known is true worship.

"Thus, the circle closes in on itself, unifying the first temple with the last one.

"But between the first and the last there are a multitude of temples, a multitide of symbols, and diversity.

"For each one of us, the temple is its own secret place where at every moment the sacrifice of the perishable to the Imperishable must be accomplished. *Joyous* sacrifice attracts Presence.

"Your body is the external temple in which the life-giving Spirit effects its work of integration and continual assimilation through your organs. It is for you to transcend this work by reintegrating the two aspects of your entity.

"Each man who prepares their union carries in himself the true temple, because he progressively learns how to 'know what he worships.'

"His high priest is his Permanent Witness. The worshipper in him is his Human Consciousness, which at the highest level *become conscious* of the lower levels, and, from this fact, is the immediate intermediary between his natural being and his supranatural Being. It is the entrance to the temple, in which the exoteric teaching is recorded.

"It's in this Human Consciousness that the emotional shock reverberates. These shocks can open for him the door to the Sanctuary by giving the 'high priest' the power of helping him to *surpass himself.*

"But the intelligent Automaton can oppose this. This is the critical point in the match between the Automaton and the Permanent Witness, which is itself the intermediary between Human Consciousness and the Divine Spiritual Witness."

Dominique paused and cast a profound look at his audience. "How can I make you experience this subtle moment of tension which is the great step between the psychic and the spiritual? Dare to try it with me, dare to go beyond comprehension . . . dare to break the 'sound barrier' in order to know your reality. So much the better if you experience in your solar plexus the anguished trembling of the horse which finds itself faced with an obstacle that is too high, but still wants to jump! Allow your psyche to vibrate in the joy of surpassing yourself. Bear this instant of emotion. . . .

"Those of you who have lived it have understood these emotional shocks: the awakening of a dormant consciousness."

Maître Pierre looked with breathless amazement at Dominique. "So that was the mystery on the other side," he murmured in a choked voice.

"Yes," answered Dominique gently: "the mystery that it was necessary to *accept* in order to find the Master who's been waiting for you."

The poignant surprise of Maître Pierre had touched the others. The Master took advantage of this to direct their attention to the initiatory value of emotion, consciously employed as an instrument of mastery.

"I would like you to learn to evoke Maître Jacques with you. That is, to evoke within you a state 'in which you must take refuge to watch your mind functioning, while remaining completely attentive to the voice of your intuition.'

"This is possible if you consciously accept the emotional reactions that can result from a new understanding. Then you will assimilate the substance of the teaching, and will no longer confuse Knowledge and Awareness.

"Listen to what I still have to tell you *in this spirit*, and allow your own Light to enliven it. For once I am asking you to project before you a mental image: the synthetic image of your human 'robot.' I say *robot* because it is constituted in such a way that it can function like an Automaton, even in the absence of its Immortal Being.

"Before you is a goodfellow of flesh, supported by goodfellow skeleton, irrigated by goodfellow blood vessels and lymphatic tissues, innervated by many goodfellow currents of energy, of which the most obvious (the goodfellow of nerves) is the only one perceptible to your eyes. The most subtle is composed of invisible current (*nadis*) and centers of spiritual energy (*chakras*) which are conductors, generators, and condensers of *prana*,[7] but I won't talk at all about that, because the manipulation of this pranic fire can be mortally dangerous for someone who has not acquired the mastery of his physical body and his psyche.

"Your goodfellows of flesh and blood, vessels and nerves, are the support and the container of *the Functional Man*, whose organs are the incarnation of Universal Functions.

"However, if the synthetic functioning of your other 'goodfellows' is

7. *Prana*: Cosmic energy which has become vital energy.

indispensable to the existence of your being, your 'Organic Man' has a fundamental value, because he is the summary and the synthesis of the animal and animating functions of Creation.

"However, these organs are in a hierarchy according to their participation in spiritual or pyschic life, or simply in the mechanistic life of the individual.

"The king of the organism is the heart, because it is the body of the incorporeal Heart, the temple of the Spiritual Witness.

"The lungs, organs of breath, are the servants of the heart, with which they constitute the serene trinity of the regenerative function.

"The complementary organic trinity could be called 'the trinity of conflicts,' because it includes the three seats of emotion: the Western liver, the Eastern spleen, and the mysterious abdominal center.

"The serene trinity is passive in relationship to the emotional trinity, whose organic activity is often upset by the contradictory impulses taking place within it.

"However, the passivity of the heart is its obedience to the rhythm of the individual. The cause of the conflicts is the resistance of the Automaton to the rhythm and tendencies of the Permanent Witness. When the instructions of the latter triumph over the resistance of the Automaton, Harmony is established between the two trinities and the 'Seal of Solomon' is enacted.

"But this Great Work demands an intense desire to transcend oneself and a clear vision of the constitution of the 'robot.'

"Its complex body is dominated by the cranial sphere—the 'leader' of this robot. The cranial sphere contains the control panel of the 'goodfellow' of energy. All the functions of the Organic Man are reflected in his cerebral localizations. The lunar brain is a *mirror*, as suits the mental organ. And this mirror immediately reflects the volitions and impulses of the Automaton with their bilious reactions, which are immediately aggravated by the motives we invent for them cerebrally. This is where we get the well-known bile-brain circuit[8] which complicates all our conflicts.

"However, the intuitive function and the Spiritual Being also have their seats there: the pituitary and the pineal glands are situated at the center of the two cerebral hemispheres.

"If you have projected before you, as in a mirror, an image of your robot, turn him around now and transpose him into yourself. Without thinking of the 'goodfellows,' become conscious of the Function Man, whose emotional trinity establishes contact between your three states: physical, pyschic, and spiritual.

8. See *The Opening of the Way*, p. 103.

"Concentrate your attention on the organic seats of emotion, and become aware of what in you has become conscious of them: it is the Human Consciousness, one or another of whose aspects is affected, according to the emotional seat that influences it.

"The *abdominal* seat influences the instinctive consciousness: either naturally (by immanent danger, for example) or artificially by mental imagination.

"The *hepatic* influences the *moral* Human Consciousness: either in the harmonious sense, under the influence of the Permanent Witness, or in a disharmonious way, under the impulse of personal tendencies, or under the influence of conventional morality.

"The *splenic* seat influences the *emotional* consciousness: either in its natural instinctive sentiments or in its artificially cultivated attachments, or by the conflict between these emotional impulses and the aspiration toward Immortal Being.

"These are only examples to show you that these differences are witnesses to two possibilities: the autonomy of Human Consciousness, or its distortion by a foreign influence. It is autonomous if it is the inscription of its own experiences, which are added to its innate consciousness, and which teach it to discern their healthy or unhealthy effects: in other words, it's the karmic consequences of what it has recorded. It is not autonomous when it is distorted by a foreign influence that violates its impressions in an erroneous way (imposed beliefs, fraudulent examples, education that stifles its spiritual call). This deformation of Human Consciousness is condemned in the Gospel: 'woe unto him who offends one of these little ones.' The 'little ones' are people who follow simply and without deception the law of their innate consciousness and their spiritual impulse. This malediction is very heavy for those who, by vicious instinct or by intransigent sectarianism, stifle or deform human consciousness!"

Dominique's attention was drawn to the distraught expression on Jean-Jacques's face.

"Woe unto him who offends . . ." murmured the pilot. "I have never understood it as a deforming power over someone else's consciousness. To stifle or to falsify his experience is to put it in peril and turn it away from its divine soul. It's horrible to think that so many people today are running the risk of such a curse, through proselytizing vice, or through the will to dominate. . . ."

"Or simply to commit a destructive act for the mere emotional excitment," finished Dominique. "Perhaps now you'll understand the major role of emotion. It can be an *effect*, a cause, and a new effect: it *is* the psychic reaction of a consciousness awakened by a moral shock, be it accidental or intentional. It *becomes* the motivation of the behavior aroused by this reaction. The effect it has on the sensitive or sexual nerves makes it look once again for satisfaction in pleasure, or in sensual exaltation. Thus, it's through ignorance or through the refusal to 'transcend' it that one wastes the fire of Heaven. . . .

"This is one of the keys to the crazy incoherence of our current society. The precipitated rhythm of this end of an age instinctively distresses it. A vague foreknowledge of a need to *surpass* this disturbs it, without enlightening it on the behavior necessary to accomplish it. Men whose vital sense has not atrophied give in to the impulse of haste and *excessive* actions, which create exciting emotion. This is where they get their taste for risk, dangerous sports, horrifying or cruel spectacles, brawls, or exasperating rhythms.

"However, all these extravagances are only the camouflaging of their subconscious impulse: to transcend their mediocrity. The error stems from the ignorance of the goal of this transcendence. The value of the sense of excess, like the value of the emotions, depends on the state to which it leads you.

"We're no longer speaking about emotional irritability, which depends on the abdominal center and which one must learn to master. What's important here is to discern the quality of emotions that affect Human Consciousness:

"In its moral sense (seat of the liver and of the spleen); in its affectivity (seat of the spleen); through egotistical will, or in the conflicts between its impulses and those of the Permanent Witness (seat of the liver); and finally, its spiritual aspiration.

"One must take into account: the emotional seat from which impulse emanates; then the aspects of consciousness between which the conflict exists.

"The organic reactions caused by emotions must be discerned in order not to allow them to distort psychic reaction. It's on this point that we must concentrate our attention.

"The beneficial effect of an emotional shock is the breaking of the egotistical, mental, or affective obstacle which is opposed to the transcendence necessary for our suprahuman realization.

"If we put emotion at the service of sexual or mental expectations, only our Automaton profits from it. But if our Human Consciousness is constantly oriented toward its suprahuman goals, it will use emotional shock as a springboard to cross over the frontier of our mediocrity."

"A springboard," Thomas repeated under his breath, "which allows us to go beyond our human possibilities . . ."

"To gain access to suprahuman possibilities," finished Dominique.

"But this program should not be utopian. Therefore, you must put it in relationship to the sense of *sacrifice*, which explains the value of the emotional shock and the condition of its effectiveness.

"To sacrifice a lower value to a higher value is to give substance and power to the *desire* which has been 'sacrificed.' If this higher value is of a spiritual order, the spiritual power is attracted by this desire, and gives to the sacrificer a power of domination over his lower states.

"Here's an example of something I witnessed. It was during the last war. A soldier who was badly wounded in the lung was brought to the operating table. There was no anesthesia. The surgeon informed the wounded man that he would have to be brave. The soldier asked for a moment to prepare himself. He closed his eyes, concentrated . . . then he firmly said: 'Go on, Major, and do it fast!' As he felt the first incision of the scalpel, he let out an impassioned scream: 'For the flag! . . .' Then he underwent the painful operation without flinching. His ecstatic smile never left him.

"What happened? The fervor of the sacrifice to a patriotic ideal had created such an intense emotional shock that the ardor of his mystical joy had transmuted his pain."

The men gathered around Dominique listened respectfully.

"It's always through an excessive gesture that one can force the passage to a higher state: it's 'excessive' in relationship to the state that one wants to transcend.

"However, the state that goes beyond your perishable humanity does not mean an amelioration of what has conditioned it. Instead, it's a radically different state: it's different in its way of vibrating and in its immortal character, just as what is Real differs from what is relative. Therefore, it imposes a different rhythm.

"It's a new state of being in which the human animal becomes the passive support of the nonmortal being, because Human Consciousness, freely enlightened by the Permanent Witness, imposes its directives on the Automaton. Then the emotional being, mastered in its lower aspect, is subjugated by human consciousness, which uses emotional shocks to detect egotistical impulses and to awaken the intuitive function. The mind is therefore reduced to its goal of transcriber, and human consciousness, progressively rectified by the Permanent Witness, is integrated by it, thus fulfilling the goal of incarnation: Total Consciousness, in other words, the anthropocosm."

"Isn't this the state of consciousness defined by Maître Jacques, in which our clear-sighted vigilance can at the same time 'watch the mind functioning' while constantly listening to the Permanent Witness?" said Thomas.

"It's exactly that," answered Dominique. "It's the reestablishment of the harmonious order, where the elements that make up man gently fulfill the roles that were primordially assigned to them.

"However, in our present condition there is so much resistance that our life is too short to acquire this mastery through mediocre efforts and small, virtuous progress. Mastery of self obtained by force of will *constrains* instead of transcending. It's always the ego that is looking at itself and flattering itself for its success: the personal rhythm remains unchanged, and this mediocre rhythm keeps us prisoners of our *natural* possibilities, which we must transcend. We await death while running in place with all these small efforts; its the sad end of our lost experience. . . .

"It's laziness to *resign oneself* because one doesn't have the courage to take the *leap* to attain the highest destiny! It's necessary to *leap* above our habits, our atavistic chains, our small egotistical passions; to *leap* above the mind with its rational reticence, above the fear and the doubt for which it is responsible. Why is it that we can pass into the astral without difficulty when we dream? Simply because the mind at sleep does not offer opposition to it. For the same reason, the sleepwalker can walk along a high and narrow ledge without danger.

"In order to pass into the intuitive state one must leap over the obstacle of one's thoughts: deliberately deny them, by making the gesture, which is excessive because it is absurd, of 'listening to silence.' What is the process of the miracle if not the 'excessive' faith in the spiritual possibility of achieving what is naturally impossible?

"What is effective meditation? It is the mediating state between the natural human state and the suprahuman state. However, it's only effective if we can go beyond the mental.

"There are three ways of achieving this: through the monotonous repetition of mantric words, which has the effect of tiring the mind; or the intense and *patient* desire for union; or finally through emotional shock, which can allow one to enter suddenly. That is the goal of this conversation: I offer you the possibility of doing this.

"If you have *heard* me, you now have the ideas necessary for becoming conscious of your diverse emotions. Now it's up to you to assemble them, to constantly return to them in order to learn how to master them. I've shown you the way, because we have during this conversation, *experienced several aspects of meditation*. Know how to find them in your 'secret place.'

"When you have awakened Maître Jacques within you, you will have an ally who will know how to provoke the opportunity for you to experiment with emotional shock. Do not refuse him out of faint-heartedness.

"People who armor themselves against emotion, whether from deference to public opinion or fear of temptation, become hardened into a coldness that sterilizes all spiritual impulse. Don't forget that the Spirit is a *Fire* which demands to be fed so as not to be smothered by our mediocrity.

"*Mediocrity is the greatest obstacle to our reanimation.*

"Therefore, meditate on the strange evangelical statement: 'Joy shall be in Heaven over one sinner that repenteth, more than over ninety and nine just persons, *which need no repentance.*' These words are obviously not an invitation to licentiousness! They are only a warning against the danger of the *lukewarm feeling due to a comfortable security which is the enemy of all risk.*

"The suprahuman realm is 'going beyond' our lower humanity. We can only attain it by breaking the chains and overcoming the obstacles that keep us from it: that is, by the sacrifices and superefforts that allow us to go beyond our natural possibilities. Our two Witnesses provoke these impulses, but who will furnish the exaltation necessary for their execution?

"What gives the victor of a dangerous exploit the courage to go beyond difficulties? It is the exaltation of emotional joy produced by the risk, by going beyond fatigue or excessive suffering: in every case, it is the shock caused by the breaking of an impossibility.

"All those whose Human Consciousness thirsts for the Immortal and the Divine are driven to shed their mediocrity. Today, this need to go beyond has become a *major necessity* for the elite. By *elite*, I mean people who are guided by their Permanent Witness, who by this fact are *called* to transcend their lower humanity and enter into the suprahuman.

"Do not perceive this ambition as a pretentious utopia: it's the *immediate duty* of all those who have the possibility of achieving it. The duty is immediate because time is running out. Today we are already in a tragic period of change in the zodiacal rhythm. Even more serious, this is the critical age of humanity, an age of judgment in which those who can transcend themselves will receive a push forward, whereas those who fall behind will suffer the fate of the masses. This is the great confusion which characterizes the end of an age. *It's now that it must happen: the suprahuman kingdom is not located beyond the Earth. It leads beyond Earth, but it is on the Earth that the human elite must first attain the kingdom in order to be integrated into it beyond the Earth.*

"The suprahuman is the culmination of our human destiny, the summit, and this summit is the point of departure for a higher spiritual state.

"The possibility is within us from the moment we are animated by our two Witnesses. Their Presence is the suprahuman seed which makes earthly man participate in this supernatural state, which becomes his home when he is delivered from his mortal body. Physical death then becomes the joyous and glorious *birth* of his realized being, liberated from the world of conflict."

The radiant face of Maître Dominique reflected the serenity of his certitude, but an exaltation came over his listeners. Swept up into this emotion, they made use of this springboard to make themselves "go beyond."

"The joy that illuminates you at this moment is waiting for you each time you go beyond an impossibility. And if this impossibility is an obstacle to Divine Presence, the sacrifice that allows you to surmount it attracts the Divine in the human.

"Then you are no longer searching for the true temple. The symbol of the Solar Heart will be reality: The Temple of the All-Powerful. . . ."

Dominique, his eyes closed, listened within himself, and the silence surrounded them.

"Have you already experienced it?" he murmured.

His voice became more somber, warmer, and more penetrating: "It's there we must concentrate in order to enter into the suprahuman. It is the sanctuary where we make contact with the Divine Power within us. It's there that our thirst for love finds its legitimate object in our *Spiritual Complement*. It's there that we can create our serenity in giving it, through an act of denial, the mediating role in all our conflicts.

"It is the secret *naos*, the tabernacle of all prayer and all communion . . . in Spirit and in Reality."

Prayer . . . communion . . . in spirit and in reality . . . The magic of the words and the intonation prolonged their lasting effects. They continued to vibrate in the striking silence. . . .

Beyond thought and time, the four disciples, united in the vision of the Master, had penetrated without difficulty into the secret place of Silence.

19

The Christ Principle

"Welcome, gentlemen. I wanted to bring you together around a traditional tree for this Christmas Eve." Dominique invited his guests into the studio, which was softly lit with small multicolored lamps. Comfortable chairs were scattered around a brazier, and the fragrance of punch mixed with the aromas of incense and spices.

In the background were two large panels representing two different trees: on one side a date palm tree, on the other side a strange green tree that evoked the image of a maple tree whose trunk has been replaced with an Osirian column. On the ground, between the two trees, was a nest of woven straw that seemed to incubate the fire which lit it from within. The joyous music of childlike Christmas carols was softly diffused from the radio.

Dominique allowed his guests to sharpen their curiosity about this unexpected decor. His cunning laughter suddenly alerted them.

"My Christmas tree seems to have struck you dumb," he said as he passed around some cigarettes. "I'd like each one of you to give me your reactions."

"It's a strange Christmas tree!" exclaimed Dutheil. "If indeed it is a Christmas tree, what are you symbolizing by the duality . . . ?"

"What do you think, Jean-Jacques?"

"The column of Osiris and the palm would lead me to look to Egypt for the key to your enigma," answered the aviator. "Is there also an Osirian Christmas?"

"It's the straw nest that intrigues me," murmured the doctor. "It's like a strange manger in which the inner fire replaces the Christ Child."

"Congratulations, Thomas," answered the sculptor as he lit his pipe. "It's this newborn fire which is the link, and the key to my two symbolic trees.

"The origin of Christmas as the festival of the Nativity dates far before our Christian era. The cult of Mithra, the unconquered Sun, celebrated the beginning of his ascension and the return of life on December 23 (the winter solstice). At midnight, lights and great cries of joy welcomed the newborn Sun and his Mother, the Celestial Virgin: 'The Virgin gave birth, the Light grows!'

"However, the Christian Christmas did not exist until much later, because the early Church had not given a precise date to the birth of its Christ Child. The custom became established little by little, among the Eastern Christians, of celebrating it on January 6. It wasn't until the fourth century that the Western Church moved the date back to December 25 to replace the pagan feast of the birth of the Sun, whose cult was formally condemned by Pope Leo the Great (ninth century).

"Thus, the Christian ritual of the Divine Nativity also rejoined the Egyptian ritual, the Feast of Khoiak, which on the same day celebrated the resurrection of Osiris, that is, his reanimation by the solar light.

"Osiris, *Neter* of Nature, is the principle of perpetuity—that is, of the cycles which are continually renewed. He is the vital Principle, which in all of dualized Nature is perpetually being born, vegetating, growing, dying, and being reborn. That's why we find in certain tombs of Osiris the silhouette of a conifer whose symbol makes this tree the ancestor of our Christmas tree. Its trunk is replaced by the *djed* of Osiris, his spinal column, to which the four physical elements give stability.

"The Osirian world is that of earthly existence. What links our Christmas tree to the tree of Osiris is that both are illuminated by the awakening of the new fire. This fire is manifested in the star of the Magi on January 6, Epiphany. On this date, the sun, crossing the apsis, starts to prolong the day, and the mornings and the evenings are lengthened. That's why we have the tradition of keeping the Christmas lights until this date."

"These comparisons are as informative as they are picturesque," said Thomas.

"We can be even more specific," continued Dominique. "Let's do a bit of synthetic symbolism. Christmas-Khoiak is the instant when the fire of the seed, buried at Saint-Michel, has conquered the infernal dragon and reanimated the germ of the seed in which Osiris is resuscitated with the sun. The Cosmic Power Michael has transformed sterile Satanic fire into living Luciferian fire; the Cosmic Power Osiris has triumphed over the

Sethian fire, and earthly vegetation once again continues on its course with the reascent of the sun."

"This similarity between the two myths fascinates me," exclaimed Dutheil as he rose to examine the two trees in detail. "But I don't get the significance of the palm."

"I put it opposite the Osirian tree, since the sun of daylight is in opposition to the nocturnal sun of the *Dwat*, just as the kingdom of heaven is different from the earthly kingdom. Moreover, the date palm tree, whose leaves are lunar[1] and whose fruit is solar, unites the two natures in its mercurial substance.

"In the legend of Saint Christopher, who carries the Divine Child across the river, 'Christopher, the traveler' leans on a palm tree, which he uses as a cane. In this *hermetic* allegory, the Egyptian palm tree links the Horian myth to the Christian symbol. And we've already seen that Christ is, for our theology, what Horus was for Egyptian dogma.

"However, notice that Jesus is referred to as the Son of David (Daud), that is, of the human line of Daud, for which he is the transcendent culmination of Osirian humanity. Moreover, just as Christ, in Jesus, allies the Divine with the human, so does Horus fulfill this union in the human being.

"Thus it's Horus and not Osiris who is parallel to Jesus Christ. That's why the Christian Christmas differs from the Egyptian Khoiak. Their similarity is limited to the idea of a renewal of life, which is brought to Earth by a Divine Power to which the Celestial Virgin gives birth. But the resurrection of Osiris is a rebirth in earthly existence. It's the *annual* reanimation of plant life.

"The solar symbolism of the Christic Christmas has a specific cosmic significance: it's the entrance of the sun into a new zodiacal sign, that of Pisces, which characterizes the Christian era. It's the beginning of another cycle, whose symbolism is suitably colored with this new phase of Cosmic Harmony.

"Its teaching reveals and *disseminates the possibility* of Redemption. However, this mystery was already known in Egypt, under the name of 'Horus the Redeemer,' but was revealed only to those initiated into the temple."

Dominique stood up, listening to the bells of Notre Dame, which were ringing a full peal. "It's midnight, gentlemen. Let us take a moment to welcome the Christian mystery.

"Christmas . . . the arrival of the first-born of the new era. Adam,

---

1. See *Her-Bak: Egyptian Initiate.*

fallen from nobility by his birth in the world, which separates Earth from Heaven, finds his nobility again in the birth that unites Heaven and Earth.

"Six months before Christmas—when the solar light prepares its progressive descent into the darkness, where it will gestate the seed conceived by the Virgin in the spring—an old, sterile woman gives birth to John the Baptist, the Precursor, in the barren mountains of Judea.

"John, Precursor of the Light which is still gestating in the darkness, is the predestined witness from the time of his birth, since the visitation of the Virgin had filled him with the Holy Spirit in his mother's womb. . . .

"The Precursor grew up in the desert and fortified himself there in Spirit so that he could separate the pure from the impure in every being who allowed himself to be immersed in the waters of the Jordan.

"John the Baptist is the Precursor of the Logos of Christ. His presence *in* the river Jordan waters the mountainous desert, 'makes the hills low and fills the valleys,' so that there is no more opposition or division between what is High and what is Low in order to 'prepare the way' for our Savior and so that the 'unified' Earth opens itself and generates salvation.[2]

"And the seed of salvation, gestated in darkness, emerges from the shadows during Christmas night, when the sun, having arrived at the lowest point of its journey, announces the renewal of light by its ascension.

"The Divine Child was born amid the dung of the stable in the straw manger where animals ate . . . surrounded by an ox and a gray donkey, ancestor of the ass that later on would carry him to the Temple under the crossed palm fronds. . . .

"Christmas . . . Why have the angels, messengers of Light from above, come down into the Earth's night, awakening the guardians of the Ram's flock, if not to announce the birth of a Mediator between inaccessible Heaven and the human herd, which is lying in wait for a new fire?

"*Agni*, the lamb, the Heavenly Fire reanimating the fire of the exhausted Ram . . . the lamb, son of the Ram . . .

"Jesus, son of David, the Shepherd . . .

"The Lamb, conceived six months after his precursor, to be baptized by him in the waters of the Jordan.

"Then Jesus, the new pastor, having sojourned forty days in the desert, will choose the *fishermen* to feed his flock."

Dominique fell silent, allowing his friends to meditate on his words.

2. The Christmas Mass liturgy.

They waited in vain for a commentary. When Maître Pierre started to distribute the punch, each one took his place around the brazier.

The grave smile of their Master gave a strange solemnity to this moment.

"Do you understand the importance of Christmas for our current times?" he continued, lighting his pipe.

"On the great heavenly clock a rotation of the zodiacal sundial is completed. Two thousand years ago, the sun, leaving the region of the constellation Aries, the Ram, moved into the celestial house under the influence of the constellation Pisces, the Fish. In zodiacal symbolism, which expresses the typical influences of each sign, Pisces is a double sign, so its influence on earthly humanity has been *dualistic*. It characterized the entire Christian era, forming the analytic mentality and dialectic thought, in science and theology alike. And it was an era of conflict between contradictory opinions, between materialism and spirituality, between compulsory beliefs and 'free thought.' There was a rivalry of doctrines in which each religion tried to impose its particular faith on the *masses*.

"However, our destiny, under the influence of celestial houses, is leading us into a new adventure, because the time had come for the sun to enter into another region (designated by the sign of Aquarius). The passage from one sign to another is always a disconcerting experience for humanity. It brings a different rhythm, a new impulse, to which we must adapt our behavior. Otherwise, we will remain in a state of upset.

"The sign of Aquarius, whose influence we are beginning to feel, irresistably incites us to individualism. Even entire peoples and races undergo the effects of this incitement, which is expressed by a sudden will for independence. And although the gregarious instinct of the masses continues to group men into parties (political, social, or religious), a critical sense is developed in the individual as an instinctive rebellion against our doctrines of divine threats.

"This new orientation, which the masses undergo as an opposing current to outdated concepts, is experienced by more conscious beings as an urgent need to engage their personal responsibility in choosing their direction and their experiences.

"But this choice requires knowledge of the various states of consciousness of our being, and of their relationship to the cosmic influences of our age.

"Just as in springtime, Nature stimulates the vegetal and animal kingdoms to be fruitful, so in the precessional season of Pisces, Cosmic

Harmony calls for the development of the human mind. Likewise, during the precessional season of Aquarius, this new accord of Cosmic Harmony provokes in earthly man the awakening of his instinctive primitive consciousness.

"This influence is corroborated by a reaction to our exaggerated cerebral development. The mind has intervened between our instinct and its intuitive overdevelopment, and has dominated them to the point of stifling them. However, the excessive advances of rational science have proved impotent in resolving man's problems. To find a solution, man will be forced to awaken his faculties of direct contact with Nature, in order to go on to awaken his intuitive faculties.

"Just as the activation of mental faculties aroused intense intellectual curiosity, so is the current provocation to the awakening of consciousness beginning to provoke an *individual quest* for knowledge. This is where Maître Jacques will play an important role, because this individual quest demands the constant intervention of the Permanent Witness. Otherwise, it can be led astray by erroneous mental concepts."

"For a long time I confused intuitive consciousness with cerebral consciousness, but the latter is, as you say, only a record of our mental operations," said Jean-Jacques.

"That's true," continued Dominique. "But for 'apprentices' I can't repeat enough that consciousness is a state of identification. To become conscious of anything is to recognize in oneself this identity: it is to *experience*. The artisan who identifies with the material with which he is working *experiences* its nature and reaction in himself. He becomes conscious of it. Likewise, the animal trainer *experiences* the reactions of the beast. In each case the awakening of the instinctive consciousness takes place. In a more subtle way, this will be the awakening of our intuitive faculties, whose exercise creates in us the intuitive *state*.

"Consciousness by identification is undeniable as long as the cerebral consciousness doesn't intervene, except as an observer. That's why the individual quest for knowledge demands the subjugation of the mind, which must only play a role of transcriber."

"This means that the freedom of individual search cannot be confused with the 'free thought' of the rationalist dialectician," intervened Jean Thomas.

"They must never be confused," agreed Dominique, "any more than rational logic should be confused with vital logic, because it dismisses (as being irrational) the mysterious functions of the Spirit in Nature. These mysterious functions, which are inherent in the laws of Cosmic Harmony, have been taught in each great era of humanity through symbols, which have *initiated* only those with 'ears to hear.' For the others, these symbols have become historic myths or humanized stories, on which religion has elaborated (to legitimize its power) dogmas and laws that conform to its particular interpretation of the initial Revelation."

"Is it necessary to look for wisdom in the sacred texts of past ages?" asked Thomas.

"It is fruitful if one studies true traditions and not arbitrary interpretations. That's why the symbol is the best guardian of the intention of the initiator. But those who have cultivated the Intelligence of the Heart will know how to decipher what is suitable for their times. For example, in the Gospel, the words of Jesus to the woman of Samaria are suitable for the 'time that will come' (our own age)."

"Must we think that is was exclusively reserved for this age?" asked Thomas.

"Not at all," retorted Dominique. "The revelation of fundamental realities is universal. Therefore it's valid for all times, but only for those who are able to understand that 'the time is come.' However, humanity is now entering a phase in which its elite will be disposed to receive it. That's what is meant by 'the time that will come.'

"With what we have seen of the impulses given by the Age of Aquarius, the double precept taught to the woman of Samaria becomes vital: it's our new duty to 'know what we worship' and to 'worship in Spirit and in Truth.' It's no longer the submission to an imposed belief which only the guardians of the herd have the responsibility for. It's the knowledge acquired through the individual experience of an actual rebirth, of our double Element of Immortality, our *Spirit*, which is our Spiritual Witness, and our *Truth*, which is our Permanent Witness.

"That is the new meaning of Christmas for the Age of Aquarius. It's the arrival of a period favorable to this rebirth and to the development of our suprahuman possibilities."

"And I understand its importance," said Thomas. "Christmas is no longer a festival particular to one religion. It's a cosmic event that concerns the entire elite of humanity."

"That's right," answered Dominique. "However, you must observe that the principle of the incarnated Christ, whose realization in conscious men is their redemption, was particularly taught in the Judeo-Christian New Testament.

"It's true that in Egypt we find the principle of Horus the Redeemer, who has 'issued forth from the human body.' It's true that the Buddha gave the example and the means of spiritual reintegration. However, it's no less true that the teaching of these realities was expressed each time in a way that corresponded to humanity's state of consciousness. Moreover, this state was dictated by Heaven.

"This is also true for the Christ Revelation, whose *human* symbolism was in part adapted to the Judaic mentality, just as Jesus based his messianic authority on the Prophets of Israel. On the other hand, his teaching was new in relation to the *earthly* Law of Moses: he announced a 'new convenant' of the Divine with the human for the work of redemption. The Christ Principle was the key to this.

"The *exotericism* of this Revelation brought to the Christian Church a moral law of love, altruistic brotherhood, and simplicity, which were opposed to cerebral complexity. This program, as you see, was an antidote to the harmful aspects of the influence of Pisces. But when you see how this pure mysticism was rationalized by coercive dogmatism, it's not surprising that the 'Rock' on which the Church was built was the same Rock (Peter) that Jesus criticized: 'for thou savorest not the things that be of God, but the things that be of men.'[3]

"The *esotericism* of this Revelation was essentially given in the stories of the Passion of Jesus. However, in this Passion, the role of denial is attributed to Peter. And it's John (and not the leader of the future Church) who was present at the crucifixion of Jesus.

"In other words: Peter (strongly attached to Judaic Law)[4] was the representative of the Messiah (son of David) for the materialistic Age of Pisces, whereas John received the spiritual testament of Jesus Christ the Savior for his future coming: 'If I will that he tarry till I come . . . ,' said Jesus to Peter in speaking of John. 'Till I come' means until the future time (our current time), the last time of the Christ realization in humanity."

"This point of view explains the coexistence of Christianity of the Judaic mentality, whose historicity personifies and particularizes, and of the spirit of Wisdom which, through its cosmic symbolism, universalizes the Christ Principle," said Jean-Jacques.

"You've lost me, my friend!" said Dutheil. "I can understand the initiatory value of a teaching based on the immutable foundations of traditional Wisdom, but how can I believe in a doctrine that imposes belief in the historic reality of the stories in the Gospels when there is no authentic proof of Jesus' family, of his place of birth, or even of the exact dates of is life?"

"The critics of the Gospels have a good case," said Jean-Jacques. "I have searched in vain for some irrefutable point in the multiple controversies launched by these deniers. The serious critics (who are too often merely

3. Mark 8:33.
4. He upholds, against Saint Paul, the practice of circumcision; he refuses to eat the meats forbidden by the Mosaic Law.

commentators) are very well armed with documents, but they end up with contradictory conclusions, which give way to confusion between the initiatory Messiah of evangelical doctrine and the Messiah that the Jews were expecting to deliver them from Roman domination and to reestablish the Kingdom of Israel. Some even identify Jesus with John the Baptist and with the author of the Book of Revelation. . . . Jesus remains a historical engima."

"I wanted to go back to the sources," continued Dutheil. "I immersed myself in the study of gnostic texts (either known from ancient times or recently discovered), the Apocrypha, the sayings of Jesus (the Logia), the Secret Communion and other supposedly secret teaching of Jesus, which often modified the sense of the canonical Gospels. I came out of all this totally confused."

"But there must be some historic witness to an event that must have shaken up pagan society," said Thomas.

"From the first century on," answered Jean-Jacques, "many writers (including the Roman Tacitus) spoke of the 'new Christian sect' and of its founder, Christ. The members of this new sect were either tolerated or (as with Tacitus) considered traitors, and were prosecuted for their crimes by the Roman government.

"No one can determine with certainty the source of the Gospels. However, from the second century on, the Christian community acknowledged the oral tradition and the first versions of the stories that constitute the *foundation* of the canonical Gospels."

"Didn't they ever find other manuscripts that could corroborate this?" said Thomas, surprised.

"More that two thousand of them," answered Dutheil. "The oldest, called the *Codex Vaticanus*, belongs to the Vatican and seems to be the most authentic, and the *Codex Sinaticus*, discovered in a monastery in the Sinai, dates from the fourth century. Even in these two texts, there are variations and different interpretations. Various testimonies (including that of Bishop Papias, in 140 A.D.) place the writing of the three Synoptic Gospels of Mark, Matthew, and Luke before this date. Their texts, and that of John (the author who is most disputed), have predominated over the other Gospels and various writings that the Church has eliminated.

"But in-depth studies have shown that the present texts underwent corrections, interpolations, and even some deletions, made in various periods, through ecclesiastical control, according to the theological opinion of the moment."

"Then how can one consider them a Revelation?" exclaimed Thomas.

A burst of sarcastic laughter came from Maître Pierre, who was rekindling the fire under the brazier. "How amusing!" he said as he passed around the punch. "My Master, Pierre du Coignet,[5] has played his role of separating the separative fire very well, don't you think? It's the role of the seducer who provokes dialectics in order to legislate beliefs . . . who, to 'save souls,' invents the constraints of the Inquisition and of excommunication. The Master of Truth may have conquered Satan by resisting the temptation of the three powers, but you can't say as much for those who succeeded him!"

"It's no less true," remarked Dutheil, "that the Christian religion spread to the four corners of the Earth, despite the thoughts and errors of its own ministers with their schisms, their scandals, their fratricidal wars, and their multiple theological disputes."

"It is really incomprehensible," said Thomas. "But what's most incredible to me is that anyone could base his faith on stories whose authenticity cannot be proved."

"And what's that to you?" retorted Dominique gruffly, interrupting the discussion, which he had been attending silently.

"What do I care about the historical reality of events when their most minor episode is a symbolic teaching?

"What surprises me is that having observed the persistence of Christianity, despite the errors of its leaders, you haven't looked for the explanation in a cause that is independent of men's behavior. If this behavior was influenced by the characteristics of the celestial house which dominated during the age of Pisces, the Christ teaching would have likewise provided the necessary antidotes to the harmful aspects of this influence.

"The mental and dualizing Satan of Maître Pierre was only the expression of an *inevitable* force, a natural rhythm, the rhythm of a new age, like the one we are currently undergoing; whereas the compensating impulse emanated from a *conscious* force, a Divine Consciousness, which provided those who were receptive to it with the means of escaping this infernal trap. The means consist in the affirmation of their suprahuman destiny, the way that leads them to it, and a new spiritual influx.

"This periodic manifestation of Providential Wisdom always translates itself into a symbolic teaching adapted to the needs of the times. This teaching becomes *revelation* for those who 'hear' its initiatory meaning. But it turns into a ferment of discord for sectarian leaders, and for the 'Scholars of the Law.'

"This double effect is inherent in the duality of the human being: what is Spirit is in accordance with the vital reality of the symbol; what is mental takes pleasure in interpreting the value of the 'letter.'

"This allows us to understand the fruits of Light or error in evangelical teaching."

5. See Chapter 3.

"It's enough to teach me to no longer confuse mystical works with 'political' works," said Thomas. "But didn't the Gospels also have a 'political' aspect?"

"You've touched on a critical point, my friend. The founder himself answered: 'My kingdom is not of this world.' But the masses are of this world. However, he also said: 'I am come not for the world, but for those who are not of this world.'"

Dutheil, puzzled, asked Dominique: "Why haven't you talked about the personality of this founder during the course of your explanations?"

Dominique took time to relight his pipe. Then he answered gravely: *"The position of the Savior, which is imposed on him by Christian dogma, places the Christ outside of time and space.*

"The episodes in the life of Jesus which are related in the Gospels are typical images of the spiritual evolution toward the suprahuman, an evolution that is pushed to the point of the *Christ Realization*, preached by Saint Paul as the ultimate goal of the Christian: '. . . until Christ be formed in you.'

"Let us carefully follow the steps of this evolution.

"At the age of twelve, Jesus manifests his precocious consciousness in the Temple of Jerusalem by his questions and answers to the Scholars of the Law. Likewise, in the Egyptian Temple[6] the age of the first manifestation of the Pharaonic Prince was also twelve years, because, for the *Royal Man* that he represented, this age is considered the first step toward his realization: the integration of his immortal *Ka*, that is, the integration of his Permanent Witness, whose presence manifests itself through the child's discernment.

"The baptism by John the Baptist in the waters of the Jordan marks a second stage: when Jesus was leaving the water, the Spirit descended *upon* him 'like a dove.' This is a beautiful image for his Spiritual Witness, who comes to hover over him and to inspire his mission. And 'the Spirit driveth him into the wilderness,' where his Human Consciousness, becoming aware of new powers, *suffered* and *rebelled against* the temptation to use them for personal power."

"If Jesus was God from the moment of his birth, I don't understand how his Human Consciousness could have suffered temptation," said Thomas.

"For the moment, it's not important," answered Dominique. *"I'm not questioning here the dogma of the immaculate conception of a Divine Child, any more than I am the historical reality of Jesus.* I'm looking at the

6. In the Temple of Luxor. See R. A. Schwaller de Lubicz, *The Temple of Man* (Paris: Dervy-Livres, 1977).

spiritual events of his life, as related in the Gospel, and I'm observing their progressive evolution. The fact that it is a matter of progressing toward the definitive Christ state is verified by the Gospels, since Jesus formally forbade his disciples to say that he was the Christ until the moment of his realization (his Passion).

"Everything occurred as if he were a being predestined by his spiritual realization and incarnated to accomplish his Christic perfection, through which he became the *Mediator* between the Divine and the human.

"Thus, I don't have to worry about historic authenticity: the symbolism of his teaching corresponds integrally to the reality of such an evolution, and the wisdom of its expression gives it an initiatory value that goes beyond any historical account.

"The interest of this development resides, on the one hand, in the progression of the states of reintegration and, on the other hand, in the veiled teaching of the two aspects of the Soul-entity (for Jesus as well as for men): *spirit* and *soul* correspond respectively to the Spiritual Witness and the Permanent Witness. The role of human consciousness is clearly perceptible, for example, in the episode of the three temptations: they can only affect this consciousness."

"It's obvious," said Thomas: "the two divine elements of the soul cannot be 'tempted.' But why aren't these important realities explicitly taught?"

"They have always been taught, but symbolically. The initiatory trials of the ancient mysteries experimentally revealed the difference between human consciousness and the two aspects of the divine soul."

"The Hindu masters of yoga also teach it in their methods of spiritual reintegration," remarked Dutheil.

"If you look carefully, you will also find indications of this in the symbolism of the Gospels, and this 'Reintegration' is nothing else but the *Christ realization*. In the Gospels it is pushed to its ultimate fulfillment. But just as the Hindu methods and Egyptian myths express many points of view which are complementary without being contradictory, so do the four Gospels express four aspects of a single Reality (which are emphasized by the four symbolic animals attributed to the four evangelists).

"I'm asking you not to let your attention wander, but to concentrate on what we are talking about today: the progressive stages of Christ Realization," continued Dominique.

"Note first that (according to Matthew) when John the Baptist refused to baptize Jesus, Jesus demanded it, because he said, 'it becometh us to fulfill all righteousness.'[7] In other words, he who was later to 'baptize in

7. Matthew 3:14–15.

the Spirit' (when he himself had become it) first had to be baptized by *his* *Precursor* (John the Baptist, symbol of the Permanent Witness).

"It was only after his temptation, after the submission of his Human Consciousness, that Jesus was able to choose his disciples and undertake his mission. Then his miracles were witness to his suprahuman power and the *inferior* forces, demoniacal, human, and terrestrial.

"A short time later, a new phenomenon manifested a higher step: his transfiguration on the mountaintop in the presence of three disciples; Peter, James, and John. 'His countenance was altered,' shining 'like the sun,' and 'his raiment was white as the light.'[8]

"It's obvious, is it not, that this transfiguration expresses his illumination by the Spirit of Light: his Spiritual Witness. However, near Jesus there appeared in glory two companions 'who spake of his decease.' Peter, heavy with sleep, mentioned Moses and Elijah, 'not knowing what he said.'"

"Could we say that Peter, James, and John represented the projection, in 'sleeping' humanity, of the luminous triplicity which in the symbol of Moses-Elijah-Jesus makes of Jesus the 'Lord'?" asked Thomas timidly.

"Don't be afraid to say it, my friend, because in having grasped that, you have understood the meaning of the Master: the man whose Human Consciousness has become suprahuman, whose conflicts are arbitrated by Maître Jacques, and whose Divine Consciousness *understands* his coming Passion and death, which he can envisage with detachment because he has within him the seed of resurrection.

"And now that you've unveiled the deep meaning of this image, observe the details that confirm it. Make a parallel of the two triplicities: Moses-Elijah-Jesus and Peter-James-John; but notice that spiritual state of the first three and the human character of the second three.

"Once this difference is established, you can situate Jesus (in the first triad) as *illumined* by his Spiritual Witness. Likewise, John (in the second triad) symbolizes the Spiritual Witness. Elijah and James symbolize the soul, that is, the Permanent Witness. Likewise, Moses (who doesn't enter into the Promised Land!) and Peter (with his faults) are the perfect image of human consciousness.

"The Permanent Witness is represented by Elijah and James. Regarding Elijah, note that Jesus insisted that John the Baptist was the Elijah who had to come before the revelation of the Messiah. However, here he affirms that *'Elijah is come already.'* Obviously, the Baptist had to come before the Transfiguration.

"In the human triplicity the Permanent Witness is represented by

8. Matthew 17:2; Luke 9:29–31.

James,[9] brother of John, whose Spirit is the Spiritual Witness of the initiated. However, these two disciples, James and John, are called the 'sons of thunder.' Aren't they, indeed, 'fallen from Heaven'? Aren't they two aspects of one Heavenly Entity?

"I'm not making up anything. I'm just underlining important points in the Gospel.

"Now we are going to find the same human triplicity, Peter-James-John, in the scene of the agony in the Garden, but we will not see the luminous triplicity there. In this great test, Jesus at first seems upset, 'sore amazed' and 'very heavy' (according to Mark 14:33). He is so lacking in spiritual force that three times he seeks help from his three disciples— but they *were too sleepy* to be able to help him! It was then, in the excess of his weakness, that Jesus found the courage *to go beyond himself*."

"Why do they speak of agony here?" asked Thomas.

"Because Jesus seems to be abandoned by his Divine Soul, without which he could never undergo the anguish of Human Consciousness, which bolts when faced with approaching suffering: 'Father, if thou be willing, remove this cup from me.'[10]

"However, you must realize that even after the stage of Transfiguration, Jesus had warned his disciples that 'I have a baptism to be baptized with.'[11]

"What is baptism if not regeneration? To be baptized is to receive a new influx of life which engenders a superior state of being compared with the preceding state.

"The baptism in water (John the Baptist) was a baptism of 'purification' which put the animal-human being in touch with his soul (his Permanent Witness), which could rectify his human consciousness and show him his goal. That was the role of the precursor.

"The second baptism is the influx of the Spirit (the Spiritual Witness) symbolized by the transfiguration.

"The third (the new baptism that Jesus was waiting for) would be the reunion of Soul and Spirit, which could not be definitively joined until the cause and the consequences of their separation in this incarnation had been exhausted. This is the meaning of 'purification of the flesh and blood' (in other words, the animal nature) symbolized by the trials of agony (the sweating of blood)[12] and the Passion.

---

9. James the Greater, the same as Santiago de Compostela.

10. Mark 14:36; Luke 22:42.

11. Luke 12:50.

12. Blood carries the animal soul; the "sweating of blood" therefore signifies the rejection of animal nature.

"Understand the meaning of this agony: the painful state of the physical and psychic individual momentarily isolated from his soul and his spirit. The soul and the spirit are waiting for his renunciation of the 'personality' to terrestrial existence and the total abnegation of Human Consciousness by unifying himself with his Permanent Witness: 'Not what I will, but what thou wilt!'

"It's only then that the 'angel' (his Divine Entity)[13] comes to strengthen him. It's a *superhuman state*, attained by *going beyond* human nature.

"The trial will come to an end only at the crucifixion. However, listen to the last words, which reveal the two Witnesses at the supreme moment: first Jesus is saddened by the departure of his Soul (his Permanent Witness): 'Eli, Eli, why hast thou forsaken me?'[14] And in order to make this symbol more precise, the Gospel has it repeated by a soldier who is present: 'This man calleth for Elijah.' Then, before dying: 'Father, into thy hands I commend my spirit.'[15]

"Then everything is fulfilled because the Spiritual Witness of Jesus will wait 'near the Father,'[16] the Permanent Witness, the *soul*, which according to canonic tradition descended into hell 'for three days.'"

"Does this sojourn in hell mean the purification of the Permanent Witness?" asked Dutheil.

"Obviously," confirmed Dominique. "He must detach himself from what Egyptian symbolism calls 'the dust of the earth and the thirst to live.'

"However, Jesus had already explained the character and the necessity of the trials of the Passion: the Son of Man must suffer, be denied and despised. In other words, the last stage of Christic Realization demands the surpassing of what is human, then of what is suprahuman, by the elimination of all particularization and by identification with the Impersonal Divinity (the 'will of the Father'). Only then will Christ be able to rise up to the right hand of the Father.

"But you must understand this return to the 'right hand of the Father.' It is not annihilation 'in the Father,' but an active state of Divine Consciousness enriched by the consciousness acquired in the human state and by the unification of the two Witnesses."

"Is that what is meant by the 'meditation' of Christ, a meditation that is possible through his participation in what is human and what is Divine?" suggested Jean-Jacques.

13. These two Witnesses assembled, but not yet unified.
14. Matthew, 27:46, 47.
15. Luke 23:46.
16. "Near" refers not to a place but to a state.

"That's right," answered Dominique. "And the liturgy places this return, which is the 'glorification' of Christ, forty days after Easter, the feast of the Ascension. However, what takes place between the resurrection and the ascension is worth close consideration:

"The first words of the resurrection are addressed to Mary Magdalene (*who did not recognize his human form*): 'Touch me not,' he said, 'for I am not yet ascended to my Father.' The Spirit of Jesus was therefore not yet reintegrated. But, he added: "Go to my brethren, and say unto them, *I ascend unto my Father*, and your Father; to my God, and your God.'[17] And when later on he appeared to his Apostles, having become Christ through his total reintegration, he declares his realization and the power resulting from it. This power was no longer superhuman but Divine: "All power is given unto me in Heaven and on earth.'"[18]

"What strikes me in your point of view," said Dutheil, "is the lack of confusion between the metaphysical aspect of the Son, the second person of the Trinity, and Jesus who was sent by His Father and whose Christ initiation is related, and whose Divine Father is also our Father, . . . as He sends His Apostles into the world, Jesus, Son of God (according to his own words 'as all those who do the will of God')."[19]

"What you say is confirmed by the words of Jesus: 'My Father is greater than I,'" agreed Dominique. "It's obvious that this 'I' refers to the still-perfectible being of Jesus, and not to the Son of the Supreme Trinity, since Catholic dogma affirms the absolute equality of these three Divine Persons!

"It's the word *Father* which has created the confusion. Between the Principle of the Absolute Divinity named Father in the Christian dogma of the essential Trinity, on the one hand, and 'Our Father who is in Heaven,' on the other, there is the same difference as that between what is 'inconceivable' and what is 'conceivable.' It is not a difference 'in itself,' but only in the way that it is considered.

"When I address myself to the 'Father who is in Heaven,' I am situating a Power in a *state of being* that is superior to mine. This is not heresy if I don't confuse the Power that I implore with the inaccessible and unnameable Absolute, and if, on the other hand, I don't attribute a personal existence to the Father but instead conceive Him as the original Active Cause from which everything that lives emanates.

"Then He is the 'living God' whose 'will' is Cosmic Harmony, and the return to Unity of what had been dualized, and of which each Soul-entity

17. John 20:17.
18. Matthew 28:18.
19. John 14:28.

is the 'Son.' But each Soul-entity incarnated in the human must 'take up his cross'[20] despite Jesus. This means that he must follow the steps of 'Christification.'

"That is the evangelical teaching. And you will find confirmation of it in Saint Paul's assertion that for a short time 'Jesus was made a little lower than the angels.'[21] By 'angels' one must understand the Heavenly Entities whose two complementary aspects are not separated,[22] whereas they are separated in the human state of Jesus."

"Many things become clear *if one takes as the connecting link the real constitution of the human being*," said Jean Thomas.

Jean-Jacques and Dutheil solemnly agreed. But Maître Pierre suddenly rebelled against Dominique: "I understand the teaching through the symbol, but why do you so adamantly deny the historical reality of the Gospel?"

"I don't deny it. *I'm not at all concerned about it*," retorted Dominique firmly. "If you want to examine the human life of Jesus, you will be up against the divergences in the four Gospels (starting with the contradictory data of his two genealogies according to Luke and Matthew). On the other hand, you'll be up against a total silence which surrounds the years between the first manifestation of his consciousness in the Temple of Jerusalem and his baptism by John the Baptist.

"The legend that attributes to him an Essene or Egyptian initiation remains in the realm of hypothesis. And what difference does it make if he was instructed by the sages or by his own revelation? Even the identity of the human personality that is attributed to him is likewise of no importance to me.

"One thing is certain: *someone* wrote (or caused to be written) these Gospels, and the teaching they constitute is witness to undeniable Knowledge. *Someone* situated the Messiah of the New Revelation at the date of the arrival of the new aeon (the new Age of Pisces). *Someone* surrounded him with twelve apostles, as was suitable for a solar (Horian) Christ emerging from the lunar world (Mosaic-Osirian) of Israel.

"The initial exoteric aspect of evangelical preaching provided a mystical impulse whose repercussion made of Jesus Christ the Lord of the Age of Pisces. His esoteric aspect (often stifled by theologians) inspired the Master Builders of the cathedrals and the philosopher-sages of the Middle Ages. The exactitude of his symbolism makes Christianity the legitimate Revelation succeeding all previous Revelations: the Egyptian Revelation

20. These words of Jesus are quoted in the four Gospels immediately before the Transfiguration, and obviously signify that one must imitate the *steps* followed by Jesus.

21. Hebrews 2:9.

22. They are together but not merged.

whose Horian aspect was the prelude of Christ, and the Revelation of Moses which was the heritage of Osirian Egypt.

"In view of all this, I don't think I have to search for historical reality. Besides, it's impossible to establish one with any certitude! That I myself believe in the human existence of the Master of Wisdom whose spiritual accomplishment made him Mediator is not important either for you or for me, because no conviction, no matter of how strong it may be, will awaken *the inner Revelation of the value of the Christ Reality 'in itself.'*

"*This Revelation is independent of all historical contingency. It is a vital Reality*, because it is inherent in the suprahuman destiny of humanity. Each man who attracts to himself, even if only slightly, the two elements of his Divine Soul, makes this become living Reality, just as for the seed in the state of germination, the realized plant that must issue from it is a living reality.

"Man's mistake is to believe that he is fully realized when he attains physical and intellectual maturity. But that is only the realization of the mortal support of the immortal being that wants to blossom in him. This immortal being is the Christ seed, *ours*, yours, and mine, since it is (through our Number-entity) our spiritual identity. This is also, however, the object of the evangelical drama. . . ."

"If I understand correctly, you're not speaking of Jesus, but of Christ, who has become, through Jesus, the Cosmic Principle," intervened Dutheil. "But then how can one attribute the Christ Principle to identical realizations, for example, of the Horian Principle or of that realized by Buddha?"

"You're making several mistakes, my friend. The universal cannot be limited to the particular. Besides, if you personify Jesus, you cannot say that Christ *became, through him*, the Cosmic Principle. But the Christ Principle 'was able to' incarnate in Jesus, who was then able to 'Christify' himself by the elimination of all that was not Christ in him. In this sense it's obvious that this Realization can be called Horian or Buddhist, or any other name that the highest mystics might call it.

"The etymological meaning of the word *Christ* is 'anointed.' Theoretically, sacramental unction has as its goal anointment with the spirit through the intermediary of a quintessential substance, whose subtle quality makes it a penetrating *carrier* of the 'grace' with which it has been impregnated.

"The Lord's Anointed is he who is penetrated by the Lord. The man who has integrated his Divine Soul is 'anointed by his own Lord.'

"In extreme unction, Christ is, in reality, the 'efficacy' of unction. Thus, one could say that the Christ Principle is the manifestable quintessence of the Divine."

"I'm beginning to see my error," said Dutheil. "It stems from the confusion between the person of Jesus and the abstract principle of the Christ. But should I give this abstract principle one of the names attributed to it by another tradition of mysticism if I'm to avoid this error?"

"I don't understand you," retorted Dominique. "The word *Christ* sufficiently defines the two aspects of this Divine Reality, which, contrary to your assertion, is *not an abstraction*. If you take it in the sense of 'unction,' its esoteric significance refers to the positive reality of the spiritual and (in the best sense of the word) magical powers affirmed by these words of the realized Christ: 'All Power is given unto me in heaven and in earth.'

"This should be understood in the sense of a Mediator between man and the Father, because, as totalized universalized Consciousness, Christ participates simultaneously in what is human and what is Divine. It's also a *Positive Reality*, because this state of mediator is the *means* of redemption for all those who follow the steps of this transcendence."

After a few minutes of reflection, observing the dreamy silence of his friends, Dominique took up the thread of his discourse.

"What I've just explained might appear to be fastidious repetition, but if you'll give me your attention, you might perceive an unexpected point of view. Saint Paul, in his Epistle to the Hebrews, uses the biblical symbol of Melchizedek to teach the difference between the *ordinary* action (that is, continual action) of the Logos and the *extraordinary* and transcendent action of Christ Power. First he emphasizes the Melchizedek must not be considered a mortal man, but the principle of perpetual animation: Melchizedek . . . 'without father, without mother, or without descent, having neither beginning of days nor end of life; but made like unto the Son of God; abideth a priest continually.'[23]

"Then he draws a parallel between the perpetual sacrifice of Melchizedek (the continual incarnation of the Logos-Spirit in all of Nature) and the exceptional sacrifice of Christ whose transmutative quality can transcend that which the first sacrifice could only animate.

"To avoid a material interpretation of these 'sacrifices,' Paul differentiates between the ritual animal sacrifices performed by the Levitical priests ('after the order of Aaron'), who were governed by the *old covenant*, whose law, he said, 'made nothing perfect.'[24]

"Between the old and the new covenant, Paul places Jesus in his imperfect state, susceptible to temptation, as the *precursor* of the Christ that he must become and that, as such, still belongs to the 'order of

23. Hebrews 7:3.
24. Hebrews 7:19.

Melchizedek.' However, Melchizedek corresponds to Osiris, whose continuous sacrifice of reanimation causes all renewal in Nature. In biblical symbolism this Osirian role is that of the old covenant of the Old Testament—that is, the Common Law which is only 'an example and shadow of heavenly things.'[25]

"Paul repudiates not only this imperfect way, but, for the disciples of Christ perfection, he even rejects the first principles of the doctrine of Christ, which are repentance from dead works, and faith toward God, the doctrine of baptisms . . . resurrection of the dead, and eternal judgment."[26]

"How can Paul, the pillar of the Church, deny the first bases of its foundation?" exclaimed Dutheil.

"Paul does not *deny* them," answered Dominique. "But in relation to the way of Christ realization whose apostle he makes himself, he posits them as *preliminary means* from which one must no longer fall away if one wants to attain the higher state.

"His insistence is of great interest in clearly showing the three stages of the work of 'Christification':

"The first stage is the 'precursory' state of Jesus, which is still imperfect enough to fear death (Hebrews 5:7). Then come the first steps of his spiritual rebirth, in which he places himself 'outside the world' (while living in this world) and is united with the Father, with those of his disciples who are not 'of this world' either. Finally, there is the total realization of the Christ state, which gives him 'all power in heaven and in earth' and allows him to affirm the permanency of his Presence unto the end of the earthly world.

"Don't forget that Paul, the pillar of the Church, is formally opposed to the other 'pillar,' Peter, whose preaching was based on the first precepts. Paul goes so far as publicly denouncing Peter for not walking 'uprightly according to the truth of the gospel.'[27] He clearly affirms his independence from the teachings of Peter. He declares himself directly illuminated by Christ, whose way of perfection he preaches.

"However, despite the divergences that separate Peter and Paul, the Church associates both of them as 'the two founders on whom the Church is solidly established.'[28] It's their divergences that characterize the two ways which these two Apostles represent.

25. Hebrews 8:5.
26. Hebrews 6:1–2.
27. Galatians 2:14.
28. Dom Lefèvre, *Daily Missal.*

"The first way, which is that of Peter, is the *preliminary* way which rests on the observance of doctrines and precepts. It uses sacramental means of purification, such as baptism and penitence (confession). This is the way of the Law, the common way, accessible to the *many* followers of the Christian doctrine, the way of the 'herd' because it replaces personal responsibility with submission to the 'responsible shepherd' and also replaces individual Knowledge (acquired through the illumination of consciousness) with adherence to imposed dogma.

"The second way, that of Paul, is the way of Christ Realization. This Realization cannot take place through ritual, precepts, or dogma, but occurs through the direct action of 'grace'—that is, the action of *the soul and the Spirit*, whose conscious reintegration opens for the human being the access to the suprahuman.

"This opening can be progressive or sudden, as with Saul on the road to Damascus. In any event, it presupposes 'predestination' or, as Paul says, a previous sanctification.

"But do not see favoritism of destiny in this predestination, a 'choice' determined by divine predilection: the words *choice, election*, and *predestination* express the consequence of a disposition that has been previously acquired through the trials of the present life, or partially realized in a former incarnation.

"This disposition[29] is the submission of Human Consciousness to the directives of its Divine Soul (the Permanent Witness), which can then progressively enlighten it."

"In conclusion," said Thomas, "the existence of these two ways renders the Christian religion as accessible to the Many as to the Few. Paul's strict selection only concerns the followers of the perfect way."

"Exactly," agreed Dominique. "The Christian apostolate addresses the masses as well as the individual, affirming as an article of faith that anyone who receives baptism is a Christian. However, that is only an *adoption*, which offers the baptized person participation in the spiritual benefits of worship—ritual and sacramental—means that Paul classified as preliminary precepts and not as effective means of Christ Realization.

"The facts have justified Paul. In the multitude of baptized people, rare are those who do not rest in the illusory security of imposed observance. Most people have lost the essential goal of their existence: to integrate their immortal being into their mortal person.

"However, the work of integration is strictly individual, and demands

29. The disposition that Paul calls "Sanctification," which is a prerequisite for Christ Realization.

from each one the free intervention of his Divine Consciousness (his Permanent Witness), outside of all doctrinary constraint, and under one's own responsibility."

"Then what is the use of the preliminary path of worship and dogma?" said Thomas, surprised.

"That serves to '*prepare* the way of the Lord',"[30] answered Dominique. "It awakens in Human Consciousness the sense of relationships between what is Divine and what is human."

"Careful, now," retorted Dutheil. "Whoever is seeing 'relationships' is supposing there is a state of separation between the things that one wants to connect."

"That's correct, my friend, but one can answer that the human masses, under the influence of the mind, are unable to conceive what is Divine except in opposition to what is human. Now Peter's way addresses itself to the masses. His religious goal is to provoke the desire to approach Divinity. His method is to impose the thought of salvation on men through the intervention of religion in all the circumstances of life (salvation being conditioned by obedience to the laws of the Church). His ecclesiastical goal is to attract the greatest possible number of sinners to save. It's Peter's net, the fisherman's net, that gathers without discrimination all types of fish but, on occasion, exceptional specimens as well. Don't forget that the ring of the leader of the Church is the ring of the fisherman.

"The way of Peter is the human way. The way of Paul leads to the surpassing of what is human."

"Isn't his method that of the Christian monasteries?" asked Dutheil.

"Theoretically, it's the goal of the monastic orders. But in practical application, the dominance of dogma and the absolute obedience to the superior of the monastary prevents the free expression of the Permanent Witness."

Jean-Jacques apologized for interrupting Dominique and said: "If the way of Saint Paul leads to the suprahuman, how would you describe John's way? I'm surprised you haven't said anything about his teaching, which is so clearly different from that of the other evangelists."

"I am silent on that matter," answered Dominique, "for the same reason the Church is; the Church places the Gospel of John *outside the Mass* (when the service is finished). It's a different way and a different teaching.

"First, note that the Eucharistic Last Supper included the breaking of the bread and its consecration. This doesn't exist in the Gospel according

30. John the Baptist in Matthew 3:3.

to John, who in place of the Last Supper gives the great sacerdotal prayer where Jesus affirms *the perfect Union of the Son with the Father and with men who have come from the Father.*

"Also note that his story of the Passion does not relate any of the three facts which in the other Gospels characterize the separation of the Soul and the Spirit: anguish, agony, the two sayings of Jesus crucified: 'Eli, Eli, why hast thou forsaken me?' and 'Father, into thy hands I commend my spirit.'

"The Gospel of John limits itself to what confirms his way. His way is not the *human effort* of the sinner who is returning toward God (the way of Peter). Nor is it the *suprahuman effort* to give full powers to the two reintegrated Witnesses (the way of Paul). Instead it's *the divine state of Union*, which is virginal because it is never violated. It is a state of absolute Love in which the human is constantly absorbed and transmuted with the Divine, without effort and *without personal will.*

"The way of Paul teaches one to form Christ in oneself, as Jesus formed Christ in himself. This formation consists of reuniting the two divine elements in the human being, whose unification is Christ Realization.

"The way of John does not have to reintegrate what was never separated: it's the identification of the Logos and the Father *from the Beginning.* It's the same identification in men 'born of God,' that is, men in whom the immortal being was totally incarnated from the moment of their birth.

"Everything in John is a matter of identification, with no separation whatsoever, not even differentiation or comparison. Paul compares and differentiates the way of Peter and the way of perfection, whereas John does not compare. He is content to preach the unique commandment of all-powerful Love, the only thing capable of realizing without disjunction the miracle of unity."

"Seen from this angle, the often shocking divergences between the four Gospels take on a very coherent, intentional character—and the initiatory meaning of Christ gets an unsuspected boost," remarked Jean-Jacques after long reflection.

"We can be even more precise," answered Dominique, "if we dare to abandon the sentimental aspect, which reduces the role of Jesus Christ to the measure of our human concept: If we consider the incarnation of the Spirit (the Divine Logos) as the creative Cause of all Nature; if we conceive the incarnated Soul-entities as the human manifestation of the multiple expressions of the Divine; if we see their incarnation as their initiation into the Consciousness of the anthropocosm; if we look at the misadventures of their avatars as the education (good or bad) of the human consciousness that each divine soul tries to enlighten . . . then we will be able to conceive Cosmic Work as the continual repetition of the Action and the Passion of the Logos incarnated in Matter. We will see it successively awaken all the aspects of functional consciousness throughout the different realms of Nature. And we will see it finally undergoing the persecution of the dualizing Mind in the human kingdom.

"This is the process of *natural* Becoming, which is earthly, human, and Osirian, and whose horrifying perpetuity can only be conquered by the suprahuman work of progressive 'Christification.'

"The sages of Egypt called this suprahuman task the solar work, or the Horian work. The Christian heritage called it the Way of Christ, and one can say that *every man who progressively incarnates his Immortal Entity is of the Christ race and participates in the development of the Christ Principle in earthly humanity.*"

Dutheil, astonished, objected: "Isn't Christ his own perfection in himself? Who, then, could still participate in his realization?"

"How difficult it is for personal man to conceive something impersonal!" sighed Dominique. "Try to do this by looking at an individual example:

"A man who begins to realize the union of his two Witnesses is already becoming a spiritual sun, and his radiance is proportional to his impersonality. If he is able to eliminate his divergent wills, and if his human consciousness identifies with that of the Permanent Witness, he participates in Divine Harmony (the will of the Father) without losing any of the qualities of his Number-entity: on the contrary, it's the enrichment of his consciousness through the 'passion' of his human existence.

"However, the highest level of this realization is the Christ state, that is, the Christification of that which the Logos incarnates, of that which undergoes the passion of its earthly avatars, of that which becomes conscious of all consciousness and 'strong from all strengths,' having acquired in this 'passion' the power over lower forces. And this Christ state is able to attract and transcend all that follows the same movement of anti-egotistical expansion. Its culmination is the return to the 'right hand of the Father,' which is the *conscious* return to the Divine Source."

Dominique stopped speaking, retired deep within himself, then resumed speaking, giving value to each word:

"Be careful," he said. "In expressing myself thus, I was speaking of the Logos and of Christ as much in the universal sense as in the sense of the achievement of regenerated man. But also know that in both these cases I'm speaking of an actual reality which is experimentally verifiable. In both cases I am speaking of a Divine State, conscious of all consciousness, in which all opposing particularities are dissolved, and which, considered in terms of our humanity, leads and unifies all those who break their chains to enter into the suprahuman."

"The state you're speaking of is a state of perfection," objected Thomas. "How can one imagine the possibility of our imperfect and mortal being entering into this state?"

"I beg your pardon, dear friend. This imperfect being is only the support, the carcass of our Spiritual Entity. It's to this Entity that Divine Nature, and the supernatural possibilities which flow from it, belong. But the relationship between the two is Human Consciousness, which is the crystallization of the experience acquired by mortal person.

"Human Consciousness is the living imprint of the multiple *impressions* fixed by complex experience of life. It is the *reflection* of it."

"Do you mean the mirror?"

"No, for the mirror *reflects*, whereas, human consciousness *is made from this reflection*. If you move a mirror, it will no longer reflect the same images. However, Human Consciousness keeps the impressions until they are modified or replaced by others that are vitally more profound. This is why it is correctable and perfectible.

"The summit of its perfection will be its identification with the Divine Consciousness of man, his Permanent Witness, whose Presence it attracts through its intense desire to be enlightened by it.

"This unification is a step in Christification, whose realization is the conjunction of the 'humanized Divine' (the Permanent Witness) with what is universally Divine (the Spiritual Witness). But are you aware that this realization is not only a personal achievement but also affects and enriches all those individuals who are themselves on the way toward realizing it?

"And I'm not speaking here of the individual interchange between beings who radiate their spirituality. I'm speaking of their cooperation in increasing the intensity of a spiritual sphere which nourishes and transcends human beings gifted with an identical aspiration.

"If you can free yourself from the mental obsession with time and space, you'll become conscious of this sphere of Power whose concrete image is given to us in the lower kingdoms of Nature.

"If, for example, we're speaking of the vegetal world (or kingdom), we are speaking about everything on Earth that is of a vegetal nature and that undergoes the laws of this kingdom. This goes for the physical conditions of its growth as well as for the influences of the stars that govern its course. However, these heavenly influences provoke the same reactions in all the subjects of the same species (taking into account modifications caused by the particular locality). In other words, these life-giving influxes envelop our globe with a vitalizing atmosphere where all vegetal forms commune as each one, according to its species, gathers the influx that corresponds to its aspirations.

"I chose the vegetal kingdom as an example because its docility toward the influence of stars and seasons can be easily checked. Make the same efforts yourselves to transpose this into the transcendent state of the supra-human *kingdom*: then perhaps you'll be able to perceive the reality of an 'atmosphere' of a spiritual order, a sphere of influence that is no longer astral but divine, with which we cooperate through our effort to transcend at the same time as we participate in the regenerating Power that it engenders by the very fact of this *communion*."

A ray of comprehension illuminated Thomas's expression.

"If man could truly count on such hope . . . ," murmured Dutheil.

"It's not hope," said Thomas; "it's *certitude*! Our Master is not preaching 'virtuous efforts' to us by evoking a glittering hypothetical paradise. He is showing us a *law*, immanent in a state of being which, if I have understood, is the kingdom of realization that we are waiting for. . . ."

"A kingdom or a state of being *which is already yours, if your Divine Entity* inhabits you, my friend," confirmed Dominique with warm emotion in his voice.

"Don't you understand the imperative character of the law of attraction which leads all that is governed by the same aspirations into the same current? Just as in the genesis of an egg or a cloud, all the elements that participate in its formation also participate in the multiple vital currents engendered by the casual center of this genesis, so (even more so) in the Great Work of Christification, a continual cooperation is established between every human being who forms in himself his own Christ and the prototypical Center of this perfection.

"*For this center is the highest Power of salvation emerging from dualized Nature. It is the Solar Christ whose transmutative virtue is the ferment of rebirth for the Divine World.*"

Plan de Grasse
Christmas 1959

THE WORKS OF
R. A. AND ISHA SCHWALLER DE LUBICZ

A NOTE ON THE WORKS OF
R. A. & ISHA SCHWALLER DE LUBICZ

Inner Traditions is privileged to present a rare moment in the full understanding of Western civilization. After many years of studying the medieval legacy in religious, Hermetic, and esoteric fields, and their manifestation in the Gothic cathedrals, R. A. and Isha Schwaller de Lubicz experienced a recognition of that same expression in the monuments of the pharaohs.

Their work represents the first important breakthrough in our comprehension of Egypt since Champollion deciphered the Rosetta Stone. This penetration of the monuments' symbolism and intuitive reading of the glyphs situates Egypt, not Greece, as the cradle of our Western heritage. Often in the style of an oral teaching, their work serves as a guide that will initiate the reader into the authentic tone, structure, and mentality of the Egyptian wisdom.

Both R. A. and Isha Schwaller de Lubicz were masters of a broad spectrum of knowledge. Familiarity with *any* discipline will enhance the understanding of their work, be it philosophy, astronomy, geology, biology and, for the very perceptive, poetry and art. Yet it is not the de Lubiczs' grasp of the many departments of knowledge alone which is masterful, but their transcendent understanding which qualifies them to question the achievements of our civilization. The work of R. A. and Isha Schwaller de Lubicz offers direction not only to the spiritual seeker, but to the scientist and the philosopher as well.

THE OPENING OF THE WAY: A PRACTICAL GUIDE TO THE WISDOM OF ANCIENT EGYPT By Isha Schwaller de Lubicz. Translated from the French by Rupert Gleadow.

In the *Her-Bak* books the author transmitted in a fictional context the atmosphere and teachings of ancient Egypt based on her extensive research and collaboration with R. A. Schwaller de Lubicz. In *The Opening of the Way*, the author has provided a practical guidebook to the wisdom of ancient Egypt. It is solidly based on the spiritual realities that were the functional pillars of the Temple as well as the basis of the Western spiritual tradition. It is meant to help the reader gain access to the dynamic unity that produced the greatest of all known civilizations, at the same time explicating the many mysteries given form in *Her-Bak: Egyptian Initiate*. This book teaches what the ancient Egyptians called "the intelligence of the heart," the master of harmony both in our body as well as our connection to the heart of the world.

ISBN 0-89281-015-7   QUALITY PAPERBACK $8.95

HER-BAK: THE LIVING FACE OF ANCIENT EGYPT by Isha Schwaller de Lubicz. Translated from the French by Charles Edgar Sprague. Illustrated by Lucie Lamy.

Here is a vivid re-creation of the spiritual life of ancient Egypt. Isha Schwaller de Lubicz brings to life the world of ancient Egypt as seen through the eyes of the young Her-Bak, candidate for initiation into the sublime mysteries of the Egyptian temple. Her fictional account is based upon years of on-site research in the temples of Luxor and Karnak under the direction of her husband and teacher, R. A. Schwaller de Lubicz. She traces Her-Bak's development through progressively advanced stages on the path to self-knowledge and cosmic wisdom. We follow his spiritual ascent, sharing his doubts, his discoveries, and his ultimate triumph, which wins him an audience with Pharaoh himself. In the second volume, his spiritual quest finds its culmination in the wisdom and science of the Inner Temple.

ISBN 0-89281-003-3   QUALITY PAPERBACK $8.95

HER-BAK: EGYPTIAN INITIATE by Isha Schwaller de Lubicz. Translated from the French by Ronald Fraser. Illustrated by Lucie Lamy.

This second and independent volume presents Her-Bak's initiation into the Inner Temple and his progressive penetration of the esoteric aspects of the Egyptian Mystery teachings. Her-Bak's story shows the evolution of one individual's life through the phases of temple training. By temple, we are to understand the entire structure of Egyptian science and wisdom, approached through the "intelligence of the heart." The living temple is Man, as he embodies cosmic principles and functions. Through the teachings given by the Egyptian sages, he is led to knowledge of what we call salvation or redemption—the triumph over death. This work is an authentic reconstruction of the sacred science and spiritual disciplines as taught in the temple of Karnak. Fifteen years' research in the temples and tombs of Egypt enabled the author to decipher the hidden meaning of hieroglyphic symbolism. The exceptional circumstances of her sojourn in Egypt, under the tutelage of her mentor and husband, R. A. Schwaller de Lubicz, placed the key in her possession.

The Commentaries, available here in English for the first time, contain a systematic exposition of the metaphysical and psychological ideas woven throughout Her-Bak's narrative and yet can stand alone as a self-contained study of Egyptian teachings and their relationship to the esoteric traditions of other major world cultures. The aim of *Her-Bak* is to share with the reader this experience of initiation into the Mysteries of the Inner Temple.

ISBN 0-89281-002-5   QUALITY PAPERBACK $8.95

SACRED SCIENCE: THE KING OF PHARAONIC THEOCRACY

by R. A. Schwaller de Lubicz. Illustrated by Lucie Lamy. Translated from the French by A. and G. VandenBroeck.

The royal principle, in humanity as well as in nature, is capable of transforming the imperfect elements of a type into the perfection of its own nature. This process of transformation is a science, held sacred by the sages, and is the concern of the pharaonic texts cited in these pages. Schwaller de Lubicz contrasts two poles of mentality, the modern and the ancient Egyptian, or pharaonic. Our rationalistic mentality is oriented toward the acquisition of technological data and its utilitarian application. Under the pretext of facilitating life, the unbridled search for new inventions hones man's egotism and leads him to destruction. Opposed in the extreme, the pharaonic mentality, based on a gnosis (a knowledge of causes), shows its *certitude* by the aim and directives it assigns to earthly existence.

ISBN 0-89281-007-6 CLOTH $16.95

SYMBOL AND THE SYMBOLIC: ANCIENT EGYPT, SCIENCE, AND THE EVOLUTION OF CONSCIOUSNESS by R. A. Schwaller de Lubicz. Translated from the French by Robert and Deborah Lawlor. Illustrated by Lucie Lamy.

R. A. Schwaller de Lubicz spent fifteen years studying the art and architecture of the Temple of Luxor. In *Symbol and the Symbolic*, he explains that true progress in human thought can be made only if we call upon the "symbolizing" faculty of intelligence, the faculty developed and refined in the Temple Culture of ancient Egypt and reflected in the hieroglyphs that have come down to us undisturbed. The mentality of ancient Egypt, argues the author, helps to free us from our present intellectual impasse, while "symbolism" must be recognized as the intuitive means of overcoming the limitations of reason.

Schwaller de Lubicz contrasts two opposing views: the analytic, mechanistic mentality of modern science and the synthetic, vitalist mentality of ancient Egyptian Sacred Science. He posits that only a symbolic mentality, like that cultivated in the Egyptian Temple, can think without objectifying and therefore can synthetically conceive the paradoxes inherent in the intimate life of matter, or nature in its ongoing genesis. Modern science has evolved to a new opening of consciousness confronted with paradoxes that reason alone cannot contend with. It will have to rise to a symbolic mode in order to integrate the complements in vital phenomena.

ISBN 0-89281-022-X QUALITY PAPERBACK $5.95

THE TEMPLE IN MAN: SACRED ARCHITECTURE AND THE PERFECT MAN by R. A. Schwaller de Lubicz. Translated from the French by Robert and Deborah Lawlor. Illustrated by Lucie Lamy.

The work of R. A. Schwaller de Lubicz constitutes a major breakthrough in our understanding of ancient Egypt. His many years of research in medieval hermeticism and its expression in cathedral architecture led him to the discovery that the very same principles informed the sacred architecture of ancient Egypt.

This insight prompted him to undertake fifteen years of on-site research at Luxor Temple. He measured the entire temple, including every block and inscription, and proved that the plan of the temple was rigorously based upon human proportions and designed to symbolically represent man. Each detail of masonry and symbolic art expresses an element of the Egyptians' comprehensive knowledge of man's physical and spiritual anatomy. The human being embodied in the geometry of the temple's architecture is Pharaoh, symbolic of the Perfect Man. In Egypt, Pharaoh represented the final stage of man's evolution, his ultimate divinization.

ISBN 0-89281-021-1   QUALITY PAPERBACK $6.95

NATURE-WORD by R. A. Schwaller de Lubicz. Translated by Deborah Lawlor. Introduction by Deborah Lawlor. Preface by Christopher Bamford. Published by Lindisfarne Press.

In this remarkable work, composed immediately upon his return from Egypt in 1952, the noted French esoterist and hermetic philosopher conveys insights derived from a lifetime of experience and study in the ancient and sacred traditions of humanity. His theme is "the intelligence of the heart," the innate, functional consciousness or way of thinking that is in harmony with Nature and so enables one to understand Life and living things.

The first part of the book, written in a single, uninterrupted flow of inspiration, takes the form of answers from the word of nature to questions posed by the rational mind.

The second part of the book consists of philosophical reflections on the first and proposes the practice of Imagination as a way of evolutionary development. Many traditions have spoken of a "higher consciousness," but Schwaller de Lubicz's attempt to formulate in *modern* terms an alchemical science of qualities, functions, analogies, and signatures is unique. He writes: "Nature has shown me a great mountain crowned with a peak of immaculate whiteness, but she was unable to teach me the way leading to it. I had to seek beyond her. It was a long search. . . ."

ISBN 0-89281-036-X   QUALITY PAPERBACK $6.95

Please order from your bookstore or send the price of the book plus $1.00 for the first book and $.50 for each additional book to cover postage and handling to

Inner Traditions International
377 Park Ave South
New York City, New York